Rebel Guerrillas

ALSO BY PAUL WILLIAMS
AND FROM McFARLAND

*Frontier Forts Under Fire:
The Attacks on Fort William Henry (1757)
and Fort Phil Kearny (1866)* (2017)

*Jackson, Crockett and Houston
on the American Frontier: From
Fort Mims to the Alamo, 1813–1836* (2016)

*The Last Confederate Ship at Sea:
The Wayward Voyage of the CSS Shenandoah,
October 1864–November 1865* (2015)

*Custer and the Sioux, Durnford and the Zulus:
Parallels in the American and British Defeats
at the Little Bighorn (1876) and Isandlwana (1879)* (2015)

Rebel Guerrillas
Mosby, Quantrill and Anderson

Paul Williams

McFarland & Company, Inc., Publishers
Jefferson, North Carolina

LIBRARY OF CONGRESS CATALOGUING-IN-PUBLICATION DATA

Names: Williams, Paul, 1946 March 14– author.
Title: Rebel Guerrillas : Mosby, Quantrill and Anderson / Paul Williams.
Description: Jefferson, North Carolina : McFarland & Company, Inc., Publishers, 2018 | Includes bibliographical references and index.
Identifiers: LCCN 2018046645 | ISBN 9781476675732 (softcover : acid free paper) ∞
Subjects: LCSH: Guerrillas—Confederate States of America—Biography. | Mosby, John Singleton, 1833–1916. | Quantrill, William Clarke, 1837–1865. | Anderson, William T., 1840–1864. | Soldiers—Confederate States of America—Biography. | United States—History—Civil War, 1861–1865—Biography.
Classification: LCC E467.1.M87 W56 2018 | DDC 973.7/3013092 [B] —dc23
LC record available at https://lccn.loc.gov/2018046645

BRITISH LIBRARY CATALOGUING DATA ARE AVAILABLE

ISBN (print) 978-1-4766-7573-2
ISBN (ebook) 978-1-4766-3410-4

© 2018 Paul Williams. All rights reserved

No part of this book may be reproduced or transmitted in any form or by any means, electronic or mechanical, including photocopying or recording, or by any information storage and retrieval system, without permission in writing from the publisher.

Front cover: *insets, left to right* Col. John S. Mosby, C.S.A. (Library of Congress), William Clarke Quantrill (author's collection), William T. "Bloody Bill" Anderson (State Historical Society of Missouri); *foreground* The sacking of Lawrence by Quantrill's raiders (*Harper's Weekly*, September 5, 1863, via Library of Congress)

Printed in the United States of America

*McFarland & Company, Inc., Publishers
Box 611, Jefferson, North Carolina 28640
www.mcfarlandpub.com*

Acknowledgments

I would like to thank a number of helpful organizations, in particular the Virginia State Library, Richmond; Kansas State Historical Society, Topeka; Kentucky Department for Libraries and Archives, Frankfort; Mississippi Department of Archives and History, Jackson; National Archives and Records Administration, Washington, D.C.; Cornell University, Ithaca, New York: Library of Congress, Washington, D.C.; University of Missouri, Columbia. I would also like to thank those diligent researchers and authors who have paved the way with their own research both in print and online, probing the careers of Mosby, Quantrill and Anderson.

Table of Contents

Prologue   1

1. "A well-marked passion to fight": Mosby, 1833–1854   3
2. Lawrence, 1856   9
3. "It means bloody war": Mosby, 1854–1861   18
4. "Bleeding Kansas": Quantrill, 1837–1861   24
5. "An opportunity to strike": Mosby, 1861–1862   36
6. "Cutthroats are coming!" Quantrill, 1861–1862   46
7. "Gratification at my success": Mosby, 1862   59
8. "There would be no prisoners": Quantrill, 1862   66
9. "A prize in the lottery of life": Mosby, 1863   75
10. "We'll descend like thunderbolts": Quantrill and Anderson, 1863–1864   101
11. "An honorable foe": Mosby, 1863–1864   122
12. "I will kill you for being fools": Quantrill and Anderson, 1864   129
13. "Wipe Blazer out": Mosby, 1864   143
14. "The optics of the dead": Anderson, October 1864   168
15. "Unconquered": Mosby, 1865   174
16. "Dark clouds are above me": Quantrill, 1864–1865   181
17. "The South was my country": Mosby, 1865–1916   190

Chapter Notes   197
Bibliography   204
Index   209

Prologue

The American Civil War, or the War Between the States, was fought from 1861 to 1865. Vast resources were brought to bear, creating landscapes of massed blue and gray armies, rows of roaring cannon, cavalry charging, banners streaming in the wind, battlefields strewn with fallen men and dead horses scattered about.

But there were other less spectacular aspects behind the big scene. Small bands of Confederate horsemen caused havoc behind Union lines. An isolated outpost may be hit in the dead of night, or a steam locomotive may crash from displaced rails, the carriages plundered, or a wagon train may go up in flames. Many Southern men, not inclined to formal discipline and fighting in massed ranks, preferred this mode of combat. They wished to fight as partisans, or guerrillas, engaged in furtive, hit-and-run warfare. But love of country was not the only driving force. Many were influenced by the chance of plunder, far more rewarding than a common soldier's pay.

Men from the South, brought up in rural communities where fast horses and guns were a way of life, were well suited to guerrilla warfare. The famous "Swamp Fox" of the American Revolution, Francis Marion, was from South Carolina, the first state to secede from the Union, the first state to open fire on the Stars and Stripes. He provided a model and inspiration. In the spring of 1862 the Confederate government introduced the Partisan Ranger Act. This recognized official guerrilla bands who, while remaining largely independent, were intended to cooperate with local military commanders by harassing the Yankees behind their lines. The stealthy horsemen caused the redeployment of enemy regiments and damaged their morale. Despite this, many military minds saw guerrilla warfare as a retrograde, lowly form of combat, beneath the dignity of honorable gentlemen. And the ferocious actions of some Confederate guerrillas tended to prove their point. The Yankees were infuriated, but at the same time turned a blind eye to the depredations of irregular units serving under the Stars and Stripes. Federal partisans called Red Legs and jayhawkers operating in the west conducted their own cutthroat war.

Federal authorities often treated rebel guerrillas as outlaws, issuing orders that they be shot on sight. And guerrillas could retaliate by showing the black flag: no quarter given, Yankee captives paying the price. But there were, in reality, two guerrilla wars waged with a different set of rules. In the east, despite the savagery, there were constraints. As the Yankees invaded the South they put barn and outbuilding to the torch but, in most instances, left women and children with a roof over their heads. Along the Kansas-Missouri border a far harsher war was fought. The family home was not sacrosanct, just as likely to be plundered and burned as barns and crops. The precedent had been set before the war when the free-state town of Lawrence was sacked by proslavery forces determined to have Kansas enter the Union as a slave state. This sparked "Bleeding

Kansas"—a western civil war that preceded and helped ignite the big event five years later.

Over the course of the war thousands of men in hundreds of guerrilla bands took to the road, their exact numbers not known. Some preferred to be called rangers, raiders, or scouts. John Singleton Mosby caused havoc in the east, while William Clarke Quantrill and William T. Anderson spread terror in the west. Out of the thousands involved, these three men were to become best known for the guerrilla wars they fought, controversial to the present day.

Note: Period spelling and grammar in quotations are often incorrect, so numerous that the customary "sic" has been excluded.

1

"A well-marked passion to fight"
Mosby, 1833–1854

April 14, 1853. "Two students had a falling out a few days ago and one shot the other with a pistol," wrote medical student Sylvester Albert to brother Bob: "The ball entered the side of his face, glanced around the lower jawbone and entered the side of his neck and finally lodged in the muscles on the back of his neck. The wound is not dangerous and he is recovering very fast. There will be a scar left and his face is full of powder so close was the pistol when fired. They have got the fellow that shot him in jail and think he may go to the penitentiary. Both are of this county."[1]

The victim was George Turpin, a student at the University of Virginia. The "fellow that shot him" was fellow student John Singleton Mosby. Young Mosby had been in trouble with the law before this event, and the shooting of Turpin was a prelude to even more turbulent times ahead.

The gun-wielding student was from an old Virginia family whose origins can be traced back to early colonial times. Edward Mosby had migrated from England to the New World in 1635, settling in Charles City County. John Mosby was born at Edgemont, Virginia, on December 6, 1833, to Alfred Daniel and 18-year-old Virginia McLaurine Mosby. There would be 11 children, of whom nine would grow to adulthood. Baby Cornelia had died before John's arrival, and Isabella would die aged five. "He is a remarkably fine child larger now than my dear little Cornelia was at her death," wrote Mosby's mother. "He has fair skin and hair and very dark blue eyes. Some say it will be black though I don't think so myself. He is right pretty, but not so much as my other baby was."[2] Virginia Mosby claimed to be a descendant of Rob Roy MacGregor, the famous Scots outlaw and folk hero.[3] If so, it could make John Mosby a distant relative of the famed Jim Bowie who died at the Alamo. It has been claimed that he too was descended from Rob Roy. Perhaps this is mere myth, but both John and Jim were Southerners who certainly displayed the fighting spirit of a man hailed as "the Highland Rogue."[4]

Despite his mother's positive description, young Mosby grew to be of slight stature, and of somewhat frail health. But he survived in a time of high infant mortality. "I still cherish a strong affection for the slaves who nursed me and played with me in my childhood," Mosby recalled.[5] His first school was in Nelson, Virginia. As a matter of routine, he was accompanied to and from the schoolhouse by a young slave of similar age. Mosby enjoyed his friend's company, and the time came when he begged him to stay all day. Some older students saw Mosby sharing his dinner with the slave, and decided this pair should be the object of some fun. The slave was seized, made to stand on a block, and knocked down to the highest bidder. Mosby, thinking the charade was real, was "distressed at losing such a dutiful playmate." To his relief, however, his friend was set free at day's end. But, rattled by the experience, "he never spent another day with me at the schoolhouse."

The schoolmaster had not intervened. Each midday he would return home for dinner and a drink. But, on at least one occasion, he "took an overdose of whiskey," and the boys found him passed out on the roadside. John Mosby saw his first ever drunken man when they carried him back into the schoolhouse. He eventually came to, and the lessons resumed. "The school closed soon after," recalled Mosby. "I don't know why."[6] But it was a sobering lesson for young Mosby, and he would become a teetotaler for life.

The young student attended his second school, a log structure in Fry's Woods, alongside the family farm. A formidable schoolmistress ruled the roost, "a most excellent woman," recalled Mosby, possibly tongue-in-cheek. She "whipped her son and me for fighting. That was the only blow during the time I ever went to school."

John Mosby was one of thousands of students who read the work of Samuel Griswold Goodrich, a prolific author of the day. He wrote more than 170 books under his better-known pseudonym of Peter Parley. These included what are considered to be the first American textbooks.[7] "In my books were two pictures that made a lasting impression on me," recalled Mosby. One was of General Wolfe dying at Quebec, and another was of Israel Putnam riding down a long flight of stone steps, the British cavalry left behind. The first book Mosby ever read purely for his own enjoyment was the *Life of General Francis Marion* by Mason L. Weems. He actually shouted aloud when he read of the famous Swamp Fox, outwitting the British during the Revolution. "I did not then expect that the time would ever come when I would have escapes as narrow as that of Putnam, and take part in adventures that have been compared with Marion's," he recalled.[8]

The Mosby family purchased a farm of nearly 400 acres, Tudor Grove, four miles south of Charlottesville, Albemarle County.[9] "I went with my father to our peach orchard on a high ridge," recalled Mosby, "and he pointed out Monticello, the home of Thomas Jefferson, on a mountain a few miles away, and told me some of the history of the great man who wrote the Declaration of Independence."[10]

Raising sheep, cattle and hogs, and growing corn, oats and wheat, Alfred Mosby prospered and in three years paid off the mortgage on the family farm.

At the age of ten Mosby commenced attending school at the Grove, a small brick building in Main Street, Charlottesville. Of slight build, and having no interest in playing sports, no one could imagine that this young man would ultimately emerge as a born combat leader. He did, however, excel at literature, and loved ancient history. "I was born a Greek," he said. But, despite being a lightweight bookworm, or perhaps because of it, Mosby grew up to reveal a somewhat bellicose nature and, despite a nurturing home environment, came to view the world as a hostile place. He heard stories of Indian fights, and battles with British redcoats in days gone by. Many old timers still had a trusty flintlock over the mantelpiece, and when Mosby was 13, the United States went to war with Mexico.

Mosby enrolled in the University of Virginia, founded in Charlottesville in 1819 by Thomas Jefferson, on October 3, 1850. He joined the Washington Literary Society and Debating Union, specialized in languages and literature, and passed Greek and Latin with flying colors. Some other subjects, like mathematics, were a different matter.[11]

On April 1, 1851, at the age of 17, Mosby participated in an April Fool's Day "calathump"— a boisterous party where the students, disguised by masks, would make their way through the streets of Charlottesville yelling, blowing horns and whistles, and sometimes discharging firearms. Town Sergeant George Slaughter took exception to the din. He seized one noisy student, threw him to the ground, and started beating him. Mosby ran to the rescue, and found himself locked up after breaking a gun stock over Slaughter's head. Fellow student, and later the surgeon of Mosby's command, Aristides Monteiro, felt that the prisoner had "the least expectation that the world would ever hear from him again." But, on the other hand, he had "a well-marked ruling passion to fight on all possible occasions."[12] A jury found Mosby guilty as charged. He received a fine of $10 which, all things considered, would seem a light punishment for the offence. Perhaps the judge felt Slaughter's aggression had been unjustified.

During October of 1852 another calathump was organized and, amidst the turmoil, Sergeant Slaughter was struck with a wooden table leg by Mosby's friend, Charles Wertenbaker. Mosby was called to appear as a witness to the event but, not wishing to incriminate his friend, failed to show up. He was summonsed to attend when the circuit court was next in town, but the matter blew over with time; all charges were dropped. Some of the local upright citizens, however, were beginning to take a dim view of Mosby's antics. A potential serious troublemaker was in their midst, it would appear.

And much more trouble arrived the following year. Mosby held a party at Tudor Grove, his parents' home, on Saturday, March 26. Two violinists were invited. But fellow student George Turpin, son of an inn keeper, had planned to make use of their talents the same night. He was most displeased to learn from violinist John Spooner that Mosby had them booked for the evening. "Don't you know that Mosby don't care anything for you," said Turpin, "but he only wants you for your musical accomplishments?"[13] Mosby, once informed, felt honor bound to request an explanation, despite Turpin's reputation as a pugnacious bully. He had slashed one student with a knife and beaten another with a rock. Nevertheless, on March 28, Mosby sent a note via a friend. Turpin read the note. "I will see the damned rascal and eat him up, blood raw, on sight," he said.[14]

"I must be prepared to take the fare that others have received at his hands," said Mosby. After morning classes the following day, the wary student returned to his boardinghouse for lunch. But Turpin was in the dining room with another student. Mosby took in his adversary's size and strength, and decided that being eaten "blood raw" was to be avoided at all costs.

It was then that Mosby borrowed the pepperbox pistol. A confrontation took place on a staircase outside the dining room. "I believe you have been making some assertions," said Mosby. Turpin took one look and charged. Mosby whipped the pistol from coat and fired as they clashed.

Young Mosby chose a pepperbox pistol rather than fists to settle his clash with a fellow student at the University of Virginia (author's collection).

Turpin was tended by a medical student until a doctor arrived. Mosby, meanwhile, traveled to Tudor Grove with a friend. But the long arm of the law followed and he was placed under arrest that same evening. Taken to the county jail, he was denied bail, and indicted by a grand jury for "malicious shooting," which carried a sentence of one to ten years in prison, and also "unlawful shooting," which was punishable by one to five years in the state penitentiary or, at the discretion of the jury, up to 12 months in the county jail and a fine not exceeding $500. Mosby's father dug deep and employed three eminent defense lawyers, led by none other than Shelton Farrar Leake, then serving as Virginia's first lieutenant governor.[15] The prisoner appeared before Judge Richard H. Field on May 17, 1853, and pled not guilty to both charges. Appearing for the prosecution, however, was William J. Robertson, the attorney for Albemarle County. Robertson was a lawyer of considerable esteem who would later successfully represent Custis Lee, son of Robert E., who took legal action against the U.S. government for seizing the family home, Arlington, during the Civil War.[16] Robertson would be elected the first president of the Virginia Bar Association, and his own home would be listed on the National Register of Historic Places in 1999.

Three eyewitnesses testified, two for the defense, and one for the prosecution, but all agreed that Mosby did not fire until Turpin charged. On May 24 both the defense and prosecution summed up their cases, and the jury of 12 retired to make their deliberations. But agreement was not easily reached. Four argued for acquittal on the grounds of self-defense, six considered him guilty of unlawful shooting, the lesser charge with a light sentence, but the remaining two said he was guilty on both counts, and should get a lengthy sentence in the penitentiary. Unable to agree on the first day, the judge informed the jury if a verdict was not reached, Mosby would be imprisoned for six months awaiting a new trial. The following day the jury reached a compromise, and filed back into court. The verdict was innocent of malicious shooting, but guilty of unlawful shooting. This meant 12 months in the county jail, and a $500 fine plus court costs. But at least Mosby would escape the penitentiary, and would have no record as a convicted felon.

Some years later, during the coming war, Judge Field asked Mosby to dine with him at his home. He told the now famous soldier that he always believed Mosby did the right thing in shooting Turpin.[17] Perhaps Mosby's new place in the world influenced Field's opinion. The judge would be one of those who, like Mosby, initially argued against succession, but became a staunch Confederate once the war began. He paid a heavy price, however. Both his sons killed on the battlefield, and he died impoverished shortly after the last shots were fired.[18]

To add to Mosby's woes, the University of Virginia had expelled him before the trial. This left Mosby with a bitter taste for years to come. But his actions had, no doubt, rekindled bad memories within the university. In 1840, Professor John A.G. Davis, while attempting to enforce discipline, had been shot and killed by student Joseph Semmes.[19] The shooter skipped bail and, in 1847, ended his own life with a shot to the head. Mosby must have known of these events, and this, no doubt, influenced a low tolerance of dangerous gun play by the university. In 1915, however, the famous old rebel, aged 81, would be asked to give a talk at the university about his wartime exploits. He readily agreed, but "I am a no better person now than when I shot Turpin," he informed the crowd.

Mosby was placed in the relatively airy debtor's cell of the local jail, located near the courthouse. His sentence was to date from May 25, the day the jury handed down its verdict. Before long prosecuting attorney William Robertson dropped by to see how the young prisoner was faring. He received a pleasant welcome from Mosby, who appeared to hold no grudge, and said that he too wished to study law. Impressed by Mosby's positive attitude,

Robertson offered to help him along the way. A long and firm friendship had begun.

Nine jurors, not happy with the trial's outcome, asked Mosby's lawyer, Shelton Leake, to prepare a petition requesting Mosby's release. Leake agreed. The document claimed that one juror, John Hamner, displayed "feelings of dislike and prejudice" against Mosby's father. A separate petition was also circulated, and Alfred Mosby obtained 298 signatures, including 105 students from the university. Medical opinion was obtained from the family doctor that, after three months in jail, Mosby had developed a serious cough. His health, and possibly even his life, were in danger. Leake wrote a letter summarizing the court testimony, and requesting that John Mosby be pardoned.[20]

Mosby's father and brother, William, before the war. In 1863, aged 18, "Willie" joined Mosby's command and later served as adjutant (*The Memoirs of Colonel John S. Mosby*, 1917).

In late June Alfred Mosby met with Governor Joseph Johnson in Richmond. The governor pointed out, however, that the evidence Alfred now presented was from one side only. He had received a letter from one juror, D. W. Maupin, who disputed the assertion that Hamner had made a statement attacking Alfred Mosby, and he opposed a pardon being granted.[21] Another resident also wrote claiming that many of the students who signed the petition were minors, and "troublesome," like Mosby himself. He deserved to remain behind bars. Despite this, Johnson said that if Leake's summary of the court testimony could be corroborated by Judge Field, William Robertson or the clerk of court, he would grant a pardon. Alfred returned to Charlottesville, elated, thinking the pardon as good as done; his son would soon be free. But no transcript of the proceedings had been taken, and the three men concerned declined to validate Leake's version of the testimony.

Mosby's mother, Virginia, wrote an impassioned plea to Governor Johnson for her son's release. She compared his imprisonment with the days of the French Bastille, and the following Reign of Terror (when thousands of people were beheaded). Johnson, no doubt, could scarcely credit such a comparison, but at least he could see the mother's anguish. Virginia wrote on, saying that while asleep she had dreamed of approaching Johnson, a "man alive to all the finer feelings" only to be turned away, but upon leaving his office, he called her back and said he would grant the pardon. She fell to her knees "with a heart overflowing with gratitude and love for you which were so very powerful as to awaken me." The whole family was in the deepest distress, she wrote, "and now most Honorable Sir if you have any mercy left do if you please relieve my son from the bonds put upon him by injustice. I can say no more but only hope."

Johnson's secretary of state, George Munford, replied that the governor felt for Mrs.

Mosby, and the case would be reviewed when either testimony from one of the three named officials, or a transcript of the trial was received. Leake wrote to back to Munford saying this could not be achieved, but then made an offer that would appear bizarre to say the least: If Munford would intervene on Mosby's behalf, and Munford found himself in jail at any time, Leake would do his utmost to get him released![22] It seems highly unlikely that Munford would have been flattered with such an offer. What did Leake think the secretary of state was? Perhaps it comes as little surprise that the governor again declined to pardon Mosby on August 16, 1853.

And that was not all. The young offender found himself moved from the relatively comfortable debtor's cell to the cold, windowless accommodation at the rear. His mother, appalled at these conditions, wrote to Governor Johnson once more, reiterating past arguments, and saying she was afraid for his life. "My son is of a very weak constitution, ... he has been delicate from his birth." Another rejection, she wrote, "would be too over power my heart." Johnson, meanwhile, had personal problems of his own. He returned to the family home in Bridgeport where his gravely ill wife lay dying. Perhaps this personal trauma softened his heart. On December 6, two days before his wife passed on, Johnson asked George Munford to write to Virginia with happy tidings; her son was to be pardoned, after all.

"Your letter was in indeed and in Truth a messenger of glad tidings and great joy," replied Virginia, "and has brightened up many sorrowful hearts, it is as a ray of sunshine in our hitherto overcast & burdened minds, and I can never feel grateful enough to our Noble Governor for what he has done." The pardon became official on December 23, and the $500 fine was reimbursed on February 16, 1854.

On May 30, 1854, the Kansas-Nebraska Act was signed by President Pierce and came into law—but only after much heated debate. This fundamentally altered the future of slavery in the United States, and would ultimately have serious ramifications for every person in the country, including John Singleton Mosby.

2

Lawrence, 1856

Two years following the Kansas-Nebraska Act, May 21, 1856—Former United States senator David Rice Atchison sat astride what he termed his "splendid Arabian charger" in front of about 800 motley dressed volunteers. He was a founding member of the Law and Order Party, which encouraged proslavery migrants to settle in Kansas, and impress their own brand of "law and order." Although now on Kansas soil, the men he now faced were mainly from the neighboring state of Missouri, where slavery was a legally established institution. They carried muskets, revolvers, Bowie knives, and even had artillery on hand.

"Gentlemen, Officers and Soldiers," said Atchison, "this is the most glorious day of my life! This is the day I am a border ruffian!"

Hats were waved and the crowd burst into cheers and shouts. They were "border ruffians," one and all. The term had been coined by Horace Greeley's *New York Tribune*,[1] and although it was intended as an insult, the Missouri men adopted "border ruffians" with relish, and today they were going to live up to the name. They were determined that Kansas Territory would be admitted to the Union as another slave state. Missourians crossing the border to illegally swamp the bona fide Free-Soil vote had ensured that the current legislature was in favor of the South's "peculiar institution."

But then the Free-Soilers had elected a separate government of their own.

The proslavery legislature had issued warrants for the arrest of certain individuals involved, and ordered the removal of two newspapers and the fortified Free State Hotel located in Lawrence, a bastion of antislavery settlers.

Atchison went on to thank the U.S. marshal mounted alongside for inviting him to speak. "Men of the South, I greet you as border-ruffian brothers." Once again their were shouts of approval as hats were waved and muskets raised. "Boys, I am one of your number today, and today you have a glorious duty to perform, today you will earn laurels that will ever show you have been true sons of the noble South!" Atchison said that they had endured privations but would be "compensated by the work laid out by the marshal.... Faint not as you approach the city of Lawrence, but remembering your mission act with true Southern heroism, and at the word, spring like your bloodhounds at home upon that damned accursed abolition hole; break through everything that may oppose your never flinching courage! Yes, ruffians, draw your revolvers and Bowie knives, and cool them in the heart's blood of all those damned dogs, that dare defend that damned breathing hole of hell."

Amidst shouts of approval, Atchison continued his rant. He assured the men that the assault about to take place had the backing "of the administration of the U.S." They would be paid as U.S. troops, "besides having an opportunity of benefitting your wardrobes from the private dwellings of those infernal nigger-stealers. Courage for a few hours and the victory is ours, falter and all is lost." Atchison went on, urging the crowd "never to slacken or stop until every spark of free-state, free-speech, free-niggers, or free in any shape is quenched out of Kansas." He pointed to a flag rustling slightly in the cool morning breeze. "Yes, that large red flag denotes our purpose to press the matter even to blood,—the large lone white star in the centre denotes the purity of our purpose, and the words 'Southern Rights' above it clearly indicate the righteousness of our principles."

He turned to a man mounted alongside. "Follow your worthy and immediate leader, Col. Stringfellow!" Atchison yelled. John Stringfellow was a doctor turned newspaper editor and militia officer. The mob erupted in cheers. "He will lead you on to a glorious victory and I will be there to support all your acts and assist as best I may in all your acts, and assist completing the overthrow of that hellish party, and in crushing out the last sign of damned abolitionism in the territory of Kansas." A hearty three cheers erupted from the crowd, and the order was given to move out.[2]

"Imagine a fellow, tall, slim, but athletic," recalled lawyer and newspaper reporter William Phillips, "with yellow complexion, hairy faced, with a dirty flannel shirt, red or blue, or green, a pair of common-place, but dark-colored pants, tucked into an uncertain altitude by a leather belt, in which a dirty-handled Bowie knife is stuck, rather ostentatiously, an eye slightly whiskey-red, and teeth the color of a walnut. Such is tour border ruffian of the lowest type ... but there is every shade of the border ruffian. Your judicial ruffian, for instance, is a gentleman.... As 'occasional imbibing' is not a sin, his character at home is irreproachable; and when he goes abroad into the territory, for instance, he does not *commit* any act of outrage, or vote himself, but after 'aiding and comforting' those who do, returns, feeling every inch a *gentleman*. Then there is your less conservative border ruffian *gentlemen* ... so far from objecting, rather like to take a hand themselves; but they dress like gentlemen, and are so, after a fashion. Between these and the first-mentioned large class there is every shade and variety; but it takes the whole of them to make an effective brigade: and *then* it is not perfect without a barrel of whiskey."[3]

Sheriff Sam Jones led 20 armed men in advance. He was going to demand the surrender of all weapons from the Free State Hotel. Resistance was expected, thus giving an excuse for the main force to initiate an attack and "cool" their Bowie knives "in the heart's blood of all those damned dogs."

But those Free-Soilers most likely to make trouble had already taken to their heels. Jones made the demand, and no resistance occurred. As he was backed by American law as it stood at the time, one brass howitzer and some small arms were surrendered by the Lawrence "Committee of Safety." But then the militia moved into town. They were going to carry out their orders, come what may. The hotel had been "constructed with a view to military occupation and defense, and regularly parapeted and port-holed for the use of cannon and small arms, and could only be designed as a stronghold to resistance to law," so the proslavery grand jury of the district court of Douglas County had decreed. This noxious citadel was to be removed. The two local newspapers, the *Kansas Free State* and the *Herald of Freedom*, were to meet a similar fate for having issued "publications of the most inflammatory and seditious character, denying the legality of the territorial authorities, advising and demanding forcible resistance to the same, demoralizing the public mind, and rendering life and public property unsafe, even to the extent of advising assassination as a last resort."[4]

Hotel proprietor Shalor Eldridge was given time to have people remove themselves and personal property, and the ruffians wheeled four cannon into position across the road. The doors of the newspaper offices were flung open, the offices ransacked and the presses smashed. The metal type faces were carted to the river and thrown in along with books and other paperwork. Those not moved were piled into the street and set ablaze.[5]

"Men endeavored by argument, and women by tears, to alter the determination, of Jones, but in vain," the Committee of Safety later reported to the Federal government: "The work of pillage had commenced. The contents of the printing offices had been scattered in the streets, and the red flag planted on the roof, first of the office of the *Herald of Freedom*, and afterwards of the Free-state Hotel. The family of [*Herald* editor] Mr. G. W. Brown were driven from their home, and the immediate pillage of the hotel was prevented only by the resolute interference of a few citizens, aided by some individuals of the mob, who kept a strict guard at the doors, and insisted that the families of the proprietors should have the time promised them by Jones in which to collect their most necessary effects and leave. At last the cannons were placed and ready, and it was announced to Colonel S. W. Eldridge, that the bombardment would commence in five minutes. His wife and children were driven off between files of United States bayonets, and amidst the yells of the impatient mob."

A cannon boomed, but the first ball flew harmlessly over the roof. The elevation was lowered, and the firing resumed. Fragments flew from the wall, but "it was solidly built of stone and concrete, consisted of three stories above ground, had a breadth of five windows in the front, and six windows on either side of the house," recalled one witness.[6] Despite repeated hits, the walls remained standing, the cannon too light for the job. More drastic action was required. Barrels of gunpowder were carried inside and the fuses lit. The explosion echoed along the street as fire and smoke blew the windows out., but the haze cleared to reveal the stubborn walls still intact. Bundles of paper stock from the pillaged newspaper offices were carried inside and set alight. The flames took hold, then spread through the shattered interior, and soon the building was ablaze from stem to stern. The roof fell in, sending up a shower of sparks and cinders amidst billowing smoke, and the walls, already weakened from cannon shot and explosion, finally caved in. Only one corner section was left standing, the rest a pile of smoldering rubble.

"The happiest moment of my life," shouted Sheriff Jones.

"The work of pillage spread through the whole town," continued the Safety Committee report, "and continued until dark. Every house and store which could be entered was ransacked, trunks broken open and money and property taken at will. In one house over $2000 was stolen. The house of [supposed Free-Soil governor] Charles Robinson was pillaged and burned to the ground. Towards evening the forces were drawn off to their camp, and the sack of Lawrence was concluded."[7]

Despite the destruction, the invaders had taken no lives, but two of their own had come to grief. One died after accidently shooting himself through the shoulder, and another was killed by a falling brick from the Free State Hotel.

An English visitor to the region, Thomas H. Gladstone, arrived in Kansas City the following night, and recalled that he would "never forget the appearance of the lawless mob that poured into the place, inflamed with drink, glutted with the indulgence of the vilest passions, displaying with loud boasts the 'plunder' they had taken from the inhabitants, and thirsting for the opportunity of repeating the sack of Lawrence in some other offending place. Men, for the most part of large frame, with red flannel shirts and immense boots worn outside their trousers, their faces unwashed and unshaven, still reeking with the dust and smoke of Lawrence, wearing the most savage looks, and giving utterance to the most horrible imprecations and blasphemies: armed, moreover, to the teeth with rifles and revolvers, cutlasses and bowie knives,—such were the men I saw around me."[8]

The sack of Lawrence was a milestone event that led to the outbreak of the Civil War five years later. The Kansas-Nebraska Act of 1854, proposed by Senator Stephen Douglas of Illinois, stipulated that the issue of slavery would be decided by the residents of each territory as it became a state of the Union, "popular sovereignty," as it was known. This repealed the "Missouri Compromise" of 1820, which forbade slavery west of the Mississippi River north of latitude 36° 30',[9] with the exception of Missouri. Had this law remained, Kansas would have come into the Union as a free state as a matter of course.

The Kansas Nebraska-Act was a potential boon for Missouri slave owners. If Kansas was a slave state, they could expand their holdings across the border. The vast majority of Southern congressmen backed the Kansas-Nebraska Act, and enough northern politicians were won over by Douglas to carry the day. The issue being decided by the people of each state instead of latitude was democracy at work, he argued. The act passed in the House of Representatives by a vote of 113 to 100, and the Senate by a vote of 35 to 13. President Franklin Pierce signed the act into law on May 30, 1854.[10] This outraged antislavery politicians, and led to the formation of the Republican Party, opposed to the extension of slavery. At this time Harriet Beecher Stow's famous book, *Uncle Tom's Cabin*, was the most widely read novel in the country. It fanned the abolitionist cause, and was later claimed to have been a primary cause of the Civil War. The Kansas-Nebraska Act, far from settling the question, would give rise to "Bleeding Kansas" as coined by Horace Greeley of the *New York Tribune*.[11]

The Missouri River flowed west to east through the state of Missouri. It was along these banks that hemp and tobacco were grown on plantations employing large numbers of slaves. Other farmers across the state ran smaller farms with just a few slaves raising hogs and growing corn. But most white settlers owned no slaves. In 1860 there were about 25,000 slave owners out of a total population of 1.2 million, 75 percent of whom had Southern ancestry.[12] The only large city, with a population of about 160,000, was St. Louis, where

The sacking of Lawrence in 1856 sparked the "Bleeding Kansas" episode, a prelude to the Civil War (based on a daguerreotype, this drawing appeared in *Kansas: Its Interior and Exterior Life* by Sara T.D. Robinson, 1857).

the Missouri and Mississippi joined. Sustained by a manufacturing base, it was a vital port, and during the Civil War became a construction base for Union ironclad river steamers. The free state of Illinois was on the opposite bank, a lure for escaped slaves. One St. Louis newspaper stated that if Kansas should become a free state, "Missouri will be surrounded on three sides by free territory, where there will always be men and means to assist in the escape of our slaves.... This species of property would become insecure if not valueless in Missouri." Senator and slave owner David Rice Atchison declared he would "extend the institutions of Missouri over the Territory to whatever sacrifice of blood or treasure," and he would see Kansas "sink in hell" before being admitted free.[13]

Once the Kansas-Nebraska Act came into force, it was not only slave holders from Missouri who set out for greener pastures to the west. Many in the northern states were determined to see that Kansas would be settled by Free-Soilers, and emigration societies raised money for their support. During the summer of 1854 six parties, totaling about 700 people, set out from Boston. They were sponsored by the Massachusetts Emigrant Aid Company, organized by ardent abolitionist Eli Thayer, the founder of the Oread Institute, an impressive castle-like structure in Worcester housing a school for young women.

On July 28, 29 people, Thayer's first arrivals, arrived by steamboat in Kansas City. They traveled 40 miles west through Kansas Territory to a location selected by an advance party under Dr. Charles Robinson. A settlement was founded on a plateau between the Kansas River on the north and "Mount" Oread, actually a high hill, to the south. The settlement was named Lawrence in honor of Amos. A. Lawrence, a Boston financier who had bankrolled the expedition.

Believing that the "pen is mightier than the sword" the new arrivals' arsenal included a printing press which would soon publish the *Herald of Freedom*. Thayer explained that he wished to "show the superiority of the free labor civilization; to go with all our free labor trophies; churches and schools, printing-presses, steam-engines, and mills; and in a peaceful contest convince every poor man from the South of the superiority of free labor."[14] Thayer may have wished for a "peaceful contest" but such was not to be. As more settlers arrived and Lawrence grew it became the recognized "Yankee Town" by Southern sympathizers. With time, Lawrence became the center of the abolitionist movement from where gangs known as jayhawkers operated. During the coming conflict they would raid proslavery settlements freeing slaves, but also pillage for personal gain under the pretext of fighting for the Union. At the same time, proslavery gangs called bushwhackers would pillage Free-Soil homes and settlements under the pretext of fighting for the Confederacy.

On November 29, 1854, David Atchison and his colleagues arranged for thousands of Missourians to cross the border and cast votes for the first Kansas delegate to Congress. Antislavery voters found themselves intimidated at the ballot boxes, especially in proslavery towns such as Leavenworth. It came as little surprise that proslavery Democrat John W. Whitfield won the election, and despite protests regarding electoral fraud, Whitfield took his Congressional seat.

On March 30, 1855, the election for the first territorial legislature took place. Once again thousands of proslavery Missourians crossed into Kansas and cast illegal votes. A mob destroyed the presses of the *Parkville Luminary* after publishing an attack on the machinations of David Atchison and his cohorts. In Leavenworth free-state lawyer and journalist William Phillips threatened to have the election declared null and void. Kidnapped and taken into Missouri, he was shaved, tarred and feathered. Using a black auctioneer, Phillips was put up for sale in a mock auction where one cent was the only bid.

It comes as little surprise that the vast majority of seats went to proslavery candidates.

Andrew H. Reeder, appointed by President Pierce as the first territorial governor, was aware of the fraud, up to 80 percent of the vote considered bogus. Free-state activist Dr. Charles Robinson offered to provide Governor Reeder with a bodyguard if he declared the election void, but the governor took a fence-sitting position and approved all election results, except those districts with the most obvious fraud.

"It looks very much like war, so I am ready for it and so are our people," Charles Robinson wrote to Eli Thayer. "Wouldn't it be rich to march an army through the slaveholding States and roll up a *black cloud* that should spread dismay and terror to the ranks of the oppressors? Cannot your secret society send us 200 Sharps rifles as a loan till this question is settled? Also a couple of field-pieces? If they will do that, I think they will be *well used* and preserved."[15] The Sharps rifle was a state-of-the-art breechloader, far more effective than the common muzzleloader of the day. George W. Deatzer traveled east to procure the weapons, and in the meantime fortifications in Lawrence were under construction. This included the concrete and stone Free State Hotel. Before long the new rifles arrived in boxes labeled "books" and a cannon arrived in a crate labeled "machinery."

New elections were held in the obviously fraudulent seats on May 22, and more free-staters gained seats. On July 2 the legislature met in the settlement of Pawnee, Governor Reeder's desired capitol, where he held substantial real estate interests. The first order of business by the proslavery majority was to oust the new free-state members and reinstate the proslavery candidates elected in March. Then the "bogus legislature," as the free-staters called it, passed a bill moving the government to Shawnee Mission, near Kansas City on the Missouri Border. Once there, it was decided to move to the proslavery settlement of Lecompton.[16] On August 14 an "act to punish offences against slave property" was amongst the first laws passed. The death penalty was proscribed for anyone raising a rebellion of colored people, be they slave or free, the furnishing of arms for such, or incitement to rebellion in speech or writing. Any person leading slaves to freedom "shall suffer death or be imprisoned at hard labor for not less than ten years."[17]

On August 16, at the urging of the proslavery lobby, Governor Reeder was removed from office by President Pierce. Indicted by a local grand jury for high treason, and in fear of his life, Reeder scurried from Kansas in May of 1856 disguised as a wood chopper. He resumed his law career in Pennsylvania, and became involved with the new, antislavery Republican Party.[18]

During 1855 the population of Kansas doubled to more than fifteen thousand. Most were opposed to slavery, and for those moving to Lawrence the sturdy Free State Hotel provided accommodation while homes were being established. Among those who arrived was a man destined to be dubbed by many as the "Grim Chieftain of Kansas." James Henry Lane had held the rank of colonel during the Mexican War, then served as lieutenant governor of Indiana, and congressman from 1853 to 1855. One of those northern politicians who voted in favor of the Kansas-Nebraska Act, he was reputed to have said, shortly after arrival, "I would just as soon buy a nigger as a mule." But, sensing the general tide, Lane threw in his lot with the Free-Soil crowd. Noted for fiery speeches that galvanized audiences, "he talked like none of the others," one settler recalled. "None of the rest had his husky, rasping, blood-curdling whisper or that menacing forefinger, or could shriek 'Great God!' on the same day with him."[19] Jim Lane would become a stalwart of the Free State Party, formed at the Big Springs Convention on September 5, 1855. But there was division within the ranks. Many Free-Soil settlers were not interested in black freedom. Morally inclined abolitionist migrants from the East verbally clashed with Westerners who wished to exclude black emigration and suffrage. They saw blacks as competitors in the Kansas labor market.

To counter the Free State Party the proslavers formed the "Law and Order Party" at Leavenworth the following month, David Rice Atchison prominent amongst the founding members.

On November 21, 1855, a land claim dispute resulted in Charles Dow, an antislavery man, being shot and killed by proslavery advocate Franklin Coleman at Hickory Point, about ten miles south of Lawrence. Dow surrendered himself to Samuel Jones, the proslavery Douglas County sheriff. Jones had moved from Virginia to Westport, Missouri, with his family in 1854, where he served as postmaster. He had crossed into Bloomingdale, Kansas, where he and cohorts destroyed a ballot box during the "Bogus Legislature" election earlier in the year. Jones' proslavery activities were noted by acting governor and fellow Virginian Daniel Woodson, who appointed him as the first sheriff of Douglas County, Kansas. Jones was described by one free state reporter working for the *New York Tribune* as "the immortal bogus Sheriff Jones, a tall, muscular, athletic loafer, with a cruel Mephistophelean expression, clad in the Border Ruffian costume-blue military overcoat, large boots, skull cap and cigar in mouth." But "beauty is in the eye of the beholder" and free-state Lawrence settler Samuel Tappan had kinder words: "Permit me to refer to Samuel J. Jones, bogus sheriff of Douglas County, who in many ways was a remarkable man, as all the early settlers can testify. A man of undoubted courage, and what was not usual with his clan, chivalric and kind, while a most intense partizan."[20]

Dow's killer, Franklin Coleman, was released on bail by a proslavery judge. In response, Free-Soilers put Coleman's cabin to the torch along with those of several other proslavery men. The alarm went out, and Sheriff Jones set out with a posse to track the culprits down. Dow's friend Jacob Branson found himself under arrest, but the road to Lecompton was blocked by free-state men at Blanton's Bridge, just south of Lawrence. They forced Jones to release the prisoner, and he made haste to proslavery Franklin to rally support. Seven cannon and two wagonloads of guns and ammunition were hauled from the Federal arsenal at Liberty, Missouri, and soon a small army of over 1000 border ruffian militia under David Atchison marched towards Lawrence, bent on destroying the "Yankee town."

James Henry Lane ready for action. The "Grim Chieftain" of Kansas led jayhawker raids into neighboring Missouri (Library of Congress).

Word spread and 500 armed defenders poured into Lawrence where the fire-breathing Jim Lane put his military training to use. Under his direction, picks and shovels flew in the construction of four circular earthen breastworks 75 feet wide, connected with rifle pits, and women went to work preparing cartridges and weapons.

By December 3 Atchison's border ruffians were camped six miles east of Lawrence on the Wakarusa River. Fueled by a plentiful whisky supply, they were eager to fight. The governor asked Colonel Edwin Sumner at Fort Leavenworth to intervene with Federal troops, and President Pierce telegraphed Sumner with instructions to do so. But Sumner, nicknamed "Bull Head," refused to become involved except through the usual chain of command, orders from the War Department.

Atchison, meanwhile, demanded that the men who had rescued Branson be handed over along with the shipment of Sharps rifles. Charles Robinson, elected "major general" of the Lawrence defense, denied that the rescuers were in town, and claimed he was not in a position to surrender the rifles because they were private property. Territorial governor Wilson Shannon arrived and commenced negotiations, but on December 6 rival patrols exchanged gunfire, resulting in the death of Free-Soil advocate Thomas Barber. Shannon, however, defused the lethal situation by negotiating with Lawrence's Committee of Safety. They denounced Branson's rescue and promised no further interference with due process of law. A treaty was signed on December 8 and the situation was further cooled with the arrival of a freezing snowstorm. The Missourians packed their tents and headed for home, thus ending what became known as the "Wakarusa War."[21]

But the free-staters still refused to recognize the "Bogus Legislature." They elected a government of their own on January 15, 1856, under the "Topeka Constitution," drafted the previous year. This outlawed slavery, but those who wished to exclude blacks altogether won the day. Indian males, on the other hand, who had adopted white civilization were to be included. An election night brawl saw the death of a proslavery man, and the following day the alleged culprit was mortally wounded while being placed under arrest. Charles Robinson was elected governor, and the constitution was forwarded to Washington with a request for Kansas to be admitted as to the Union as a free state.

President Pierce was appalled, and promptly declared the Topeka Constitution to be an act of rebellion. On July 3 the House of Representatives, on the other hand, voted to accept the document and admit Kansas as a free state. This, in turn, was blocked by the Senate, leaving the whole situation in limbo, the "Bogus Legislature" being the recognized legitimate government while Kansas residents continued to arm themselves for their own civil war.

Sheriff Jones, meanwhile, had unfinished business. He rode into Lawrence to arrest Sam Wood, who had led the Jacob Branson rescue. Jones quickly found himself surrounded by a mob who taunted him, knocked him down, and stole his revolver. He returned a few days later with a posse of four men. But a repeat performance ensued, and the posse left town empty handed. Jones returned with 11 Federal troopers. Six arrests were made, but that night Jones made the mistake of exposing himself in the military camp. A gunshot rang out, and he fell with a bad wound to the back.

"ABOLITIONISTS IN OPEN REBELLION" screamed the proslavery *Atchison Squatter Sovereign*. "SHERIFF JONES MURDERED BY THE TRAITORS & HE MUST BE AVENGED."

Despite a bullet lodged near the spine, Jones survived, and was soon planning his own revenge, backed up by such firebrands as David Rice Atchison. A Lecompton grand jury indicted Charles Robinson, James Lane and several other outspoken Free-Soil advocates for treason, and decreed that the *Kansas Free State* and the *Herald of Freedom* newspapers were to be removed for using "inflammatory and seditious language." Also, the Free State Hotel, "designed as a stronghold for resistance to law," was to be demolished.

Thus occurred the first sack of Lawrence, on May 21, 1856.

But retaliation was swift. A few days later antislavery fanatic John Brown and four of his sons murdered five proslavery settlers with broadswords in what became known as the "Pottawatomie Massacre." The battle lines of Bleeding Kansas were drawn.

And soon to be embroiled was one William Clarke Quantrill, at the time of the Lawrence attack, living back east in Ohio, and only 18 years old.

3

"It means bloody war"
Mosby, 1854–1861

Following John Mosby's pardon for shooting George Turpin, his family struck out for fresh pastures some distance from Charlottesville. As Mosby had carried a gun to his dispute with Turpin, it comes as little surprise that some felt the young troublemaker should have stayed behind bars.

A new farm was purchased in Fluvanna County, and Mosby, a budding lawyer, continued his legal studies. On September 4, 1855, he was examined by three judges including Richard Field, the man who had sentenced him to jail. He passed, and left home at the age of 22 to set up his own law practice in Howardsville, Albemarle County.

Business was sparse for the new lawyer in town, but a ray of sunshine entered Mosby's life in the form of Mariah L. Pauline Clarke. The attractive Kentucky girl, 19, was visiting relatives when the two met in June of 1856, just one month after the sacking of Lawrence had caused a stir in the newspapers. The ever present slavery debate was slowly but inevitably coming to the boil.

Pauline's father was Beverly Leonidas Clarke. A Virginian by birth, he had moved with his parents to Kentucky in 1823. Clarke had graduated from the Lexington Law School in 1833, and served in Congress from 1847 to 1849.[1]

Pauline returned to Kentucky, but the tyranny of distance proved no barrier to the young pair. Mosby was entranced with the intelligent young lady who shared his love for literature and history, and, with the feelings reciprocated, the couple were married in a Roman Catholic ceremony at the City Hotel in Nashville, Tennessee, on December 30, 1857. Dignitaries included Senator Andrew Johnson from Tennessee. Although from the South, Johnson would remain loyal to the Union during the coming war, and become president of the United States on the assassination of Abraham Lincoln.[2]

In November of 1858 John and Pauline left Howardsville and moved to Bristol, a rapidly growing community straddling the border between Virginia and Tennessee. With only two other lawyers in town, business was brisk, and by this time there was a welcome addition to the family, May Virginia, born on March 10, 1858. She was joined by a brother, Beverly Clarke, born on October 1, 1860. Also in residence was John's teenage sister Blakely, Pauline's teenage sister Delia, and Aaron Burton, a slave owned since childhood by the Mosby family. At the age of 86, Burton would have kind words for his former master. "I raised Colonel Mosby. I loved him and was in all his battles. When the war was over Colonel John told me that I was free and could go and do as I pleased…. He is a good man and was a great fighter."[3]

The presidential election of 1860 saw four candidates. The Democrats were split between those wishing to preserve the Union and those who wished to secede to form a confederacy of proslavery states. Pro–Union Northern senator Stephen Douglas, and Southern vice president John C. Breckinridge, both Democrats, ran against each other. The Constitutional Union Party ran John Bell, and the newly formed Republican Party, dedicated to restricting slavery to existing states, ran a Kentucky-born lawyer named Abraham Lincoln.

The policies of Breckinridge and Bell were seen as those most favorable to Southern interests, and Mosby found himself a lonely voice in Bristol when he voted for the Vermont-born Yankee Democrat Stephen Douglas, a man who favored the Union remaining intact. As votes were cast orally (there was no secret ballot), Mosby's fellow Southerners knew where he stood. "Do you know what succession means?" he asked J. Austin Sperry, editor of the *Bristol Courier*. "It means bloody war, followed by feuds between the border states, which a century may not see the end of." Mosby would gladly "hang a secessionist" if he could. Sperry replied that he could not see why "secession should not be peaceable," and asked Mosby what side he would take. " I shall fight for the Union, of course, and you?" Sperry replied that he would fight for "my mother section," and should they meet in battle, "I would run a bayonet through you." "Very well," said Mosby, "we'll meet at Philippi" (conflict between opposing Roman armies in 42 BC).[4]

Abraham Lincoln was elected president on November 6, 1860. South Carolina led the split by seceding from the Union on December 20, and Mississippi, Florida, Alabama, Georgia, Louisiana and Texas all followed by February 1, 1861. Abraham Lincoln was sworn in as the 16th president of the United States on March 4 and as part of his inaugural address declared, "I have no purpose, directly or indirectly, to interfere with the institution of slavery in the States where it exists. I believe I have no lawful right to do so, and I have no inclination to do so."[5]

Despite this assurance, it was anti–Yankee passion that ran high throughout the South. Most believed that the South's "peculiar institution" was threatened under a Lincoln administration. The voices of logic were shouted down.

"In April 1861, came the call to arms," recalled John Mosby. "On the day after the bombardment by South Carolina and the surrender of Fort Sumter that roused all the slumbering passions of the country, I was again attending court at Abingdon, when the

Mosby's wife, Pauline, was a well-connected and sharp-witted match for her dashing husband (author's collection).

telegraph operator told me of the great news that had just gone over the wire. Mr. Lincoln had called on the States for troops to suppress the rebellion."[6]

Two days later the Virginia convention voted in favor of secession, already a forgone conclusion. The bands had already starting playing "Dixie's Land" and "The Bonnie Blue Flag" as a joyous throng marched on the state capitol building in Richmond. The Stars and Stripes fell to be trampled in the dust while the rebel Stars and Bars was raised on the flagstaff. A 100-gun salute roared in honor of Fort Sumter's surrender. Richmond would soon be proclaimed the capitol of the Confederacy. Southern firebrands, spoiling for a fight, greeted these events with joy, a chance for adventure and glory while ridding themselves of the damned Yankees. More sober souls, however, shook their heads with apprehension. The country's heavy industry, capable of producing shot, shell, rifles, railway locomotives and marine steam engines was almost wholly located in the North. Only one Southern foundry was capable of producing heavy cannon, the Tredegar Iron Works in Richmond.[7]

Mosby was in a dilemma. After saying he would gladly hang a secessionist, his beloved home state of Virginia had "gone South." He and many other Virginians who had not wished to see the Union split could not now consider fighting against their home state, friends and neighbors. "The people of Virginia," recalled Mosby, "in response to the President's call for troops to enforce the laws, sprang to arms to resist the Government. The war cry 'To arms!' resounded throughout the land and, in the delirium of the hour, we all forgot our Union principles in our sympathy for the pro-slavery cause, and rushed to the field of Mars."

Even before Virginian secession, Mosby had enlisted in the Washington Mounted Rifles at the request of William Blackford, a former university classmate. But he "was so indifferent about the matter, that I was not present when the company organized"—hardly an auspicious beginning for a rebel chief, but still, the die was cast. The company mustered in Abingdon, and "William E. Jones was made captain. He was a graduate of West Point and had resigned from the United States army a few years before," recalled Mosby. "Jones was a fine soldier, but his temper produced friction with his superiors and greatly impaired his capacity as a commander."[8] Jones was a bitter man. Shortly after his marriage in 1852, his wife Eliza had been swept from his arms and died during a shipwreck. As a result, he became "embittered, complaining and suspicious."[9]

"Grumble" Jones, as he was known, drilled Mosby and the other green recruits of the Washington Mounted Rifles. Perhaps some would make good soldiers. At least Jones had seen action, having fought Indians before leaving the army in 1857. "Captain Jones had strict ideas of discipline, which he enforced," recalled Mosby, "but he took good care of his horses as well as his men. There was a horse inspection every morning, and the man whose horse was not well groomed got a scolding mixed with some cursing by Captain Jones."[10] Later on two men were caught pillaging dry goods. Jones forced one to wear a women's hoop skirt around his neck, and the other to ride around all afternoon holding the stolen parasol over Grumble's head.[11] But "Jones was very kind to me," recalled Mosby. Perhaps the captain recognized in Mosby someone of education and intelligence like himself, which would contrast sharply with some farm boy recruits who could scarcely read and write. And "no man in the South was better qualified to mould the wild element he controlled into soldiers," recalled Mosby. "His authority was exercised mildly but firmly, and to the lessons of duty and obedience he taught me I acknowledge that I am largely indebted for whatever success I may afterwards have had as a commander."[12]

Editor Austin Sperry was surprised to have a soldier "in the bob-tailed coat of a cavalry private" walk into his office at the *Bristol Courier*. "How do you like my uniform," the new arrival asked.

"Why, Mosby! This isn't Philippi, nor is that a Federal uniform."

"No more of that," the recruit replied. "When I talked that way Virginia had not passed the ordinance of secession. She is out of the Union now. Virginia is my mother, God bless her! I can't fight against my mother, can I?"[13]

The Washington Mounted Rifles received orders to leave Abingdon and muster in Richmond. While infantry from the same area traveled by rail, Jones knew a 300-mile ride would be a good training exercise for his recruits. But Mosby now had to say goodbye to his beloved Pauline and children, a depressing experience. Perhaps the gloomy weather and rain as the company rode out on May 30, 1861, was an ill omen for the Southern cause. But, as Jones "had been an officer in the army on the plains, we learned a good deal from him in the two weeks on the road, and it was a good course of discipline for us.... The men boiled with enthusiasm, the only fear being that the whole thing would blow over before they reached the firing line. At Wytheville, on our third day's march to Richmond, we got the papers which informed us that the war had actually begun in a skirmish at Fairfax, where Captain Marr had been killed. We were greatly excited by news of the affair." There was one man, Mosby remembered, "who was conspicuous on the march; he rode at the head of the column and got the bouquets the ladies threw at us; but in our first battle he was conspicuous for his absence and stayed with the wagons."[14]

Bad weather along the trail seemed to have no ill effect on Mosby's frail health, as disclosed in letter written to his "Dear Ma," after arrival in Richmond on June 17, 1861. "I reached this place yesterday evening. We had been 18 days on the road. We generally slept on the ground at night & I never before had such luxurious sleeping. I had no sign of a cold although it rained most of the time. I fattened every day, our march was a perfect ovation. The people threw open their doors to us.... I wish you would send me something to eat, the food here is very rough—nothing but fat salt meat & cold hard bread.... Mr. Palmer says ours is the finest company that has come to Richmond, not in dress (for I can tell you we look like savages) but in fighting qualities."[15]

Recruits, both North and South, joined the military in droves. But this provided a vexing problem as the armies grew: an acute shortage of trained officers. The only way to fill the gap was to recruit educated professionals such as lawyers, teachers and managers to fill the gap. These civilians would have to study military tactics, and learn on the job. Many would prove to be excellent soldiers and rise to senior ranks above their West Point contemporaries. While camped near Richmond, Mosby ran into a well-connected friend, Tim Rives, who wanted him to apply for an officer's commission. He offered to set up a meeting with Virginia governor "Honest John" Letcher.[16] But "I declined and told him I had no military training, I preferred serving as a private soldier under a good officer. I had no idea then that I should ever rise above the ranks."

The company rode from Richmond to Ashland, and Mosby wrote to Pauline: "Ma and Pa came down to Richmond Sunday and came out here to see me. Left yesterday evening. Ma brought me a box of nice things to eat.... I like a soldier's life far better than I ever dreamed I would. And were it not for the uneasiness and anxiety of mind which I know it gives those who are near and dear to me I would be perfectly happy." A few days later he added an update before posting: "We have been ordered to march to Winchester on horseback. We start tomorrow. We'll soon be among the Yankees.... We are armed with sabres, pistol, and Sharps carbines—a short rifle three feet long. Can shoot ten times a minute." Being issued with these carbines was a great compliment, Mosby recalled, "as arms were scarce in the Confederacy. We had been furnished with sabers before we left Abingdon, but the only real use I ever heard of their being put to was to hold a piece of meat over a fire for frying."[17] Like all good cavalrymen, Mosby kept a saber jangling by his side for at least the early part of the war. It was part of the mounted warrior image, when all said and done. "But when I became a commander, I discarded it ... certainly the sabre is of no use against gunpowder." New uniforms arrived, fresh from the penitentiary where prisoners toiled on behalf of the Confederacy, whether they liked it or not. "They were a sort of dun color," Mosby recalled. But the uniforms did not go down well with the men, who preferred more colorful garb. With mutiny threatened, the drab clothing was discarded and piled up in the camp. By war's end the rebels would not be so fussy, donning anything they could lay their hands on rather than go naked. This included captured Yankee blue. But Mosby and his friend Fount Beattie had no problem with the new uniform. Perhaps some inner voice told Mosby that this "dun color" was, in fact, excellent camouflage for his future role. The blue Federal uniforms, by contrast, stood out amidst the foliage. It would not be until the end of the 19th century that the American brass saw the wisdom of rebel ways and introduced camouflage colors like those worn by the Confederacy.

John Mosby first laid eyes on James Ewell Brown "Jeb" Stuart on July 9 at Bunker Hill, in the Shenandoah Valley. "I had never seen Stuart before," recalled Mosby, "and the distance between us was so great that I never expected to rise to even an acquaintance with him.... At the beginning of the war he was just twenty-eight years old. His appearance—which included a reddish brown beard and a ruddy complexion—indicated a strong physique and great energy." Jeb came from a distinguished Virginian military family. His great grandfather had commanded a regiment during the Revolution, and his father had fought in the War of 1812. He graduated from West Point in 1854, at that time superintended by Robert E. Lee. Stuart saw service in Bleeding Kansas and was wounded while fighting Cheyenne tribesmen in 1857. In 1859 he served as Lee's aide-de-camp when John Brown was captured at Harpers Ferry.[18] He resigned from the U.S. Army when Virginia seceded, and was commissioned as a lieutenant colonel in the Confederate Army.

The Washington Mounted Rifles were to be absorbed into the 1st Virginia Cavalry regiment, commanded by Stuart, who would be promoted to full Colonel the following week. The very next day Jones's company was ordered to scout towards Martinsburg. Near Snodgrass Spring, the rebel horsemen could see the white tents of General Robert Patterson's Federal troops scattered on the hills around the township. Mosby now had his first close contact with the enemy, but it was no menacing Yankee regiment spoiling for a fight. Two bluecoats had strayed outside the Union picket lines. As the Confederates closed in, the Yankees saw the danger and took to their heels. "They ran

The dashing Jeb Stuart impressed John Mosby, and in time they became a mutual admiration society (Library of Congress).

across the field, but we overtook them," recalled Mosby. The sorrowful captives were taken back to Stuart's camp. "Since then I have witnessed the capture of thousands, but have never felt the same joy as I did over these first two prisoners," he recalled.[19] "I got a canteen from one—the first I had ever seen—which I found very useful in the first battle I was in."[20]

And that first battle, the first major clash of the Civil War, was less than two weeks away.

4

"Bleeding Kansas"
Quantrill, 1837–1861

Kansas, May 1856. The Pottawatomie massacre of five proslavery settlers caused outrage, and John Brown found himself hotly pursued by Deputy Marshall Henry Pate with a force of 50 men. Pate ransacked Free-Soil homes as he nabbed anyone who could have been involved. Amongst several prisoners were two of Brown's sons.

In response, Brown rounded up an armed party of 29 supporters and led a counter-attack. On June 2 they caught up with Pate's force camped alongside the Santa Fe Trail, near the village of Black Jack. In the pre-dawn light, Brown split his force into two groups, one under his own command, and the other under compatriot Sam Shore. Despite being outnumbered, they charged downhill towards Pate's camp. The crackle of gunfire split the morning stillness, and the surprised Missouri men scrambled for cover. Assuming they were under attack by a larger force, they returned a hot fire from a creek bed and gullies. As the sun rose, the haze of gun smoke obscured the smaller enemy numbers, and Pate raised a white flag. A parley was required. He met Brown, who demanded unconditional surrender. Pate refused, returned to his lines, and the rifles cracked once more. About half of Pate's border ruffians, however, mounted up and galloped off. They'd had enough shooting for one day. Brown ordered several men to Pate's rear and, once there, his son Frederick yelled out, "Hurrah! Come on, boys! We've got 'em surrounded; we've cut off all communication."

An outfoxed Pate assumed enemy reinforcements had arrived. Again the white flag was waved. They met, and Brown made an offer Pate could not refuse. His head would be blown off unless he surrendered. A disillusioned Pate agreed to release Brown's sons in return for safe passage for himself and his 22 remaining men. The "Battle of Black Jack" was the first gunfight between pro and antislavery forces, argued by some to be the real opening shots of the American Civil War.[1] There were no deaths on either side, but four of Brown's men received bullet wounds.

The Free-Soil Topeka Constitution was declared invalid by the United States Congress, but on July 4, 1856, Independence Day, the illegal Topeka Legislature met. Colonel Edwin Sumner arrived with two companies of the 1st U.S. Cavalry with a cannon in tow. The meeting was broken up, but the Free-Soil men responded with raids on the proslavery settlements of Franklin, Fort Saunders and Hickory Point.

On August 30 proslavery Virginian lawyer John Reid led a force of about 400 men and one cannon towards the Free-Soil township of Osawatomie. Reid had received word that John Brown and his brood were in town. Brown's son, Frederick, was the first to fall, shot and killed by the gun-toting Rev. Martin White who was acting as Reid's guide after being forced from town due to his proslavery stance. News traveled quickly to Brown, who rallied 40 men for the town's defense. A furious gunfight took place costing the lives of another five free-staters, and two of Reid's men. When Brown's ammunition ran out, he ordered his outnumbered force to disperse. He hoped Reid would make a futile pursuit, but he stayed to burn the town. A few buildings sheltering women and children were spared, and Reid moved off with several prisoners leaving a ruin of fire and smoke behind.[2]

William Clarke Quantrill, 19 years of age, rode into the toxic atmosphere of Bleeding Kansas five months later, March 1857. "As I remember him," wrote one acquaintance, "he was about five feet ten inches tall, rather slight of stature, weighing, perhaps, 150 pounds, walked with an easy, slouchy, gait, head bent a little forward, eyes cast downward, hair of a yellowish-brown color, cut straight around the neck about even with the lower part of the ear, the end of the hair turned under towards the neck. He wore a drab corduroy suit with pants tucked into tops of his high heeled boots: also a drab slouch hat."[3]

Born on July 31, 1837, in Dover, Ohio, Quantrill was the son of Thomas Henry Quantrill, a tinker, and his wife, the former Caroline Cornelia Clarke. He was the eldest of eight children, four of whom died in infancy. The family tree included individuals of dubious repute. One uncle was a pirate operating off the Texas coast, and grandpa Thomas Quantrill was a philanderer, professional gambler and horse trader who made a dishonest dollar whenever the opportunity arose. Thomas Henry's brother, Jesse, was a fraudster who married a gullible young lady for her money, then lost the lot in failed business pursuits.[4]

Young William Quantrill showed early signs of following in the family's dubious footsteps. A teenage girl was locked by persons unknown inside a church when she was sounding the bells. Twenty-four hours passed without food or water before the distraught young lady was found. A reward of $100 was offered for the culprit, but never claimed. Years later, in Kansas, Quantrill admitted that it was he who had performed the deed and thrown the key away.[5]

His father, Thomas Henry, followed the family tradition by stealing funds from the Canal Dover Union School, of which he was a trustee, to pay for a tin-smithing manual he had authored. But Fellow trustee Harmon V. Beeson discovered the fraud. Thomas decided to remove the evidence and visited Beeson with a derringer. But Beeson managed to knock his antagonist down with an iron poker before a shot could be fired. Thomas recovered and managed to stay out of jail, but managed to bring more trouble on his head. He took a decided dislike to a local artist, Mrs. Roscoe, who gave painting lessons. And, worse still, she was married to a pretentious Frenchman. Such a conceited creature needed to be brought down. Word soon spread that Mrs. Roscoe was a woman of easy virtue. Furious, she caught up with Thomas on a street corner, bullwhip in hand. The cutting weapon cracked as the defamed lady took her revenge.[6]

Caroline Quantrill was later described by an acquaintance, Mrs. Francis Thompson, as "a good cook and housekeeper, and that to get his victuals properly cooked seemed all about Thomas H. Quantrill cared for.... She was of a solitary turn, of a brooding disposition, never going to visit her neighbors, but sometimes attending the Presbyterian church."[7]

Despite his shortcomings, Thomas managed to retain a respectable veneer, apparently, as he was appointed principal of the Dover school. It can only be assumed suitable candidates were in short supply. This was convenient for his eldest son, William, who, upon graduation at the age of 16, secured a position from his father teaching the junior grades.

Thomas, however, was not in good health. He died of consumption on December 7, 1854, a blow to the family who depended on his income for survival. To make ends meet,

Caroline took in borders, and a sister took in sewing. Young William, meanwhile, decided to head west. He joined Miss Mary Clapp, a teacher, who was traveling to Illinois to join her family, former residents of Dover. Once there, perhaps he could find business opportunities to help support the family.

Steaming by rail across flat, grassy plains, they arrived in Mendota, Illinois, on August 8, 1855, and Quantrill wrote: "Dear mother…. We travelled by day & night ever since we started not having stopped half an hour in one place. Tomorrow I am going to hunt something to do. We are both well except that Mary was looking out of the window of the car while we were going along the shore of Lake Michigan when a spark of fire flew in her eye & made it a little sore." But no spark flew between the young couple. Mary soon married a prominent Illinois farmer and settled with him in Mendota. "I have $6 of my money left & maybe the next time I write I can send a little along," continued Quantrill. "I am about 600 miles from home." He said that there were two schools there, and "probably I can get one of them." Returning to teaching seemed the best way of making a dollar before moving on to make his "fortune."[8]

Quantrill's next letter asked his mother to find any documents proving a Quantrill family member had fought in the Texas war for independence from Mexico. Such soldiers were entitled to generous land grants in Texas, and Quantrill knew someone who could well be interested in buying such property. The chances of such a long shot bearing fruit would indicate a desperate search for ways to make "my fortune." He also wrote asking for copies of his father's book, the "Tinman's Guide." He had sold his own copy, and felt there would be a good market for them in Chicago where there are "many tin shops." He was teaching, and was paid every three months "$25 a month & boarded." Quantrill supplemented his pay and honed his shooting skills with hunting forays. He wrote to a friend, Edward Kellam, "Here a man who understands the business can shoot from 50 to 60 prairie chickens every day & get $1.50 per dozen all he can shoot. There is a place 16 miles from here called inlet pond, where there are thousands of ducks and geese. I was up last Saturday & I killed 2 geese and 11 ducks, but the fellow that was with me killed 9 geese and 32 ducks. We got 50 cts apiece for the geese & 25 cts for the ducks. If you was here we could go every day."[9]

As winter set in Quantrill began to realize the streets out west were not paved with gold. His prospects for anything better than basic survival were slim. "You may expect me home early in the spring," he wrote to his mother, "for I was dunce to go away for I could have done just as well at home as out here…. I will turn over a new leaf entirely. You said the children had the ague; you must try and cure them if possible & this is the last winter you will have to keep borders if I keep my breath. I feel I have done wrong in going from home & hope you will forgive me for it."

But soon an alarming piece of gossip circulated in Dover. William Clarke Quantrill was being held out west for having killed a man. What precisely happened has never been confirmed. Employed at a lumber yard, one version had Quantrill shooting an intruder in self defense after being woken in the office during the night. Another version had him being found during the day standing over a dead man behind a woodpile with a smoking gun in his hand.[10] His mother received a letter dated February 21, 1856, from Fort Wayne, Indiana, which seemed to confirm a basic truth in these rumors. "I suppose you thought I was dead, but not so." He apologized for the long delay between letters, but "something has happened to me." He was not going to give details now, but "you will not think so hard of me when you know it all."

John Mosby and William Quantrill both shot their first men while still teenagers. But, unlike Mosby, Quantrill's shooting had been lethal. It seems ironic that Mosby's wounding of his opponent saw him convicted and land in jail, while Quantrill was released following his lethal shooting. He was only 18, and there were no witnesses to contradict his claim of attempted robbery.

Quantrill resumed teaching near Fort Wayne with 35 to 40 students, and "they say I'm the best teacher they ever had." He was still planning to return home in the spring to support the family. "The next time I will tell you all about what has happened. But I want you never to tell any body else whoever it may be for my sake."[11]

Quantrill did not return home in the spring. He stayed on in Fort Wayne and furthered his education in a city school with the study of Latin, chemistry, trigonometry and physiology. Based on this, it would appear he considered teaching to be his future. Unforeseen twists and turns, however, can alter life's outcomes to a momentous degree. But during 1856 he did travel back to Ohio and reunite with his family. He soon secured a position teaching to the south of Dover in the Blicktown district while his mother continued to take in lodgers, and his sister still helped out with her sewing. But it was still a basic hand-to-mouth existence for the Quantrill family.

William Clarke Quantrill, like John Mosby, shot his first man while still in his teens (Wikimedia Commons).

Harmon Beeson, the man who had beaten Quantrill's derringer-toting father with an iron poker, made plans to head for Kansas. His son, Richard, and Colonel Henry Torrey were to accompany him. Richard had been a school friend of Quantrill, and he asked to go along.[12] The sacking of Lawrence and the troubles of Bleeding Kansas were well known, so it was quite possible that these men from Ohio, a free state, were aiming to reinforce the antislavery cause. If so, they had no idea that taking William Clarke Quantrill along was like the wooden horse being taken into Troy. Quantrill agreed to work for his passage, and the party set off in late February 1857.

On March 15, the travelers disembarked from a steamboat in Independence, Missouri, where they purchased two teams of oxen and headed southwest. In Franklin County, Kansas, they selected a well-timbered site with rich soil and rolling grass on the Marias des Cygnes River, an ideal place for farming. Beeson and Torrey paid a resident squatter $500 each for a claim of their own, and $250 each for a claim for Quantrill. A cabin was erected on Torrey's land, and from there they went to work. On May 16, 1857, Quantrill wrote to his mother describing progress on the farm: "I have just finished a hard job of rolling logs at a clearing around our cabin, which we are going to put in potatoes. Yesterday we just finished planting a Ten-acre field of corn on the prairie, which Mr. Torrey & I plowed. Next week we are going to commence a 20 acre field, so that we will have corn enough for next winter at least." He encouraged his mother to sell their property in Ohio so they could purchase a 160 acres for a farm in Kansas of their own. Despite the stories of violence, he claimed "all is peace and quietness here now, & it will remain so without doubt. Why, not less than 50,000 people from the North have come into this Territory this spring so that

Kansas will soon be a State among States & able to maintain her own rights." Quantrill left a good description of life in a frontier cabin: "We live on side meat—bacon about four inches thick; corn cakes, beans, few dried apples occasionally, & fish & squirrels when we can get them which we have pretty good luck doing. Our house is built of round logs with a fire place made partly of stone; a floor made of puncheon that is split boards about 3 inches thick. Our furniture consists of 2 stools made out of puncheon, 3 trunks & a table made when we wish to use it by putting a board (which we found in the river) across the 2 trunks. Our walls are decorated with guns, boots, side meat, skillets, surveying chain &c. The only job that we have to do that we all dislike, is dishwashing which Mr. Beeson is doing now. We have to take turn about at it; no one will do it more than twice in succession. Our stock consists of 3 yoke of cattle, six pigs & about 2 dozen chickens. We will have by fall 3 times as much stock if we have good luck. All I want is for the rest of you to be here, and we will live twice as fast."[13]

Despite the apparent tranquil relationship, a financial clash erupted when Quantrill decided to sell his claim. As tensions rose, he moved in with another settler, John Bennings, and the dispute was taken to a "squatter's court" of respectable citizens. The verdict was in Quantrill's favor, and the other two were ordered to pay him $63 in two installments. But the required funds were either not on hand or deliberately withheld, as the first payment was not made. Quantrill decided to take matters into his own hands, and purloined a yoke of oxen from Beeson, and blankets and pistols from Torrey. Beeson caught up with the culprit and put a pistol to his head. Quantrill led Beeson to his oxen, and returned the pistols to Torrey. The blankets, however, disappeared until they were found some time later, worse for wear, in a hollow log. Quantrill eventually received half the money owed, probably from Torrey, because they resumed a tranquil relationship. Beeson, on the other hand, would never have anything good to say about William Clarke Quantrill.

Quantrill moved in with some young men from Dover who built a cabin on Tuscarora Lake, Johnson County. At this stage his attitude towards slavery was what one would expect from an Ohio boy. To his approval, the proslavery settlers were being swamped by Free-Soil people, but the influx resulted in further violence. In the Spring of 1858 proslavery settlers were driven from the area around Fort Scott, Kansas, into Missouri by jayhawker leader James Montgomery. In retribution, on May 19, Georgia proslaver Charles Hamilton led a party back into Trading Post, Kansas, and herded 11 men into a gulch near the Marias des Cygnes River. Five were shot and killed while five others, wounded, survived by playing dead. Another was left unharmed amidst the bodies. The "Marais des Cygnes Massacre" caused outrage, and Quantrill had no time for Southern sentiment, as revealed in a letter written to a friend in Dover on January 22, 1858. The proslavery Lecompton Constitution had been rejected by an election on January 4, and Quantrill was delighted, making reference to the "Lecompton swindle." He was impressed with the fiery Jim Lane "as good a man as we have here ... his presence is enough to frighten 100 Missourians. The settlers shot two men and wounded 4 or 5 but in self defense, it is a pity they had not shot every Missourian that was there." Digressing from politics, Quantrill went on to comment on the local lady population, "a man can have his choice for we have all kinds & colors here Black White and Red But to tell you which I like the best is a mixture of the two latter colors if properly brought up for they are both rich and good looking & I think go ahead of your Dover gals far enough. You and the rest of the boys there must attend to the girls well while we are here in Kansas and tell them we are going to marry squaws & when they die we are coming to old Dover for our second wives so they must not despair."[14]

According to hearsay, Quantrill was thrown out by his Dover friends due to stealing firearms and provisions from cabins in the area. He went to ground for a few weeks, but resurfaced at the home of John Bennings, who had provided a home during his dispute with Torrey and Beeson. The word had got around that he was not to be trusted, however, and he packed his swag and left the district. He turned up at Fort Leavenworth and hired out to help drive cattle to Fort Laramie.

Around this time cavalry trooper R. M. Peck encountered "Charley Hart" at Fort Bridger in what is now Wyoming. Using an alias lends credence to the theft allegations. Perhaps the Quantrill name was best buried for the moment. "I could see nothing heroic in his appearance, but considerable of the rowdy," Peck recalled in 1907. "He was apparently about twenty-two or twenty-three years of age; about five feet ten inches in height, with an ungraceful, slouchy walk; and by no means prepossessing in features." Having "struck it rich" in a gambling spree, Quantrill was decked out in new clothes: "a pair of high-heeled calf-skin boots of small size, bottoms of trousers tucked into boot-tops; a navy pistol swinging from his waist belt; a fancy blue flannel shirt; no coat; a colored silk handkerchief tied loosely around his neck; yellow hair hanging nearly to the shoulders; topped out by the inevitable cow-boy hat."

Peck described an encounter where Quantrill calmly pulled his gun on the dealer to make sure he handed over his winnings. The dealer had his own pistol within reach, and "Charley" wanted no arguments. After pocketing the money, Quantrill threw the small change into the air, and watched as the crowd scrambled for the coins. He gave the dejected dealer a $20 gold piece for his trouble, and departed. But, if what Peck heard is true, Quantrill must have wished he had kept the lot. His luck at the tables turned sour next day, and he departed flat broke.

Upon return to Leavenworth, Quantrill hired out once more on a cattle drive to supply troops involved in a small war with Mormons in Utah. They had set up their own colony, and refused to recognize the government of the United States. The town of Leavenworth was a proslavery stronghold, and the men Quantrill signed to drive cattle with were of the violent, border ruffian class. He had been rejected by his former Free-Soil compatriots, and now heard the proslavery point of view.

On January 9, 1859, he wrote to his mother telling of his time in Utah where he worked as a quartermaster's clerk. He was fired, however. It "was all my own fault," he wrote, without revealing the reason. He then found work as a cook, but after praising the Mormons in previous letters, now considered them "great rogues and rascals." Perhaps, however, this did not include the ladies: "I have a notion to marry 4 or 5 women here if I can for here is the only place I will have a chance I suspect, the Mormons have from 3 to 8 on an average."[15]

Quantrill arrived in Lawrence, Kansas, on July 30, 1859—minus Mormon brides. He put pen to paper and wrote to his mother once more, the first letter since January. He described being one of seven survivors from a gold mining expedition of 19 men to Pikes Peak, Colorado. He mentioned "cold weather & starvation and Indians" and "I dug out $54.34 & worked 47 days which money hardly paid my board and expenses." This excursion seemed to have a deep impact, as in future letters he would make reference to the hardship and freezing conditions. He wrote to his sister, "My dress consisted of a complete suit of buckskin; pants, coat, moccasins, a red woolen shirt, a fur cap, a large leather belt in which is a large pistol and knife; and then mounted on an Indian pony, with my rifle laying across the saddle, ready for use in a moment's warning. We look rough enough, for we do not shave or cut our hair, and to a person not used to such sights, we look like ruffians."[16]

Quantrill seemed to have a guilty conscience about deeds of his recent past. He wrote to his mother: "I expect every body thinks and talks hard about [me] but I cannot help it now it will be straight before another winter passes." When returning to settled territory, Quantrill's horse and possessions were stolen by Indians when he was out of camp, and a friend was badly wounded and left for dead. Leaving his friend with appropriate medical care in Lawrence, Quantrill headed for Osawatomie, Lykins County, the free-state town burned by Jim Reid's border ruffians three years earlier during their attempt to catch John Brown. The wily abolitionist had escaped to fight another day, and on December 20, 1858, led a raid into Missouri. One slave owner was killed, and 11 slaves were freed. The governor of Missouri put a price of $3000 on Brown's head.

As Quantrill found employment as a teacher at a private school in Stanton, Kansas, Brown was in Virginia formulating final plans for his assault on the Federal arsenal at Harper's Ferry. He was going to arm slaves in a massive rebellion that would end the South's "peculiar institution" once and for all. Brown's party was attacked by troops under Robert E. Lee. The fiery old abolitionist was captured, tried for treason, and hanged on December 2, 1859.[17] While many in the North considered Brown a martyr, his actions were despised in the South. The raid and hanging widened the rift between North and South, and helped spiral the march to war.

Less than two months after Brown's hanging, Quantrill wrote to his mother again. This revealed a homesick young man who had undergone a radical shift in thinking from a few years earlier, and perhaps Brown's raid and trial for treason had been the final straw. "You have undoubtedly heard of the wrongs committed in this territory by the southern people, or proslavery party, but when one once knows the facts they can easily see that it has been the opposite party that have been the main movers in the troubles & by far the most lawless set of people in the country. They all sympathize for old J. Brown, who should have been hung years ago, indeed hanging was too good for him. May I never see a more contemptible people than those who sympathize for him. A murderer and a robber, made a martyr of; just think of it."[18]

On February 8, Quantrill wrote home again. "It is a pleasant morning, this; the sun is just rising, its light causing the trees, bushes and grass to glitter like brilliants, while the hanging sheets of frost drop from them, announcing his warmth, then silently melting away. I stood in my schoolhouse door, and viewing this it made me feel a new life, and merry as the birds. But these feelings and thoughts are soon changed and forgotten, by the arrival of eight or ten of my scholars, who come laughing and tripping along as though their lives would always be like this beautiful morning, calm and serene. And I wish that I could always be as these children. But I have been so no doubt, and I have no reason to expect it a second time. Every year brings its changes and no two are alike…. When my school is finished, I will be able to tell you better what my plans are for the coming year. One thing is certain: I am done roving around seeking a fortune, for I have found where it may be obtained by being steady and industrious. And now that I have sown wild oats so long, I think it is time to begin harvesting; which will only be accomplished by putting in a different crop in different soil." These hardly seem the words of a man whose name would soon be reviled. Little wonder his mother had trouble accepting that Quantrill, the murderer of Lawrence, and her beloved, poetic son were one and the same. But "there is no news here but hard times, and harder still coming," Quantrill wrote, "for I see their shadows; and 'coming events cast their shadows before,' is an old proverb. But I do not fear that my destiny is fixed in this country, nor do I wish to be compelled to stay in it any longer than possible, for the devil has got unlimited sway over this territory, and will hold it until we have a better set of men and society generally. The only cry is, 'What is best for ourselves and our dear friends.'"[19]

When the school term ended Quantrill rode for Lawrence, about 40 miles away. Having procured work with a surveying team on the Delaware Indian reservation about four miles from town, he moved into the cabin of John Sarcoxie, the son of a chief.[20] When visiting Lawrence, Quantrill encountered a group of border ruffians at the ferry crossing on the Kansas River. They got to talking, and Quantrill heard of easier ways of making money than being steady and industrious. "Coming events cast their shadow before"—and falling in with the border ruffians did just that.

On June 23 Quantrill wrote to his mother again. He said he had sent some money with previous letters, but as he had not heard from her, he supposed they had not been received. He said he would send more once he had heard from her. He talked in general terms about the weather, and apologized for "my short and badly written letters, for I stop at taverns & never can feel at home enough to collect my thoughts & write an interesting letter." The letter finished with "P. S. I will here say that I will be home any how as soon as the 1st of September & probably sooner by that time I will be done with Kansas."

But Kansas had certainly not done with Quantrill. He was at a turning point in his life, and that letter was the last word Caroline Quantrill would ever hear from her son. Perhaps he could not bring himself to write a pack of lies, talking of industrious plans or coming home, while he had decided on a life of crime.

While continuing to live with John Sarcoxie, Quantrill also took a room at the Whitney House in Lawrence. Except for a few confidants, he told people his name was Charley Hart, a detective working on behalf of the Delaware Nation. But while consorting with border ruffians in various crimes, Quantrill played a double game, also riding with abolitionists on raids into Missouri. His deeds caught up with him, however, when Douglas County Prosecutor Samuel Riggs issued a warrant for the arrest of "Charly Hart" on charges of "burglary and larcent, in breaking open and stealing from a powder-house of Tridenour & Baker; for arson, in setting fire to a barn in Kanwaka township this country, and for kidnapping."[21] Sheriff Walker was given the warrant to serve, but seeing his approach, Quantrill dashed into the wagon shop of a Free-Soil associate, John Dean, and bolted the door behind him. By the time Walker and his deputy smashed their way in, the bird had flown. A search about town was made, but the fugitive had found refuge in the home of an antislavery friend where he spent the night. Next day Dean arranged a wagon, and Quantrill, lying low, was spirited safely out of town.

Charley Hart's double-game could not last. He had been helped out of town by Free-Soil men, and there had been other actions on his part that did not add up for his proslavery cohorts. His claim that he only mixed with the antislavers as a spy had been stretched beyond breaking point. He realized that, in the short term at least, he would have to rub shoulders with the Free-Soil jayhawkers. But it was the ideals of the proslavery bushwhackers that remained close to Charley's heart.

Abraham Lincoln was elected the sixteenth president of the United States on November 6, 1860. While the South fumed at this result, and the war clouds gathered, Quantrill devised a plan to regain the favor of his former bushwhacker friends. James Morgan Walker had a 1900-acre property in Missouri with 26 slaves, and about 100 horses and mules. And he kept a hoard of gold under lock and key—or so rumor had it. Quantrill proposed to his jayhawker associates that they raid Walker, free the slaves, and pillage the house and farm. Apart from one horse-drawn wagon to carry loot, he proposed that they approach on foot. Stolen horses would provide their escape.

Quantrill and three others, Edwin Morrison, Charles Ball and Chalkley Lipsey, set out together while John Dean, who had saved his hide in Lawrence, and Albert Southwick brought the wagon along some distance behind. On December 10 they neared Walker's farm and, while supposedly reconnoitering, Quantrill slipped away. He arrived at the home of Walker's son, Andrew, and offered to lead his companions into an ambush. In return, he would be require protection from the Kansas jayhawkers once they learned of his treachery. His father would be informed, Andrew said, and he would do what he could to protect Quantrill.

That night Quantrill lead Ball, Lipsey and Morrison towards the homestead through a drizzling, cold rain. Dean and Southwick were nearby with the wagon, ready to load the plunder. But, based on Quantrill's betrayal, three of Walker's neighbors, guns in hand, were waiting in a harness room alongside the front porch. Andrew Walker and another man, John Tatum, were on the porch hidden behind a loom. Quantrill and the three unsuspecting cohorts strutted onto the porch. Quantrill had Morrison stay there as a lookout, while he, Ball and Lipsey drew their revolvers and barged inside.

"We have come to take your niggers to Kansas," Quantrill said to Morgan Walker and his wife. "We also want your horses and mules and what money you have in the house." According to Andrew Walker, "my father replied that if his niggers wanted to go to Kansas they were at liberty to do so, but he did not see any reason why those who did not want to go should be compelled to leave him, and he thought he should have his money and stock left him." Quantrill told Ball and Lipsey to join Morrison and round up the slaves while he held a gun on Walker and his wife. They stepped outside, and in the next instant the blast of Tatum's shotgun rent the air. Morrison, hit by 19 buckshots, died where he fell. Ball and Lipsey scrambled from the porch as a hail of lead erupted from Andrew Walker and the three men in the harness room. Lipsey fell with buckshot in his thigh and groin, and cried for help. His friend Ball turned back and pulled him to his feet. They staggered through the darkness towards the wagon, only to find it gone. After having his boot heel shot away, Dean had scrambled aboard, flicked the reins, and dashed off. Southwick, left behind, ran for his life after the wagon. Ball heaved the bleeding Lipsey through the drizzling rain into the darkness of the woods and escaped—for the moment.[22]

Morrison's body was dragged from the porch and laid out in the harness room. Quantrill looked down on the bloody corpse, and condemned him as a blaggard jayhawker who had made attacks on honest Missourians. By morning the word had spread and local farmers arrived, guns in hand, bent on revenge. Some were not happy with Quantrill's account, and felt a quick lynching should be his lot. Upon arrival in Kansas, Quantrill claimed in desperation, he and his brother had been ambushed by jayhawkers on the Santa Fe Trail. His brother had been killed, while he was wounded and left to die. He had joined the jayhawker band responsible in order to take revenge, and killed the guilty one by one. Those he had led into the ambush were the last of them. But not all listeners were convinced by this tale that sounded like a dime novel plot. Andrew Walker was obliged to fend off repeated demands for a necktie party at Quantrill's expense.

Ball, meanwhile, had helped the badly wounded Lipsey onto the neighboring farm of George Rider. The following day he managed to steal one of Rider's horses and shoot a hog, and they remained concealed in the woods. But next morning, one of Rider's slaves saw smoke from a small cooking fire. He soon found them, and Ball told the slave would be freed and taken to Canada if he stole a wagon and team and escaped with them. The slave appeared to agree, but dashed to the homestead and reported their presence. Rider promptly sent word to Walker. "My father, brother, Quantrill and myself went out where they were," recalled Andrew Walker. "They drew their pistols and my father and myself fired on them killing them both. Quantrill did not kill either of them. Southwick [actually Lipsey] was so badly wounded that he could not stand. They had stolen a horse the night before and had it tied in the brush near by. They were to leave that night."[23] Quantrill would later claim that he personally killed the wounded Lipsey with his Colt in retribution for the supposed murder of his brother.

Dean and Southwick, meanwhile, escaped back to Lawrence. Dean, once he heard of Quantrill's treachery, would spread the story that the coward had refused a challenge from Ball to a fair fight. One can hardly blame Dean for hating Quantrill. Apart from the treachery, it was Dean who had spirited the traitor out of Lawrence, avoiding Sheriff Walker.

The Jackson County sheriff took Quantrill to Independence, Missouri, where he wrote an account of the affair. He claimed to have been born in Hagerstown, Maryland, a slave state. To have admitted being from antislavery Ohio would have undermined his supposed proslavery credentials. Word of the raid spread around town, and there were many who wished to see Quantrill hang. He was placed behind bars in protective custody until the excitement died down. Andrew Walker took him out that evening, and they shared a hotel room for the night. But next day a rabble gathered in the town square intent on lynching Quantrill. "The people had not got to fairly understand the matter," recalled Walker, "and they hardly knew themselves what they were going to hang him for, only for the fact he was in bad company and there was naturally a prejudice against Kansas men, as there had been a great deal of trouble between Kansas and Missouri. The crowd was mostly proslavery men."[24] Walker stood before them and shouted that they would hang Quantrill over his dead body. The mumbling and cursing mob could see Walker meant what he said, and slowly dispersed.

It would seem Quantrill could charm anybody when required. Walker not only saved his skin, but also bought him a new suit of clothes, "of which he was badly in need," Walker recalled. They returned to the farm, but Morgan Walker was justly concerned that Quantrill's presence would attract abolitionists seeking revenge with guns and flaming torches. He gave Quantrill $50, a fleet but one-eyed mare named Black Bess, and bade him God speed.

A week later, on December 20, 1860, news of South Carolina seceding from the Union swept the country. Would the other slave states, including Missouri, follow? On January 4, 1861, Missouri's new governor, Claiborne Fox Jackson, gave his inaugural address. He advocated that Missouri "stand by her sister slave-holding states ... with whose institutions and people she sympathizes."[25] But neighboring Kansas, now dominated by antislavery settlers, was admitted to the Union a few weeks later as a free state. Charles Robinson was elected the first governor, and jayhawker chief Jim Lane as senator.

And to Missouri governor Jackson's displeasure, elections for a constitutional convention held in February of 1861 brought surprising results. Despite Missouri's outspoken proslavery element, most settlers did not own slaves, and few outright secessionist delegates were elected. Most successful candidates were Unionists, either staunch or conditional.[26]

Keeping well clear of Lawrence, Quantrill stayed on the move over the next few months, staying with various friends, including Henry Torrey, whose blankets and pistols he had once stolen. Once the dust had settled, however, he moved back to Johnson County, Missouri, and batched with a friend, Mark Gill. The Walker family, living close by, now supplemented Quantrill's needs once more. Anna Walker, Morgan's daughter, recently divorced due to her "extracurricular" activities, was back home. Quantrill made her acquaintance, and the two were soon sharing much more than poetry and yarns. She had affairs with other men over the next few years, and upon her father's death following the war, the enterprising lady used her talents and inheritance to set up a bordello at Baxter Springs.

Quantrill, now well known as a bushwhacking, proslavery man, spent time with his friend John Bennings, now residing near Stanton, Kansas. Jayhawker leader Eli Snyder, residing at Osawatomie, got wind of Quantrill's arrival at Benning's cabin on March 25, 1861. Snyder had sworn revenge against the turncoat, and he rode with 12 others to Stanton where Justice of the Peace Sam Houser swore out a warrant for Quantrill's arrest on horse stealing charges. Snyder wanted Houser to deputize himself and his men to serve the warrant, but Houser, no doubt assuming the culprit would be shot for "resisting arrest," ordered that Constable E. B. Jurd do the job. Jurd, however, was only too happy to deputize Snyder's party to back him up.

Before dawn the following morning Quantrill was awakened by the distant, shouting voice of Constable Jurd demanding Quantrill's surrender. The bleary-eyed bushwhacker peered out through a window and saw Eli Snyder amongst the posse. He yelled back that he would rather go down fighting than be murdered by Snyder. The constable convinced Quantrill it was in his best interest to negotiate. Allowed into the cabin, Jurd promised Quantrill safe passage, and soon emerged holding his Colt up for all to see. The culprit was coming out, unarmed, he said, no one was to shoot. They set out for Stanton, and Snyder attempted to goad the prisoner into a fight as they rode. Quantrill refused to take the bait, so Snyder decided to shoot him anyway. The captive's life was spared when a posse member knocked Snyder's revolver to one side, and the shot went wide.

Once in Houser's office, a "very pale and nervous" Quantrill still found himself under threat. A pistol, pointed at his head, misfired when the trigger was pulled. The percussion cap guns of the day were more reliable than the old flintlocks, but still not perfect. Then galloping horsemen and rattling vehicles came down the street. A gang of 17 proslavery men from Paola had arrived, and they demanded Quantrill's immediate release. Snyder backed down, and Justice of the Peace Houser agreed to commit the outlaw to the safety of the Paola jailhouse. The jubilant victors rode out, Quantrill not believing his luck, no doubt. Once in his Paola cell, the prisoner was provided with a pistol and Bowie knife for self protection. Behind the scenes, strings were pulled, and a few days later the cell door swung open and he walked free. A writ of habeas corpus had been filed on the grounds that his arrest had been "malicious, false and illegal." Quantrill was wined and dined at Torrey's Hotel, but he was advised to head for Missouri post hast. As he mounted Black Bess, Snyder and an armed party galloped into town with a fresh arrest warrant issued by the Douglas County court in Lawrence. Patting his buttocks in contempt, and waving his Colt in the air, Quantrill galloped off. He disappeared in a cloud of dust towards the Missouri border, Snyder's party unable to pursue, their horses spent.[27]

A few weeks later, on April 12, the guns around Charleston Harbor roared, and shot and shell rained down on Fort Sumter. "I did not know one could live such days of excitement," recalled Mary Chesnut, wife of a Confederate officer. "Some one called 'Come out! There is a crowd coming.' A mob it was, indeed, but it was headed by Colonels Chesnut and Manning. The crowd was shouting as showing these two as messengers of good news. They were escorted to Beauregard's headquarters. Fort Sumter has surrendered!"[28]

On April 15 Abraham Lincoln put out a call for 75,000 volunteers, and the electric telegraph rattled the news to the west. Quantrill moved South for a brief time with his friend, Mark Gill, who felt there was less chance of his slaves being freed in Texas. Quantrill soon rode north again into Indian Territory where he befriended Joel Mayes, of mixed Cherokee and Scots blood, who formed a company of pro-Confederate Cherokees. Riding with them, Quantrill learned the skills of scouting and ambush.

In Missouri and Kansas, meanwhile, pro and antislavery men rushed to join regular army forces, Union and Confederate—or irregular jayhawker and bushwhacker bands. The saga of Bleeding Kansas was about to move into a even bloodier, more lethal chapter, one in which William Clarke Quantrill would take center stage.

5

"An opportunity to strike"
Mosby, 1861–1862

"There's Jackson standing like a stone wall," cried General Bernard Bee. "Rally behind the Virginians!" The disorganized and retreating Confederates on Henry House Hill took heart, regrouped and counter attacked through the battle smoke.[1] General Bee had said the famous words, but for him they were of little avail. He was mortally wounded amidst the fighting, and died the following day.

That morning, July 21, 1861, Jeb Stuart had divided his cavalry regiment. While one half took part in a dashing cavalry charge that had halted a Union advance, the other half, including John Mosby's company, had been left in reserve. "For two hours we sat there on our horses," Mosby wrote to Pauline, "exposed to a perfect storm of grapeshot, balls, bombs, etc. They burst over our heads, passed under our horses, yet nobody was hurt. I rode my horse nearly to death on the battlefield, going backwards and forwards, watching the enemy's movements to prevent their flanking our command."[2] The rebel horsemen would receive praise for holding their ground under this barrage, but not all could stand the strain. One man, recalled Mosby, "fell off his horse—commenced praying; the surgeon ran up,—thought he was shot: examined him, told him he was only scared to death."[3] As the First Battle of Bull Run, or Manassas, as the rebels called it, raged on, the Confederates were reinforced by fresh troops arriving by rail. After fierce fighting, what had looked like a Union victory turned into a Union rout.

"On to Richmond," Horace Greeley's *New York Tribune* had thundered before the unexpected defeat.[4] Simply capture the rebel capitol, and the war would be virtually won. A half-trained army with inexperienced leadership had marched south. While the rebel army was little better off, those defending their hearths and homes from invaders generally tend to have the edge. The Bull Run fiasco was the result.

But, as the Yankees fled, Captain William "Grumble" Jones looked on through gritted teeth. Where were the orders to pursue? His commander, Marylander Major Robert Swan, "halted us in a field within fifty yards of Kemper's guns, which were firing on the retreating troops," recalled Mosby. "I was near Captain Jones. He rose in his stirrups and said indignantly, 'Major Swan! You can't be too bold in pursuing a fleeing enemy. But he made no impression on Swan.'" No man or horse in Jones' company received a scratch from enemy action, Mosby recalled.[5] Instead of pursuing the enemy, "After dark Swan marched us back over Bull Run…. He did a life insurance business that day." But then, in a letter to his wife a few days later, Mosby wrote, "in a moment we were in full pursuit, and as we swept by the lines of our infantry, at full speed, the shouts of our victorious soldiers rent the air. We pursued them six or eight miles till darkness covered their retreat."[6] It would appear that Mosby could not admit to his wife missing the exciting pursuit. Either way, he stated that, some considerable time later, he had the pleasure of carrying "an order from Jones who had become a colonel, for Swan's arrest."

Once the battle smoke cleared, the rebels picked their way across the fields where the Yankees had fled helter-skelter back to Washington, 25 miles to the north. They had abandoned everything, "arms, wagons, horses, ammunition, clothing, all sorts of munitions of war," recalled Mosby. "We took enough arms, accoutrements, etc., to equip the whole army. They were splendidly equipped, had every imaginable comfort and convenience which Yankee ingenuity could devise."[7] Mosby lamented the fact that the repulse had not been followed up with a far more aggressive pursuit. He felt Washington could have been captured, and the Yankee government forced to recognize the Confederacy.

Uniforms on both sides at this early stage had not become standardized. Many volunteer companies wore individual apparel in various colors, and some rebel battalions had been adorned in Union blue. As a result, friend had sometimes fired on friend while, on other occasions, fire was withheld when the enemy advanced. And the Confederate "Stars and Bars" national flag looked markedly similar to the Federal Stars and Stripes through a haze of dust and smoke. General Beauregard soon remedied this by designing a new flag for use in combat,[8] a blue St. Andrew's Cross adorned with stars against a red background, the famous Confederate battle flag.

There was much reorganization and finger pointing in the North after Bull Run, and Horace Greeley disowned the "On to Richmond" articles, not written by himself while he was recuperating from an injury. But it was he who had set the tone. Greeley had initially attacked the Lincoln administration for moving too slowly, and was obliged to fend off accusations that much of the blame lay with him.

The Federal Army of the Potomac was formed under the leadership of General George B. McClellan. He ordered two divisions of bluecoats into Virginia, and Confederate general Joseph E. Johnston moved his soldiers north to counter the move, with headquarters in Centreville. Jeb Stuart's cavalry took position at Fairfax Court House, a Virginia hamlet of about 300 people 15 miles from Washington. It was here that Captain John Marr had been killed during a clash the preceding June, the first Confederate officer to die in the war.

The opposing armies dug in and drilled—and drilled. McClellan's organizational capabilities were beyond reproach, and he was beloved by the troops. But the big guns remained silent over the next few months. Skirmishes did occur, however, and the threat of death was always there. "It was after dark," Mosby recalled. "When riding along the road a volley was suddenly poured into us from a thick clump of pines. The balls whistled around us and Captain Jones' horse fell shot through the head. We were perfectly helpless, as it was dark and they were concealed in the bushes. The best of it was that the Yankees shot three of their own men—thought they were ours."[9] Other minor clashes occurred, and on one occasion Mosby was "knocked senseless" when his horse fell and rolled over him. But not all contact with the enemy meant bloodshed: "Some of the Yankees came to my picket post under a flag of truce,—stayed all night,—ate supper with me; and we treated each other with as much courtesy as did Richard and Saladin when they met by the Diamond of the Desert."

The visitors may have been less relaxed had they known they may fall victim to Mosby at another time. His lethal Sharps carbine had an optimum range of 1000 yards, and he delighted in shooting Yankee pickets from a distance. "I took deliberate aim & fired at them with more eagerness than I ever did at a squirrel," he wrote Pauline. She wrote back regularly, keeping him abreast of events at home.[10]

With Mosby through all this was Aaron Burton. Although a slave, there was a considerable bond between the two men. "Aaron considers himself next in command to Captain Jones," Mosby wrote to sister Liz,[11] and in another letter to Pauline he mentioned Aaron "doctoring the sick men during the battle. He is a good deal thought of in the company."

On November 18 Mosby took part in what he considered to be, at the time, the "most dashing feat of the war." He described how an 80-man cavalry scout under Lieutenant Colonel Fitzhugh Lee, nephew of Robert E., attacked an equal force of Yankees protected by a thicket of pine trees. "We charged right through them and they poured a raking fire into our ranks," Mosby wrote Pauline. He and his friend Fount Beattie "in the ardor of pursuit" became separated and came across two Yankees in the woods. A demand for surrender was ignored and one aimed his rifle at Beattie. Mosby fired his pistol but missed. The Yankee fired but, despite being at close range, his bullet only cut a few leaves. Mosby scrambled from his horse, steadied his carbine against a tree, and fired. The Yankee fell, and Beattie fired at the other man, but missed. Then a South Carolina rebel rode up and shot the surviving Yankee dead. "The man I killed had a letter in his pocket from his sweetheart Clara,"[12] Mosby recalled without apparent regret. By this time he had become hardened to the realities of war. It was kill or be killed. There had already been many grieving sweethearts, both North and South, and there were many more yet to come.

But Mosby did have regrets over other aspects of the war. When viewing Washington, D.C., "we could see it distinctly," he wrote Pauline, "with all their fortifications and the stars and stripes floating over it. I thought of the last time I had seen it, for you were there with me, and I could not but feel some regrets that it was no longer the Capitol of my Country, but that of a foreign foe."[13] Perhaps the Stars and Stripes over the capitol also reminded Mosby of those prewar days when he had offered to hang any man who favored secession.

Fitzhugh Lee led several companies of the 1st Virginia Cavalry on a scouting expedition. A flicker of red against the Virginia green was seen in the distance, but it was not enemy fire. The Yankee Brooklyn 14th Chasseurs Regiment wore red caps and breeches with a blue jacket. According to legend, at Bull Run Stonewall Jackson had cried, "Hold on boys. Here come those red-legged devils again." While most volunteer companies discarded their individual uniforms for standard Yankee blue, the Brooklyn Chasseurs kept their more colorful garb until mustered out in May of 1864.[14]

"As soon as we got in sight of them we charged," recalled Mosby. A portion of the "red-legged Yankees" were in a thicket, and some rebels dismounted and charged into the woods on foot, carbines in hand. A sharp fight ensued, prisoners were taken, and Mosby found a copy of the *Washington Star* at the enemy campsite. It carried the riveting news of two Confederate envoys to Great Britain having been taken from the British ship R.M.S. *Trent* by the U.S.S. *San Jacinto* on November 8, 1861. This could have serious, negative ramifications for U.S. and British diplomatic relations, and strengthen the bond between London and the Confederacy. Although not given full status as an independent nation, Britain recognized the Confederacy as a legitimate "belligerent power," a halfway measure. The Confederacy not only craved full recognition from the world's most dominant power, but hoped it would go to war with the United States to break the Yankee blockade on Southern ports. This would allow cotton to be freely shipped again to British mills which were in dire straits since the blockade was enforced. Many politicians there assumed the South would prevail, especially after Bull Run. The correspondent for the *London Times* wrote that every foreign diplomat, except one, agreed that "the Union is broken for ever, and the independence of the South virtually established."[15] An air of deep gloom shrouded Washington.

The North's free press was an important source of intelligence, and Mosby handed the captured paper to Fitzhugh Lee. "Colonel, here's a copy of to-day's paper," he said with pride. But Lee did not take the paper. "The ruling passion strong in death," he coldly replied.[16] This was an old saying used over the years by various people, meaning that a person's "ruling passion" cannot change even if it costs your life. Religious zealots, for example, would burn at the stake rather than recant. Mosby had achieved a reputation as being the first to get his hands on enemy newspapers, which meant putting his life at risk, thus the "ruling passion strong in death." Fitz Lee was a West Point officer who believed in honorable battle along conventional lines. He was no Swamp Fox man. The world of spies, guerrilla warfare and groping about in the woods was repugnant to him. Stunned with the rebuttal, Mosby gave the paper to Grumble Jones who dispatched it to General Johnston's headquarters at Centreville.

"The last time I went on picket was the 12th of February (1862)," recalled Mosby. "By this time Stuart had been made a brigadier-general, and Jones was colonel of the regiment." Mosby had never met Jeb Stuart, but on February 12 he received orders to report face to face after escorting two ladies to their destination behind the lines. "I left my horse with my friend Beattie to bring back to camp, and took my seat in the carriage with the ladies."[17] One would expect an officer to be given this task, but Private Mosby knew one of the ladies, having often dined in the family home at her father's invitation. No doubt Mosby, despite being a mere private, was an acceptable dinner guest as he was an educated man with a certain decorum.

With the ladies safely delivered, Mosby traveled back to Stuart's headquarters at the Grimsby House through falling snow and a chilly breeze. He delivered his report to the general, and requested a pass to get safely back to camp, about four miles away. But Stuart would not hear of it. He said Mosby must stay the night and return in the morning. "There could have been nothing prepossessing in my general appearance to induce him to make an exception of me," recalled the astonished private, "for I was as roughly dressed as any common soldier." That evening Mosby found himself sharing a fireside with Generals Stuart, Smith and Johnston. "I felt just as much out of place and uneasy as a mortal would who had been lifted to a seat by the side of the gods of Olympus." He dined with the gods that evening, not saying a word, and was sent for the following morning to break bread with the gods once more. "But now my courage rose; I actually got into conversation with Joe Johnston, whom I would have regarded it as a great privilege the day before to view through a long-range telescope." And there was no need for Mosby to plod on foot back to camp through the ice and snow. Stuart loaned him a horse. Private Mosby had met the great Jeb Stuart face to face, and such small events can influence outcomes. It's not what you know, but *who* you know, when all said and done. "So here began my friendship for Stuart which lasted as long as he lived."[18]

But an even bigger surprise awaited Mosby on return to camp. It seemed the gods of Olympus were smiling on him these days. He was summonsed to Colonel Grumble Jones' tent and "by coincidence" received his first promotion to adjutant, with the effective rank of lieutenant. "I was as much astonished as I had been the night before to be asked to sit at the table with the generals," he recalled. He was delighted to receive the promotion, but it did have pitfalls: "I never could repeat the formulas of the regulations, and for this reason I remember the few weeks I served as an adjutant with less satisfaction than any other portion of my life as a soldier."

And there were other reasons for dissatisfaction, not only for Mosby. As he received his promotion, an obscure Union general named Ulysses S. Grant was firing on Fort Donelson near the Tennessee-Kentucky border. He had already taken Fort Henry on February 6, and Fort Donelson fell on February 16, with more than 12,000 men taken prisoner, an entire army lost, and the strategic Cumberland River opened to Yankee navigation. Throughout the North, bells rang, champagne corks popped, steam whistles shrieked and guns boomed.[19] This was their first great victory, and "Unconditional Surrender" Grant became a celebrity. But Mosby refused to be dispirited. "The idea of giving up or abandoning the field should never enter a Southern man's head," he wrote to Pauline. "To be sure there must be a costly sacrifice of our best blood, but the coward dies a thousand deaths, the brave man dies but one."

The new adjutant may not have liked paperwork, but every cloud has a silver lining, as they say. The job brought him into further personal contact with Jeb Stuart. The two developed a rapport, and Mosby was dispatched on several scouting expeditions at Stuart's behest. His reports proved reliable, establishing a bond of trust.

On March 17, 1862, McClellan finally moved against the rebels with a massive army of over 120,000 men, the largest ever seen on the American continent. The Confederates, unsure of the enemy tactics, fell back from Centerville, bluecoats in pursuit. "General Johnston wants to know if McClellan's army is following us," Stuart said to Mosby, "or if this is only a feint he is making." Stuart did not order Mosby out, but the eager adjutant took the hint. "I will find out for you," he replied, "if you will give me a guide." Mosby set out on horseback with the guide and two other men, and skirted around the enemy flank, coming up in their rear. Riding from tree grove to hillock, dismounting, and observing, then mounting once more, they found this was an isolated body of troops that had no line of communication with Washington, and had already started falling back. Yankee cavalry kept in sight in an attempt to conceal the retreat. "Of course, I was proud to have made the discovery," Mosby recalled, "and I rode nearly all night to report it to Stuart." General Ewell's division had been deployed to repel the mock advance across the Rappahannock, a waste of time and men. "Our cavalry was immediately ordered in pursuit," recalled Mosby, "and I went with it." He wrote to Pauline saying they

Ulysses S. Grant, despite accusations of drunkenness, achieved early victories in the West that helped offset Union defeats in the East (Library of Congress).

took "about 30 prisoners, 16 horses, arms, etc. General Stuart was so much pleased with my conduct that he wrote a report to General Johnston commending me very highly and also recommending my promotion."[20]

But there was no promotion—and Mosby was about to lose what rank he held. McClellan's main thrust was, in fact, on the Virginian peninsula between the James and York Rivers in an attempt to capture Richmond. Once discovered, Joe Johnston's army, including Stuart's cavalry, moved to defend the capitol. In April the regiment was stationed just outside Yorktown, where news arrived that the Confederate Congress had just introduced conscription for the first time in American history. All able bodied men between 18 and 35 could be called up for military service—unless you own 20 slaves or more. Democracy had had been flushed away, apparently, and rich men were exempt. Many rebels deserted. To calm ruffled passions, the troops were allowed to elect their own officers. The result was Fitzhugh Lee replacing Grumble Jones as colonel of the 1st Virginia Cavalry. Shortly before the change of command, Adjutant Mosby had said to Lee, "Colonel, the horn has blowed for dress parade." The prim and proper Lee exploded, "Sir, if I ever again hear you call that bugle a horn I will put you under arrest."[21]

Mosby did not continue on as adjutant once Fitz Lee took command. Whether he resigned or was pushed is obscure. In his 1898 *Reminiscences* he wrote, "Fitz Lee did not reappoint me as adjutant, and so I lost my first commission on the spot where Cornwallis lost his sword. This was at the time an unrecognized favor. If I had been retained as adjutant, I would probably have never been anything else."[22] These are the words of a man given the sack. But in his 1917 *Memoirs* Mosby reproduced a letter written to Pauline: "Immediately after the election I handed in my resignation of my commission. The president had commissioned me for the war, but I would not be adjutant of a Colonel against his wishes or if I were not his first choice."[23] Perhaps, as with his contradictory accounts of Bull Run, Mosby put on a brave face when writing to his wife.

Mosby found himself relegated to the ranks once more, but Grumble Jones did well, being appointed colonel of the 7th Virginia Cavalry. He whipped his troops into shape, never losing a fight, and in September was promoted to brigadier general at the request of Stonewall Jackson. Despite this, however, he had no time for Jeb Stuart and an insulting letter written to him resulted in Jones' court martial. He was found guilty, but rather than lose a good man, Robert E. Lee had Jones transferred to command the department of Western Virginia. He was killed while leading a charge during the Battle of Piedmont, a Confederate defeat, on June 5, 1864.[24]

Just five days after the Conscription Act, President Jefferson Davis introduced the Partisan Ranger Act of April 21, 1862. This allowed for "bands of partisan rangers, in companies, battalions, or regiments, to be composed of such members as the President may approve." They would be entitled to the same pay and conditions as regular soldiers, and be paid the full value of any arms or munitions captured from the enemy and delivered to "quartermasters at such place or places may be designated by a commanding general."[25] This, no doubt, fired the enthusiasm of a man like Mosby who found formal military proceedings not to his taste. It provided a chance for a small, independent commands to operate away from more conventional souls like Fitzhugh Lee.

But there were those who did not agree. Units calling themselves partisans were already on the road, with and without official approval, and commanding General Joseph Johnston had complained of handbills and newspaper ads for partisan recruits. This, he felt, would cause men to desert who could see a lucrative chance for plunder with rather than meager army pay. Others felt the same way, and General Heth had already given orders, on April

2, to disband two Virginia State Ranger units, considering them mere plunderers rather than legitimate troops.[26]

The day following Mosby's demotion, he was appointed to Stuart's staff as a courier. The man who once rebuffed the idea of becoming an officer had by now tasted power, and gained confidence in his own abilities. Stuart, however, was unable to secure him a commission. But he well knew Mosby's qualities, and often gave him scouting responsibilities far in access of a mere private. This led to some thinking Mosby was a captain or lieutenant. "This was the origin of my partisan life, that was far more congenial to me than the dull, routine work of an adjutant," Mosby recalled.

On May 31 General Johnston was severely wounded at the Battle of Seven Pines, one of a series of struggles to halt McClellan's thrust to capture Richmond. The next day Jefferson Davis' military advisor, Robert E. Lee, took command, and the force confronting the Yankee juggernaut was renamed the Army of Northern Virginia.[27] On June 9 Jeb Stuart and John Mosby took breakfast alone, and the scout was asked to find out if McClellan was fortifying along the Totopotomoy Creek on the Federal right flank. "This was the very thing I wanted: an opportunity for which I had pined. In a few minutes I was saddled. I rode over the camp to the 1st Virginia and got three men from my old company, who had marched with me from Abingdon the year before—Pendleton, Crockett and Williams. We started off as joyful as if we were going to a wedding."[28] But, deterred by a flag of truce on the road, preventing troop movements, they were unable to proceed. "I did not want to go back without something," Mosby recalled, and they set off to scout in another direction. The change of plans worked to their advantage. They penetrated the Yankee lines and discovered that, for several miles, the enemy right flank had only cavalry pickets to guard the line of communication to their major supply depot, called the White House, on the Pamunkey River. It was well to the rear of McClellan's lines, and there were no infantry to be seen. "Here, it seemed to me," Mosby recalled, "was an opportunity to strike a blow."

He rode back to Stewart posthaste and, exhausted and hot, dismounted. Mosby delivered his report lying down. "A martinet would have ordered me to stand in his presence," Mosby recalled. Stuart listened with intense interest, had Mosby write it out, and galloped off to Robert E. Lee's headquarters. The document would give Mosby credit if things went right—or someone to blame if things went wrong. Stuart was soon back rapping out orders for an advance to the enemy's rear. Based on the report, Lee had ordered him to probe the strength of McClellan's right flank, gather supplies and cattle, and do what damage he could without undue hazard to his command.[29]

Stuart's Ride

During the dark, early hours of June 12 no "horn" sounded Boots and Saddles, despite intense activity in the rebel cavalry camps. All taking part in Stuart's expedition had been ordered to prepare as quietly as possible. The buoyant young general led his 1200 men and two cannon through Richmond northwards towards Louisa township, with scouts and flankers out. He hoped to give the impression to prying Yankee eyes that they were marching to reinforce Stonewall Jackson in the Shenandoah Valley. The rebels then turned eastwards, and camped northwest of Hanover Court House for the night. Next morning "without flag or bugle-sound we resumed our march," recalled Stuart. Scouts reported no serious obstacle between them and Old Church, directly in the enemy's rear. Yankee cavalry were seen at Hanover Court House, but they fell back as the rebel column turned south. At the township of Haw's Shop the Confederates charged Yankee pickets who fled in "wholesome terror," according to Stuart.

Captain William Royall, commanding two squadrons of the 5th U.S. Cavalry, got wind of the enemy movement, and moved up from Old Church to confront Stuart's advance. Rebel Captain William Latané of the 9th Virginia Cavalry drew his saber and led the attack

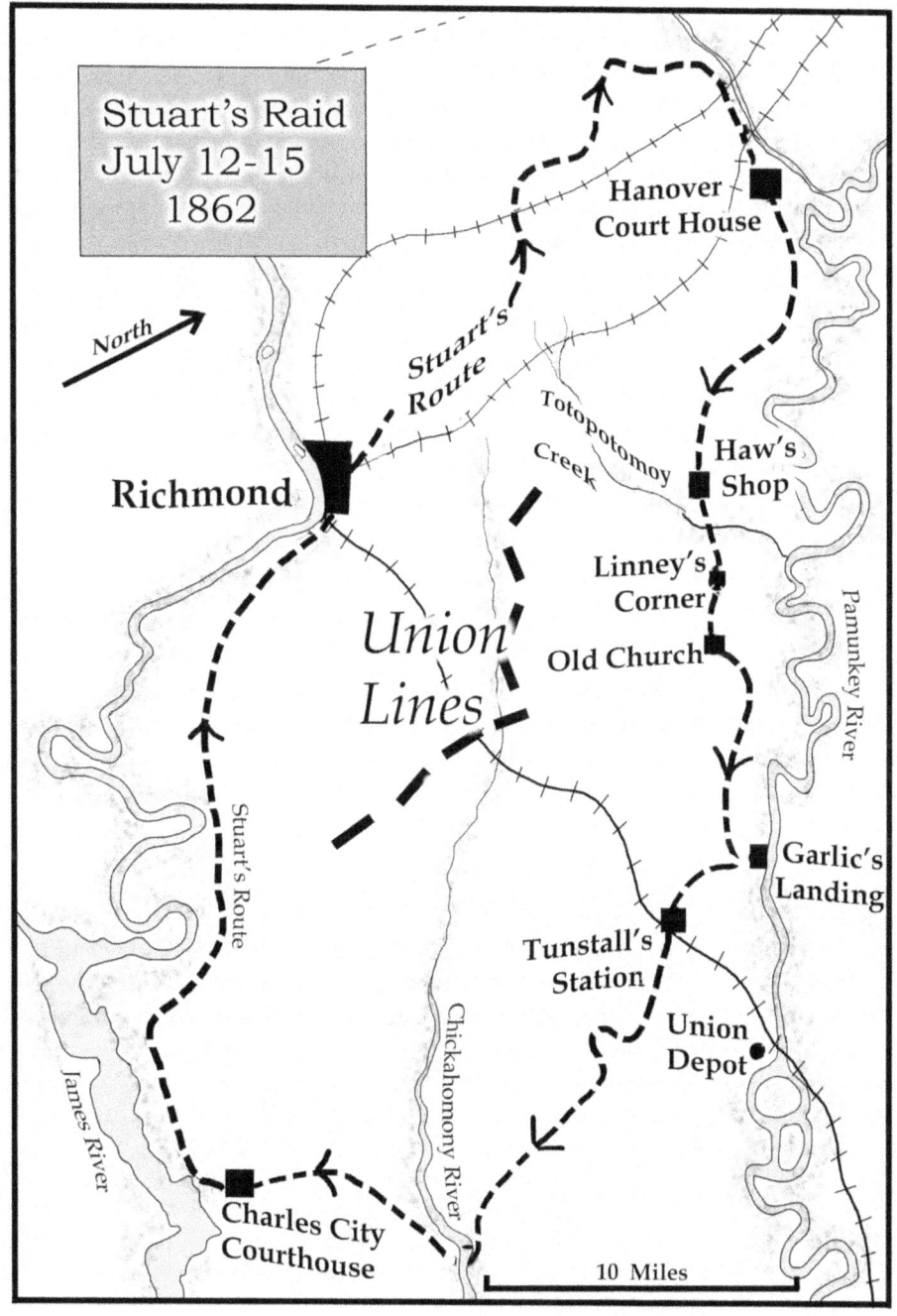

Stuart's Raid, July 12–15, 1862 (author's rendition).

against the Yankee line. Royall saw him coming but wisely relied on his pistol rather than the blade. Latané was shot dead from his saddle as he slashed at Royall with his saber. But Royall was badly wounded by another rebel before he could fall back. The Yankees fled under the rebel onslaught leaving their well stocked camp at Old Church to the raiders. The Confederates dismounted and feasted on luxuriant provisions rarely seen in ne of their own camps. What they could not carry off went up in flames. Several Union officers and enlisted men were taken captive, along with horses, arms and five cavalry guidons.

But what to do now? Old Church was as far as Lee had authorized Stuart to proceed. The alerted Federals, however, could move in behind, cutting off retreat. Stuart had suggested to Lee another option: continue right around McClellan's army, doing what damage they could. Guarding McClellan's rear were cavalry commanded by General Phillip Saint George Cooke, Jeb Stuart's father-in-law, a Virginian who had stayed loyal to the Union. This, according to Stuart, was a decision he would "regret but once, and that would be continually." Perhaps this prediction urged Stuart on. "In a brief and frank interview with some of my officers I disclosed my views," he later reported, "but while none accorded a full assent, all assured me a hearty support in whatever I did."[30] Mosby later claimed that Colonel Fitz Lee was opposed, while Robert E. Lee's son, Colonel William Lee, was in favor.[31] Mosby felt that Stuart never had the slightest intention of turning back, otherwise "he would have left pickets behind him to keep the way open. But he did nothing of the kind."

"Just before Stuart gave the order for us to move," recalled Mosby, "he turned to me and said, 'I want you to go on some distance ahead.'" "'Very well,' said I, 'but give me a guide.'" With two soldiers who knew the local roads, Mosby led the advance. They soon captured a Yankee sutler's wagon and, in the distance, the masts of two schooners could be seen at Garlick's Landing on the Pamunkey River. Yankees there were hard at work unloading supplies for McClellan's troops. Mosby sent one soldier to alert Stuart, about two miles back, then pushed on alone, leaving the other man to guard the sutler and his valuable goods. Mosby captured another sutler's wagon, but a bugle call alerted him to the presence of Yankee cavalry drawn up in battle line near the York River Railroad tracks. His horse was too tired to run, so he simply drew his saber and flashed it about his head, as though beckoning more troops on. Fortunately for Mosby, the rebel advance guard came into view and the Yankee squadron to his front promptly "vanished from sight." Stuart soon arrived with a battalion of dust covered horseman, all bent on destruction. A detachment was detailed to deal with the schooners, and the sky was soon black with smoke as the vessels went up in flames along with a wagon train of supplies. "Capturing watercraft was a novel experiment in cavalry tactics," observed Mosby.

"A few picked men," reported Stuart, "including my aides, Burke, Farley and Mosby, were pushed forward rapidly to Tunstall's to cut the wires and secure the depot." The handful of infantry guarding Tunstall's Station were captured by the advance guard without a shot being fired, and the rebels soon set about placing logs over the tracks. But, before the job was complete, "a train of cars came thundering down from the Grand Army," reported Stuart. The engineer was in no mood to stop, and gave his locomotive full steam ahead. Logs went flying as the iron horse crashed through. The train, with Federal troops on board, steamed on amidst a gauntlet of gunfire, the rebels riding alongside. The feisty engineer paid for his bravado when he was shot by Captain Farley. Some bluecoats returned fire while others jumped out and others lay flat to avoid being hit.[32] But nothing could stop the lumbering train, and it soon disappeared down the track "with extraordinary speed" in a haze of steam and smoke.

As night came on, the rebels spent some time tearing up rail lines, and chopping down telegraph poles. The railroad bridge over Black Creek went up in flames along with an immense wagon train which, "illuminated the country for miles." But they also had time to indulge themselves. "That night was a feast for Stuart's cavalry," recalled Mosby, "Champagne and Rhine wine flowed copiously."[33]

At midnight the rebels continued their historic ride around McClellan's army, prisoners carried double on captured mules. The Yankee cavalry was thwarted by orders to move no faster than supporting infantry. They had little hope of catching Stuart's rapidly moving horsemen, despite the rebels having to reconstruct a destroyed bridge over the Chickahominy River. Timbers were ripped from an old warehouse and, "It seemed to rise out of the water like magic," conjured up by Lieutenant Redmond Burke of the 1st Virginia Cavalry. By 1 p.m. on June 14, the Confederates were safely across, and Burke saw his newly built bridge go up in flames to prevent pursuit. A few shots fired across the river by Yankee artillery came far too late.

The rebels rode on to Charles City Courthouse, well within Confederate territory. The exhausted but jubilant horsemen had been in the saddle for 36 hours, and could now afford the luxury of sleep. Stuart rode ahead and reported to Lee's headquarters at daylight the following morning, then rode back to join his men. On July 15 Stuart lead his cavalry back into Richmond where they received a joyous welcome from crowds thronging the streets. They brought with them 165 prisoners, 260 horses and mules, and numerous arms. Millions of dollars in damage had been done, and Stuart felt this raid would compel McClellan to detach up to 15,000 men to guard the Yankee rear. The only Confederate casualty had been Captain Latané.

John Mosby was one of those singled out by Stuart for "conspicuous and gallant service." Stuart referred to him in his report as a captain "without commission."[34] Robert E. Lee in his General Orders of June 23, listed Mosby as one of the "privates" who received special commendation. It seems that Mosby was a private, but acting as a captain with Stuart's blessing, and one newspaper went for something between captain and private: "After destroying the enemy's camp near the old church, Lieutenant John S. Mosby, aid to General Stuart and who had been most daring and successful as a scout was sent on in advance, with a single guide, towards Tunstall Station, to reconnoitre and ascertain the position and force of the enemy. On his way he met two Yankees whom he took prisoners and sent to the rear in charge of his guide. Alone he pushed on and overtook a cavalryman and an artilleryman of the enemy's forces, having in charge a quartermaster's wagon and stores. Lieutenant Mosby dashed up and, drawing his pistols, demanded their surrender. The New Yorker surrendered at once, but the Pennsylvanian, beginning to fumble for his pistol, the lieutenant made a more emphatic demand for his surrender, and at the same moment compelled him to look quite closely into the muzzle of his pistol. All this time there was drawn up, not four hundred yards distant, a company of Yankee cavalry in line of battle. In a moment a bugle sounded as for a movement on him, when, anxious to secure his prisoners and stores, Lieutenant Mosby put spurs and galloped across the field, at the same time shouting to his imaginary men to follow him, when none of the Confederate cavalry were in sight and the swiftest more than a mile in the rear. The Yankees, hearing the word of command and apprehending the descent of an avalanche of Confederate cavalry upon them, broke line, each man galloping off to take care of himself. The wagon, prisoners, and stores were then secured and among them were found forty splendid Colt's pistols with holsters, besides boots, shoes, blankets, etc., etc."[35]

The daring ride around the Yankee army made McClellan look foolish, and Jeb Stuart a hero. It also brought "Private—Lieutenant—Captain" Mosby into the public eye—a man to be watched.

6

"Cutthroats are coming!"
Quantrill, 1861–1862

On March 19, 1861, the Missouri State Convention voted decisively for Missouri to stay within the Union. Despite many delegates favoring Southern principles, amongst other concerns, it was felt that the bordering free states, Kansas, Illinois and Iowa, would invade Missouri if war broke out. William Clarke Quantrill was not pleased with the result. And he was not the only one. Governor Claiborne Jackson's democratic ideals, if existent, went out the window when he ordered the state militia to mobilize and seize Federal arms on behalf of the Confederacy. Missouri was going to secede whether the electorate liked it or not.

But Captain Nathaniel Lyon of the U.S. Army had other ideas. He was no stranger to the smell of gunpowder, having fought Seminoles and Mexicans, and taken part in the "Bloody Island Massacre" of Pemo Indians in California. On May 10 he ordered Federal troops to surround the militia mustered at Camp Jackson on the outskirts of St. Louis. Outgunned and outnumbered, they surrendered without a shot being fired. The militia were escorted through the city streets as a hostile proslavery crowd gathered and pelted the Federal troops with stones and any other object that came to hand. Then someone shot an officer, and the "St. Louis Massacre" followed. The troops opened fire and 28 civilians were killed along with many more wounded. Two soldiers died in the exchange, and the following day two more were killed along with four civilians in another clash. A wave of pro-rebel sympathy swept the state, and many who had favored conditional union now came out for secession.[1] The Confederate victory in Virginia at Bull Run on July 21 was a huge boost to Southern moral, and more fence-sitting Missourians took up arms for the rebel cause.

Most prominent of these was former Missouri governor, Sterling "Old Pap" Price. Having been a victorious general during the Mexican War, Jackson placed him in command of the pro-southern Missouri State Guard. He, Jackson and Secretary Thomas Snead met with Nathaniel Lyon, now promoted to brigadier-general in the Union Army. They urged Lyon to allow Missouri to remain neutral, and have no more Union troops march into the state.

"Rather than concede to the state of Missouri for one single instant the right to dictate to my Government in any manner however unimportant," replied Lyon, "I would see you and you and you and every man, woman and child in the State dead and buried—This means war!" He "turned on his heel and strode out of the room, rattling his spurs and rattling his saber," recalled Snead.[2]

Price and Jackson were forced to flee from Jefferson City, the capitol, as Lyon advanced with Union troops. The convention reassembled and installed Hamilton Gamble as the legitimate pro–Union provisional governor of Missouri. Gamble had previously served as the chief justice of the Missouri Supreme Court, and his appointment was immediately recognized as bona fide by the Lincoln administration. This enabled the raising of pro–Union militia for service within Missouri, and volunteer regiments for the Union Army.

General Ben McCulloch, however, led Confederate troops from Texas and Arkansas into Missouri where they joined forces with Price's State Guard. Serving under Price, William Clarke Quantrill saw his first action at the Battle of Wilson's Creek on August 10. The fighting started when Nathaniel Lyon, although outnumbered, struck the rebel camp. One Federal column under Colonel Franz Sigel had initial success, but was hit with a counter-attack by McCulloch when the German troops stopped to loot the rebel camp. McCulloch drove them from the field, and then turned to aid Price who was fighting other bluecoats under General Lyon. Having received no word from Sigel of his defeat, Lyon now continued the fight against the entire enemy force. Dead and wounded littered the ground as "Bloody Hill" became the center of conflict. Price dashed about on horseback encouraging his men to fight. "Don't lead us, General," his men cried, "don't come with us! Take care of yourself for the sake of us all! We will go without you!"[3] But Old Pap stayed to the fore and received a side wound for his trouble. Lyon also dashed about on horseback, but the bullet that struck him in the chest took his life. Major Samuel D. Sturgis, later commander of the 7th U.S. Cavalry,[4] took command and ordered a general retreat.

Price's victory brought in a wave of recruits, and he laid siege to Lexington, Missouri, on September 13. Author John N. Edwards, in his 1877 book *Noted Guerrillas*, stated that Quantrill displayed "conspicuous daring" during the fight: "Mounted on a splendid horse, armed with a Sharps carbine and four navy revolvers, his uniform a red shirt, and for oriflamme a sweeping black plume, he advanced with the farthest, fell back with the last, and was always cool, deadly and omnipresent. General Price—himself notorious for being superbly indifferent under fire—remarked his bearing and caused mention to be made of it most favourably."[5] Edwards' assertion may be true, but no verifying mention of Quantrill's performance at Lexington has ever been found.[6]

On September 20 the rebels advanced behind dampened hemp bales, captured from a warehouse on the riverbank. Pushed forward by teams of three men on hands and knees, the bales absorbed the enemy balls and bullets, and heated shot failed to ignite the dampened straw. The Yankee ammunition ran low, and it was not long before the white flag was seen. Price commended Colonel James Mulligan for his spirited defense, and when he refused to take a parole, had him escorted in Price's own buggy to the safety of Union lines. Rebel governor Jackson was present, and ordered "Mulligan's brigade to be drawn up in solid column to hear a speech from him," reported *Harper's Weekly*. "He then addressed them in harsh language, demanding what business they had to make war in the State of Missouri, adding that when Missouri needed troops from Illinois she would ask for them. After upbraiding them for some length of time, this wretched traitor at last told them they might go home, when they dispersed with feelings which can be more easily imagined than described. If Governor Jackson falls into the hands of any of the Illinois Volunteers he will have a hard time."[7]

Three days layer, on September 23, General Jim "Grim Chieftain" Lane struck Osceola, Missouri, with 1200 jayhawkers. The town was an affluent trading center on the Osage River, and the warehouses were stocked with provisions and valuable goods. The bank was cleaned out, and wagons were loaded with pillaged spoils as men became roaring drunk on captured liquor. Despite efforts to prevent them, "the boys filled their canteens and 'tanks' with the stuff," recalled Captain Henry Palmer of the 11th Kansas Cavalry, "more deadly for a while than rebel bullets, and nearly 300 of our men had to be hauled from town in wagons and carriages impressed into service for that purpose. Had the rebels then rallied and renewed the fight we would have been captured and shot."[8] But it was nine local men who were captured by Lane, given a drumhead court-martial, and shot.

Many residents were Union sympathizers with men fighting in blue, but no distinction was made when it came to looting and putting homes to the torch. Jim Lane later boasted of causing one million dollars damage, and his own loot included $1,000 in gold, a pile of silk dresses, a piano, and a fine carriage. Every shop and warehouse was set ablaze, only a few houses and a livery stable left standing once the smoke had cleared. No doubt he felt well justified by Lawrence having been sacked in 1856. What else could rebels expect?

Their incendiary work done, Lane's Brigade continued north, and the raid was a blessing for about 200 slaves who went with him, free at last. The jayhawkers camped outside Kansas City, and were described as "a ragged, half-armed, diseased, mutinous rabble." Lane was described by Lieutenant Thompson of the 3rd Iowa as "the last man we would have taken for a general. He had on citizens' pants, a soldiers' blouse, and a dilapidated white hat. He rolled under his dark brows a pair of piercing eyes, and between his jaws a huge quid of tobacco."[9]

On September 27, 38,000 bluecoats commanded by General John C. Frémont marched from Jefferson City towards Lexington to attack Price's army. Scouts brought word to Price, and he abandoned Lexington, retreating south to Neosho. Frémont got wind of the move, and followed. Price's withdrawal to the southeast corner ended Confederate control of most of the state, leaving only rebel guerrilla bands to defend the Southern cause. But their numbers grew as recruits, appalled by the likes of Lane's Brigade, flocked to their ranks.

During Price's retreat to Neosho, a shortage of food caused many local recruits, including William Quantrill, to leave the column and fend for themselves. The settlement of Blue Springs, Jackson County, Missouri, was named for the abundant fresh spring water of the Little Blue River. It was here that Quantrill arrived to be sheltered by friends amongst the Southern sympathizing inhabitants.

Word arrives that Kansas jayhawkers were raiding settlements along the border. The Walker farm was near Blue Springs, and Andrew Walker mustered a party of about a dozen men, including Quantrill, to hunt them down. Walker's party arrived at the De Witt homestead, recently plundered, then rode to the home of Strawder Stone, also pillaged. "Mrs. Stone got angry with them and talked pretty sharp to them," recalled Walker, "and one of them struck her on the head with his pistol." The jayhawkers were overtaken at the Thompson homestead and the avengers struck. Mrs. Stone's attacker was shot and killed while the others, despite some being wounded, got away. Next day, the authorities took Stone and Thompson into the Independence jail while they investigated the death, and the two wounded men would soon die. But, taking a leadership role, Quantrill rode into town and swore out an affidavit before Justice of the Peace Hightower. He and others were responsible for the death at Thompson's house, he said, and the two men in custody were released. Once all facts were considered, no official action was taken against Quantrill, but "then the Federals in Independence wanted Quantrill," recalled Walker, "but he kept out of their way. I give you these details because I want the public to know just how Quantrill began his celebrated career as a guerrilla and bushwhacker."[10] Under pressure from his father, Walker retired from the band to follow his own path during the war, which at one time included being forced to serve in the Federal Army.

Apart from being a crack shot and excellent horseman, Quantrill had learned military organization while serving with Price, and ambush tactics from his native friends in Indian Territory. He emerged as the leader, and at the end of 1861 his band consisted of 15 men: George Todd, Fletch Taylor, William Gregg, William Haller, Joe Gilchrist, Perry Hoy, John and James Little, Joe Vaughan, James Hendricks, John and Ed Koger, Harrison Trace, Olive Shepherd, and George Maddox. At the outset, Quantrill's closest friend was Jim Little, but those who to rose to leadership roles in the short term were Todd, Haller and Gregg. Many more would join, but these 15 formed the core of what became known as Quantrill's Raiders. Of them, George Todd would emerge as the most conspicuous. A 20-year-old Canadian-born stone mason, handsome and blond, Todd was described as bad tempered and brutal, but an excellent shot and fearless in combat.[11]

Towards the end of December 1861, a deserter from Old Pap's rebel army, George Searcy, went on a robbery spree near Blue Springs, and made a foolish attempt to bushwhack the emerging bushwhacker chief himself. Quantrill was not amused. The robber was tracked down and given a token trial. "Not so fast, gentlemen," Searcy had said as a rope was placed around his neck. "It's a shame to die until red hands have a chance to wash themselves." But "four guerrillas dragged on the rope," recalled a witness. "There seemed to be—as his body rested at last from its contortions—the noise as of the wavering of wings. Could it be that Searcy's soul was taking its flight?"[12]

Searcy's victims were delighted for the return of their stolen horses, mules, mortgage papers and other property. Perhaps Quantrill, having a dubious reputation from Charley Hart days, was attempting to reinvent himself as a latter-day Robin Hood.

A few days after Searcy's demise a Federal patrol riding the road to Independence was passing through Manasseh Gap. Bullets flew as Quantrill's band opened fire. Several Yankees were wounded and the others quickly surrendered. They were all paroled and allowed to go free after being relieved of their arms. This was the first clash between bluecoats and Quantrill's Raiders, and the word quickly spread. This new menace on the prairies was to be destroyed at all costs. But it would prove to a long and costly contest that would see repercussions for decades to come.

At this early stage of the war Quantrill did attempt to behave by the rules: taking prisoners, giving paroles and offering to exchange prisoners. But that first sacking of Lawrence in 1856 had set an example that liberated the vengeful passions of jayhawkers in the Bleeding Kansas conflict that followed. In Missouri and Kansas, far more vicious guerrilla warfare would occur than that practiced by Mosby and others back east where house burning and giving no quarter were considered only an act of last resort.

On Christmas day, 1861, Quantrill told his men to go home. Freezing weather had set in. They would reform when the temperatures rose and they could take to the road once more. He returned to Blue Springs, but not all in that bastion of rebel support wished to see the Confederacy flourish. Riley Alley was, covertly, one such inhabitant, and he invited Quantrill and his men to attend a ball at his home. The festivities were well under way when Yankee troopers burst in with revolvers drawn. They found a few known rebels, but most, wary, had stayed well clear. Suspect male guests were loaded into wagons and taken to Independence. Riley Alley, having to appear as a victim, was taken along. Soon released, his subterfuge had fooled no one, and he fled the area to avoid Quantrill's retribution. One rebel taken prisoner, Sol Basham, was put on trial and spent the remainder of the war in the Rock Island Penitentiary.[13] The others were threatened, and 15-year-old Frank Smith was told, "You damn little rebel, I'm going to let you go, but if I hear of you getting into anything down there at Blue Springs, or taking any part in assisting the rebel cause, I'll send down and have you brought in here and will cut your damn head off." The budding young rebel, thus pushed, promptly joined Quantrill.

The incident found its way into a song written by Ed Koger, a banjo playing member of Quantrill's band.

> Old Rile Alley gave a ball,
> The Feds came down and took us all
> Over the ice and over the snow—
> Sing-Song Kitty, won't you kiss-me-o'
> Old Rile Alley gave a ball,
> planned to catch Quantrill and bushwhack all,
> But Quant was smart and didn't go—
> Sing-Song Kitty, won't you kiss-me-o![14]

Among new recruits for Quantrill in late January were John Jarrett and his brother-in-law, Thomas Coleman Younger, who had only just turned 17. "He was an exceedingly handsome fellow, stalwart, alert and intelligent and every inch a soldier. He wore a black slouch hat, dove-colored trousers and a colored shirt. Around his waste, suspended from a glossy black belt, was a brace of fine revolvers," recalled Confederate Major Warren Bronaugh of the 16th Missouri Infantry. "This alert and entertaining young picket was no other than the now famous Cole Younger, whose name for daring and endurance is known in every state and territory of this union."[15] Younger himself recalled, "I cannot remember when I did not know how to shoot. I hunted wild geese when I could not have dragged a pair of them home unaided."[16]

In early February of 1862 Yankee General John Pope received a report from Captain W. S. Oliver of the 7th Missouri Volunteers. It contained not only the first surviving official mention of William Clarke Quantrill, but also a hint of the hardships endured by troops engaged in pursuing rebel guerrillas:

> I have just returned from an expedition which I was compelled to undertake in search of the notorious Quantrell and his gang of robbers in the vicinity of Blue Springs. Without mounted men at my disposal, despite numerous applications to various points, I have seen this infamous scoundrel rob mails, steal the coaches and horses, and commit other similar outrages upon society even within sight of this city. Mounted on the best horses of the country, he has defied pursuit.... I mounted a company of my command and went to Blue Springs. The first night there myself, with 5 men, were ambushed by him and fired upon. We killed 2 of his men (of which he had 18 or 20) and wounded a third. The next day we killed 4 more of the worst of the gang, and before we left succeeded in dispersing them. I obtained 6 or 7 wagon loads of pork and a quantity of tobacco, hidden and preserved for the use of the Southern Army, and recovered also the valuable stage-coach, with 2 of their horses. I was absent a week, and can say that no men were ever more earnest or subject to greater privations and hardships than both the mounted men and the infantry I employed on this expedition. Quantrill will not leave this section unless he is chastised and driven from it. I hear of him tonight 15 miles from here, with new recruits, committing outrages on Union men, a large body of whom have come in to-night, driven out by him. Families of Union men are coming into the city tonight asking of me escorts to bring in their goods and chattels, which I duly furnished.... My men are without boots and shoes, and the long march in the snow and cold from Morristown and this last severe expedition has filled the hospital, as you are aware from the report of the post surgeon, heretofore transmitted. Three are confined to their beds with broken limbs and two with small-pox. They cannot be removed in my wagons. Others may come down in a few days. I applied to General Hunter for shoes, &c. He replied that all my supplies of that sort must be obtained through you. Saying nothing, general, about the deplorable condition which the withdrawal of my force will leave this people in, is it not pertinent for me to ask how I can move my command in its present condition on this frozen ground and snow? I assure you, sir, nothing do I more desire than to rejoin my regiment,

but if I go now my men must travel with frozen feet, and my sick I must leave behind for aught I see. I am not insensible, and cannot be, to the appeals which pour in upon me from the many Union men of this vicinity to remain, but I have no duties to discharge transcending your command, and do not ask for delay on that account.... Hoping this presentation of facts will excuse me from moving until at least I obtain further commands from you, and awaiting your further orders, I remain, with great respect, your obedient servant,

W. S. OLIVER,
Captain, Comdg. Detached Battalion Seventh Mo. Vols.

P.S.—I omitted to say I find that I had 1 man killed and 2 wounded during the expedition referred to.[17]

Captain Oliver may well have been frustrated with Quantrill's exploits to date, but far worse was to come. Less than three weeks after he wrote this report the residents of Independence scattered as a band of 16 wild horsemen galloped down a fog shrouded street. Feeling confident, the rebels occupied the northeast corner of the town square. But then something stirred in the mist, Ohio cavalry materializing from the southwest. The bluecoat regiment had passed through town shortly before, and citizens had ridden out to give the alarm.

The rebels opened fire, then turned and fled into the countryside with the Yankees in close pursuit. One trooper caught up with William Gregg who turned and pointed his pistol at the Yankee's ear. *Click, click, click.* It misfired three times, and Gregg found himself under saber attack, but "the only harm he did was to blacken my arm from elbow to wrist," he recalled.[18] Two others, Gabriel George and Hop Wood, were not so lucky, and died where they fell, and Black Bess was shot from under Quantrill. Despite a leg wound, he managed to scramble amidst boulders and make his escape, while the remainder of his men used tactics employed by Indians when eluding the enemy. "It was harder to trail one man than a company," Cole Younger recalled, "and every little while the company would break up, to rally again at a moment's notice."[19]

"Cutthroats are coming!" It was March 7, 1862, in the small township of Aubry, Kansas, near the Missouri border. In an upstairs bedroom of the local tavern, Abraham Ellis jumped from his bed, "But before I could dress the house was surrounded & they were yelling and screaming & swearing like Devils—and five men who were in the lower rooms started to run across the fields but were soon overtaken and butchered there were five of us up stairs (all travelers) & about thirty were riddling the house with bullets.... I was carelessly looking out at the window up stairs & Quantrell saw me through the window & gave me a dip— he made a good shot—(or as he afterwards expressed it, a dam'd good shot) I was struck in the center of the forehead where the brains of most men are supposed to be located—I fell and was supposed to be dead." Ellis' life had been saved by the ball slowing as it passing through the timber window sash first. The other men "then went down stairs & surrendered & in a few moments Quantrell & two others of the gads hill Band Came up stairs—each had a revolver in his hand—with the hammer raised They were trembling like criminals & Swearing like Devils ... as soon as they got within about four feet of me they all pointed their revolvers at my head ... one of them balled out—If you have any money God damn you give it to me in a minute or I'll blow you to *Hell* and as I had no hankering after [that] place—I passed over ... $250.00 they then passed on & searched the rooms & I heard one of them say, that he had found a pocket book & that it was a dam-d fat one—They then ordered me down stairs & said that I was not dead by a dam-d sight—I then crawled down stairs & was helped into a chair & in a few minutes Quantrell came down & then recognized me." As it turned out, Ellis had formerly served as a Lykins County superintendent of public instruction, and met Quantrill when he was teaching school in Stanton. They had shared

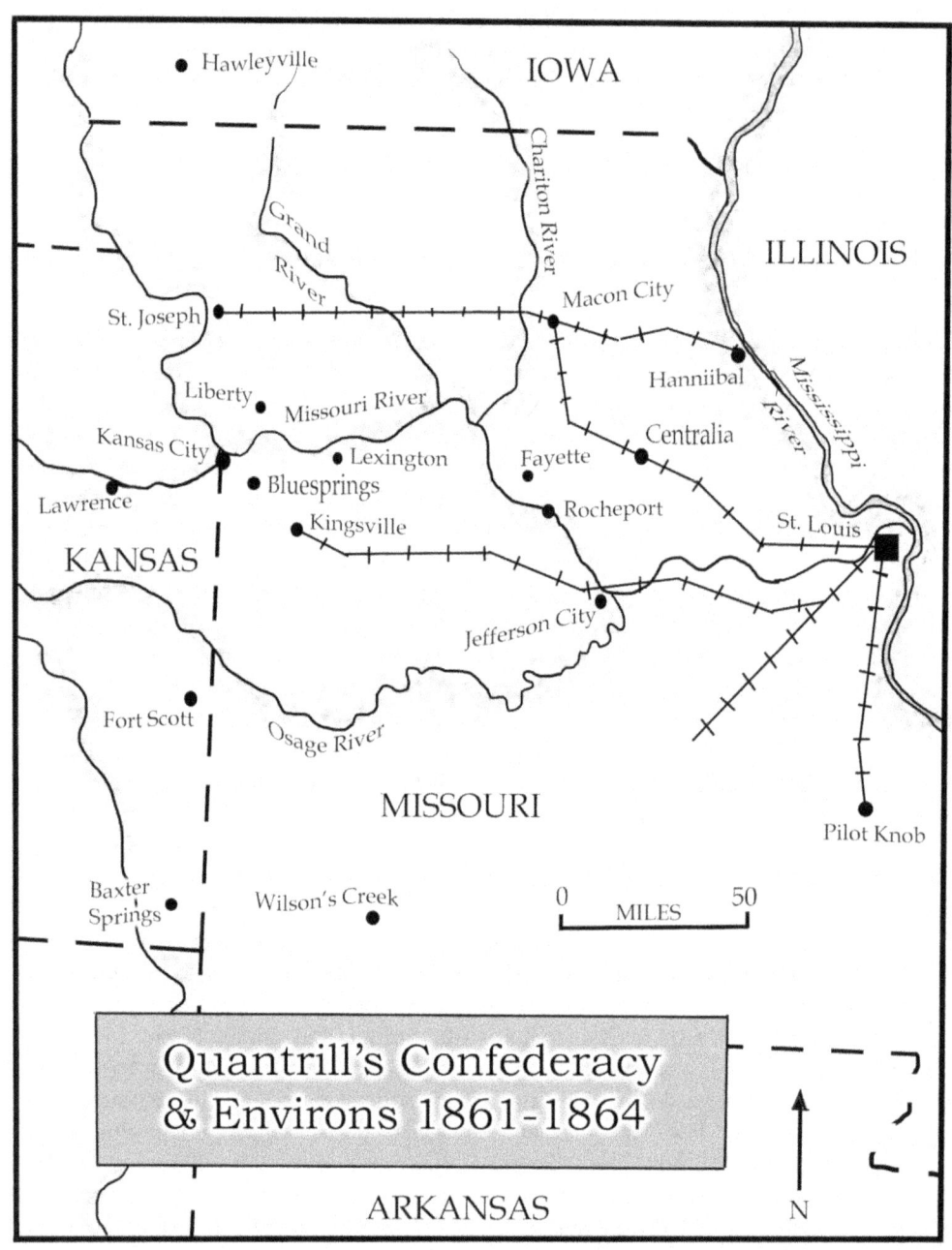

Quantrill's Confederacy and Environs, 1861–1864 (author's rendition).

a room in a boarding house for a night, conversed till after two in the morning. Ellis had found the future bushwhacker to be "an interesting and educated man." He recalled Quantrill at that time as "a well built man light hair blue eyes—round face, pleasant countenance, with little or no beard." But in Aubry, "he had Mustash & Side whiskers & both had a red tinge & at that time, he had assumed the appearance of a desperado."

According to Ellis, Quantrill "got a cloth and some water and & washed my face & said he did it himself & was dam-d sorry for it—as I was one of the Kansas men he *did not* want to hurt." Quantrill assured Ellis that none of his property would be touched, but the victim, the pistol ball still imbedded in his forehead, passed out and lay "on the frozen ground for about four hours senseless and motionless & to all appearances dead."[20]

Lieutenant Reuben Randlett of the 5th Kansas had shared a room with Ellis and, discretion being the better part of valor, had come downstairs and surrendered. After having a revolver thrust into his mouth and another against his head by two bushwhackers, he was questioned by Quantrill. The officer should be spared, he decided—for the moment at least. Randlett was ordered to mount his horse, and as he and Quantrill rode out he saw the wounded Ellis hitching up his team. But then he fell to the ground, and Randlett assumed Ellis to have died where he fell. As the bushwhackers moved back into the countryside they left at least five murdered men behind them, and had pillaged every store and house. Smoke billowed from one building set ablaze.

Ellis, still breathing, was picked up by townsfolk, and three days later an army surgeon extracted the bullet and skull fragments from his forehead. The wound healed, but with a large concavity quite apparent, he became commonly known as "Bullet Hole" Ellis. "The only redeeming traits I ever saw in Quantrell," Ellis recalled, "was that he showed by his kindness to me, after I was wounded that he was not entirely a Demon—But history will record him a desperately bad man—a highway robber, of the darkest shade & a desperate leader of a set of the most desperate Demons that ever disgraced the name of man—infinitely worse than he was."[21]

Lieutenant Randlett, taken off with the bandits, was fortunate to find favor amongst his captors. "He was a splendid fellow and we all became very much attached to him," recalled William Gregg. "We allowed him the liberty of the camp and lines, and his uniform alone distinguished him from one of our men."[22] At one point Randlett was taken to a hilltop to watch a skirmish between the guerrillas and Kansas Red Legs who had been raiding in Cass County. A few of the enemy were wounded before being driven off.

The guerrillas were surprised to have two Yankee deserters arrive in camp. They claimed they wished to join the Confederate Army, and had heard that Lieutenant Randlett was Quantrill's prisoner. They even offered free advice: string the officer up without delay. Following Quantrill's interrogation in a farmhouse, the deserters found themselves being questioned by another man. Little did they know this apparent rebel was, in fact, the Yankee they had advised hanging clad in bushwhacker clothes. Following the interview, it comes as little surprise that Randlett had little good to say about his former comrades in arms. They were either thieves or spies, he told Quantrill. As Randlett rode off with his captors he heard shots ring out behind him.

But Randlett had only been spared from the same fate for a particular reason. Quantrill wrote to Fort Leavenworth requesting his exchange for one of his own men, Brady, previously captured. He received no reply, and Randlett sent a letter of his own. Colonel John McNeil wrote back directly to Randlett on March 17, saying he had sent Randlett's letter up through the chain of command. As yet he had received no reply, "but I can assure you that you will soon be liberated and if the party who holds you dares harm a hair of your head they will one and all be hung when taken which is now only a matter of time and that time short."

Quantrill took Randlett to Independence and gave him a ten-day parole to negotiate Brady's release. Once released, word got round that Randlett was in town, and he was threatened by a proslavery mob. An old man named Perry with Union leanings helped Randlett escape to Kansas City where he was shown into the presence of Colonel McNeil.

The colonel broke into a flurry of abuse against Quantrill, and informed Randlett that he was to act as guide on an expedition to destroy the guerrilla band. Randlett said he was honor bound not to do so, and refused to comply. Tempers rose as hot words were exchanged and Randlett shouted, "I will not go, and damn you, you can't make me go." As he bolted from the building he knocked Colonel William Weer from the sidewalk. Once equilibrium was restored, Randlett repeated his story to Weer who said orders had just been received to remove McNeil from command, and he had nothing more to say on the matter. Ironically, Weer would be removed from command himself later the same year during an expedition into Indian Territory. Despite a victory over the rebels at Locust Grove, Weer's drunken behavior led to mutiny amongst his officers and he was placed under arrest. Although praised for gallantry later in the war, he would be court-martialed and cashiered for misappropriation of funds.[23]

Randlett rode to Leavenworth and spoke to General Sturgis, repeating Quantrill's request for Brady's release. But Sturgis said that that there could be no bargaining with someone of Quantrill's breed, a mere outlaw as far as he was concerned. Randlett could do as he pleased, but Sturgis advised that he not return to the guerrilla band. Randlett, however, felt honor bound to do so, and rode back to Independence, now occupied by 1200 Union troops. Attempts to locate Quantrill's band went nowhere, however, and he returned to Kansas City, never to meet Quantrill again.

Rebel guerrillas, "will not, if captured, be treated as ordinary prisoners of war, but will be hung as robbers and murderers." So decreed Major General Henry "Old Brains" Halleck, commander of the Department of the Missouri. The time had come for affirmative action against the likes of Quantrill, and Attorney General Edward Bates backed Halleck up.[24]

But, in Halleck's defense, he had no time for pro–Union jayhawkers either. "These men do not belong to this department, and have no business to come within this State," he wrote in January 1862. "I have directed General Pope to drive them out, or, if they resist to disarm them and hold them prisoners. They are no better than a band of robbers. They are driving good Union men into the ranks of the secession army." Halleck warned that if the government allowed jayhawkers such as James Lane and Charles Jennison to operate with its approval, "it may resign all hopes of a pacification of Missouri."[25] Charles "Doc" Jennison was head of the jayhawker "Red Legs," so called due to the custom of wearing red leggings to distinguish friend from foe. But, to Halleck's frustration, Lane and Jennison had contacts of their own, and could not be simply driven out.

Only five days after Halleck's decree to hang rebel guerrillas, Quantrill and his band crossed the broad waters of the Missouri River. Their target was Liberty township, about 14 miles from Independence. John McCorkle, who would join Quantrill later the same year, described how such operations were performed: "We would get into the skiffs, take a horse that was used to swimming by the bridle and then tying a horse to the tail of a horse ahead of him, start across the river, making the horses swim behind us and in this manner I crossed sixty horses at one time."[26]

In Liberty, one bluecoat was captured and summarily shot after refusing to divulge the whereabouts of his comrades, a futile gesture, as it turned out. The other eight soldiers were soon located in a fortified brick building. Shots echoed through the streets for three hours before the besieged Yankees waved a white flag. Fortunately for them, Quantrill had not heard of Halleck's order, so they were paroled and allowed to go free. The proslavery element in town wined and dined the victors before they recrossed the Missouri.

But then Quantrill read of Halleck's decree in the St. Louis *Missouri Republican*. He drew a line in the dirt and rode his horse across it. "Now boys," he said, "I accept the challenge. All of you who wish to remain and fight with me ride over on this side of the line. All of you who wish to leave the outfit go ahead and nothing will be held against you. Every man now will make his own choice"—or so the story goes.[27] This sound remarkably like the legend of William Barret Travis at the Alamo. It makes sense that Quantrill would have given his men the choice, as described in William E. Connelley's 1910 book *Quantrill and the Border Wars*, but this makes no mention of any line.[28] Quantrill's precise dialogue and the supposed line would appear to be a later myth repeated as fact. Whatever the case, over 40 men decided to stay with him, while between 15 and 20 decided to go. But as Halleck warned, continued depredations by jayhawkers proved to be effective recruiters for the Confederacy, and they returned to Quantrill's ranks within a month.

"Boys," Quantrill shouted, "Halleck issued the order, but we draw the first blood." He had just shot and killed an unarmed Union sergeant captured on a bridge over the Little Blue. It was March 22, 1862, a few weeks after Halleck's decree. Far from discouraging rebel recruits, Quantrill now had over 100 riders with him Also captured were the bridge toll keeper and his young son. Accused of being a spy, the toll keeper was given a perfunctory trial and shot in front of the boy.

The bold cavaliers rode off leaving the bridge in flames, two dead men and one traumatized orphan—good training for events to come. That evening they split into four groups and Quantrill led 21 men to the farm of David Tate, about three miles south of Little Santa Fe. They ate and bedded down for the night leaving two men outside. But, in need of sleep themselves, these pickets soon nodded off.

A few hours later Quantrill was startled to hear loud thumping on the front door, Yankee major James Pomeroy demanding admittance. News of the Little Blue bridge killings was out, and Tate, a known rebel sympathizer, was wanted for questioning. Pomeroy did not know his quarry was inside until bullets fired by Quantrill splintered the door. The unhurt major ran back to his men, two companies of the 2nd Kansas Volunteer Cavalry, and ordered them to fan out. The rebels, ignoring Pomeroy's offer to have women and children evacuate, scrambled to barricade the doors with furniture and opened fire. The Yankees shot back, and the shrill screams of the Tate women could be heard from inside. Pomeroy ordered a cease fire, and the non-combatants dashed out through the door. Once clear, the firing resumed, but two rebels slipped out a window and surrendered themselves. From them Pomeroy learned that he had the guerrilla chief himself boxed in. "Come out, Quantrell," he shouted, "I have the house surrounded by 500 men."[29] But the only reply was another blast of gunfire from the windows. Pomeroy and Private William Wells moved forward with bundles of kindling in hand. Flames would force the rebels out. But the rebels saw their move and delivered a hot fire of their own. Pomeroy limped back with a thigh wound, and Wills with a wounded arm and a load of buckshot to the groin. Pomeroy would recover, but Wills died the next day.

Captain Amaziah Moore, assuming command, sent for reinforcements and made another attempt to set the house on fire. Lessons had been learnt, and this time flames took hold. Moore yelled out another demand for surrender, but Quantrill was not done yet. The Yankees were startled when a section of weatherboarding at the rear broke open. "Steady boys, follow me," Quantrill shouted.[30] The rebels ran out, those with shotguns to the fore, and those with pistols behind. Astonished, the Yankee line split as the rebels shot left and right. Most made it to the woods but the Rollen brothers were cut down. Colonel Robert Mitchell soon arrived with reinforcements and assumed command. "The others escaped," he reported," and though the woods were carefully scoured, no traces of them were found. While firing was taking place several men were seen to fall in the house and the prisoners stated when they were first taken that there were four or five wounded. Five bodies could be distinctly seen in the flames." Interestingly, Mitchell referred to the bushwhackers as "Jayhawkers," indicating confusion about who exactly was a bushwhacker and a jayhawker at the time. For some, both had been dumped in the same category of undesirables, apparently.[31]

Colonel Mitchell marched out on a search at dawn the following day. As he approached the Wyatt farm, George Todd and 11 men fled into dense undergrowth on foot, but the troopers dismounted and gave chase, capturing three guerrillas on the run.

Quantrill, meanwhile, found refuge at the home of David Wilson in Jackson County. He sent word for his men to regroup at the headwaters of the Little Blue, then moved from farm to farm, one step ahead of Yankee troops. The rebels mustered once more, but most had lost their horses while escaping on foot. Quantrill told them to return when they had procured fresh mounts by fair means or foul.

On March 26 the Yankee garrison in Warrensburg came under attack by Quantrill leading 200 mounted men—or so the *Kansas City Journal* and *Liberty Tribune* reported. But it was impossible for Quantrill's Raiders to be involved only four days after the Tate farm fight. By now Quantrill had become so notorious that many preferred to think he was behind every attack, even if he was miles away at the time.[32]

Only four days later, Captain Albert Peabody of the 1st Missouri Cavalry received word that Quantrill, with 60 men, was camped in the area around Pink Hill. Peabody split his force of 65 men into two detachments, and set out to hunt the rebels down. Quantrill, with only 30 men in reality, was sheltering in the two-story log house of Sam Clark. Peabody's command arrived and saw three men in the yard. When bluecoats rode over to investigate, the windows erupted with gunfire. The Yankees shot back, wounding John Kroger, in the yard, before he could take cover. While some bushwhackers shot from doors and windows, others dug plaster from between wall logs to form loopholes. Peabody, his men dismounted and spreading out, sent word for Lieutenant White's detachment to join the fight. The firing echoed across the hills, and the Yankees soon found themselves under long range fire from proslavery farmers attracted by the gunfire.

White's detachment arrived over an hour later, and Peabody led a mounted charge. Met by a hail of bullets, he was driven back, his horse wounded three times. Quantrill decided to try for the rebel horses in the barn, 70 yards off, and detailed Todd and half his men to deliver covering fire from the top windows. The rebels bolted from the house only to find their timing badly misplaced. Peabody was just launching a second assault. The rebels halted in their tracks and dashed back to the cover of the house.

Quantrill realized the horses were too far off, the only hope of escape being on foot to nearby woods. Quantrill had several men feign a charge from a side door, drawing the Yankees' fire, before darting back inside again. As the troops reloaded their single-shot rifles, the rebels bolted from the house en masse and dashed to the woods at the rear. They scattered through the trees and regrouped on a high bluff overlooking Ball Ford on Little Sni Creek. Then 50 Yankees under Captain Murphy arrived at the ford, on their way to reinforce Peabody. As the troopers crossed the rebels opened fire and men splashed into the shallow water below. Murphy rode about rallying his men and attempted to attack the rebel position, but became pinned down at the base of a cliff. But then the bushwhackers found themselves outflanked as Peabody, in pursuit, arrived hot on the guerrillas' trail. The rebels fired a last few shots then scattered through the trees and undergrowth, making their escape on foot.

The guerrillas had lost their horses and saddles again, and would have to procure replacements. Their numbers were also down. Six bodies were found in the log house, and it was rumored that two of those who escaped later died of their wounds.[33]

Quantrill had learned that sleeping in houses was dangerous. This luxury became a death trap. On the stormy night of April 15, however, the bushwhackers again took shelter in a house, the abode of Jordan Lowe. The weather was so appalling that the Yankees would also take shelter, it was assumed. But Lieutenant George Nash of the 1st Missouri Cavalry, once informed of Quantrill's situation, was not going to let cold winds and rain dampen his ardor in any way. The storm calmed at about 4 a.m. and Nash quietly approached with 30 men. The rebel horses, tied to a fence outback, were taken in hand as the house was surrounded.

As first light glimmered, a burst of Yankee gunfire splintered the wooden walls. Quantrill must have cursed his own bad judgment as he leapt for his revolvers. For a third time in four weeks he was surrounded in a house by Yankee troops. The rebels returned fire, but by now Quantrill had learned that attack was the best form of defense. The rebels bolted from the building, but George Todd, Joe Gilchrist and Andy Blunt were left behind. Firing from the loft, they had not heard the order to bolt. Cole Younger turned back and warned them to get out. Younger and Todd made it to safety, but Gilchrist was killed and Blunt taken prisoner. The Yankees fired at the bushwhackers as they were "flying to the brush, about 20 rods from the brush, killing 4, wounding 4," wrote Nash's superior, Lieutenant Colonel Egbert Brown, "and capturing 5 prisoners, all the horses, accoutrements, most of their arms and clothing [leaving them] barefooted and coatless."[34] Blunt was shown no mercy, shot after capture and left lying in the dirt, presumed dead. But, made of sturdy stuff, he was still alive. Once the Yankees left he managed to crawl to a nearby farmhouse where he was nursed back to health. The Yankees must have been astonished to see Blunt riding with Quantrill once more, returned from the dead.

And Lieutenant Nash was haunted by another ghost before his days were done. On June 5, 1862, he pursued guerrillas who had robbed a quartermaster train north of Sedalia. While tracking them, Nash ordered William Field, a prominent landowner, shot on suspicion of helping the bushwhackers. Influential friends were outraged, and Nash found himself arrested for murder. He absconded during the trial, however, and reenlisted under the name Charles Hill. Recommended for an officer position in a newly formed colored regiment, the escapee wrote to the authorities under his real name requesting a pardon, only to find himself placed under arrest once more.[35] He was dishonorably discharged, and sent to Gariot Prison in St. Louis until being paroled in 1863.[36] He ultimately became a rancher in Arizona, but disappeared without trace in 1897.

Bushwhacker William Gregg later described the three house sieges as "a series of surprises, in each case losing our horses, which was a great drawback, however, we soon got onto the enemies tactics, and never afterwards did we lose horses in any considerable number, but often beat the enemy out of theirs."[37]

On April 21, 1862, six days after the Lowe house fight, General James Totten, commander of the District of Central Missouri, issued Special Order No. 47. This listed the depredations of "guerrillas, marauders, murderers and every species of outlaw" infesting southeast Jackson County. Farming and legal pursuits had been disrupted due to "a well-known and desperate leader of these outlaws by the name of Quantrell, and the whole country reduced to a state of anarchy ... murderers, marauders, and horse-thieves, will be shot down by the military upon the spot when found perpetrating their foul acts." Anyone found supporting "these outlaws in their lawless deeds will be arrested and tried by a military commission for their offences."[38]

Ironically, on the very same day, Jefferson Davis announced the Partisan Ranger Act which attracted the attention of Private John Mosby in Virginia. The act blurred the line between bandits and partisans, as the former could claim to be the latter, especially out west where the relative civilities of warfare practiced in the east were often ignored. It comes as little surprise that Yankee authorities declined to recognize rebel guerrillas as legitimate soldiers, regardless of any act laid down by the Confederate Congress.

The revolvers of the era still required each chamber to be loaded with ball and powder, then compressed with a handle-operated ramrod beneath the barrel. A separate percussion cap placed at the rear of each chamber provided ignition. Quantrill and Todd rode to Hannibal, Missouri, to procure a fresh supply of percussion caps. A bustling Mississippi river port, Hannibal would later become the boyhood home of Mark Twain and provide the setting for *Tom Sawyer* and *Huckleberry Finn*. Still later, it would be home to the legendary "Unsinkable Molly Brown" of *Titanic* fame. But Quantrill was already creating a legend of his own as he and Todd returned to Jackson County with a fresh supply of the vital caps. By then his men had procured new mounts by fair means or foul, new recruits had joined the ranks, and Quantrill was set to deliver a new reign of terror on the Missouri plains.

7

"Gratification at my success"
Mosby, 1862

Following Jeb Stuart's famous ride around McClellan's army, the Confederate secretary of war, George W. Randolph, agreed to see John Mosby. He carried a letter of introduction from Jeb Stuart which praised his work, "and, in my estimation, fairly won promotion. I am anxious that he should get the Captaincy of a Company of Sharpshooters in my brigade, but the muster rolls have not yet been sent in. I commend him to your notice."[1]

But still Mosby received no promotion.

Jeb Stuart was the hero of the day. One would think those in the corridors of power would have been only too pleased to grant him this request. Perhaps there were others, like Fitzhugh Lee, who the unorthodox Mosby had rubbed up the wrong way, others who had enough clout to block this upstart from progressing beyond the ranks. Mosby was a teetotalling, non-smoking, oddity who had no time for sport. And this strange character received considerable press for his exploits on Stuart's raid. Perhaps jealousy played a part.

Following Robert E. Lee's victory over McClellan in the Seven Day's Battles, General John Pope, a bombastic braggart, was placed in charge of new force being raised in the north, the Army of Virginia. McClellan, still commanding the Army of the Potomac, was not happy with this turn of events. "Pope will be thrashed," he wrote to his wife. "Such a villain as he ought to bring defeat upon any cause that employs him."[2]

Pope said that he was not concerned with lines of retreat or entrenchments to hold ground, and implied that the troops in the western theater of war under his command had done far better than those in the east. He was hated by all who served under him, from generals to drummer boys. On July 14, 1862, the new commander decreed, among other things, "Let us look before us, and not behind. Success and glory are in the advance, disaster and shame lurk in the rear."[3]

Mosby saw his chance with the Partisan Ranger Act of April 21. The Confederate Cavalry were only doing routine picket duty, and Mosby asked Jeb Stuart for 12 men to penetrate the enemy's rear. He would provide, "disaster and shame" for John Pope. But "judged in the light of what is before us now," Mosby recalled, "it looks strange that I was refused…. I had to beg for the privilege of striking the enemy at a vulnerable point."[4]

Perhaps those who disparaged Mosby had reached Stuart's ear. Perhaps the upstart private was a bit too sure of himself. Stuart claimed he needed every man for his coming campaign, but offered to give Mosby a letter of recommendation to Stonewall Jackson, "who, no doubt, would give me the men I wanted." Stuart was not only refusing Mosby, but was prepared to have him move to another command. Considering his former praise for "Captain" Mosby, this appears to be strange behavior indeed. Mosby, however, had little choice. He accepted the letter, "the best I could get," and set off on July 19, 1862, with Mortimer Weaver, a club-footed courier exempted from military service.[5] Stuart's letter read, "The bearer, John S. Mosby, ... is en route to scout beyond the enemy's lines towards Manassas and Fairfax. He is bold, daring, and discreet. The information he may obtain and transmit to you may be relied upon."[6] This recommended Mosby as a scout, not for partisan warfare which is what the ambitious rebel had in mind.

They spent the night at a farm house near Beaver Dam Station on the Orange and Alexandria Railroad. Before joining Jackson, Mosby intending visiting his family and parents, by rail, who were staying near Lynchburg. The next morning he sent Weaver with their horses directly to Jackson's camp at Gordonsville, then made himself comfortable to await the train. His colt revolvers were unbuckled and placed alongside the haversack containing the letter to Jackson.

"Here they are!" someone shouted.

Robert E. Lee was impressed with Mosby's observations regarding Yankee troop movements at Hampton Roads (Library of Congress).

Mosby looked around to see that Yankee cavalry also operated in the enemy's rear. He bolted for nearby trees, but found himself overtaken by galloping hooves and surrounded by horsemen in a cloud of dust. General Pope had ordered General Rufus King to make a raid on the Confederate railroads, and impede communications between Richmond and Jackson's army in the Shenandoah Valley. "So while we were destroying culverts and bridges," recalled Union Lieutenant Willard Glazier, "others were playing mischief with the telegraph wires: others still were burning the depot, which was nearly full of stores, and a fourth party was at the lookout. During this affray we captured a young Confederate officer who gave his name as Captain John S. Mosby. By his sprightly appearance and conversation he attracted considerable attention. He is slight, yet well formed; has a keen blue eye, and florid complexion; and displays no small amount of Southern bravado in his dress and manners. His gray plush hat is surmounted by a waving plume, which he tosses as he speaks in real Prussian style. He had a letter in his possession from General Stuart, recommending him to the kind regards of General Lee [Jackson]."[7]

Private Mosby had not been able to accept his lack of promotion. After all, he had been listed as a "captain" in Stuart's report. But whatever his rank, if he is to believed, Mosby was treated as an honored officer and gentleman, not just one more private. "The colonel and captain treated me with great courtesy. General King, before whom I was carried, ordered my arms to be restored to me," he wrote to Pauline. "You need feel no uneasiness about me.... Colonel Davis, who captured me, offered to lend me Federal money. I thanked him, but declined."[8]

A prisoner having his revolvers returned seems most unlikely, but if they were, he did not get to keep them. Mosby later stated that the Colts lost during his capture needed to replaced.

During the war's early days an exchange of prisoners was common practice, but largely disbanded later during the conflict for a variety of reasons. This included a refusal by the Confederacy to exchange black soldiers taken captive. Mosby was held in the Old Capitol Prison in Washington, but soon put aboard a steamer with others listed for exchange. The craft steamed down the Potomac to Hampton Roads, Virginia, held by the Federals. Here his "keen blue eye" saw blue clad troops aboard transport ships. Where were they headed? Despite McClellan's defeat in the Seven Days Battles, his men still sat entrenched on the Peninsula. "If they were reinforcements for McClellan," recalled Mosby, "it would indicate that he would advance again on Richmond from his new base on the James. On the other hand, if they sailed up the Chesapeake, it would show they were going to join Pope, and McClellan would be withdrawn from the peninsula."

The troop transports weighed anchor and moved off. The captain of Mosby's vessel had expressed his support for the South, so Mosby asked him to find out where the troops were headed. "When he returned," Mosby recalled, "he whispered to me that Aquia Creek, on the Potomac, was the point. That settled it—McClellan's army would not advance, but would follow the transports northwards."[9] During that night the steamer carried the prisoners up the James River to the point of exchange. Mosby, unable to sleep through sheer excitement, sat on deck all night watching for the morning star. He was first down the gangplank early the following morning and, telling the Confederate Commissioner he had crucial information for General Lee, was allowed to proceed without delay. The hot August sun beat down as he trudged on foot towards Lee's headquarters, 12 miles away, and he lay by the roadside to rest. A Confederate horseman of Wade Hampton's Legion saw the forlorn soldier and, upon hearing his story, allowed him to ride while he walked alongside. When they reached camp, another horse was provided, and both rode to headquarters where Mosby requested an urgent meeting with General Lee, but "in the imperious tone customary with staff officers, he said that I could not see the general." Mosby's protest fell on deaf ears, but as he walked off another officer, having heard the exchange, told him to wait. Very soon the commanding general looked up from a map in his quarters to the rather scruffy soldier who said he had important news. Mosby was awed, but "General Lee's kind, benevolent manner put me at my ease." Lee listened, but would he believe Mosby's tale? To add credibility, Mosby said he was the same man who had been on Stuart's ride around McClellan. "Oh, I remember," said Lee. Mosby was flattered to be asked where he thought the next Federal advance against Richmond would come from. Mosby gave his opinion, and Lee had a staff officer dispatch a courier to Stonewall Jackson, about 80 miles west of Richmond, near Gordonsville. Since the destruction of the Beaver Dam Railroad Station where Mosby was captured, Lee could not trust the telegraph line, and mounted couriers were kept on the move.

As Mosby was about to depart, he opened his haversack and placed a dozen lemons on Lee's table. Purchased at Fort Monroe en route from captivity, they were a rare treat in the South due to the Yankee blockade. Lee, surprised at such a gesture, said he had better give them to the sick and wounded, "But I left them and bade him good-by," recalled Mosby. "I had little expectation of ever seeing him again."

"As soon as Jackson got the news," recalled Mosby, "he hastened to strike Pope at Cedar Mountain before reinforcements could reach him." Mosby's story had tended to confirm other reports Lee had on hand. Pope had sent troops to take Gordonsville, but Jackson moved against the isolated and outnumbered Yankees under General Nathanial Banks. On August 9, however, the Confederates were surprised to find themselves under a savage, headlong assault by a force half their size. They fell back, and even Jackson's old Stonewall Brigade was put to flight. But Jackson rallied his troops and, supported by A. P. Hill's Division, the Yankees were driven back several miles until reinforced. Jackson had triumphed, and he held his position for two days expecting a further Union assault which never came. When he heard that Pope's main force had arrived at Culpepper Court House, he fell back to a more defensive position behind the Rapidan River.

By now it was apparent that McClellan's troops on the Peninsula were being withdrawn. The fight at Cedar Mountain confirmed that Northern Virginia would be the next battleground.[10]

Following his meeting with Lee, Mosby traveled home to procure a fresh horse. On August 17 he returned to the army and encountered Stuart and staff as they arrived by rail from Richmond. Stuart had received orders from Lee to organize another raid, and any thought of Mosby joining Jackson was forgotten as he requested Mosby's services once more. No doubt Lee had told Stuart of Mosby's vigilance and report on the enemy troop transports. It would appear that Mosby's capture had worked in his favor; such are the ironies of fate.

"Stuart was to meet Fitz Lee at Verdiersville," Mosby recalled, "and I went with him. I had no arms—I had lost my pistols when I was captured at Beaver Dam—but trusted luck to get another pair."[11] But the following morning more losses were in store. They slept the night on a house porch, and as dawn approached, Mosby was told of mounted men on the road. He and another man rode out to investigate. "They had not gone 100 yards before they were fired on and pursued rapidly by a squadron," Stuart wrote to his wife, "I was in the yard bareheaded, my hat being on the porch, I just had time to mount my horse and clear the back fence, having no time to get my hat or anything else. I lost my haversack, blanket, talma, cloak, and hat, with that palmetto star—too bad wasn't it? I am all right again, however, and am greeted on all sides with congratulations and 'where's your hat!' I intend to make the Yankees pay for that hat."[12] Mosby escaped, but also lost his haversack and telescope.

On August 22 Stuart set out with his command to raid Pope's headquarters at Catlett's Station. As he galloped past Mosby he called out, "I'm going after my hat." The rebel horsemen, riding through torrents of rain on a dark night, had virtually given up hope of locating their goal, but then heard a distant voice singing "Carry me back to old Virginny." The singer turned out to be an African-American who had known Stuart in Berkeley County. He was pleased to see him again, and led the rebels to Pope's camp.

The slumbering Yankees were horrified to hear bugles calls and rebel yells as the gray-clad cavalry galloped in. The camp was quickly taken amidst chaos, rain and lightning bolts. Pope, however, was not amidst the prisoners, being absent, and the rain prevented the burning of a robust railway bridge. Axes were put to work, but this was abandoned when bluecoats opened fire from concealed positions. Stuart's hat and cloak were not found, but he did have the pleasure of capturing 300 prisoners, numerous horses, mules, wagonloads of supplies and Pope's $350,000 money box. And, most satisfying of all, Pope's hat and best dress uniform coat. To the delight of citizens, the elegant trophy with its glittering brass buttons and epaulettes was soon on display in a Richmond shop window.[13]

On August 28–30 the armies of Lee and Pope clashed at the Second Battle of Bull Run. Again the Yankees were repulsed, but without the same degree of carnage during the retreat. "The Confederates were disappointed," recalled Union general George Gordon, "many of them scolded bitterly. Rarely had a better opportunity offered for the destruction of an army." Mosby rode with Stuart to the signal station on Clarke's Mountain "where we could see Pope's army retreating and his trains scudding back to the Rappahannock."[14]

"Our arms have been crowned with a glorious victory," Mosby wrote to Pauline. "Our army is now marching on towards Leesburg, and we all suppose it will cross into Maryland. I have escaped unhurt, though I got my horse slightly shot in the shoulder and had a bullet through the top of my hat, which slightly grazed my head.... I have a very good Yankee horse, also two fine saddles and two pistols I captured. With one man I captured seven cavalry and two infantry."[15]

The Confederates were jubilant with this latest success, and it looked more than ever to the nations of the world that the Confederacy would prevail. The Federals "got a very complete smashing," wrote British prime minister Lord Palmerston to Foreign Minister Earl Russell, "and it seems not altogether unlikely that still more greater disasters await them, and that even Washington or Baltimore may fall into the hands of the Confederates. If this should happen, would it not be time for us to consider whether ... England and France might not address the contending parties and recommend an arrangement upon the basis of separation?"[16]

But Palmerston did not comprehend the determination of the tall, stooped man who paced the War Office in Washington during every battle, awaiting the rattle of the telegraph to bring the latest news. "I expect to maintain this contest until successful, or till I die, or am conquered, or my term expires, or Congress or the country forsakes me," wrote Lincoln. The second defeat at Bull Run did not change a thing.

George McClellan was brought back to replace the defeated and deflated John Pope. What to do with yet another defeated general? Pope was sent west to Minnesota where the desperate Dakota tribe, deprived of food held by traders, had killed hundreds of settlers in a bloody uprising.

Lee, meanwhile, had decided to invade Union soil. On September 4, 1862, his troops made the move singing "Maryland, my Maryland." He fought McClellan's army at Sharpsburg, near Antietam Creek, on September 17, 1862. Stuart's cavalry was deployed in the West Wood on the extreme left of Stonewall Jackson's line, and Mosby served as a courier. He rode with Stuart past some batteries Jackson was directing "and I stopped a minute to look at the great soldier who was then transfigured with the joy of battle." But no doubt that joy abated somewhat when Lee ordered their retreat back into Virginia. After savage fighting that saw the bloodiest day in American history, McClellan had won the day. "I rode on and overtook Stuart," Mosby recalled, "but the killed and wounded were strewn on the ground 'like leaves of the forest when autumn hath blown,' and I had to be careful not to ride over them. Whole ranks seemed to have been struck down by a volley."[17] Mosby saw a Confederate officer bending over a wounded Yankee colonel demanding his formal surrender. Stuart ordered the officer away, and Mosby rolled a blanket under the colonel's head. He needed water, and Mosby took a canteen from a dead man, but first offered it to another wounded Yankee nearby. "No," he said, "take it to my Colonel, he is the best man in the world." The colonel was Isaac J. Wistar of the 71st Pennsylvania Infantry. He recovered to be promoted brigadier general later the same year. After the war Wistar became president of the Pennsylvania Canal Company, and in 1869 he and Mosby enjoyed a friendly reunion.[18]

Lee retreated, and McClellan let him go. Perhaps it was memories of being savaged by "Marse Robert" on the Peninsula that prevented an effective pursuit. Best not to tempt fate, despite having thousands of fresh bluecoats on hand who had not taken part in the fight. As it was, he could claim a victory, nobody could complain about that—except Abraham

Lincoln. Pursuit of the defeated rebels was "all easy if our troops march as well as the enemy," he wired McClellan, "and it is unmanly to say they cannot do it." But McClellan did not budge. Lincoln visited the troops and, observing the vast camp from a hilltop with his friend Ozias Hatch, asked, "Hatch, what is all this?" "Why, Mr. Lincoln, this is the Army of the Potomac." "No, Hatch, no. This is General McClellan's bodyguard."[19] Lincoln returned to Washington and again urged McClellan to move against Lee. The general claimed his horses could not pursue Lee because they were "broken down from fatigue." Lincoln wired back, "Will you pardon me for asking what the horses have done since the battle of Antietam that fatigue anything?"[20]

Lincoln sacked McClellan for a final time. He was replaced by Ambrose Burnside, who was reluctant to take command. But rather than have the job go to General "Fighting Joe" Hooker, a rival, Burnside agreed to take it on.

Mosby's horse had been disabled during the battle, and he visited his parents to procure a fresh mount. He rejoined Stuart on November 5, and was sent with two men to scout behind the Yankee army at Rectortown. During this, he learned of Burnside's promotion and sent word to Stuart. The courier rode past five Yankee cavalrymen on the road, who merely said, "Good Morning." Being well within Union lines, perhaps they mistook his Confederate uniform for dusty civilian clothes.

Burnside devised fresh plans and set his troops in motion, skillfully masking their movements, to the frustration of Robert E. Lee. Several scouting parties were dispatched, including Mosby with another man, and they correctly reported that the Yankees were moving towards Fredericksburg, Virginia. Major General Henry "Old Brains" Halleck, previously chasing guerrillas out west, had been moved east as the Union commander-in-chief, and now had Mosby to contend with instead of Quantrill. Halleck ordered General Franz Sigel's 11th Corps closer to Washington for defense against any surprise move by Lee. Sigel moved to Fairfax Court House, with cavalry pickets covering territory to the west. Lee was unsure of Sigel's intent, and Stuart dispatched Mosby with nine men towards Manassas to determine his plans. "There was a Yankee regiment there," he wrote to Pauline on November 24. "We came upon ten. We charged them with a yell. The Yankees ran and stampeded their whole regiment, thinking all of Stuart's cavalry were upon them." The following month he wrote again, "I reckon you saw the account in the Richmond papers of my scout and stampede of the Yankees near Manassas.... General Lee sent me a message expressing his gratification at my success."[21]

Mosby had managed this ploy with a handful of men 35 miles inside enemy lines, turning a scouting foray into a raid that had made fools of the Yanks. Stuart and Lee now knew that Mosby was one of a rare breed with an inexplicable quality that put them above the rest. "His piercing eyes flash out from beneath his brown hat, with its golden cord," recalled one observer, "and he reins his horse with the ease of a practiced rider.... His activity of mind and body,—call it, if you choose, restless, eternal love of movement, was something wonderful."[22]

On December 11, 1862, it was Ambrose Burnside's turn to confront Robert E. Lee. The Union army crossed the Rappahannock at Fredericksburg on pontoon bridges only to be mown down in futile assaults against the entrenched rebels. Lee watched the blood-soaked shambles from his hilltop command post. "It is well that war is so terrible," he said, "or we should grow too fond of it."

One division under George Meade on the Union left flank briefly penetrated Jackson's line, only to be repulsed with a savage counterattack. On December 15 Burnside called off the offensive, and the bluecoats retreated back across the Rappahannock through a chilly rain. A rare appearance of the Northern Lights this far south caused the rebels to think that God was on their side. The Federals had suffered 13,000 dead, wounded and missing to the rebels 5,000.

"If there is a worse place than hell," said Lincoln, "I am in it."[23] Following the success at Antietam, the president had revealed his plans for the Emancipation Proclamation, freeing all slaves in the rebellious Southern states. For the British or the French to side with the Confederacy in any way would be morally wrong. Fredericksburg, however, made it look once more that the Confederacy could win the war, in which case the Proclamation would be a waste of time.

As winter settled in the two armies sat encamped on opposite sides of the Rappahannock. The opposing pickets saw no use in killing each other, that would not win the war. Far better to swap coffee for tobacco and listen to the military bands serenading each other across the river. A Union band might play "Dixie" as a tribute to the enemy, then a rebel band might strike up "Yankee Doodle" in response.

The ever restless Jeb Stuart, however, felt a raid on Burnside's line of communication with Washington would give the Yankees a Christmas they would rather forget. The grayclad horsemen moved out, and Union supply wagons were soon in flames while others were driven off to supply Lee's army. A Federal cavalry regiment was put to flight through their own camp where "we got all their good things" recalled Mosby. "The 17th Pennsylvania Cavalry just passed through here," the Fairfax telegraph tapped out to Washington, "furiously charging to the rear."

Stuart lead his command back to the Confederate lines, but Mosby stayed behind. He had been allowed off the leash with several men to cause mischief with the Yankee outposts, a turning point in his life. "I had the good luck, by sheer chance," recalled Mosby, "to come across a forester named John Underwood who knew every rabbit-path in the country."[24] Underwood was a 25-year-old rebel sympathizer residing in Fairfax County. "I was largely indebted to his skill and intelligence for whatever success I had in the beginning of my partisan life." With Underwood's assistance, Mosby's small band of marauders surprised three Yankee outposts over two nights, capturing 20 cavalrymen and their horses. The prisoners were paroled at Middleburg before their horses and accouterments were divided up between Mosby's men.

Stuart "was so satisfied with our success," recalled Mosby, "that he let me have fifteen men to return and begin my partisan life in northern Virginia."[25]

8

"There would be no prisoners"
Quantrill, 1862

While Mosby's partisan life was just getting started, the notorious Quantrill's was well under way. As sunshine thawed away winter's frost and snow, his guerrilla band struck Yankee detachments, supply trains and the stage coach lines. During June Captain J. F. Cochran arrived at Harrisonville with two dead men slung over their saddles and another three wounded. He was escorting a mail carrier with 24 men of the 7th Missouri Cavalry. The advance guard of six men had been ambushed by Quantrill. "I was about fifty yards in the rear with 18 men," Cochran reported. "We charged into the brush and routed them and then dismounted and searched the brush, and fired at them a number of times. I do not know what their loss was, as I had to leave to take care of the mail. The mail is safe."[1]

Cochran's commanding officer, Lieutenant Colonel James Buel, stationed at Independence, was far from happy with this state of affairs. "The mail arrived safely at Harrisonville," he reported, but "The carrier dared not come back with escort. I am unwilling that any more of my men shall be murdered escorting this mail. I have therefore ordered it to be carried for the present by secessionists. I shall hold them accountable for its safe transmittal."

Confederate colonel Upton Hays arrived in Jackson County from Arkansas in late June. He met with Quantrill and requested that he draw Federal troops away while he carried out recruiting for the regular army. The guerrilla chief went to work with his usual zest, and caused havoc into Cass County. Even river traffic was not immune, and the raiders captured and pillaged the steamboat *Little Blue*.[2] Major Eliphalet Bredett, 7th Missouri Cavalry, set out in pursuit with 110 men. "Arriving at Wellington," he reported from Camp Powell at Lexington on July 3, 1862, "I made prisoners of 54 men (all charged with aiding and abetting the rebellion) and sent them under a guard of 12 men to this post. At Napoleon I made prisoners of 25 men, 3 of whom had just returned from the rebel army, and the others had been implicated in the affair of capturing and plundering the steamer *Little Blue*, committing also outrages on 40 sick soldiers on board. I prosecuted a general search of the town for contraband articles, which I found in various quantities secreted in cellars, hay-stacks, and outhouses, and sent these, together with the prisoners, to this post."[3]

But, despite a wider search, he did not catch the elusive Quantrill. Colonel Hays requested an escort while he carried out his recruiting duties, and Quantrill provided George Todd and 35 men. This left him with about 65 bushwhackers to continue diverting Yankee troops.

In early July the raiders were camped alongside Sugar Creek near Wadesburg, Cass

County. As Dawn's first light glimmered in the east, there was a mad scramble for guns as shots rang out. A detachment of the 1st Iowa Cavalry charged from the trees. The rebels returned a withering fire and the bluecoats fell back in disarray. But they were only the advance guard of a far larger force under Lieutenant R. M. Reynolds. Another attack, however, was also beaten off. Reynolds, losing heart, beat a hasty retreat back to camp at Clinton where his superior, Major James Gower, was most displeased with the lieutenant's performance. Gower took to the road himself and arrived at the campsite with 293 men. The rebels were, of course, long gone, and Gower sent out patrols to track them down. Captain Martin Kehoe picked up the trail, and sent word for Gower to hurry on. The force, men and horses exhausted, regrouped at the Hornsby farm in Jackson County where the rebels had eaten just a few hours before. Gower ordered his command to rest there for the night.

The Sears Farm

Quantrill, meanwhile, spent a rainy night in the woods before riding to the Sears farm, owned by a Yankee sympathizer. The plan was to burn him out, but first they spread their soaked coats and accouterments to dry in the morning sunshine. Then bluecoats arrived. Without waiting for the rest of the command, the ambitious Captain Kehoe had mounted his company at dawn and followed the trail. Upon seeing the rebel pickets, he sent word back to Gower for reinforcements. The pickets saw the bluecoats and Quantrill had their precious horses taken to a ravine while the remaining men took position behind a log fence. Kehoe ordered a saber charge to be met with a blaze of gunfire and six troopers dropped from their mounts to die where they fell, while nine others managed to stay saddled despite their wounds. Kehoe hit the ground with a bullet in his shoulder as his horse, also shot, rolled in the dust. The remaining bluecoats reigned their mounts around and fled back down the road, leaving their wounded commander to fend for himself. He staggered after his men, all thoughts of a glorious victory gone with the wind. The six riderless horses continued on to be let in through the farm gate and gratefully added to the rebel stock. The dead troopers were stripped of arms, and also their canteens, found to contain whiskey rather than water.

But then shots rang out and guerrilla John Hampton spun to the ground, killed, and George Maddox and William Tucker were wounded. Kehoe's men had opened fire with rifles out of range of the rebels' pistols. Quantrill led a charge, killing two more Yankees, and the rest fell back. The rebel casualties were placed in an ox-drawn wagon and taken away. Quantrill watched through his powerful spyglass as the Yankees withdrew to a log farmhouse. But then he saw something else, a rapidly approaching dust cloud on the horizon—Yankee reinforcements, no doubt.

Quantrill quickly considered his options, and ordered his men into the ravine sheltering the horses. Flanked by thick brush, it was roughly 50 feet wide and five to six feet deep, a natural earthwork suitable for defense. Yankee Captain William Martin's Company G of the 1st Iowa Cavalry saw the move and charged the ravine. Despite his shoulder wound, Captain Kehoe rejoined the fight on a borrowed mount only to have it too shot from under him as the guerrillas opened fire.[4] Martin dismounted his men and charged on foot "not firing a shot until I reached the brink of the precipice, when I opened a volley of fire upon their lines, which were formed not more than 15 feet from my line, which produced a most dreadful effect. I at once cried to my brave men to charge the ditch.... Then ensued a hand-to-hand and bloody struggle for the mastery of the defile; but my gallant men drove them from their strong position with not more than half their number of men they had on their side."[5]

The bushwhackers retreated through the brush only to be met with troops deployed by Major Gower. A blast of gunfire drove the rebels back towards Martin's command. Breaking through Martin's advancing line, they reoccupied the ravine but, as the bluecoats charged once more, fell back to another ravine. "By a succession of charges and repulses we eventually disbursed them in every direction," reported Martin, "every man seeking flight in every direction without regard for anyone else. Thus ended the bloodiest and most sanguinary guerrilla battle that has ever been fought in the State of Missouri, or probably in the United States, according to the numbers engaged." From start to finish the fight had lasted one and a half hours.

But, once again, Quantrill, despite a thigh wound, had made good his escape along with most of his men. William Gregg led over 20 out on horseback while others escaped on foot. They scattered through the brush and trees taking some of their wounded along as they went. The jaded Yankees rested for an hour, then rode out, gathering a few loose horses, but the guerrillas had disappeared. From start to finish, the Yankees had lost 11 killed and 21 wounded. They captured 30 horses, saddles, blankets, coats, guns, a mail bag, the company roll, "overcoat, and spy-glass, recognized by one of their wounded as belonging to Quantrill."[6]

Major Gower estimated the rebel loss as 18 killed and 30 wounded, the true number unknown. But the bushwhackers admitted it was their hardest fight ever, and were astonished at the Yankee performance—probably fueled by the whiskey found in canteens, they preferred to think.[7] But Quantrill, at least, had learned to avoid pitched battles, stick with hit-and-run. Despite this example, however, some of his comrades were slow to learn.

As the guerrilla chief nursed his wounded thigh in a secluded farmhouse, those men who had lost equipment and horses went out on the prowl to procure more. George Todd returned from his escort duties with Colonel Hayes, and in late July was out on a scout with his friends Ed Koger and John Little. As their horses drank at a well-used ford on the Little Blue, fire and gunsmoke erupted from the riverbank foliage. Koger and Little splashed dead into the stream while Todd, unscathed, reigned his horse about and escaped into the woods. But in the dash Todd attempted to jump his horse between two boulders. Amazingly, the horse became wedged there, forcing Todd to flee on foot. The unfortunate horse was later found in the same place, apparently having starved to death.[8]

The Yankee commander at Independence, Lieutenant Colonel Buel, had dispatched a company under Lieutenant Aaron Thomas to lay the trap. Thomas and his men were elated with the success; all those hours of waiting had paid off. But the lieutenant would soon pay a heavy price.

Only July 22, 1862, Union general John Schofield issued General Order No. 19. This required all able bodied men in Missouri to join the state militia "for the purpose of exterminating the guerrillas that infest our state." This proved to be a great recruitment incentive for the Southern cause. Rather than serve the Yankees, many young men joined the guerrillas or enlisted with Colonel Upton Hayes' regulars. Within a few weeks Quantrill ranks had grown to 300 men.

Colonel Buel had conveniently camped most of his troops in a field half a mile from Independence. Buel himself was stationed in the second story of the Southern Bank near the southwest corner of the town square. The town garrison consisted of 21 men billeted across the street, and 24 stationed at the jailhouse one block north of the square.

Confederate Colonel John Hughes arrived from Arkansas with 75 men on a recruiting drive. But, with more ambitious plans in mind, he asked Quantrill to cooperate in the capture of Independence. Word leaked out and ardent Union citizen, Mrs. Wilson, tried to warn Colonel Buel. "Madame, we have heard such reports several times lately, and don't you see we are here yet." Stop worrying and go home, he advised. A lawyer friend of Mrs. Wilson also tried to warn Buel, but to no avail. Captain William Rodewald, commander of the headquarters guard, took a different view. He felt the lady knew what she was talking about and ordered his men to stay on the alert that night.

Shortly before four the following morning, August 11, one of Rodewald's pickets saw horseman moving up Spring Branch Road into the public square. He shouted "Halt!" three times, but they kept on coming. He fired a shot before bolting back inside the guard quarters, and the men upstairs opened fire on the shadowy figures in the street. "For God's sake, don't fire, it's your own men!" a rebel shouted.[9] The confused Yankees ceased firing, and Rodewald led a squad out of the building for a closer look. Confederate regulars under Colonel Hughes were moving through the square, and Rodewald recognized one former resident as an enemy soldier. He gave the order to open fire and several Confederates died where they fell. Both guerrillas and regulars counterattacked, but over the next two hours Rodewald held the crossing of Lexington and Liberty streets. Confederate Major Hart was killed, and the Yankees captured 12 other rebels.

At the jail one block away, meanwhile, George Todd approached with a guerrilla squad. Lieutenant Charles Meryhew, in charge of the guard, ordered one volley fired, then fled, not stopping till he arrived in Kansas City with a handful of men. Todd occupied the jail and smashed down cell doors with a sledge hammer. He freed two prisoners accused of being bushwhackers, and then discovered town marshal James Knowles cooling his heels in one of his own cells. Knowles had been arrested for killing a drunken Irishman, and it was a known fact that he had alerted Buel to the river ford where Todd's companions had been killed. Todd had become obsessed with revenge over his friends' death, and took great pleasure in shooting Knowles down. After being discovered in a hotel bedroom, Lieutenant Thompson, who led the ambush, was shot and kicked down a flight of steps.

While Colonel Hughes' regulars attacked the Yankee military camp outside of town, Quantrill and his guerrillas maintained the fight in Independence. After holding his position for two hours, at 6 a.m. Rodewald was ordered by Buel to take position inside his headquarters building, the Southern Bank. From there they could fire on the rebels from the bottom and top story windows. But Quantrill ordered his men to surround the bank, and from the second story of a large brick house across Liberty Street they were able to pour fire directly into Buel's position. Wishing to show the troops now under attack outside of town that he was holding out, Buel wanted to hoist the Stars and Stripes, but he had no flag. A 16-year-old bugler, Bill Buhoe, offered to fetch Rodewald's colors from across the street. He made a mad, barefooted dash with bullets flying about him, and came panting back with the colors. But two solders attempting to hitch the flag to a chimney were quickly shot down. Then the rebels saw two more men emerge onto the roof, two rebel prisoners, and, with the guerrillas holding fire, the colors were fixed in place.

Quantrill decided to burn Buel out. Cole Younger and Jabez McCorkle piled wood shavings from a carpenter's shop against two timber doors of a building abutting the bank.[10] Once alight, the flames quickly spread. Buel waved a flag of truce, and before long was speaking with Colonel Gideon Thompson who had taken command, Colonel Hughes having been killed in the battle with the encamped Yankee troops. Buel agreed to surrender if "the officers and men of my command were to be considered prisoners of war, the property and persons of the Union citizens to be respected."[11] In other words, no one was to be handed over to the tender mercies of Quantrill.

With the terms accepted, word was sent to the embattled camp to give up the fight. Most of the Yankees capitulated, but others slipped away carrying news of the defeat to Kansas City.

The Confederates occupied the town, and Quantrill returned to the Walker homestead as a conquering hero. Despite the main fight having taken place at the Yankee camp, it was he who had forced Buel's surrender. It was amazing what a well-lit fire could achieve at the right time and place.

A few days after the battle, at the Ingram farm, Colonel Thompson officially mustered Quantrill and his raiders into Confederate service as Partisan Rangers. Elections for officers were held and 120 men cast their votes. Quantrill became captain, William Haller, first lieutenant; George Todd, second lieutenant; and William Gregg, third lieutenant. But George Todd was not happy with the result. He and Haller promptly fell out. On November 3, 1862, Haller went his own way, possibly because Quantrill let it be known that he was not happy with Haller outranking Todd, one of the flaws of officers being elected. The most popular man was not necessarily the best man for the job. Early in 1863 Quantrill heard that Haller had been killed in Cass County, Missouri.[12]

The capture of Independence sent a wave of trepidation through western Missouri. Where would be next? Kansas City? Lexington? And how come Buel had surrendered while his men were still putting up a good fight at the camp? Why had he not heeded warnings of the attack? He and another officer, Captain James Breckinridge, were accused of being in cahoots with the rebels. Breckinridge had failed to find any signs of the rebels while on patrol, and waved a white flag when the rebels first attacked the camp which was promptly pulled down by others determined to fight on. Paroled by the rebels, Buel and Breckinridge were mustered out of service and court-martialed. But, as regards Buel, the redoubtable Captain Rodewald testified, "If I were upon my oath I should say that I believe that Colonel Buel acted in good faith, and did not betray his command into the hands of the enemy. He did not display any lukewarmness during the fight, and even seized a musket and fired several shots into the rebel attacking force."[13] Both Buel and Breckinridge were acquitted. The man who had led a valiant defense from behind a stone wall at the camp battle, Captain Jacob Axline, would be murdered by guerrillas while returning home to Hickman Mills on June 3, 1864.[14]

On August 15–16 the Confederates won another victory at what was called the Battle of Lone Jack in Jackson County. About 800 Yankees under Union Major Emory Foster put up a good fight against over twice their number of Confederates under Colonel Vard Cockrell before retreating back to Lexington. Quantrill's Raiders were not present, but Cole Younger, on detachment, rode with the rebel force. The wounded Union commander and his brother, were captured: "After we were put in a cabin a Confederate guerrilla came in and threatened to shoot us both," recalled Foster. "As he stood over us, pistol in hand, the young man we had seen distributing ammunition to the Confederate line rushed in, seized the guerrilla and shoved him out of the room. Other men entered and addressed the newcomer as Cole Younger. My brother had $300; I had $700. This money and our revolvers Cole took from us at our request and delivered safely to my mother at Warrensburg, Missouri."[15]

Colonel Upton Hays turned over to Quantrill Lieutenant Levi Copeland of the Missouri State Militia, captured at Lone Jack. Quantrill sent a message to Fort Leavenworth offering to exchange Copeland for one of his own men, Perry Hoy, but the answer came in the form of a St. Louis *Missouri Republican* article describing Hoy's death by firing squad. Copeland was summarily shot along with two other prisoners. But Quantrill was still not happy. He ordered his men to mount up, and Gregg asked where they were going. "We are going to Kansas to kill ten men in revenge for poor Perry," Quantrill replied.[16]

Olathe

On the morning of September 6 the raiders crossed the border into Kansas and, as they rode, murdered ten Free-Soil farmers at their homesteads. That afternoon the raiders reached the outskirts of Olathe, the Seat of Johnson County. An Indian interpreter had told Dr. John Barton, the town's founder, that Olathe meant "Beautiful" in his native language, but the area had seen its share of ugly strife during Bleeding Kansas days, and was about to experience more.

Quantrill dispatched Gregg with 60 men to surround the town while he rode directly into town with the remaining 80. Three Yankee recruits were shot down during the advance, and the garrison of 125 bluecoats hurriedly formed in line at the south end of the town square. The rebels dismounted and, using their horses as shields, lined up on the opposite side, their guns menacing the troops. Quantrill called out with a promise of protection if they surrendered. All laid down their arms except one. He paid for his bravery with his life. The troops and male adults were placed under guard in the town square. The rebels then plundered the town, loading wagons with loot. Quantrill recognized an old acquaintance amongst the prisoners, Judge Robinson, and they chatted for some time. At one point the judge called Quantrill "Bill." The rebel politely told Robinson "to address him as 'Captain Quantrill,'" Robinson recalled. The guerrilla chief wanted respectability now, apparently, and produced "a commission from the Confederate government."[17] Robinson was treated kindly, but a few others made the mistake of objecting to being robbed and were shot down in cold blood. The rebels stayed overnight, and next day the captured bluecoats were marched out of town where, much to their relief, they were paroled rather than face a firing squad.

Quantrill led his men east back into Missouri, but the Yankees were out for his blood. On September 10 Quantrill's camp on the north branch of the Grand River was discovered by troops under Lieutenant Colonel John Burris, 10th Kansas Volunteers. Olathe being his adopted home, the Ohio-born officer had a score to settle.[18] A ten-day chase followed through Jackson, Cass, Johnson and Lafayette counties. As the Yankees pursued, they picked up abandoned stock, arms and wagons loaded with loot from Olathe. On the 19th they caught up at Smithfield. Quantrill decided to make a stand and ordered his men to dismount. They formed a defense line, and bullets flew as a brisk skirmish followed. The fight was indecisive, and the bushwhackers mounted once more. Using their old ploy to throw off pursuit, they scattered in all directions. They took their wounded, but left two dead men behind. The Yankees lost one dead and three wounded.

Burris, his men and horses exhausted, gave up the chase a few days later after combing scrubland for "detached fragments" of the band. But before returning to Kansas, "we burned the houses, out-buildings, grain, hay, &c., of about a dozen noted marauders whose premises had been favorite haunts for guerrillas." The raid provided freedom for "upward of 60 loyal colored persons, tired of the rule of rebel masters." The freed slaves "furnished their own transportation and subsistence and accompanied my command to Kansas."[19] No doubt the purloined goods helped compensate the refugees for years without freedom or pay.

On October 6 Captain Daniel David received word that Quantrill's Raiders were on the Independence-Lexington Road. David sent to Fort Leavenworth for reinforcements, then moved his cavalry squad cautiously forward. Warned by pickets, Quantrill, with 100 men, prepared an ambush. Twenty-five men would act as a decoy, and the remaining 75 would conceal themselves by the roadside to bushwhack the Yankees.

Dick Chiles had just arrived in the guerrilla camp that very morning. Although new to the band, he insisted he was entitled to lead the decoy party. His deeds of daring in the past entitled him to the honor, he claimed. Quantrill, of course, wanted either Todd or Gregg for the job, but they stood back and agreed to let Chiles prove himself.

Chiles led the party forward and called a halt at a log cabin at a bend in the road. Hiding the horses in the brush, he had the men take position behind a fence and behind the cabin. The Yankees soon appeared and Chiles gave the order to fire—but to soon. Two bluecoats fell along with half a dozen horses, and two others turned tail, but Captain David rapped out orders as the rebels fell back into the surrounding brush. "I dismounted my men and took to the brush in a like manner," David reported. "Then almost a hand-to-hand fight ensued, which lasted about 40 minutes and not any of the time more than 40 yards apart, during which time we drove the rebels from the field." David retraced his steps and took Dick Chiles prisoner. He had not only bungled the job, but had been badly wounded in the process. Shot through the lungs, Chiles would survive the war but die of the wound not long after. Of the two Yankees shot, one was dead and the other dying, and one other wounded. Yet others, more lucky, had bullet holes through their hats and clothes. David was unsure of rebel casualties, but "learned from the ladies who had come up to learn the result of the fight that Quantrill was pressing buggies and carriages to convey his wounded."[20]

Reinforced, the determined Captain David pushed his pursuit. They found the guerrilla trail, and at one stage, "Captain Johnson, ever ready with his battery, turned his little gun upon them and gave them a few canister, which sent off on a double-quick." But Quantrill always managed to stay one step ahead. His men scattered when required and regrouped once the enemy had lost their scent. David called a halt and consulted his officers. It was "almost unanimously agreed to return to camp for rest, as myself and men had been under a heavy march for three days and only eaten three meals, and our horses almost exhausted from fatigue and light forage." The weary soldiers returned to their barracks, the notorious Quantrill still on the loose. "We do not believe guerrillas can ever be taken by pursuit," David concluded, "we must take them by strategy."

With winter coming on, Quantrill decided to raid the settlement of Shawneetown, Kansas, to replenish their warm clothing stocks. On the way they attacked and burned a Union supply train, killing 15 soldiers. On October 17 they rode into town and stole clothes not only from stores but also the male inhabitants. Some who objected were shot, as did a few others who attempted to escape while being forced to load wagons with plundered goods. The bushwhackers rode out with their stolen loot, the town in flames behind them.[21] The settlement had only 20 buildings, but this was good training for a far bigger town to come.

The chill winds and snows of winter stripped leaves from the bushes and trees guerrillas used for cover. On November 3, 1862, Quantrill led 150 men south towards Arkansas. That afternoon they attacked and burned a train of ox-drawn wagons, killing several soldiers, and taking prisoner Lieutenant N. M. Newbury and four privates. A Yankee force under Colonel Edwin Catherwood set out in pursuit and a running fight ensued. It was a close chase that saw Lieutenant Newbury and one private rescued, and six bushwhackers killed. But Catherwood's men and horses were "so exhausted that I found it impractical to proceed farther without rest."[22] The simple fact was, the guerrillas were usually mounted on the best horses available, through contribution, purchase or theft. The Federal army, through its massive demands, used whatever mounts were available at the time.

On November 5 Quantrill fell in with Confederate colonel Warner Lewis, leading 300 cavalry, in southwest Missouri. Lewis suggested that they join forces and attack the Federal garrison at nearby Lamar. As the Yankees were billeted in a strong brick courthouse suitable for defense, Quantrill felt such an attack unwise, but the persuasive Lewis swung him round. Quantrill entered the town from the south at 10 p.m., as planned, and attacked. Lewis was expected from the north. The garrison, warned of the rebel advance, had barricaded the courthouse and fired back, killing two of Quantrill's men. The firing continued for some time. But where was Lewis with his 300 cavalry? Quantrill withdrew, but not before putting Lamar to the torch. Lewis never turned up. Perhaps, upon reflection, Quantrill's reservations about attacking a strong post had changed Lewis' mind—or perhaps he never had any intention of joining the raid. He may have hated civilian shooting bushwhackers and jayhawkers with equal venom, and hoped that Quantrill would never leave Lamar alive. Lewis himself, it would seem, had a strong instinct for survival. The following year he and one other man would be the only ones to escape after a Confederate party of 18 men made the mistake of starting a fight with Osage warriors.[23]

Once in Arkansas, Quantrill's band took up scouting duties for Colonel Jo Shelby's Missouri men, soon to become known as the "Iron Brigade." In mid–November Quantrill handed command of his raiders to George Todd while he traveled east to Richmond with two other men, Blunt and Higbee. He arranged a meeting with Secretary of War James Seddon, where he requested a commission as colonel under the Partisan Ranger Act. He could raise a whole regiment of Missouri men, he claimed, but said the Confederacy must wage a savage "no prisoners" war if it was to survive. Seddon replied that even war had its amenities and refinements, and in the modern nineteenth century it was simple barbarism to talk of a raising a black flag.

"Barbarism!" Quantrill replied. "Barbarism, Mr. Secretary, means war and war mans barbarism." The bushwhacker, his anger rising, went on to lecture Seddon on how the people had been robbed and wronged by abolitionists. "The cloud has burst," he said. "Do not condemn the thunderbolt." Quantrill continued his tirade.

Confederate secretary of war James Seddon had little time for Quantrill and ignored his request to be commissioned as a colonel (National Archives).

> "The world hates slavery. The world is fighting you.... I have captured and killed many who do not know the English tongue.... This secession, or revolution, or whatever you call it cannot conquer without violence, nor can those who hate it and hope to stifle it, resist without vindictiveness.... Men must be killed. To impel the people to passion there must be some slight illusion mingled with the truth; to arouse them to enthusiasm something out of nature must occur. That illusion should be a crusade in the name of conquest, and that something out of nature should be the black flag...."

"What would *you* do, Captain Quantrell, were yours the power and the opportunity?"

"Do, Mr. Secretary? Why, I would wage such a war and have such a war waged by land and by sea as to make surrender forever impossible. I would cover the armies of the Confederacy all over with blood. I would invade. I would reward audacity. I would exterminate. I would break up foreign enlistments by indiscriminate massacre. I would win the independence of my people or I would find them graves."

"And your prisoners, what of them?"

"Nothing of them; there would be no prisoners. Kansas would be laid waste at once. Meet the torch with the torch, pillage with pillage, slaughter with slaughter, subjugation with extermination…."[24]

Captain Quantrill lingered in Richmond throughout the winter. But he received no commission as colonel of Partisan Rangers. Documents dated after this period confirm that he returned to Missouri still a captain.[25] Some men who rode with him, however, like John McCorkle, later wrote of him as "Colonel" Quantrill, a title he adopted for a brief period later on.[26]

It was not long after Quantrill's departure for Richmond that George Todd decided that operating with regular army units in Arkansas was not to his taste. With a handful of other malcontents, he simply rode out one day, and headed back to Jackson County, Missouri. There's no place like home, they say, regardless of the weather. William Gregg, uninformed of Todd's departure—or desertion, it could be said—assumed command of Quantrill's Raiders on November 28, just hours before Confederate General John Marmaduke's 2000 men clashed with 5000 Yankees under James Blunt in the Battle of Cane Hill. Shelby's Iron Brigade, hotly engaged and greatly outnumbered, repelled three infantry assaults before being forced to retreat through the Boston Mountains.

By December 7 both sides had marshaled their forces and 11,059 Johnny Rebs under General Thomas Hindman tangled with 9,216 bluecoats under Generals Herron and Blunt in the Battle of Prairie Cove. The rebels were driven back to Van Buren where they arrived on December 10 in a ragged and demoralized state.

"John, let's go back to Missouri," said one bushwhacker to his compatriot John McCorkle. It seemed time to follow Todd's example. "'All right,' I replied," McCorkle recalled years later, "so six of us started back. We put on Federal uniforms as the country through which we were to go was full of Federals."[27]

The Confederacy now had no hope of ever reclaiming northwest Arkansas from Yankee control. McCorkle and his companions were not the only ones to head for home.

9

"A prize in the lottery of life"
Mosby, 1863

"My purpose was to weaken the armies invading Virginia, by harassing their rear," recalled John Mosby. A line was only as strong as its weakest point, "it is easy therefore, to see the great results that may be accomplished by a small body of cavalry moving rapidly from point to point on the communications of an army. To destroy supply trains, to break up the means of conveying intelligence, and thus isolating an army from its base, as well as its different corps from each other, to confuse their plans by capturing despatches, are the objects of partisan war."[1]

But, despite being given charge of 15 men, Mosby still only held the rank of private. Stuart's reference to him as a captain after the McClellan raid, however, along with his new command, prompted the officer who wasn't to don a captain's uniform. A visit to a photographic studio in Richmond captured the image for posterity.[2] Pauline and the children were impressed, no doubt.

On a chilly January 24, 1863, the small command moved out from Stuart's camp near Fredericksburg. When approaching Middleburg, Mosby gave orders for his men to split up and seek shelter at local farms. They were to reunite at Mount Zion Church, near Aldie, on the morning of the 26th. At about 4 p.m. two sentries at the Chantilly Church picket post in Fairfax County were astonished to find themselves staring down the barrels of Colt revolvers. They had no idea of rebels being in the area, and gave up without a shot being fired. The other ten men of their detachment, dismounted nearby, were equally surprised, and not inclined to fight. One, however, deciding to take his chances, suddenly mounted and galloped off. Mosby's revolver cracked twice, and the soldier toppled from his horse. Shot through the arm and side, he was still alive, but in too much pain to move. He was left behind to be found by other Yankees who would come looking for the lost detachment.

Mosby escorted the prisoners to Middleburg where they were paroled, and the captured horses and equipment divided amongst his command. By the following week Mosby had captured 28 Union cavalrymen and 29 horses. The legend of "Mosby's Confederacy" had taken root.

The captured detachment came under the overall command of the flamboyant Englishman, Colonel Sir Percy Wyndham. A roving soldier of fortune, he had fought with Garibaldi in Italy and received an Italian knighthood for his trouble.[3] He traveled to the United States and entered the Union service, but was perplexed by Mosby's hit-and-run tactics. He sent word that he considered Mosby no better than a common horse thief. Mosby pled guilty to the charge while pointing out that armed riders were stolen along

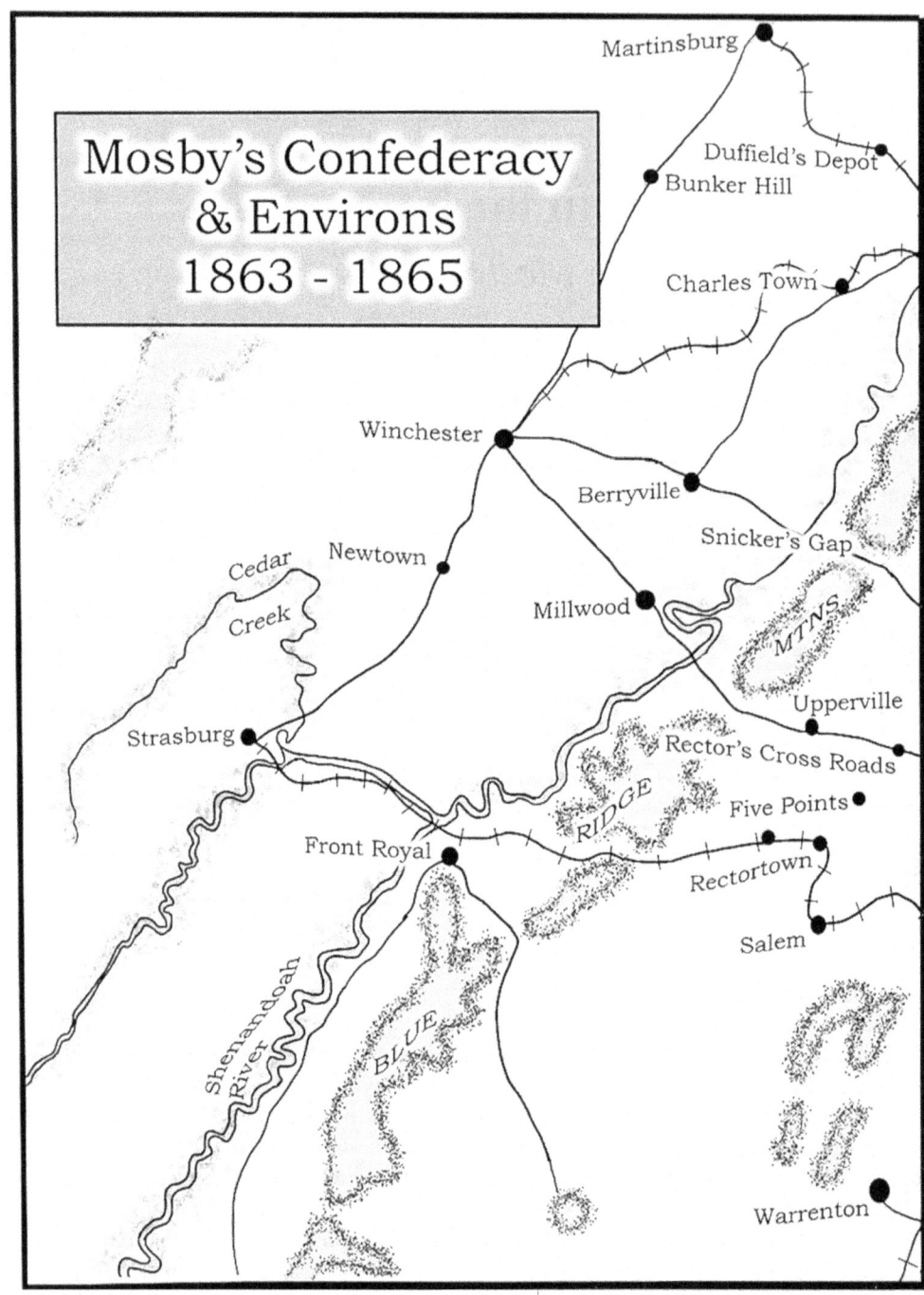

Above and opposite: **Mosby's Confederacy and Environs, 1863–1865 (author's rendition).**

with the horses. He sent word to Wyndham, through a civilian, that the Yankees of one new regiment were not worth capturing, as they were only armed with sabers and outmoded carbines. Mosby much preferred Yankees providing his men with Colt revolvers, the weapon of choice. "I think that my command reached the highest point of efficiency as cavalry

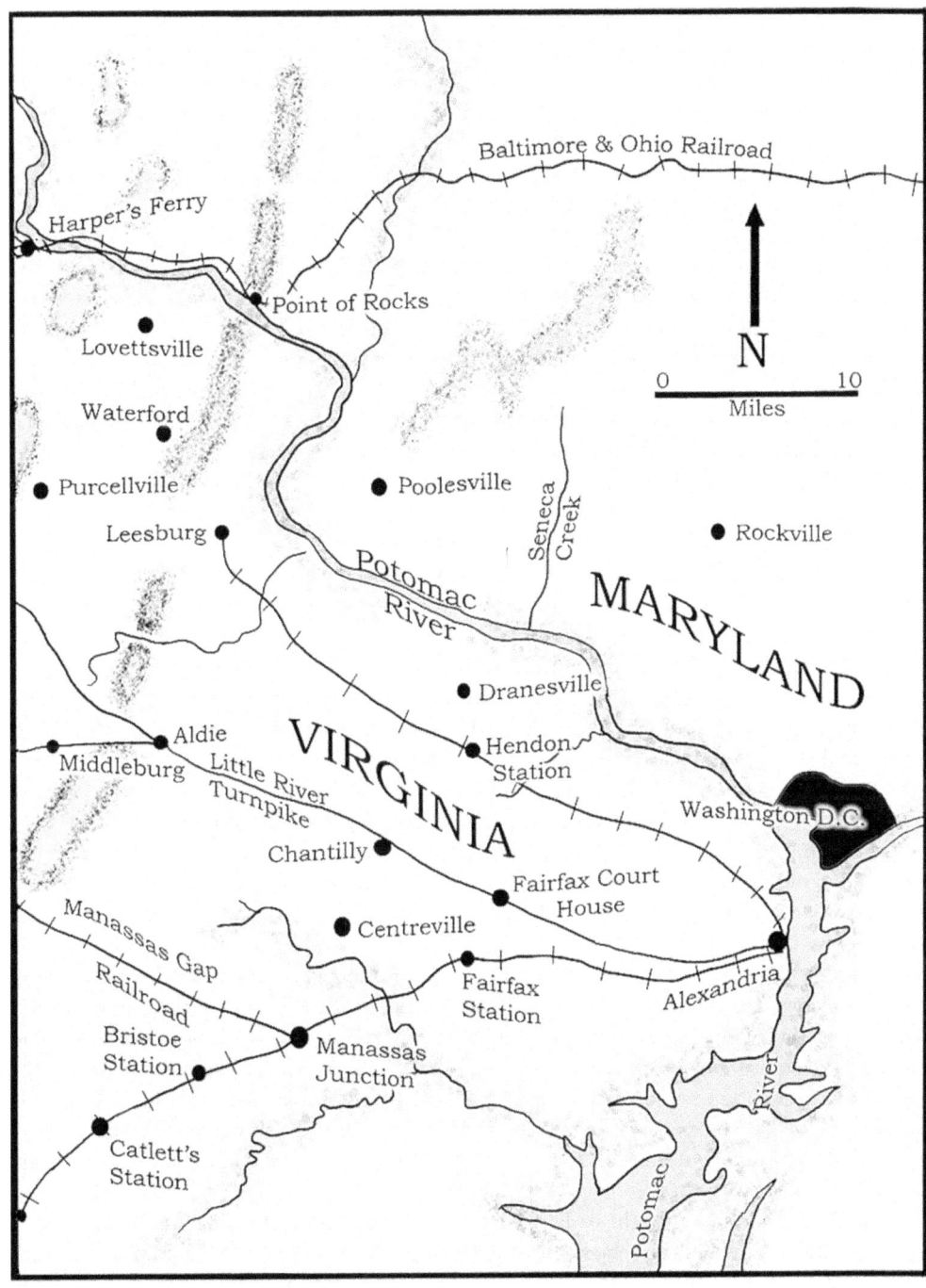

because the were well armed with two six-shooters and their charges combined the effect of fire and shock." And, furthermore, "I believe I was the first cavalry commander who discarded the saber as useless and consigned it to the museums for the preservation of antiquities. My men were as little impressed by a body of cavalry charging them with sabres as though they had been armed with cornstalks."[4]

Wyndham set out to end Mosby's career before it could get into full swing. He led his brigade to Middleburg through a chilly night, arriving at daybreak. The guerrillas were sheltering in local homes, he believed, so the town was surrounded and the houses searched. Twenty-one adult males were arrested, but the rebels escaped as they were not sheltering in town. Mosby and his friend Fount Beattie, sleeping in a nearby home, were awakened by a slave. Mosby quickly gathered his men and struck the enemy rearguard as the Yankees rode from town. One man and three horses were captured. But Wyndham did not take this insult lying down. He spurred his horse around and led a rapid counterattack. The rebels found themselves on the defensive and three were captured while the others escaped. Mosby watched the Yankee column ride off from a nearby hilltop. With those taken prisoner was his friend Fount Beattie, whose horse had come down during the skirmish.[5] But at least he was unharmed, and would soon be riding with Mosby once more after being exchanged.

Bullets flying along their streets did not appeal to the good citizens of Middleburg. Mosby was asked to desist from this mode of warfare, in their vicinity at least. Colonel Wyndham had accused the residents of harboring guerrillas and had threatened to burn the town. Mosby replied in writing: "My attacks on scouts, patrols, and pickets, which have provoked this threat, are sanctioned both by the customs of war and the practice of the enemy; and you are at liberty to inform them that no such clamor shall deter me from employing whatever legitimate weapons I can most effectively use for their annoyance."[6] But he did quietly move his rendezvous point to Rector's Cross Roads, on the Little River Turnpike, about four miles west of town.

A few nights later a bright camp fire was seen amidst the trees near Herdon Station on the Alexandria, Loudon, and Hampshire Railroad. A layer of fresh snow allowed Mosby's guerrillas to approach without the telltale snap of a twig or the crunch of a stone. And Mosby had trained his men to move in silence, using hand signals to convey orders. Thirteen Yankees were taken by surprise. One vidette was shot as he attempted to escape, but the others were taken alive. Then a squad of Union cavalry galloped onto the scene. But they found nothing. Mosby had disappeared with his captives into the night. The whole thing was a failed ploy set up by Wyndham to lure the elusive Mosby to destruction. The colonel learned he would have move much faster to catch the man who would become renowned as "the Gray Ghost."

A line of canvas-topped Federal supply wagons rattled their way towards Middleburg. Yankee cavalry, front and rear, provided the guard. Suddenly a party of mounted men appeared to their front. They charged with wild rebel yells and Colt revolvers blazing. The forward bluecoats panicked and galloped back amidst their own wagons as the canvas tops were thrown back. The panicked riders were hit with a hail of "friendly fire" as the concealed infantry, armed with Spencer repeaters, mistook them for attacking rebels. Mosby later wrote that Wyndham's attempts to kill him "struck blindly around like the Cyclops in his cave, but nobody was hurt."[7]

On the cold and wet night of February 26, 44 troopers from the 18th Pennsylvania Cavalry bedded down in the schoolhouse at Thompson's Corner on Ox Road. Their horses were tethered to trees guarded by three sentries who did their best to stay dry as rain came down. "As only a raccoon could be supposed to travel on such a night," recalled Mosby, the soldiers "would feel safe and be sound asleep, so that a single shot would create a panic."[8] With John Underwood as guide, Mosby approached with 27 men at about 4:30 a.m. His numbers were swelled from local volunteers and detached soldiers who wanted to join the fight, eager to see service with the guerrilla whose renown was on the rise. A vidette challenged their advance. "Friends" came the answer. The sentry peered into the darkness, but the approaching riders did not look at all friendly. He took hasty aim and fired before bolting back towards the school. His shot went wild, and the guerrillas charged with a rebel yell. The bleary-eyed troopers scrambled for guns and some fired wildly through the windows. The rebel line wavered for a moment. "Close on them, men," yelled Mosby, and they charged once more. This was too much for the Yankees who fled from the building on foot and out into the night. One Yankee was killed, two wounded and several taken prisoner. Forty horses were captured along with stores and equipment left behind. This attack confirmed the danger of having small, isolated picket posts far from main camps during the night, and they were ordered to withdraw till daybreak.

With Wyndham ordered away on scouting duties, Major Joseph Gilmer of the 18th Pennsylvania Cavalry led 200 men to Middleburg on the night of March 1.[9] He had orders to end "gang" leader Mosby's career once and for all. By the time the sun had risen over the cold, snow covered landscape, the Yankees had occupied the town, and Gilmer had set up headquarters in the hotel Mosby was rumored to sleep in. The troops rounded up all the adult males, mostly aged men, who were supposedly the marauders who attacked their outposts and stole their stock. Several colored women seized their chance for freedom, and asked to be taken too. "They had children," recalled Mosby, "but the major was a good-natured man. So each woman was mounted behind a trooper—and the trooper took her baby in his arms…. When they started, the column looked more like a procession of Canterbury pilgrims than cavalry." Gilmer warned the citizens again that their town was under risk of being torched, then led his command out.

Mosby galloped into town at the head of about 20 men as the Yankee column moved into the distance. The women, their men folk taken as prisoners, wailed at the loss. "The tears and lamentations of the scene aroused all our sentiments of chivalry," he recalled. Despite warnings that he was outnumbered, Mosby set out in pursuit, his small band against Gilmer's 200.

The Yankees, meanwhile, passed through the village of Aldie, five miles to the east. Warmed by an ample supply of whiskey, Major Gilmer received word of horsemen on the road to his front. The guerrilla he had been sent out to catch was about to give battle, he assumed. As Mosby himself observed, with children, women and prisoners riding double, "pistols and sabres would be of little use if an attack was made." In a panic, Gilmer turned right from the turnpike and led a headlong flight along the old Braddock Road. This had carried the British to destruction near Fort Duquesne during the French and Indian War in 1755. Now the Yankee horses sank in thawing snow, mud and slush. Firstly the male prisoners were abandoned, then the colored women and their children. "The Braddock Road had seen one such wreck and retreat a hundred years before," observed Mosby.

But the horsemen Gilmer had fled from were, in fact, Yankee allies, a detachment of 50 Yankee troopers of the 1st Vermont Cavalry, commanded by Captain Franklin Huntoon.

In the rear, Mosby's small band pressed on. Not knowing Gilmer had fled along the Braddock Road, he assumed Huntoon's Vermont Cavalry, when they appeared to his front, were Gilmer's rearguard. The rebels captured two videttes as they crested a hill, then set out after another two seen on the pike. But what looked like only two troopers from a distance turned out to be a whole dismounted squadron, their horses feeding at a large roadside flour mill. Mosby's "horse was high-mettled and ran at full speed, entirely beyond my control," he recalled. The Yankees looked around to see the rebel horsemen bearing down, Mosby and his unruly mount in the lead. A few bluecoats fired, wounding two rebels, but most simply bolted, "some hid in the mill; others ran to Bull Run Mountain near by." Captain John Woodward, however, put up a good fight till his horse was shot from under him. Pinned beneath his fallen mount, he surrendered rather than be shot. Mosby's horse did not stop, carrying him to certain destruction among yet another Yankee squad further down the road. To save himself, he jumped from his saddle and tumbled in the snow. His men galloped towards him, and the astonished bluecoats to their front turned and galloped away, the only thing pursuing them Mosby's riderless horse.[10]

The Confederates returned to the mill where some bluecoats "had hidden like rats" in the grain, recalled Mosby. They were pulled out, possibly saved from a crushing death, as the churning grind stones were in full operation. The prisoners rounded up included Captains Huntoon and Woodward, and 17 others, along with 23 horses. Mosby rode out on a borrowed mount to find his own horse. The animal was long gone, still chasing Yankees, but he did encounter Gilmer's abandoned prisoners plodding back. To Mosby's surprise he received profuse thanks for their rescue, actually effected by Gilmer's misidentification of Huntoon's allied troops.

Gilmer was court-martialed for his role in the affair. He was found "Not guilty" of cowardice, but guilty of having been drunk while on duty. "He might have done more if he had taken less whiskey along," recalled Mosby.[11] The unfortunate major was cashiered on July 23, 1863.

The drawing in of pickets during the night left gaps in the Federal defense line. This could well allow even greater damage—providing there were rebels prepared to take the chance. One such gap appeared between the infantry post at Centreville, and the 18th Pennsylvania Cavalry cantonment at Chantilly, three miles away. Major General Samuel Heintzelman, commanding the Washington defenses, was informed of the gap by the telegraph operator at Chantilly. He passed the news along, but if Colonel Wyndham ever received the news, he did nothing to fill the void.

James Ames, a Yankee sergeant from the 5th New York Cavalry, deserted his comrades and joined Mosby's band. A large, powerful and articulate ex-sailor from Bangor, Maine, he arrived in uniform without a horse, and offered his services. "I never cared to inquire what his grievance was," recalled Mosby. But this seems strange. If Ames wished to convince Mosby of his loyalty, disclosing his reason for desertion would seem the logical first step. It has been claimed he deserted because of Lincoln's Emancipation Proclamation.[12] If so, he was not the only one. Many Yankees had enlisted to save the Union, not free slaves. Despite some feeling Ames should be shot as a spy, the information he provided corroborated Mosby's impressions of Federal dispositions and gaps. Given the benefit of the doubt, Ames returned to his former regiment at Germantown with an unmounted rebel volunteer, Walter Franklin, where they stole two fine mounts before rejoining Mosby's band.

The Stoughton Raid

Sir Percy Wyndham and infantry commander Brigadier General Edwin Stoughton were not billeted with their troops. They were enjoying cozy lodgings with soft beds in the township of Fairfax Court House, several miles inside the Yankee lines. Their troops were either under canvas or in crude timber barracks spread around the countryside: three cavalry regiments and two infantry regiments at Germantown, one mile away, one infantry brigade near Fairfax Station, and another infantry brigade, with artillery and cavalry, at Centreville.[13] The once picturesque Fairfax Court House had changed hands during the war, and was now marred by ruins, deserted houses and overgrown gardens. The once fine central hotel had been commandeered as a Union Army hospital.

West Point graduate Edwin Stoughton, only 24, was the youngest general in the Union Army.[14] From an auspicious Vermont family, he had distinguished himself as colonel of the 4th Vermont Infantry fighting under McClellan during the Peninsula Campaign. The young and handsome Stoughton was popular with the ladies, so it was said, but such was not the case with the men under his command. His "most striking characteristic was his senseless profanity and West Point snobbery," recalled one man, also "ever memorable knapsack drill ... hour after hour ... often at the double quick ... carrying our whole equipment which weighed around eighty pounds." One soldier of the 12th Vermont wrote, "Some of the boys would as soon shoot him as not."[15] Another was not happy because Stoughton lived in comfort apart from his men. Five days before his capture, the soldier wrote, "if he is so fancy, that he can't put up with them, the Government had better put him out." The writer went on to complain of a woman named Ford in town who was a known spy for Stuart, yet "I understand that she and Stoughton are very intimate. If he gets picked up some night he may thank her for it. Her father lives here, and is known to harbor and give all the aid he can to the rebs, and this in the little hole of Fairfax, under the nose of the Provost-Marshal, who is always full of bail whisky. So things go, and it is all right. No wonder we don't get along faster."[16] The beautiful Antonia Ford had warned General Beauregard of the Yankee plans to move against Manassas before their disaster at First Bull Run.[17]

Stoughton arrived at Fairfax Court House during December of 1862 in command of the Second Brigade of General Casey's Division. Their prime task was the defense of Washington, 18 miles away, and they repulsed Stuart's cavalry during his December raid. Stoughton occupied the two-story brick home of Dr. William Gunnell on Main Street, almost opposite the court house, while Wyndham occupied the home of Judge Henry Thomas on Chain Bridge Road, one block away. Their staff, a military band, and a small guard detachment were also in town, along with hospital personnel. Communication with the outside world was through a telegraph office set up in a tent on the courthouse lawn. They felt so safe that Stoughton saw no problem with his mother and sister paying a visit. No doubt they were bursting with pride at Edwin's success in the military world, but events would prove that even the most favored families can suffer bitter blows.

Stoughton and Wyndham were dangerously exposed—with hindsight. The fact was, despite the lack of troops quartered in Fairfax Court House, Mosby would have to avoid up to 3000 Federal troops billeted in the general vicinity. He needed a guide to avoid their camps and pickets, and "Big Yankee" Ames proved to be just the man.

On the evening of March 8, 1863, Mosby met up with 29 men at Dover, Loudoun County, two miles west of Aldie. The volunteers were not aware of the risky venture before them. Once on the move over snow-covered ground under a misty, light rain, Mosby confided his plan to Ames. It was the big Yankee's job to guide them safely 25 miles to Fairfax Court House avoiding the enemy fortifications, camps and patrols. Mosby planned to cut the telegraph line between Centreville and Fairfax Court House, where they would have to capture the sentries without a warning shot being fired. Stoughton and Wyndham would be roused from their beds and taken back to Confederate lines, but the timing was critical. Mosby needed to arrive when the enemy were asleep, grasp his prisoners, and get clear of Yankee lines before daybreak. By then the raid would have been discovered and, even with the telegraph down, Union cavalry would be in pursuit. The chances of success seemed remote, but "the safety of the enterprise lay in it its novelty," recalled Mosby, "nothing of the kind had been done before.... Adventures to the adventurous."[18]

As they approached enemy territory, two hours precious hours were lost. The men at the rear fell back in the darkness, and Mosby soon realized they were nowhere to be seen.

Most would have abandoned the risky venture then, but the two groups circled around until contact was made, and Mosby pushed ahead. Ames guided them through the Union gap to the road between Germantown and Centreville. Here the telegraph line linking the two posts flanked the road. One agile rebel shimmied up a pole with cutters, and the wire came down. They followed the road towards Germantown, Mosby's men still oblivious to their mission, then turned off through the pines. The flickering fires of bluecoat pickets could be seen through the foliage to their left. They followed the Chain Bridge Road and the men were soon surprised to find themselves in the quiet streets of Fairfax Court House. Their entry was from the south, Union territory, to give the impression of Union cavalry arriving. The ploy worked. "It was so dark they could not distinguish us from their own people,"[19] recalled Mosby, and "the few guards stationed around the town, unsuspecting danger, were easily captured."[20] Rebel squads were sent to the officers' quarters and stables to secure their horses for the trip back. They were to rendezvous at the court house yard, where the bewildered telegraph operator was hustled from his tent. All links with the outside world went dead along with a snip of the telegraph wires. Mosby sent Ames with a squad to rouse Sir Percy from his slumbers, while he selected half a dozen men for the most important job. The young general slept in blissful ignorance of the events surrounding him. A loud knock on the door caused a top story window to open. "Who's there?" asked a bleary voice. "Fifth New York Cavalry with a dispatch for General Stoughton." Lieutenant Samuel Prentiss opened the door to find himself staring into the barrel of a Colt revolver. Mosby grasped the officer's nightshirt and whispered, "Mosby" to him as they barged inside. With Prentiss leading the way, the rebels clambered up the stairs into Stoughton's bedroom—and the end of his military career. "There was no time for ceremony," Mosby recalled, "so I drew up the bedclothes, pulled up the general's shirt, and gave him a spank on his bare back, and told him to get up." Stoughton rolled over and peevishly asked what was going on. Mosby informed him that he was a prisoner. "I then asked him if he had ever heard of 'Mosby,' and he said he had. 'I am Mosby,' I said. 'Stuart's cavalry has possession of the Court House; be quick and dress.'" Mosby had multiplied the rebel force by thousands to "deprive

Private Mosby donned the uniform of a captain for his raid on Stoughton's headquarters (*The Memoirs of Colonel John S. Mosby*, 1917).

him of all hope of escape." The bleary-eyed Stoughton asked to be taken to Fitz Lee, a West Point friend. Mosby agreed without revealing that such a meeting would take some time. All he wanted at this critical point was Stoughton's cooperation, one way or another. "Stoughton had the reputation of being a brave soldier, but a fop," recalled Mosby. "He dressed before a looking glass as carefully as Sardanapalus" (legendary effeminate Assyrian king).[21]

"I fought for success and not display," Mosby later wrote. "There was no man in the Confederate Army who had less of the spirit of knight-errantry in him, or took a more practical view of war than I did. The combat between Richard and Saladin by the Diamond of the Desert is a beautiful picture for the imagination to dwell on, but it isn't war, and was no model for me."[22] But while Stoughton dressed, the guerrilla leader took a piece of coal from the fireplace and scrawled "Mosby" across the wall.[23] This, along with his plumed hat, and the audacious raid itself, would suggest there was more "knight-errantry" in Mosby than he cared to admit.

Once satisfied that he his dignity was intact, Stoughton was taken downstairs and outside. His couriers had been taken prisoner, and the party returned to the courtyard where Mosby was sorry to learn that Sir Percy Wyndham was on a lucky streak. The colonel had departed for a meeting in Washington that very evening. But Ames had captured his horses, uniform, and two of his staff officers. This included Ames' former captain, Augustus Barker. Mosby would have liked to stay longer and destroy "the large amount of quartermaster's, commissary, and sutler's stores accumulated there," but the two hours lost in their approach left no time for such luxuries. At 3:30 a.m. the cavalcade mounted up and moved out. As they rounded the courthouse corner the order "Halt!" was heard. Lieutenant Colonel Joseph Johnson, cavalry commander in Wyndham's absence, peered out a window in his nightshirt. "The horses need rest." he yelled. "I will not allow them to be taken out. What the devil is the matter?" The horsemen stared back through the darkness and made no reply. "I am commander of this post and this must be stopped."[24] Johnson was appalled when the insolent horsemen simply laughed. Mosby ordered two men to fetch yet another prisoner and Johnson, finally realizing what was afoot, disappeared from the window. The rebels dashed into the house only to be met by his wife who "held her ground like a lioness," Mosby recalled.[25] They pushed past and searched the house, but all they found was Johnson's uniform on a chair, his hat on a table, and his watch dangling on the wall. Johnson had fled in his nightshirt and taken refuge in a nearby barn.

With no time to waste, Mosby gave the order to move on. By now the unhappy Stoughton realized that Jeb Stuart's cavalry had not occupied the town after all. Mosby's small band of 29 men had taken Fairfax Court House without a single shot being fired, a disgrace for himself

General Edwin Stoughton's military career came to a humiliating end when he was "caught napping" by John Mosby (National Archives).

and the Union Army. To baffle pursuit, the command moved off in the direction of Fairfax Station, but half a mile down the track veered right towards Centreville. With at least one prisoner for every rebel, it proved impossible to prevent Lieutenant Prentiss and some others from escaping into the darkness.

Mosby and one other man rode in the rear, and "we stopped frequently to listen for the hoofbeats of cavalry in pursuit, but no sound could be heard save the hooting of owls. My heart beat higher with hope every minute; it was the crisis of my fortunes." Mosby moved to the front where Stoughton rode under the watchful eye of William Hunter, one of Mosby's original 15. Near Centreville a challenge was heard from a Yankee picket and Captain Barker, seeing his chance, galloped off. A man rode after him and was about to fire when Barker's horse lost its footing and tumbled in a ditch. Barker was recaptured, and the command rode on without interference, despite being within sight of the Yankee fortifications. "The camps were quiet," Mosby recalled, "there was no sign of alarm; the telegraph wires had been cut; and no news had come about our exploit at the court house." Mosby led the column around Centreville, through the swift waters of Cub Run, and the eastern sky glowed with dawn's first light as they moved towards the old Bull Run battlefield. He looked at Stoughton, and could not help but feel a pang of sorrow for the man. "From the heights of Groveton we could see that the road was clear to Centreville, and that there was no pursuit," Mosby recalled, and "I knew that I had drawn a prize in the lottery of life."[26]

Mosby's capture of General Stoughton electrified both North and South. The commanders were astonished at the audacity of the raid and made no secret of it—all except General Fitzhugh Lee. When a wet and bedraggled Mosby brought Stoughton and other prisoners to his headquarters he was "treated with indifference," Mosby recalled. But Fitzhugh showered his old West Point comrade with every courtesy, and invited him and other captive officers to warm themselves by the crackling log fire.[27]

Mosby rode off in disgust, and had the news telegraphed to Jeb Stuart. The two were reunited that evening when Stuart alighted from a railway carriage at Culpepper Station. Taking a very different attitude, Stuart showered his guerrilla chief with praise, and handed him a commission as captain from Governor Letcher. But Mosby was not impressed. This was a commission in the "Virginia Troops"—an organization which did not exist. Presumably this was to cut through military red tape, as "Stuart remarked that he thought the Confederate War Department would recognize it," recalled Mosby.

A few days later the following appeared in General Orders.

> Captain John S. Mosby has for a long time attracted the attention of his generals by his boldness, skill and success, so signally displayed in his numerous forays upon the invaders of his native soil.
>
> None know his dashing enterprise and dashing heroism better than those foul invaders, those strangers themselves to such noble traits.
>
> His last brilliant exploit—the capture of Brigadier-General Stoughton, U.S. A., two captains and thirty other prisoners, together with their arms, equipments and fifty-eight horses—justifies this recognition in General Orders. This feat, unparalleled in the war, was performed in the midst of the enemy's troops, at Fairfax Court House, without loss or injury.
>
> The gallant band of Captain Mosby shares his glory, as they did the danger of this enterprise, and are worthy of such a leader.
>
> J. E. B. Stuart,
> Major-General Commanding.

"A Union Brigadier-General and Several Officers Gobbled Up" screamed the *Washington Evening Star*. "There is screw loose somewhere, and we need a larger force in front."[28]

The competence of Union leaders was put under scrutiny. The raid "reflects very uncreditably upon some of our military leaders," observed one New York trooper, "while it shows how wily a foe we have to contend with." Abraham Lincoln, with characteristic humor, said he "didn't mind the loss of the Brigadier as much as the horses." He could "make a much better General in five minutes, but the horses cost one hundred and twenty-five dollars apiece."[29] Miss Antonia Ford found herself under arrest and sent to Washington's Old Capitol Prison. "Miss Ford of Fairfax," claimed the *New York Times*, "was unquestionably the local spy and actual guide of Captain Mosby in his late swoop upon that village."[30] But Big Yankee Ames had performed that deed while an oblivious Miss Ford slumbered on through the night. Mosby denied her involvement, and no evidence could be found. Yankee Major Joseph Willard had fallen in love with the Southern belle and, despite proof of her spying activities in the past, worked hard for her release. After seven months behind bars, she finally walked free, and repaid Willard for his kindness by marrying him on March 10 the following year.

Stoughton found himself behind bars in Richmond's Libby Prison. He was exchanged two months after his capture and, his military career in tatters, resigned from the army. He practiced law in New York City with his father and uncle, but rumors persisted that his capture had been the result of an involvement with Miss Ford. Following the war he wrote to Mosby requesting a statement that she had not been involved, and he had not used profanities when taken prisoner. Richmond papers had reported that, when woken up, Mosby asked if Stoughton had heard of him. According to one account he replied, "Yes, have we caught the son of a bitch?" and another claimed, "Have you caught the damned rascal?"—bad words by the standards of the day. But in the long run it made little difference, as Stoughton died of tuberculosis on Christmas day, 1868.

Sir Percy Wyndham was a prime target in Mosby's raid, but he was absent when the rebels struck (Library of Congress).

Also derided was Lieutenant Colonel Johnson, the man who had fled in his nightshirt while his wife held the fort. "We regret exceedingly that he was not caught then and there," said the *New York Times*, "and carried into Dixie's land, in *status quo*. The appearance of a National cavalry officer, taken when on outpost duty in his nightshirt, paraded through a rebel town in the same airy costume, would not only have supplied the unfortunate inhabitants with some amusement, but served as a severer warning to his comrades left behind than they are likely to receive in any other way." The story went round that he actually hid in a water closet, and the title "Outhouse Johnson" was bandied about. He fled from Fairfax Court House to Washington in disgrace, and at the end of the year was cashiered after pleading guilty to being absent without leave and breach of arrest.[31]

Sir Percy Wyndham had been responsible for the picket deployments which left the crucial gap. For this lapse he was transferred to less responsible duties the following week, but Mosby felt the gallant cavalier had been given a raw deal. "Wyndham ought not to be blamed," he recalled, "because he did not anticipate an event that had no precedent. He did exercise reasonable vigilance. In this life we can only prepare for what is probable, not for every contingency."[32] Wyndham took part in further battles and was wounded at Brandy Station on June 9. He then served in Washington, D.C., and, after being refused a promotion, retired from the army in July of 1864. In 1866 he returned to serve with Garibaldi in Italy once more, but his adventurous career came to an appropriate demise when, in 1879, his hot air balloon ignited and crashed into a Burmese lake.[33]

Mosby's audacious raid saw a flurry of activity by Union troops. Closing the barn door after the horses had bolted, infantry were transferred from Germantown to Fairfax Court House. They fortified the town with rifle pits, and tramped through the streets on futile patrols on the lookout for Johnny Rebs long gone. Fairfax Station, three miles away, became the new, highly fortified headquarters. Major General Julius Stahel took command of the cavalry responsible for scouting and picketing, and the two brigades of 3300 men were reinforced to a division of 5200 men. Mosby's gap was closed by an infantry brigade, and a cavalry regiment was ordered from Winchester to Berryville to counter guerrilla raids in the Shenandoah Valley.[34]

Mosby was well satisfied by all this. These deployments only served to show how a small number of partisan rangers could force the redeployment of many Yankee troops from belligerent to protective duties.

Chantilly, Miskel's Farm and Other Fights

A little over a week following Stoughton's capture, the Yankee vidette at Herndon Railway Station, about nine miles north of Fairfax Court House, saw what he assumed to be the relief guard approaching across the snow-covered ground. But the blue overcoats worn by the two men in the advance concealed Confederate uniforms. The sentry quickly found a Colt revolver in his face, and was disarmed. Twenty-five men of the 1st Vermont Cavalry were relaxing in the sunshine around an old sawmill, their horses tethered to a fence. The Yankees "would not be expecting us," recalled Mosby, "as all our attacks had been at night."[35] Unconcerned, the bluecoats watched the horsemen approach. But suddenly "Charge" was heard and the howling rebels broke into a gallop. With no time to mount, the Yankees dashed into the mill and upstairs into the loft. But Mosby had no time for a siege. The real Yankee relief guard could arrive and attack his rear. Scraps of timber and shavings covered the ground story floor. At the top of his voice, Mosby ordered them set on fire. It comes as little surprise that the Yankees surrendered even before the match could be struck. The prisoners filed out to be disarmed. Then four fine horses were seen tethered outside a nearby house. The rebels rushed in to find a fine lunch spread on the table, but the room as deserted as the *Mary Celeste*. One man clambered up the stairs into the attic and called out for anyone concealed there to surrender. Ignored, he fired a shot into the darkness. There was a hurried movement, then dust and cobwebs flew as a man crashed through the ceiling into the room below. Once brushed off, Major William Wells emerged. He had stepped from a timber beam onto the weak, lathing ceiling. Three more officers emerged from the dark to be taken prisoner. They were led away, and the rebels enjoyed consuming their lunch, "by right of war," recalled Mosby. They had been detailed to investigate accusations of soldiers stealing from civilians. Despite losing their lunch, they apparently bore no grudge against their captor. Many years after the war Mosby received a letter from Lieutenant P. Cheney, one of the four. He complimented Mosby on the treatment they received which "has always been gladly remembered by us all—in every respect courteous."[36]

In this raid Mosby suffered no casualties, but bagged one major, one captain, two lieutenants, 21 men along with their arms, and 26 horses and equipment. One wounded Yankee was left behind.[37] Major Wells was soon exchanged and, for gallantry while fighting Jeb Stuart's cavalry at Gettysburg, received the Congressional Medal of Honor. Perhaps the unseemly circumstances of his capture, and Mosby's association with Stuart, had urged him to fight all the harder. He was promoted to brigadier general, brevet major general, in 1865.[38]

In mid March Mosby was planning his next assault. But he took time out for some recreational activities. On March 16 he wrote to Pauline with a request that she bring herself and the children to the home of James and Elizabeth Hathaway near Salem in Fauquier County. They lived in a fine two-story brick house on their plantation which, in 1860, employed 31 slaves. Fount Beattie often resided there, and would marry one of their daughters. The Mosbys enjoyed a fruitful reunion, and their third child, John Jr., was born nine months later.

No doubt Mosby was happy to receive the following communication from Assistant Adjutant General Walter Taylor, dated March 23: "The President has appointed you captain of partisan rangers. The general commanding directs me to say that it is desired that you proceed at once to organize your company, with the understanding that it will be placed

Too late. Union reinforcements moved into Fairfax Court House village following the raid (*The Photographic History of the Civil War*, 1911).

on a footing with all the troops of the line, and to be mustered unconditionally in the Confederate service for and during the war."[39]

"In" the Confederate service—but not "with." Although Mosby was finally a *bona fide* officer, his independent guerrilla operations would continue behind the Union lines.

Mosby met with about 60 rangers at Rector's Cross Roads. He planned to follow a similar trail to that used in the Stoughton raid, and strike two outposts of the 5th New York Cavalry near Chantilly in another daylight assault. Mosby planned to approach from the rear so the enemy would mistake them for their own cavalry. They rode 23 miles without detection, but their horses were fatigued by the time they neared Chantilly late that day. Before they could cross around to the Yankee rear, Mosby decided to abandon the attack, but some of his men had not come this far simply to withdraw. A party dashed out and attacked a seven-man picket post. One Yankee was shot and killed, and the others taken prisoner. They rejoined Mosby and began the ride back, but one mile down Little River Turnpike they topped a rise to see 200 Union cavalry in pursuit. With his horses tired out, Mosby realized he could not outdistance the fresh Yankee mounts. A stand would have to be made, and they rode on in a search for suitable defense terrain. About three miles west of Chantilly Mosby found the place, conveniently provided by the Yankees themselves. A timber abatis of sharpened spikes been placed over the road, but was now not manned. Here the rebels paused and regrouped for their defense—but for Mosby the best form of defense was attack. Some men had ridden ahead, and he dispatched another five to take the prisoners behind Confederate lines. He ordered the remainder, about 50 men, to line up behind the abatis. "I knew that when they darted out it would create the impression on my pursuers that I had drawn them into an ambuscade," recalled Mosby. "I had no faith in the sabre as a weapon. I only made the men draw their sabres to prevent them from wasting their fire before they got to closer quarters. I knew that when they got among them the pistol would be used." The Yankees, thinking they had the guerrillas on the run, were in high spirits. "I could distinctly hear their loud cheers and the hoofstrokes of their horses on the hard pike," recalled Mosby. They came over a rise about 100 yards from the rebel position. In the next instant guerrillas, brandishing sabers and venting horrific rebel yells, bolted through gaps and around the abatis. The astonished bluecoats ground to a halt, and panic gripped their ranks. "It was more of a chase than a fight for 4 or 5 miles," recalled Mosby. "My men had returned their sabres to their scabbards and the death-dealing revolver was doing its work."[40] Five Yankees were killed and several wounded as they fled. Mosby took 36 prisoners including one lieutenant, and captured 50 horses, with no loss to his command.[41]

One of Mosby's men had used his saber rather than the pistol. Captain Bradford Smith Hoskins had been decorated for his services with the British Army during the Crimean War, and arrived with a letter of introduction from Jeb Stuart. "He was a thorough soldier of fortune," Mosby recalled, "devoted to the profession of arms, and loved the excitement and danger and joy of battle."[42] But the time would come when Hoskin's reliance on the blade rather than the pistol would cost him dear.

Mosby sent word of this latest exploit to Stuart, and received the following in reply, dated March 27, 1863.

> Captain,—Your telegram, announcing your brilliant achievement near Chantilly, was duly received and forwarded to General Lee. He exclaimed upon reading it,
> "*Hurrah for Mosby! I wish I had a hundred like him!*"
>
> Heartily wishing your continued success, I remain your obedient servant,
> J. E. B. Stuart, Major General commanding.[43]

Stuart referred to Mosby as "Captain," but President Davis had authorized his promotion to major the day before, March 26.[44] News could travel slowly through the bureaucracy, and on April 7 Mosby still signed a report as "Captain Commanding." On April 22 the secretary of war instructed the adjutant general, "Nominate as major if it has not already been done so."

The Confederate authorities had received a flood of complaints from Southern citizens about the activities of undisciplined partisan rangers, a menace to friend and foe alike. Stuart wrote to Mosby "by all means ignore the term 'Partizan Rangers.' Let 'Mosby's Regulars' be a name of pride with friends and respectful trepidation with enemies."[45] Mosby, however, had no problem with being called "Partisan Ranger" or "guerrilla," or even "bushwhacker." "Now I never resented the epithet 'bushwhacker,'" he recalled, "although there was no soldier to whom it applied less—because bushwhacking is a legitimate form of war, and it is just as fair and equally heroic to fire on an enemy from behind a bush as a breastwork or from the casemate of a fort."[46] Ignoring Stuart's instruction, a report of June 10, 1863, was signed, "Respectfully, your obedient servant, JNO. S. Mosby, Major of Partisan Rangers."

The word was whispered from homestead to farm, village to town; Mosby was planning his next raid. In seems a minor miracle that news of his rendezvous were not betrayed to the Yankees. They would have arranged a hot reception if they could. It says something for the loyalty of the populace to both Mosby and the Cause at this stage of the war. On the morning of March 31, 1863, he arrived at Rector's Cross Roads amidst chilly, falling snow. The men came in—and kept coming, 69 in all, the most to muster yet. Mosby's fame was a beacon to men who wanted to serve under a leader they could trust—and the promise of booty did no harm. "I had never seen more than a dozen of them before," recalled Mosby, "and very few of them had seen each other." Of the original 15 men placed under Mosby by Stuart, about half a dozen were no longer around, having been captured while attending a dance. This was a lesson to be learned by all: don't let your guard down, no matter where you are.[47]

The others who turned up, although well-mounted and well-attired, were a motley crew, cavalry and infantry on furlough, one or two wounded with crutches tied to their saddle. And even deserters from the regulars arrived. "Once their commanders heard that I had reclaimed and converted them once more into good soldiers," recalled Mosby, "they not only made requisition to have them returned to their regiments, but actually complained to General Lee of their being with me." At this time Mosby did not question those who wished to ride with him. "I cared nothing for the form of a thrust if it drew blood," he said. "Patriotism, as well as love of adventure, impelled them. If they got rewards in the shape of horses and arms, these were devoted, like their lives, to the cause in which they were fighting."

Despite having 69 men, Mosby was not overly optimistic of achieving a great deal with this raid. The Yankees had become wary of this Swamp Fox phantom who would strike, then disappear without trace. Keeping their destination to himself, Mosby led his command towards Dranesville, 28 miles away, to strike the Union picket post there. His plan was to attack at dusk when the enemy would least expect a visit from the Gray Ghost. His previous assaults had been after dark, or in broad daylight as at Herdon Station, two weeks earlier. He arrived at Herdon to hear that the Dranesville camp, about three miles further on, had been disbanded the day before, the cavalry moving to Difficult Run, several miles away. Well named, the waters of this stream could only be crossed at a few fords, and Mosby well knew that they would be well guarded by alert Yankee cavalry. Rather than abandon the mission, however, he decided to push on to Dranesville. Perhaps he would come across an isolated Yankee command or supply train? Such a strike would make the venture worthwhile.

But no target of opportunity was found. From Dranesville they moved up the Leesburg Pike to find a camping site that would provide forage for the horses. Miskel's Farm was located in the forks of the Potomac River and Goose Creek. It was here that Mosby called for a halt at midnight.[48] The Potomac was a few hundred yards away, and Union camps on the other side were no threat. He decided videttes were not needed on the pike—a mistake, as it turned out. But he did place a guard over the horses while men took refuge from the cold in the barn hayloft, a good place to sleep for the night. He and some others enjoyed the luxury of spreading out on the homestead floor in front of a warming log fire. Using his saddle as a pillow, Mosby was soon sound asleep.

He arose at sunrise the following morning, April 1, to be told that Yankee signal flags were flashing across the river. His command had been spotted, no doubt, but who were they signaling to? Buckling on his Colts, Mosby stepped outside as one of his men, Dick Moran, came galloping in at full speed waving his hat. "The Yankees are coming!" he cried. Moran had spent the night at a friend's house near the pike and saw the approach of 150 Vermont Cavalry, commanded by Captain Henry Flint. An informant in Dranesville had revealed Mosby's location.

Mosby and those in the house made a rush for the barn, less than 100 yards away. As they arrived at the corral, the Yankees could be seen 200 yards away against a thicket of woods as they rode through a gate into the open field around the homestead. Mosby dashed about ordering his men to saddle and mount rather than open fire, but had no time to do the same himself. The Yankees poured in across the snow covered ground, and closed the gate behind them to make sure the rebels could make no escape. One squadron moved straight for Mosby's command while another moved around to the rear of the homestead. This suited Mosby. He felt the Yankees dividing improved his chances "at least fifty per cent." But his situation was one of great peril, to say the least. They were hemmed in by the junction of the two streams. "As Capt. Flint dashed forward at the head of his squadron, their sabres flashing in the rays of the morning sun," recalled Mosby, "I felt like my final hour had come."[49] And the Yankees looking on from the other side of the Potomac agreed. Their shouts and cheers carried across the river.

But Mosby was not beaten yet. As his men scrambled to saddle and mount, he threw open the barnyard gate to his immediate front. With Colt in hand, he strode forward on foot. He called out to those men who were now mounted to follow and, with "demonic yells" they did just that. They galloped out from the barnyard towards the Yankees "as reapers descend to the harvest of death."

The Yankees were surprised by the enemy charge, and their advance ground to a halt. One of the first to fall was Captain Flint, hit by several bullets. Lieutenant Josiah Grout fell from his mount with a bullet in his abdomen and another in his hip. Mosby mounted a horse offered by Harry Hatcher, and led a headlong assault. The bewildered troopers dropped from their saddles as the rebels' pistols spoke. Hatcher scrambled into the saddle of a fallen cavalryman and joined the fray as pistols banged and a stiff wind whipped the gunsmoke away. The Yankee cheering from over the river petered out as the unbelievable spectacle unfolded, a small band of rebels launching a savage assault against more than twice their number. The Union men broke and fled back towards the gate they had shut behind them. "The remorseless revolver was doing its work of death in their ranks," recalled Mosby, "while their swords were as harmless as the wooden sword of harlequin." And the Remington revolvers used by the Yankees had been carried through the cold night air, the powder and percussion caps becoming damp. "The first cavalryman I came in contact with was near the fence," recalled the very able William Chapman, "and we were not more than a yard apart. This cavalryman turned immediately towards me from the line and our pistols almost touched. A fierce wind was blowing from the west, and the brim of my Confederate cloth hat flapped down over my eyes. I knocked my hat from my head with my left hand still holding my pistol in my right and aiming at my antagonist, whose pistol snapped and mine went off. He fell at that point ... the failure of the Remington pistol to fire saved my life."[50]

The Yankee squadron moving around behind Mosby had also bolted towards the shut gate. The bluecoats piled up against the fence, the rebels shooting into their ranks. When pistols were emptied, sabers were finally drawn. The gate, designed to open inwards, finally burst open, but in the panic horses and men became crushed together in the narrow opening as they forced their way through. Once in the open, they bolted through the woods and down the pike with the rebels in close pursuit. Sam Chapman, brother of William, pursued a party of Yankees into the woods. One man turned and swung his saber delivering a cut to Chapman's head. He survived the blow to be rescued by another rebel, Hunter, and the chase continued down the pike. The roadside was strewn with dead and wounded, but many troopers threw up their arms in surrender when the alternative was death.

Not only Yankees were captured, however, as William Chapman recalled. He and another man chased some bluecoats into a field, and he attempted to use the captured Remington pistol which, "missed fire," he recalled, "and my antagonist, seeing this, closed in upon me. But one barrel [chamber] of six went off. I was taken back to the woods about 400 yards from the pike where there was another group of cavalrymen. After being held there a few minutes, I was rescued by a party of my friends who had heard of my misfortune, and with a number of prisoners captured there, we proceeded to join our comrades."[51] One Yankee jumped from his horse and, in a gesture of surrender, sat by the roadside. "You have played us a nice April fool, boys!" he called out as Mosby thundered by. The Yankees lost nine killed, 22 wounded, with 82 men and 95 horses captured. Mosby's loss was one killed and three wounded.

The Union brass were not impressed. "Had a proper disposition been made from our forces," reported General Stahel, "Mosby could not, by any possible means have escaped.... It is only to be ascribed to the bad management on the part of the officers and the cowardice of the men." An investigation was to be carried out, "and shall recommend those officers who are guilty to be stricken from the rolls."[52] Flint's second-in-command, Captain George Bean, had been amongst the first to gallop breathlessly back into the Union camp. He was cashiered for cowardice on April 28. But, as with all battles, there was conflicting evidence. Bean claimed he was in charge of a reserve force and, despite an attempt to rally the men, could achieve nothing once the troops fled. But his actions were condemned by Lieutenant Grout, who was promoted to captain three days after the fight. He recovered from his wounds to be elected governor of Vermont in 1896. The investigation concluded that Bean had made no attempt to rally the men, while Lieutenant Woodbury was shot in the head and killed while trying to do so. But Sergeant Ide, captured by the rebels, said Bean was dismissed because the army needed "a scapegoat."[53] As regards being cowards, the soldiers said they were fatigued by a long night march, and their hands were frozen by the cold. Mosby's men, on the other hand, were fresh, having enjoyed a good night's sleep.

But, the fact was, the rebels had won a notable victory despite few of them having fought together previously. It would appear that *esprit de corps* had overcome a lack of training. Mosby's men held various ranks in other units but, at this time, it was every man equal. Yet it still worked. It seemed that a certain Mosby magic flowed through the command. While the Yankees flustered and fumed over Miskel's Farm, the reputation of John Singleton Mosby soared.

General Stahel ordered General Copeland's Michigan Cavalry brigade to bring Mosby in at all costs. They scoured Loudon County, confiscating horses and food, and sweeping up those who could possibly be members of Mosby's band. Mosby's raids, wrote Upperville resident Ida Delany, "produced a retaliating raid from the Yankees in which the citizens suffer severely. Mosby having always to get out of their way." Edward Carter Turner wrote in his diary, "I did not respect the service in which Mosby was engaged. Its object was mercenary rather than patriotic. I cared nothing for the glory others seemed to see in reckless feats and hair breadth escapes." But personal tragedies can influence opinions. Turner's guerrilla son had been killed by Illinois Cavalry on April 25.[54]

During April of 1863 Major Mosby led probing forays, but the Yankees were vigilant and there was little he could achieve against the vast numbers deployed. Nevertheless, always eager for action, he proposed to Stuart a raid on the Yankee rear in Fairfax County. President Lincoln's latest hope, "Fighting Joe" Hooker was now in command of the Army of the Potomac, and was about to make his attempt to crush Robert E. Lee, encamped at Fredericksburg. On April 26 Stuart ordered Mosby to keep an eagle eye out for Hooker's troop movements and, while on the job, capture one of his railway supply trains.

Eighty men responded to Mosby's call at Upperville, and they set out on April 28. A Yankee cavalry raid, in overwhelming numbers, from Fairfax Court House, however, forced him to abandon the mission. Fighting Joe and his host of bluecoats turned up at Chancellorsville and the battle with Lee's army broke out on April 30. But most Union cavalry under General George Stoneman had been dispatched to disrupt communications and supplies in the Confederate rear. The mission had little effect, and the missing cavalry left Hooker's rear exposed.

On May 3 the guns could be heard pounding in the distance as Mosby, with 100 men, moved towards Hooker's rear to inflict what damage he could. But, attracted by the sound of a Yankee bugle, he discovered an enemy cavalry detachment at nearby Warrenton Junction. This would be easy prey, he felt. "I committed a great error in allowing myself to be diverted by their presence from the purpose of my mission," he admitted.[55] The Yankee troopers were lounging about with no sense of danger while their horses grazed. They had no pickets out. The appearance of horsemen moving from the woods about 200 yards off raised no concern; just some of their own on patrol, no doubt. But what was that? A rebel yell? They looked around in horror to see the riders charging them at the gallop. The Yankee horses took off in a stampede, and the troopers bolted into various structures including a large two-story frame building alongside the railroad. Those sheltering in houses were quickly captured, but the main body in the large building held out. Hot fire from the windows wounded some of Mosby's men. Mosby crept up and emptied his two Colt revolvers through a window. "The house was as densely packed as a sardine box," he recalled, "and it was impossible to fire into it without hitting somebody." Sam Chapman burst the door open and, followed by others, charged in. Those in the bottom story surrendered, but those above kept up a brisk fire. Mosby ordered hay from a nearby stack to be scattered about the walls and brought inside. Once alight, smoke curled up the stairs and "not being willing to be burned alive as martyrs to the Union, the men above now held out a white flag from a window," he recalled. Amidst a gray, choking haze, the surviving Yankees staggered down the stairs and across a blood-soaked floor. They carried the wounded outdoors, including their commanding officer, Major Steel, who later died.

Mosby had just captured three times his own number, but the self-gratification was short-lived. With his men spread over the field gathering scattered horses and tending prisoners, a man came galloping in with startling news. Enemy cavalry were coming their way fast. "Now we will whip them!" shouted Mosby. But such was not the case. The Yankees thundered in and, with no chance to reform and mount for a counter-attack, it was a case of every man for himself. The rebels fled, but some prisoners and horses still found themselves taken along.

The Yankees were jubilant. The notorious Mosby was not invincible after all. Two days later, Union General Stahel reported, "Our men being surprised and completely surrounded, rallied in a house close at hand where a sharp fight ensued. Our men defended themselves as long as their ammunition lasted, notwithstanding the rebels built a large fire about the house, of hay and straw and brushwood. The flames reached the house and their ammunition being entirely expended they were obliged to surrender. At this juncture a portion of the Fifth Regiment of New York Cavalry ... came to their rescue, making a brilliant charge, which resulted in the complete annihilation of Mosby's command and recaptured our men and property.... The rebel loss was very heavy, their killed being strewn along the road."[56]

Mosby claimed one man killed and 20 captured, mostly wounded.[57] And, of course, the elusive Gray Ghost had escaped once again. This was due to the Yankee horses having being "tired out by the service of the last few days," claimed Stahel. But Mosby had learned a hard lesson. Do not count only on Lady Luck—reconnoiter first. "When I ordered the charge at Warrenton Junction, I had no idea whether I was attacking a hundred or a thousand men."

Mosby's reputation had taken a hit, and on May 6 General Milroy at Winchester sent 400 infantry and 30 cavalry to ambush Mosby's command near Upperville. The cavalry feigned retreat and lured about 15 rebels into a trap, but the Yankee infantry opened an undisciplined fire too soon. They killed three of their own cavalrymen and wounded two.[58]

When Mosby called for volunteers four days later, only 37 men showed up. But if the guerrilla chief was discouraged, he still showed a brave face. After all, this was eight more men than he had when capturing General Stoughton behind Union lines.

Jeb Stuart had ordered a strike against the railroad, so Mosby and his small command rode out on May 10—destined to be an ill-omened date for both Mosby and the Confederacy. On May 10 Stonewall Jackson took his last breath, having been wounded by "friendly fire" during Lee's victory at Chancellorsville. On May 10, 1865, Jefferson Davis would be captured by Yankee cavalry while fleeing South, the last official act of the war.[59] On that same day William Clarke Quantrill would be captured in Kentucky. On May 10, 1876, Pauline Mosby would die due to complications after childbirth.

Mosby's Raiders burned a small railway bridge at Cedar Run and cut the telegraph line, but when they set fire to the Kettle Run trestle a troop train arrived. Bluecoats scrambled from the cars and managed to extinguish the flames. Mosby's men were dissatisfied with these events. Apart from doing little damage, they had gained no booty, one of the attractions of being a partisan ranger. Mosby realized that he needed to actually capture a supply train, then loot the carriages before burning them. This would provide spoils for the men, while depriving the enemy of supplies, and cause them to draw yet more troops away from the front to protect their railways. Up till now he had been a will-o-the-wisp, able to disappear, but he decided to capture a train requiring different tactics. On May 19 he requested, from Stuart, a mountain howitzer, a small 12-pounder brass cannon. It could be disassembled into sections for transport on pack animals in rugged terrain or, as in

Mosby's case, drawn by horses. Being horse drawn allowed for fast use on relatively level ground.

A 16-mile section of the Orange and Alexandria Railroad, between Bull Run and Cedar Run, was guarded by the 12th Vermont Infantry. Two companies were encamped at Catlett's Station, and another eight at Manassas Junction. Mounted patrols of the 7th Michigan Cavalry rode from Bristoe Station, and a company of the 15th Vermont Infantry acted as guards in the carriages.[60] Mosby's task was formidable. He had to avoid the cavalry and infantry patrols, derail the daily train, and neutralize the infantry guard. With the howitzer in tow, he would not be able to simply hit-and-run as on previous raids. To keep his load light, only 15 rounds were to be carried in the limber chest, enough for the train attack, but inadequate for a prolonged engagement. Sam Chapman, an artillery man, was placed in charge of the gun squad. Mosby later admitted that the enterprise was "not only hazardous but foolhardy ... it could not be done without alarming the camps, which would make my retreat difficult, if not impossible. But I thought the end justified the risk." At this time Lee was preparing for his second thrust into the North, the vital Gettysburg campaign. "An attack, even by my small band, at such a critical time, might create an important diversion in favor of General Lee."[61]

On the morning of May 29 Mosby set out with 48 men and the howitzer from Patterson's Mill on Little River, not far south from Middleburg. A march of 17 miles brought the rangers to a secluded grove within two miles of the track where they set up camp. Next morning Yankee bugles were heard sounding reveille, the nearest enemy camp only one mile away. The rebels moved along a narrow pathway through sheltering pines till they were within 100 yards of the railway tracks, about two miles from Catlett's Station. One man scrambled up the telegraph pole and cut the line, while others loosened a rail from the timber sleepers at the bottom of an incline. The howitzer was carefully positioned, and one lookout was left near the track while the other men took cover. It was not long before the lookout gave a frantic wave, and Mosby rode forward to see the locomotive huffing down the grade. It pulled one carriage loaded with sutler's goods, and nine carrying rations and forage. Thirty-one bluecoats rode onboard as guards. At Mosby's signal the loose rail was pulled away by an attached wire. The front wheels hit the gap and the train came to a steaming, grinding halt. Mosby gave the word and the Confederates charged on horseback with wild rebel yells. The rattled guards let off one wild volley, killing one horse, and a newsboy broke his leg as he jumped from the train. In the next instant splinters flew as Chapman's gun sent a shell crashing into the cars. Artillery was too much. The bluecoats jumped from the train and fled for their lives through the pines. "The guard of the 15th Vermont ran in every direction," recalled one railway man, "wonderfully demoralized and not only disgraced themselves—but the whole regt."[62]

Then another shell ripped through the locomotive's boiler. "The infernal noise of the escaping steam increased the panic among the fugitives," Mosby recalled. The sound of Mosby's gun echoed across the hills and "The long roll was beaten through the camps, and the bugles sounded—'to horse.'"[63] Meanwhile his men pillaged the sutler's car, loaded with boot leather, citrus fruits, confectionaries and fresh shad, rare luxuries for rebels due to the Yankee blockade. Each man took what he could. Then bales of hay were set ablaze, and the whole train went up in flames, smoke billowing into the sky.

So far so good. But now Mosby had to retreat with the howitzer in tow, and every good soldier holds his artillery to the last. Without the gun, the whole command could have simply vanished into the woods. The Yankee mail bags taken from the train were tied to the gun carriage, and Mosby began his retreat. But one mile down the track Yankees were seen to their front; 45 men of the 5th New York Cavalry under Lieutenant Elmer Barker were just one of several detachments closing in. But now the howitzer came into play again. The gun boomed, the shell burst, and a bluecoat was thrown as his horse came down. The Yankees scattered back down the road. The rebels advanced past the fallen horse, and Mosby sent a detachment galloping forward with wild rebel yells. Mosby pushed on, leaving the scattered Yankees behind but, reinforced by new arrivals, they regrouped and set out in pursuit. Again the howitzer was unlimbered, and again a shell burst scattered the blueclad ranks. Mosby formed a rearguard of half a dozen men and ordered the rest, with the howitzer, to get away if they could. The Yankees advance overtook Mosby in a thicket of woods. Hand-to-hand combat saw the bluecoats driven off, but Mosby's English companion, Captain Hoskins, paid the ultimate price. Relying on the saber rather than the gun, he was delivering a thrust when his antagonist shot him from his horse, just before being shot down himself. With the main Yankee force rapidly advancing, "I had no means of carrying him off," Mosby recalled, thus the mortally wounded "gallant gentleman" was left by the roadside "with his life-blood ebbing fast away." The Yankees carried him to the farmhouse of an English family named Green, where he died within a few days.[64]

Mosby and his rearguard rejoined the main party, and they rode into a lane ascending a hill with high fences on each side. This provided ideal protection from cavalry attack, and he ordered the howitzer unlimbered. The enemy could only approach from one direction, and he knew he could hold out as long as the gun had ammunition. But at this point a lack of discipline became apparent. Several rebels decided it was every man for himself, and disappeared into the woods with their booty. The reinforced Federal Cavalry came into view, and at 200 yards the howitzer boomed once more. The Yankees scattered as a shell exploded in their ranks. "We can get that gun before they can fire again,"[65] Lieutenant Barker yelled. But Chapman loaded the howitzer with grape shot, a swarm of metal balls which could cut a swath through tightly packed ranks. The Yankees obliged by charging in a column of fours instead of spreading out. The howitzer fired, men and horses fell, and Barker received two balls through his thigh. His horse, although wounded, carried him back to safety. Mosby led a counter-attack, driving them off. "They used their sabres," recalled Mosby, "and we the revolver."

But then the gun's precious final round was rammed home. Again the Yankees charged, again the howitzer belched fire and smoke. An oncoming horse was hit by the shell "which passed lengthwise through his body before bursting," recalled Chapman. Mosley led a counterattack but, as at Hendon Station, his own horse kept on at the gallop after he ordered a withdrawal. Mosby and another man, Charlie McDonough, dashed into the blue-clad ranks. Mosby received a saber blow to the shoulder a split second before he shot the wielding trooper from his saddle. Behind him, the bluecoats charged on the now defenseless howitzer. Sam Chapman was wounded with a pistol shot as he swung the rammer in a final, desperate bid to defend his gun. Fount Beattie mounted and made his escape, as did George Tuberville, who took off with the gun's two horses and the limber chest. Chapman and Dick Montjoy were both taken captive, to be later exchanged. Mosby, his horse now under control, wheeled about and charged back past the captured howitzer. He received a scratched face from a passing branch, but both he and McDonough made good their escape.

The Yankees were pleased with themselves. General Stahel telegraphed Washington: "We had a hard fight with Mosby this morning, who had artillery,—the same which was used to destroy the train of cars. We whipped him like the devil, and took his artillery. My forces are still pursuing him."[66]

"Their shouts of triumph rang through the woods," Mosby recalled, "but no further pursuit was made."[67] And he felt the loss of a howitzer was a worthwhile sacrifice. As the Yankees cheered, a column of dark smoke rose in the sky from the burning train, the freight cars, supplies and locomotive destroyed. So who had really won the day? Exactly how many casualties Mosby suffered is obscure. Some authorities say one dead, eight captured, and two wounded, including Mosby. But three days after the fight, Colonel Mann reported that Union scouts had returned to the scene where they "found and buried three more rebel dead. This makes their loss … to have been six killed instead of one as reported by me."[68] General Stahel reported four Union dead and 15 wounded but, despite their minor triumph, the Gray Ghost had escaped once more. The scar on Mosby's shoulder, however, would be a constant reminder that the "outmoded" saber could still do damage when required.

Mosby joined his family again at the Hathaway home near Salem. On the night of June 8, 1863, he was fast asleep alongside Pauline when the door flew open and he was shaken awake. Perhaps Mosby was relieved to see Fount Beattie standing over him, not General Stoughton come to wreak revenge. "Yankees are coming," Beattie exclaimed.

A detachment of the 1st New York Cavalry under Captain William Boyd arrived. A squad under Lieutenant Ezra Bailey searched the house, but by then their quarry had flown the coop. Legend has it that Mosby was perched outside the bedroom window on the limb of a large walnut tree. Unlike the unfortunate Colonel Johnson, he had escaped fully clothed, not in his nightshirt. The only occupants found were the Hathaways, and Mrs. Mosby in an upstairs bedroom with her two children. It comes as little surprise that Pauline denied any knowledge of her husband's whereabouts. "Mrs. Mosby is decidedly handsome," recalled one soldier, "and converses with more than ordinary intelligence."[69]

They took several horses from the stables, including Mosby's sorrel mare which was renamed "Lady Mosby." James Hathaway was also placed under arrest and spent some time behind bars before being released.

Over time, Mosby had observed that Yankee horsemen needed much drilling and experience before they could become good cavalry, "while, on the contrary, the Southern youth, who, like the ancient Persians, had been taught from the cradle 'to ride, to shoot, and speak the truth,' leapt into the saddle, almost as a cavalryman from birth."[70] On June 9, however, Jeb Stuart's camp was surprised at Brandy Station by Federal cavalry under General Alfred Pleasanton. The largest cavalry battle ever to take place on the American continent followed, and the smoke cleared to reveal a narrow Confederate victory. But the improved performance of the Federal horsemen shook the rebels, and greatly improved Yankee morale.

The following day, June 10, Company A, 43rd Battalion Partisan Rangers, mustered at Rector's Cross Roads. Mosby had 70 men, and they were joined by 30 Prince William County Rangers under Captain William Brawner. According to regulations, the men were permitted to elect their own officers, but Mosby was having none of that. He would appoint the officer, call for "ayes," and the election was done. And dissenters were invited to return to the regular ranks. By "Mosby's election" James Foster became captain, and Thomas Turner, William Hunter, and George Whitescarver became first, second and third lieutenants.[71]

Following Hooker's defeat at Chancellorsville, Northerners shuddered at the prospect of a possible invasion by "Marse Robert." Lincoln and his generals studied the maps—and with good reason. One smashing rebel victory in the North, the capture of Washington, and the Confederate Cause would triumph. As Lee moved up the Rappahannock towards Pennsylvania, Mosby's 100-man command moved to strike a squadron of Michigan Cavalry near the northern, Maryland bank of the Potomac. The Yankees were camped on Seneca Creek, 20 miles from Washington. Any rebel probes in this area could draw Union troops from confronting Lee further to the east. Mosby had counted on crossing the Potomac under cover of dark but, his guide having lost the trail, his command did not cross until after dawn's first light. They skirmished with a bluecoat patrol, and exchanged fire with a cavalry squadron commanded by Captain Dean on the opposite side of Seneca Creek. The Yankees lined up to do battle in a crescent shape 50 yards from a bridge crossing, but Mosby, undeterred, ordered the charge. The rebel horses clattered over the timbers, and the enemy opened fire but "not one of us was touched in going over," Mosby recalled.[72] They struck with pistols and rebel yells, and the Yankees "were driven several miles in confusion with the loss of seven killed, a considerable number wounded, and 17 prisoners; also 20 odd horses or more. We burned their tents, stores, camp equipage etc. I regret the loss of two brave officers killed—Capt. Brawner and Lieut. [George H.] Whitescarver. I also had one man wounded."[73] The Yankees reported a loss of four killed, one wounded, and 16 missing.[74]

Stuart read Mosby's report, and forwarded it to Richmond with the following endorsement: "In consideration of his brilliant services, I hope the president will promote Major Mosby."[75] But not everything went Mosby's way. On June 11 Captain J. William Foster, six men and ten horses of his command were captured by Yankee cavalry during a night raid in Middleburg. General Pleasanton occupied the town and ordered all adult males arrested, and the women were placed under virtual house arrest.

On June 17 Mosby met Jeb Stuart at the home of rebel informer, Miss Kitty Shacklett, near Piedmont Station. Mosby presented Stuart with a fine horse captured during the Seneca Creek skirmish, and Stuart gave permission for another raid on the same post.[76] Perhaps they both felt good horse flesh was worth the risk.

Dispatches Captured

Mosby set out under a blazing sun with about 35 men, but while stopped for refreshment at the home of James Gulick near Aldie, the distant sound of battle reached his ears. Yankee forces under General Hugh "Kilcavalry" Kilpatrick and rebels under General Thomas Munford had clashed. On the spur of the moment, Mosby decided to abandon his plan, and ride to the sound of the guns. Perhaps he could cause havoc behind Union lines. He led his command cross-country to a point on the Little River Turnpike about five miles east of Aldie. Here, from seclusion, Yankee cavalry movements could be observed. After nightfall, Mosby and three other men merged with a Yankee column moving west, their Confederate uniforms unrecognizable in the dark. Four hundred yards beyond the last Yankee picket posts, they saw three officers' horses, tended by an orderly, tethered to the fence outside the home of Union sympathizer Almond Birch. Mosby rode over and asked the orderly who the horses belonged to. Major William Sterling and Captain Ben Fisher of General Hooker's staff, carrying dispatches, came the reply. The loose-lipped soldier was astonished to be grasped by the collar and have a Colt revolver thrust in his face. "You are my prisoner," said the stranger. "My name is Mosby."

Sterling and Fisher's agreeable supper was followed by a shock when they walked outside: taken prisoner by the notorious Gray Ghost. But once the upset wore off, Mosby was surprised to hear them laughing. "They said they had laughed so much about hearing their people being gobbled up by me," recalled Mosby, "that they were now enjoying the joke being turned on themselves." Even war can have its lighter side, apparently. The captives were taken to a nearby farmhouse where Major Sterling was relieved of his precious satchel.

In the dim candlelight Mosby could see the documents were of extreme importance. "They contained just such information as Gen. Lee wanted," Mosby recalled, "and were the 'open sesame' to Hooker's army."[77] The dispatches revealed the number of Yankee divisions, which would enable Lee to estimate the number of men in the Army of the Potomac at that critical time. Another document disclosed a Yankee cavalry expedition towards Warrenton and Culpepper that could discover Lee's move towards Yankee soil. Mosby scribbled out a note, and sent both documents and prisoners to Jeb Stuart. Stuart acted on the information, and headed off the enemy cavalry expedition.

"Major Mosby, with his usual daring," said Stuart's report, "penetrated the enemy's lines and caught a staff officer of General Hooker, bearer of dispatches to General Pleasanton."[78] Two of Hooker's staff being captured with Union troops all about was a painful reminder of the Stoughton affair. More officers "Gobbled Up" by Mosby, wailed the *Washington Evening Star*.[79] The Yankee commanders issued orders to use strong escorts, as "the country is reported full of guerrillas." As the bluecoats advanced, orders were given to search all homes and imprison anyone deemed to be a likely rebel.

General Lee was delighted with Mosby's success, but remained anxious regarding enemy movements and objectives. He wanted information from Stuart and needed to know that Hooker's army was still in Virginia and would not "steal a march on us, and get across the Potomac before we are aware."[80] During June Mosby carried out scouting missions, and Jeb Stuart used his reports to plan his movements as the Confederates advanced to the North.

On the evening of June 22 a male slave arrived at Union general George Meade's headquarters at Aldie. Having overheard Mosby discussing his movements with Dr. Jesse Ewell, the slave divulged what he knew. Next morning Meade dispatched 103 infantry and 33 cavalry under Captain Harvey Brown to neutralize the partisan chief once and for all.

Brown stationed his men in a church and behind a fence, and placed a sentinel in a tree. The Yankees lay in wait, and before long horsemen were seen to approach. Mosby appeared leading 30 men, despite having captured two Yankees who revealed the waiting ambush. But they had said that only a small cavalry force was waiting, with no mention of the 103 infantrymen. Mosby saw the blueclad cavalry and ordered a charge. The guerrillas dashed forward with rebel yells, their Colts blazing. One Yankee cavalry sergeant was killed and several troopers wounded as they galloped back towards the concealed infantry. To Mosby's surprise a cloud of gunsmoke erupted from behind the fence. Three rebels were wounded, one with his finger shot off, and Mosby's horse was hit in the eye. The rebels turned about and beat a hasty retreat where "they found refuge in the mountains beyond," reported Captain Brown.[81] Unaware of the wounds inflicted, Meade complained that the troops "did not hit a rebel." Captain Brown complained of defective infantry ammunition due to a rain shower the previous evening. "Thus the prettiest chance in the world to dispose of Mr. Mosby was lost," wrote General Meade to General Howard on June 22.[82]

One of Mosby's wounded men, John Ballard, had been hit in the leg, the bone broken. The rough riding during their trek into the mountains made the fracture worse, and he was taken to the home of Robert Whitacre where the limb was amputated. But, surprisingly enough, the resolute Ballard was not lost to the partisan command. After recuperating, he was soon riding behind Mosby again with an artificial leg.[83]

Stuart sent Mosby out on another scout to confirm earlier reports that Hooker's troops were encamped, and not on the move. This could allow a second ride around the enemy, a repeat of Jeb's former glory with McClellan's army. After sending back couriers with current dispositions, Mosby continued on alone. He stopped at Coleman's homestead to glean any further information, and saw two unarmed Yankee cavalrymen augmenting their rations from a cherry tree. His gray uniform concealed by a waterproof "gum cloth," he rode over and asked them where they were from. "Reynolds' corps camped at Guildford," was the reply. Mosby announced that they were now his prisoners, and the appearance of a revolver deterred any argument. He attached a lead between their horses' heads so neither could bolt off alone, and the trio set out. At sunset they came across a mile-long wagon train on the pike guarded by Federal cavalry. He warned the prisoners to remain silent, and the trio rode along with Yankees troopers who had no idea that the officer in their midst was actually the notorious Mosby with two prisoners under the gun. Two hundred yards down the road, the unknown officer and what appeared to be his "orderlies" peeled off and rode away. Once well clear of the Yankee column, Mosby paroled the prisoners and let them go, but kept their horses. "Early next morning I was again at Stuart's headquarters," he recalled.[84]

Presumably this was the basis for a recollection by Miss Laura Ratcliffe, of a friend of Jeb Stuart, and noted Confederate spy. It differs in detail, but would appear to be referring to the same event: "One day a soldier on a white horse, with an oil-cloth around him, rode up to the house, and we could scarcely believe our eyes when we found it was Major Mosby. He dismounted and came in to see if we had any late papers or any news, and left his horse standing at the front door. One of my sisters was so afraid the Yankees would come while he was there that she led his horse behind the barn, and kept him there till the major was ready to start; but he did not appear the least uneasy, nor did he make a hurried visit. That evening two Yankees came to our house and told us that it was rumored that Mosby had ridden several miles with them between here and Guilford; that when he got ready to turn off he said 'good evening' and then dashed through the woods, and was out of sight in an instant. I told them the story was improbable, but suppose it was really true."[85]

Lee and the Army of Northern Virginia advanced through Maryland into Pennsylvania, and the Yankees scrambled to counter this second major invasion of Northern soil. Abraham Lincoln had little faith in Hooker after the Chancellorsville debacle, and placed George Meade in command. Mosby moved to join Lee with about 50 men, and crossed the Potomac into Maryland on July 1. "Well, I am going with you," said Big Yankee Ames. "but I will not fire a shot." He had been happy to repel Yankee invasion of the South but, retaining some spark of loyalty, would "not fight on Northern soil."

As Mosby crossed the Potomac, a rebel division approached Gettysburg, Pennsylvania. Union cavalry under General John Buford had arrived the day before, and fighting broke out. The Yankees held off three times their number until reinforcements arrived, and the Battle of Gettysburg was on.[86]

Oblivious to this action, and unable to locate Lee, Mosby contented himself with raiding Mercersburg, Pennsylvania. He relieved the locals of 218 cattle, 15 horses and 12 African Americans. As they drove the stock back towards the river border, one bitter old lady called out, "My earnest prayer is that you will not get across the river with them."

"Old lady," said Ames, "did you ever hear of Mosby?"

"Oh, then, you'll get off safely enough, I'll be bound."[87]

Major Mosby got off safely enough, but General Lee did not. On July 3 he ordered the disastrous Pickett's charge, and the rebels were mown down. The retreat commenced the following day, and over on the Mississippi "Unconditional Surrender" Grant saw the rebels lower their colors at Vicksburg after a siege of 47 days. History tells us that the Confederacy lost the Civil War on Independence Day, 1863. But if that was the case, the rebels did not know it at the time. The core of the Confederacy was still intact, and vital cities like Richmond and Atlanta were still firmly in rebel hands. If they could inflict enough damage on invading Union troops, there was still the chance the North would sue for peace.

Mosby's idol Jeb Stuart was controversially absent from Lee's army before the Battle of Gettysburg. He had crossed the Potomac at a ford scouted by Mosby, fought Union cavalry and captured supplies as he led his cavalry to the right of the Federal Army. He threatened Washington before turning south to reunite with Lee on the battle's second day. Lee had been deprived of cavalry reports on the enemy's movements, and some blamed Stuart for the defeat. Mosby felt implicated, and insisted that Stuart was, in fact, complying with his orders, not disobeying them as some would have it. Stuart would not live to see the war out, and as the controversy continued, Mosby championed his defense.

Undeterred by these reverses, Mosby continued to raid and harass the enemy, night and day, wherever possible. On July 28 he reported to Stuart, "I sent you in charge of Sergeant Beattie, 141 prisoners which we captured from the enemy during their march through this country. I also sent off 45 several days ago: included in the number, 1 major, a captain, and 2 lieutenants. I also captured 123 horses and mules, 12 wagons (only 3 of which I was able to destroy), 50 sets of fine harness, arms, etc." Stuart endorsed the report, "Mosby has richly won another grade and I hope it will be conferred." Lee forwarded this Richmond, "as evidence of the merit and activity of Major Mosby and his command."[88]

The elusive Mosby baffled the Yankees. The rebels would strike, bluecoats killed or captured, a railway trestle go up in flames, tracks torn up, then the Gray Ghost would seem to simply disappear. The anxiety of Yankee soldiers on picket duty was well founded. Fear of being killed, or "gobbled up" to rot in a prison camp, elevated their fears, and kept them always on edge. During the night a rustle of leaves in the foliage could bring on a blast of musket fire, alarming the camp, when the only offender was a stray cow, or perhaps a swooping owl. But the bluecoats had to stay on the alert. Where would the dreaded Mosby strike next? The search of homes suspected of harboring guerrillas might miss a concealed enclave beneath the porch. Clothes hanging in a closet may conceal a cavity beyond. A water tank could contain something other than water, and bales of hay in a barn may well have a cavity inside. The crinoline and petticoats of a demure Southern belle perched on a large chair may well conceal a trapdoor below.

Mosby's raids, along with those of other guerilla bands, caused the Yankees to dispatch thousands of troops from combat duties to defending lines of supply and communication in their rear.

10

"We'll descend like thunderbolts"
Quantrill and Anderson, 1863–1864

In early May 1863, as Missouri's winter chills were replaced with warming sun, Federal Lieutenant Colonel Walter King, commander at Lexington, reported that William Clarke Quantrill was back in Jackson County. Upon return from his trip to Richmond, Quantrill rejoined his old comrade George Todd and between 125 and 150 men ready for action. According to Colonel King's informer, Quantrill had received orders from General Price to "stop bushwhacking and horsestealing," and "annoy Kansas and Western Missouri" in preparation for the Confederate thrust north. Quantrill had come back to Jackson County to stay, and "seems to be rather elevated in his purpose by his six or eight months experience with the regular forces."[1] Perhaps Quantrill felt, by elevating his purpose above theft and murder, he may yet become a bona fide colonel. His previous exploits had got him nowhere, and according to Quantrill aficionado, William Connelley, he arrived "much crestfallen and discouraged. He was ambitious. Through his distorted vision he saw promotions in store for him and honors heaped upon him. He believed he had earned them and well earned them. But he had found the world larger than he believed it, and was surprised and vexed to find that the eyes of the whole Confederacy were not fixed on him and his achievements. He pined to be a hero, and was hurt to think he was not so regarded. He had not been wined and dined in Richmond."[2] And the shattering Confederate defeats at Gettysburg and Vicksburg in early July were enough to add to any rebel's gloom.

Quantrill struck a patrol of the 5th Missouri cavalry, a regiment commanded by Colonel William Penick. Five men were killed in the first volley, and the others fled, four more being overtaken and killed. The guerrillas threw the bodies into a wagon, and had a farmer take them to Penick's headquarters in Independence with a message that this is what bluebellies hunting Quantrill could expect.[3]

And virtually no settlement was safe. Newspapers screamed that troops should be out on the prairie hunting the bushwhackers down, while citizens wanted townships garrisoned. There were not enough troops to go round. Many captured guerrillas were executed without trial, or conveniently shot while "trying to escape."[4] Bluecoats burned homes of suspected rebel sympathizers.

Amidst this turmoil, Quantrill's reputation took on legendary qualities and newspapers gave him credit for various raids whether he was involved or not.

Confederate veteran Captain Z. E. Benton, many years later recalled one version of "Quantrell's Call," sung around rebel campfires:

> Arise my brave boys, the moon is in the west,
> And we must be gone ere the dawning of the day:
> The hounds of old Pennock will find but the nest,
> For the Quantrell he seeks will be far, far away.
> And when they are weary and the chase given o'er,
> We'll descend like thunderbolts down from the cloud;
> We will ride through their ranks and bathe in their gore,
> Smite down the oppressor and humble the proud.[5]

While Quantrill's life was romanticized, he took time off for a little real romance in his life. Sarah Catherine (Kate) King was the young and attractive daughter of Robert King, who lived near Blue Springs, not far from the Morgan Walker farm. In 1926 she gave an account of her times with Quantrill to a reporter with the *Kansas City Star*. Although "The Strange Romance of Quantrill's Bride" was embellished with fiction, her account provides much of what is known about her life. Sifting through the facts, it would appear she became romantically involved with Quantrill in 1863 when 15 years old, and Quantrill 25. Her parents banned her from seeing the notorious guerrilla, but where there's a will there's a way and "as is so often the case," observed the *Star* columnist, "the parental ban only served to deepen her regard for the young gallant."[6] Kate claimed they were married by a country preacher, and she used the name "Kate Clarke" for self protection. Given the moral codes of the day, the marriage may well have taken place, but no documentary proof has been found. She said she spent much time with Quantrill, and gang members later confirmed them being together. Following Quantrill's death, Kate said she purchased a boarding house in St. Louis, financed by selling jewelry he gave her. The precious stones had probably once adorned some fair lady in Lawrence, Kansas, a town ripe for picking a second time.

Perhaps it was Gettysburg and Vicksburg, along with the lack of recognition in Richmond, that prompted Quantrill's most ambitious scheme, a last chance to make a noteworthy name for himself before it was too late. How long could the Confederacy last? And things were changing: "During the year 1862 the men were kept close together and all under the watchful eye of Quantrill," recalled William Gregg. "Not so in 1863, there was Todd, Poole, Blunt, Younger, Wilson and others. Each had companies, often widely separated, and only called together on special occasions, all of whom, however, recognized Quantrill as Commander in Chief with Lieut Gregg as adjutant."[7]

Lawrence

On August 10, 1863, guerrilla chiefs, responding to Quantrill's call, rode into camp near Blue Springs. They listened as he outlined his audacious plan for an attack on Lawrence. "It is the great hotbed of abolitionism in Kansas, and add the plunder stolen from Missouri, stored away in Lawrence, and we can get more revenge and more money than anywhere else in the state." There was no doubt that Lawrence had been the seat of many jayhawker raids. "More than one anti-slavery raiding party had its origin in the town," recalled resident Erastus Ladd, "and more than one Lawrence family possessed articles of dress, furniture, and livestock which could be characterized by but one word, loot."[8]

Quantrill sounded confident, but not all there liked the odds. Lawrence was 50 miles away with a population of 3000, and if they did manage to strike, Yankee troops would be out for their blood. It would be a fighting retreat all the way back to Missouri, and the border would provide no safety. "I know," replied Quantrill, "but if you never risk, you will never gain."[9]

The debate continued, and Quantrill called one of his scouts, Fletch Taylor, to report. The town was only defended by a handful of soldiers, and not all had arms, Taylor said. For three years now there had been false alarms of a coming attack, and the locals had grown complacent. And, Quantrill argued, what better place to strike than the hometown of the dreaded Jim Lane, who waged a jayhawker war on Missouri, killing, burning and freeing slaves.

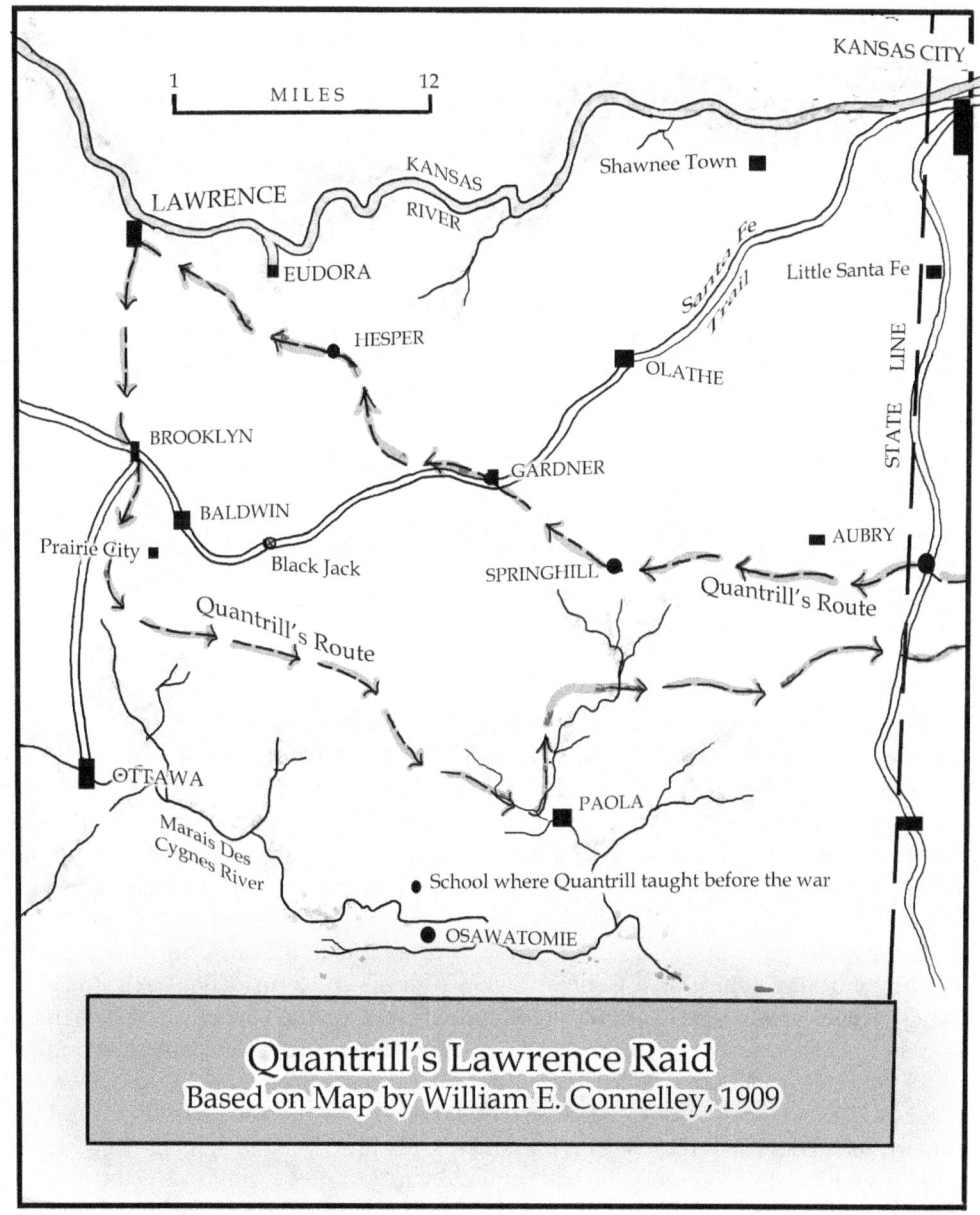

Quantrill's Lawrence Raid (author's rendition, based on a map by William E. Connelly, 1909).

A vote was taken. It was unanimous. Lawrence would be sacked again—and they'd make a proper job of it this time.

Only three days later events transpired that seemed to vindicate this decision. According to bushwhacker John McCorkle, the Yankees stationed in Kansas City, "were guilty of one of the most brutal and fiendish acts that ever disgraced a so-called civilized nation."[10] Union General Thomas Ewing had commandeered a three-story brick building in Grand Ave. for use as a jail to house female rebels. Some had been caught concealing percussion caps, lead, gunpowder and bolts of cloth used in sewing guerrilla shirts, and others were jailed because they had relatives of the bushwhacker breed. The prisoners were housed on the upper two floors while their guards occupied the first floor. There was also a cellar. What exactly this was used for is open to debate. Here bricks were removed in the wall adjoining a building alongside. Some claimed this was to create more storage space, while a doctor later testified that it was to gain access to women of easy virtue confined there. The rebels, however, insisted these walls were sabotaged to bring the building down. Cracks appeared in the walls above the cellar, and ceiling plaster fell. A merchant wasted no time in having his stock removed, and guards reported the danger, but no order was given to move the prisoners. About seventeen women and girls, one boy and one guard were inside when the whole building started to tremble. Nannie McCorkle jumped from a window. Then the building alongside the jail collapsed. This sparked a chain reaction and dust billowed from a pile of falling debris as the jail also crashed down. Four women were killed and others badly injured.

One of Quantrill's lieutenants, William T. Anderson, to become known as "Bloody Bill," had three sisters amongst the wreckage. Fifteen-year-old Josephine died; Mary was disfigured and crippled; and Julia, shackled to a ball and chain for rowdy behavior, suffered a back injury and broken legs.[11] John McCorkle's sister, Christie, cousin of Cole Younger, was also dead. McCorkle later claimed, "This foul murder was the direct cause of the famous raid on Lawrence, Kansas." But, as has been seen, the wheels were already in motion. And McCorkle recalled, "Nan Harris and Mollie Anderson [more likely Grindstaff][12] had just gone out into the hall for a bucket of water, when they heard cries from the other girls that the roof was falling. The guard, evidently repenting at the last moment, carried these two girls to safety."[13] Undermining a building to carry out murder under such circumstances would be an inventive approach to say the least. And the fact the guard was still inside and saved two girls suggests stupidity caused the collapse rather than murder. Eleven years later, Dr. Joshua Thorne, in charge of the General Hospital in Kansas City, stated that women of "ill character" were confined in the jail cellar. The guards had weakened the wall between the adjoining building by cutting three large holes through, and the cellar had become "a house of prostitution." He had visited the cellar the day before the collapse and found "many of the female prisoners intoxicated—one of the women was cutting with an axe at one of the posts in the basement."[14] He reported this to the officer on duty, and the following morning approached General Ewing with his concerns. Upon arrival back in Grand Avenue, however, he heard the crash and screams, and saw the cloud of dust rising.

Whatever the cause, the rebels chose to believe the incident was deliberate murder, and Bloody Bill Anderson would wreak a terrible revenge. Born in 1839, Anderson had moved to Kansas from Missouri in 1857 with his mother, Martha, the three sisters and two brothers, Jim and Ellis, to reunite with his father, William Anderson, Sr. Following various moves from his native Kentucky, he had acquired land 13 miles east of Council Grove. By 1860 the family was reasonably prosperous, William Sr. engaged in farming, freighting and a store on the Santa Fe Trail. But trouble struck when young Ellis shot an Indian and fled to Iowa, and Martha Anderson was killed by lightning while working outside the home. By then another child, Charles, was on the scene, only one year old. Bill Anderson, now 21, acquired his own land claim, but decided to supplement his income with horse trading. This soon mushroomed into horse stealing, the stock being sold as far a way as New Mexico.

The war's outbreak offered more promise of plunder and profit as jayhawkers and bushwhackers raided at will. When attempting to recruit a man for a raid into Missouri, Bill said, "I don't care any more than you do for the South, Strieby, but there is a lot of money in this business."

William Sr. was infuriated when an associate, Judge Arthur I. Baker, broke off his relationship with young Mary Anderson to became engaged to a schoolteacher, Annis Segur. Judge Baker also preferred charges against a cousin of the Anderson boys, Lee Griffin, a member of Bill's gang, for stealing horses from his future father-in-law, Ira Segur. On May 12, 1862, William invaded Baker's home with shotgun in hand and murder in mind. As he ascended the stairs Baker walked out and delivered a lethal blast from his own shotgun. Seen as self-defense, there was no legal retribution, and two days later Baker married his betrothed. To make things worse, Baker had horse rustling charges drawn up against Bill who, released on bond, fled with brother Jim for Missouri. The remaining family members soon followed.

On the night of July 3, 1862, Bill, Jim, Lee Griffin and another unknown accomplice paid a return visit to Baker's home. Lured into his nearby store, Baker was shot and wounded before being shut in the cellar along with his wife's 16-year-old brother George, also wounded. The store, house and barn were set ablaze.[15] Baker died where he lay, but George escaped the flames through a small window. He was found next day and told the story of Bill and Jim Anderson's first proven murders before dying of his wounds that afternoon.

A posse failed to catch the culprits before they escaped back into Missouri, and Bill Anderson became a full-time bandit with brother Jim. While supposedly partisans on the Confederate side, they robbed Southerners as well as Yankees, causing Quantrill to warn them off. They shifted their operations to other parts of Missouri, and joined a gang that operated between Warrensburg and Lexington led by a bushwhacker named Reed. "They are the basest robbers ever left at large in a civilized community," complained the *Lexington Weekly Union* of February 7, 1863. "They are the men who killed Gaston, Barker, Iddings, Phelps, King, Myers, and McFaddin.... They boast their deeds of daring and murder, their robbery of the mail and express at various times, and there is no act of villainy or cold blooded murder, where a dollar could be made, which they will not do."[16]

During May of 1863, as Quantrill was returning from Richmond, Anderson took part in Dick Yeager's guerrilla raid 150 miles into Kansas, robbing and killing. "The last two weeks have been full of terror to the citizens of Central and Southern Kansas," wrote a reporter for the *New York Times* on May 17, 1863. "The denuding of this military district of effective troops left our borders to the mercy of the guerrillas, who again swarm in Jackson and other Missouri border counties."

The Yeager raid was an education for Bill Anderson, and before long he attracted enough men to form his own gang. General Ewing received the following report from a friend, Sam Breitenbaugh, in Lexington, dated July 15, 1863: "Dear General: I left Kansas City yesterday morning on the *Ogden*. Arrived here at 5 o'clock the same day and the first news I learned was the murder of four Union men and one girl and nine wounded by the Bushwhackers, numbering 40. This sad affair took place in Freedom township, in the German settlement, some 15 miles from the city. After they executed their hellish purposes, they went in the direction of the Mound, about nine miles from town and dispersed in small bands of from five to 10 some going toward the Sni and in various directions. This band is headed by one W. T. Anderson who formerly lived in this place."[17]

The girl's death was probably not intended. White females from both sides would be robbed, but generally not targeted for violence. Apart from Victorian era chivalric tendencies, this ensured the safety of their own womenfolk. But the jail collapse was seen by bushwhackers as premeditated murder.

General Ewing did nothing to calm simmering tensions when, just four days after the collapse, he issued General Order No. 10. "Wives and children" of known guerrillas, and those "willfully engaged in aiding guerrillas," were to leave Missouri. If they failed to move promptly, they would be escorted south by troops "with their clothes and such necessary household furniture and provision as may be worth saving."[18]

That same night Quantrill, leading 150 men, rode into Captain Pardee's farm on the Blackwater River. In his pocket was a death list of Lawrence residents. Andy Blunt rode in with 100 men, and Bill Anderson with 40. The following morning the expedition set out. Scouts fanned out to detect enemy troops, and men wearing captured blue uniforms rode at front and rear. Until now, only trusted lieutenants knew the target, but late that afternoon Quantrill called an assembly at the Potter farm. Lawrence was their destination, he shouted. "Boys, this is a hazardous ride, and there is a chance we will all be annihilated. Any man who feels he is not equal to the task can quit, and no one will call him a coward." Whether or not any melted away depends on who you believe, but the command remounted and rode through the night. A little before dawn they arrived at the headwaters of the Grand River, only four miles from the Kansas border. Concealed by woods, they ate and slept till 3:30 p.m., then continued their ride. They were soon joined by Colonel John Holt with 100 Confederate recruits, and about 50 farmers out for adventure and plunder. This provided about 450 men for an expedition that was about to inflict the most notorious event of the war.

The march resumed, and at about 5:30 p.m., August 20, they crossed from Missouri into Kansas. At about seven that evening a farmer rode into the camp of Captain Joshua Pike of the 9th Kansas Regiment stationed at Aubry. The excited farmer had seen 800 guerrillas on the march, he claimed. Pike telegraphed various posts including Little Santa Fe, Missouri, from where the news was sent to Kansas City, but not read by General Ewing till 10:45 next day—as Lawrence lay in smoldering ruins.[19] Pike sent no warning to Lawrence or other towns, and remained stationary with his 100 men. But Quantrill's destination was not known, and Pike may have dismissed Lawrence being the target. Following the massacre General Ewing wrote that Lawrence "had an abundance of arms in their city arsenal, and could have met Quantrell, on half an hour's notice, with 500 men."[20] But Ewing also attacked Pike for his lack of action: "Quantrell would never have gone as far as Lawrence or attacked it, with 100 men close on his rear." Years later Pike claimed that of his 100 men, only 21 were fit for duty, and it would have been "suicide" to attack the supposed 800 guerrillas.[21]

The rebels took several men from their homes in stages and used them as guides before killing them. The last, Joseph Stone, was known to George Todd. Stone had been involved with the arrest of Todd's father in Kansas City in 1861. He was either beaten to death or shot, depending on which account is correct, but either way Stone joined the dead.[22] Quantrill also took a young boy, Jacob Rote, to act as guide. He was held captive through the massacre, but later released.

The dark command rode through Franklin township, about four miles from Lawrence, many strapped to their saddles in case they fell asleep. Dr. R. L. Williams saw them ride by, 400 guerrillas in a column of fours, with another 50 spread about the flanks. "Hurry up, we ought to have been in Lawrence an hour ago," he heard one say. "Rush on boys, it will be daylight before we get there."[23]

As a soft glow blushed on the eastern horizon, the guerrillas arrived on a ridge with a fine view of Lawrence spread before them, neat rows of brick, stone and timber buildings lining wide streets. Wafts of smoke curled from chimneys as early morning fires were lit. Somewhere a dog barked, and a few early risers moved in the streets.

The mayor's son, Hoffman Collamore, about 16, was the first to feel the guerrillas' wrath. Out riding on a hunting foray about a mile from town, he encountered the blue clad rebels riding in advance. One called out and asked where he was going. He gave a token reply, then rode on. The rebels opened fire and he galloped off, but a spray of bullets brought both him and his horse to the ground. Hit in the thigh, the boy played possum till the rebels rode on. He crawled away to eventually recover from his wound.[24]

A group of four young people out for a morning ride saw what they took to be Federals moving towards the outskirts of town. But something was not right. They appeared to be on the very best horses, Kentucky thoroughbreds, not the usual army stock, and some were out of uniform. Then the horrible truth sunk in. Attractive 19-year-old Sallie Young urged her escort, John Donnelly, unarmed and in uniform, to ride for his life while she rode to spread the alarm. Bushwhackers, as a rule, did not harm women. Four guerrillas broke off and rode towards them. Donnelly galloped off and, although pursued by two riders, made good his escape.[25] Sallie rode hard for town, but was overtaken by Frank James. He took her back to Quantrill, and throughout the morning she was forced to lead bushwhackers to the homes of those on his death list. Not knowing the pressure she was under, some survivors

The sacking of Lawrence by Quantrill's raiders—the most notorious guerrilla action of the Civil War (*Harper's Weekly*, September 5, 1863).

hurled abuse following the raid. But she had, in fact, attempted to save all she could with false information. Judge Lawrence Bailey recalled "she had used her influence to save the lives of a number of citizens, with ready invention and great presence of mind, giving such accounts of them as to induce her captors to spare them."[26] And another witness recalled, "She importuned so often for others that she was finally told by Quantrill that she must look out to save herself, as his men were becoming exasperated with her."

While Gregg rode forward with five men to scout, Quantrill questioned a farmer feeding hogs about troop dispositions in town, and where certain jayhawkers could be located. Any lies, and he was a dead man. He answered as best he could, then Quantrill moved to the farm of Postmaster Robert Miller, a friend of Jim Lane. Miller and one son, Josiah, also on the wanted list, were found to be absent. Quantrill questioned daughter Margaret, but she quickly saw through his blue jacket. "You are not soldiers," she blurted. "You are Quantrill's." The guerrilla nodded. "You have guessed right, I am Quantrill and these are my men." Her brother William galloped off to warn the township, and a party of rebels rode in close pursuit.

The Reverend Snyder of the United Brethren Church, part-time officer and recruiting agent for the 2nd colored regiment, was milking a cow on his farm to the east of town when two men rode through the gate. They produced revolvers, opened fire, and Snyder died where he fell. Brothers Solomon and Samuel Bowers, living with him, were also shot. But Solomon, badly wounded, managed to make his escape.

Quantrill, meanwhile, mustered his men. The time had come to show their true colors and the blue jackets were removed. His orders were to kill every man big enough to carry a gun, but spare the women and children. The men looked towards the large cluster of buildings spread across the plain. There could be quite a few guns in there. This was no small shanty town, to be easily taken. "Let's give it up," one man said, "it's too much." Others mumbled in agreement. Quantrill rode along the line on his superb brown gelding. "You can do as you please," he snarled, "I'm going to Lawrence." He reigned his horse about and rode towards town. The battalion watched him go, then, with a nudge of spurs, followed. They were committed now. But some still felt they were riding in the valley of death. "We are lost," one man said.[27] As the main force moved in to attack, Quantrill dispatched 11 men to Mount Oread to act as sentinels.

Erastus Ladd, J.P., was a well-known resident of Massachusetts Street: "I stepped out on the porch on the south side of my kitchen, and was standing there for a moment, when I heard, first, two or three scattering shots, followed immediately by a dozen or more in quick succession, in a south-easterly direction, but hidden from my view by houses. The shots were accompanied by cheers, or rather yells. In a few moments, as I stood looking, some three or four negroes from the camp, which was some forty rods from where I stood, came rushing by, hallooing, 'The secesh have come!' As I looked, the head of the column of fiends rushed down the street on which the camp was, full in my view, and commenced shooting down the boys in camp near by."[28]

As the survivors of the 2nd colored regiment ran for their lives, 22 white recruits of the 14th Kansas Regiment came under attack. The rebels rode through their tents with trampling hooves and men were shot down as they ran. Seventeen were killed and five wounded.

Andy Blunt's company rode through the east side of town, William Gregg led his men through the west while Quantrill led a charge down Massachusetts Street. "We saw that every man was shot down at sight," recalled Ladd. "When they had rode into the main street, and commenced their hellish work they immediately broke into squads and rushed through all the streets, killing every man they saw, probably in order to prevent any concentration or organization on our part for defense. They rode up and down the streets seeking victims." The Rev. Richard Cordley observed: "The horsemanship of the guerrillas was perfect. They rode with the ease and abandon of men who had spent their lives in the saddle amid rough and desperate scenes. They were dressed in the traditional butternut, and belted about with revolvers. Their horses seemed to be in the secret of the hour, and their feet scarcely seemed to touch the ground."[29]

Quantrill reached the river, then turned and rode back to the Eldridge House, the former Free State Hotel. The hated building, destroyed by border ruffians in 1856, had been rebuilt four stories high in brick complete with ornate iron trimmings on the facade. One again it was a prime target for bushwhacker vengeance. Inside, the panic-stricken clamor of a gong was no summons to breakfast. Someone was trying to sound the alarm. The rebels took position around the hotel, expecting rifles to appear at the windows. But the inmates, taken by surprise, offered no resistance. Frightened guests hastily donned clothes and many left their rooms to find out what was going on. They huddled in hallways chattering nervously. The dreaded Quantrill had arrived. What to do? Captain Alexander Banks, Kansas provost marshal, waved a white sheet out a window. Quantrill rode across and Banks called out, asking what he wanted. "Plunder" was the answer.

"We are defenseless and at your mercy," Banks called out. "The house is surrendered, but we demand protection for the inmates." Captain Banks "represented to Quantrell that the guests at the hotel were not abolitionists," recalled Judge Bailey, "but many of them strangers and travelers to kill whom would be held a great outrage by the country at large."[30] Quantrill agreed to spare the guests. But others in the streets had already died and he was not through yet. He turned to the bushwhackers. "Kill!" he cried. "Kill and you will make no mistake! Lawrence should be thoroughly cleansed, and the only way to cleanse is to kill! Kill!"[31] With a rebel yell, the guerrillas returned to their deadly work.

Quantrill dismounted and led a squad into the hotel. The guests' lives were to be spared, but they were to be robbed and their rooms ransacked. Guerrillas fired shots through one door, wounding one man, when the inmates refused to open up. The distressed victim came out with blood trailing down his trousers. In another room three soldiers refused to surrender. The door was smashed in by George Todd and John Jarret, and the soldiers were shot down. George Todd would boast of murdering 17 men that day. Captain Banks' life would be spared as Quantrill instructed, but Todd forced him to remove his fine new uniform, and donned it himself.

Judge Bailey encountered Quantrill at the head of a staircase. He was "about five feet nine inches in height, had gray eyes, brown hair and light complexion, but tanned or sun-browned, unshaved but with no great growth of beard, moustache or whiskers, was dressed in gray pants and hunting shirt open at the breast, with low-crowned soft hat and a yellow or gold cord around it for band. He had a revolver in his hand and another in his belt, but did not look more formidable or ferocious than many men I have met at other times and passed without fear."[32] Quantrill was talking to a hotel guest, Arthur Spicer, who had worked as a surveyor with him before the war. "We called you Charley Hart then, you know," he said. Quantrill wanted no reminders of his time as a common thief. "It makes no difference what they call me," he replied coldly. Quantrill ordered Spicer to lead his men to Jim Lane's new home. If the reluctant guide gave any trouble, he was to be shot.

Judge Bailey was aghast to hear the hotel was to be torched. "I could hear the report of the firearms, and yells from the guerrilla horsemen as they dashed along the streets, but I failed to realize the demon-like atrocities that were being perpetrated upon the unarmed and defenseless people of the town who were so unfortunate as to fall into their hands."[33]

But later many a tale was told of men managing to escape by dashing into surrounding cornfields or brush along the riverbank. From the opposite side, a small party of troops fired at rebels when they appeared. The soldiers planned to cut the ferry lines, but guerrillas did the job for them. One colored blacksmith escaped by hiding amidst tomato vines while his nearby shop burned to the ground.

The Eldridge House was set on fire and the bewildered guests filed out onto the street. Wild riders dashed about them, and one guest was shot. Quantrill yelled that they were under his protection, and had them escorted down the street to another hotel, Nathan Stone's Whitney House. "Years ago old man Stone treated me with kindness," he said, "and I'll be damned to hell if a hair on his head will be injured."[34] But before the day was over, Nathan Stone's name would be added to the list of dead.

With the guests under guard, Quantrill procured a fine buggy and a team of white horses to tour his conquered domain while his men rode in wild abandon through the streets, shooting and venting rebel yells. Men and boys in the teens were shot down as mothers and sisters screamed and cried, begging for them to be spared. Some tried to shield their loved ones from death only to be thrust aside. The guerrillas screamed their praise for Jeff Davis and the Southern Cause. Liquor stores had been raided, and some rebels were already drunk. Methodist preacher Larkin Skaggs cut down a huge Stars and Stripes and dragged it along Massachusetts Street "putting his horse through various turns," recalled Judge Bailey, "to make the old flag jump and roll by turns fifty feet behind his horse in the deep dust."

"When they came to plundering and burning, the streets were comparatively clear," recalled Erastus Ladd. "When they were near my house, or along the street, I would go into my cellar; and when they were temporarily absent, I would come up and watch the progress of affairs from the windows or porches. The first fire I saw was a large barn, about one hundred feet from my house. They had taken the only horse in it, and then set it on fire. In the course of time it came our turn. I was in the cellar. A devil came to the door with a cocked revolver in his hand, and called Eliza out. He demanded if I was in the house. She told him I was not. He demanded her money, jewelry and arms. She gave him what she had. He then broke up some chairs, and tore up some books, piled them up in the dining room, and in the kitchen, and set them on fire. He was a Perfect demon."[35]

Ladd was to survive, but elsewhere similar invasions had much more lethal outcomes. Schoolteacher Edward Fitch was a member of the home-guard and, as such, on Quantrill's death list. Drunken guerrillas burst into his home and one, with a "course, brutal, blood thirsty face—inflamed with hellish passions and strong drink," recalled his wife, Sarah, "turned & saw my Edward—oh Mother—so calm so self possessed—and without a word the deadly aim was taken—shot after shot in rapid succession—emptying his own revolver, then taking the weapon from the hand of his companion, and using all its load to make sure work of death—oh can you picture that moment—I begged, I implored—I looked around on that circle of hard cruel faces—and I know there was not help—no help—oh had God forgotten us—the match was applied to our home." Stunned with grief, she was forced at pistol point from the burning house with her two distraught, crying children. "By this time houses in every direction were burning—the crash of falling walls—the constant firing—the unearthly yells of the mounted invaders, rushing in every direction—the shrieks of the bereaved, the groans of the wounded—could anything more be added to the horrid picture." The family watched on in anguish and tears as both her husband's body and house were consumed by flames. "Oh, I feel as tho' I was crushed into dust with the weight of sorrow which has as rolled upon me," she recalled, "oh the *utter desolation*—the heart breaking despair I have endured. My brain reels!—my reason totters—had it not been for *our* children—Edwards's darlings—that I had to live for, I do not think I *could* have endured."[36]

Similar scenes were enacted in scores of places throughout Lawrence over the next few hours. Bill Anderson, enraged by the collapse of the Kansas City jail, reputedly killed 14 men himself. " I came for revenge," he told one woman, "and I have got it."[37] But this satisfaction would not last. Over the next year many more still would pay the price.

The guerrillas searched for men on Quantrill's wanted list. These were prominent soldiers, jayhawkers and abolitionists. Pastor Richard Cordley lived a little south of the city limits in New York Street. He was a prime target, guilty of holding religious services for blacks and being active in the Underground Railroad that conducted escaped slaves to freedom. But the search for this "negro harborer" failed. With his wife alongside and infant daughter in arms, he fled out the back door as the bushwhackers arrived. They escaped into the woods, but their fine stone home was looted and burned.

The architect of this mayhem, meanwhile, drove his purloined buggy up Mount Oread. The crest had earthworks seven feet high interconnected with trenches around a stone fort, now unmanned by the complacent local militia. From here Quantrill could see the smoke rising from buildings being set ablaze below. He spoke to the pickets and checked that no Yankee columns were in sight, then drove the buggy back into town.

One hotel guest later told a newspaper man, C. M. Chase, that Quantrill said he was surprised that his men were murdering people. He claimed, "They had got into the saloons, got drunk and beyond his control." Perhaps Quantrill, hearing the gunshots and screams of mass murder taking place, wished to absolve himself from blame. The attack had been successful beyond any expectations. Like Pearl Harbor 78 years later, there had been a failure of communication along with too many false alarms, and the attack had been a complete surprise. Quantrill said he had come to "destroy the town and plunder its wealth, in return for Lane burning Osceola." This had occurred two years earlier with nine men killed after court-martial—a long time to wait for such a disproportionate revenge. How many men and buildings had been destroyed by Quantrill since then? What about Shawneetown? But on the spur of the moment he may well have used this as a supposed justification. At Stone's Hotel, one former associate spoke to Quantrill. "Charlie, how could you do such a thing to a town where you have so many acquaintances and some friends?" "My men came here for revenge," he said, "and I can't stop them from what they are doing."[38] Once again, Quantrill refusing to accept responsibility for the carnage. He laid the blame on men he led with instructions to kill. "Quantrell said here, after he had satiated his hate and revenge," recalled Erastus Ladd, "'that he was now 'ready to die.' A universal shout will go up from every part of slavedom, and from the infernal regions, when this event shall have reached their ears."

But a shout for revenge would also go up. Like Admiral Yamamoto after Pearl Harbor, Quantrill was a man destined for a violent and early death.

Jim Lane was at the top of Quantrill's wanted list. But he did not want Lane shot and killed—the jayhawker king swinging from a Missouri gallows was the desired outcome. But when the first shots were heard, Lane's well-honed instinct for survival had seen him leap from bed and hack the nameplate from his front door. Barefoot and clad in nightshirt only, he bolted out the back door leaving his wife to face the guerrillas alone. He hid in a ravine for some time, then crept to a farmhouse where he borrowed a straw hat and some ill-fitting clothes. Moving on, he secured a plough horse from another property, and rode bareback around the countryside rallying men to arms.

Back in Lawrence, meanwhile, the rebels arrived at Lane's fine new abode. They treated Mrs. Lane with the utmost courtesy as they removed valuables, then set the house ablaze. Anguished over the loss of her fine piano, they attempted to save it, but abandoned the quest when the crackling flames drove them outdoors. "Give Mr. Lane my compliments," Quantrill said. Her husband would be glad to meet under "more favorable circumstances," she frostily replied.[39]

Sentries on Mount Oread reported horsemen approaching; Yankee reinforcements, no doubt. Loaded with stolen cash and plunder, the guerrillas departed amidst flames, smoke and ruins at around nine o'clock. But one man lingered behind. Larkin Skaggs had taken a ring from Lydia Stone, daughter of Nathan Stone. But this had been a gift from Quantrill three years earlier for having nursed him through an illness. Lydia had complained, and Quantrill had given Skaggs a tongue lashing while ordering the ring returned. He complied, but muttered she would be "damned sorry for it."[40] As other rebels prepared to leave, the drunken Skaggs returned to the Whitney House. Lydia was not there, but he took revenge by shooting her father down. Skaggs mounted up, but saw the home of Fred Read still standing. This too must go up in flames, he decided. The formidable Mrs. Read had seen off more than one guerrilla that day, and when Skaggs struck matches she promptly put them out. A neighbor, James Faxton, appeared at the door. "Run for your life," she shouted. Faxton ran off with the drunken Skaggs in pursuit, but he managed to escape. The frustrated Skaggs made his way back to Mrs. Read and threatened to shoot her, but then was hit with an awful realization; he was the only bushwhacker left in town. Without his murderous companions to back him up, panic set in. He mounted his horse and began to ride out only to be spotted by an armed survivor, Billy Speer, who had lost two brothers in the massacre. He opened fire and Skaggs, hit in the shoulder, fell from his horse. Troops had just crossed on the ferry, and Delaware brave, White Turkey, was with them. He shot Skaggs in the heart and scalped him, then townsfolk riddled the body with gunfire before hanging the remains from a tree. Skaggs had dragged the Stars and Stripes though town, and his body was given the same treatment, hauled behind a horse. The naked, riddled and battered corpse was thrown into a ravine, set on fire, and left for the scavengers. Skaggs was the only guerrilla killed, but John McCorkle recalled, "Tom Hamilton and another man were wounded in Lawrence; they were placed in an ambulance and brought to the command. These were placed with the advance guard of twenty men under Dick Yeager, who was appointed to pilot the command out."[41]

As the guerrillas rode out the smell of burnt flesh, gunpowder and smoke hung in the air. Women and children wept alongside dead bodies strewn about. The Reverend Cordley saw "a woman sitting among the ashes of a building holding in her hands a blackened skull, fondling it and kissing it, and crying piteously over it. It was the skull of her husband, burned with the building."[42] Many bodies were consumed by flames, and due to the heat many were buried in haste. The exact death toll is unknown, but generally placed at between 150 and 200. At least 85 women and 250 children lost husbands and fathers. One hundred and eighty-two buildings went up in flames, including 100 homes. The estimated cost of the destruction was between $1.5 and 2.5 million.[43]

A false alarm that the guerrillas were returning sent many survivors scurrying into the cornfields and woods. But scouts soon reported no rebels in sight, and a witch hunt seemed in order. A carpenter named Tom Corlew had moved his family out before the raid, and he was accused of being a Quantrill spy. Thrust before a kangaroo court, he was soon

Order No. 11. **Noted artist George Caleb Bingham's 1868 painting revealed the result of Ewing's directive (State Historical Society of Missouri).**

swinging from a barn joist at the behest of the vengeful mob who ended his contortions with a volley of shots. "I was there during the whole proceeding and went to one or two parties whom I thought might stop it, but to no avail," recalled future Kansas senator James Horton. "My recollection was that the jury found no evidence against him and so reported. His hanging was perhaps a natural outcome of the excited state of public feeling at that time, as Corlew was a Missourian and was said to have been acting with proslavery men in 1856, but I think that many people in Lawrence regretted the occurrence and in ordinary, quiet times no such termination of a trial, even by a lynch court, would have been permitted."[44]

On November 18, 1863, indictments were issued against Quantrill, Colonel Holt, George Todd, George Maddox and others who had been recognized amidst the chaos. Of these, Maddox was the only man ever tried as a result of the Lawrence Massacre. He was brought from Missouri, and locked up in a Lawrence cell on February 6, 1866. He would never receive a fair trial in Lawrence, and he was granted a change of venue to Ottawa, Kansas. The evidence was heard and a jury took only ten minutes of deliberation to bring in a verdict of not guilty. The war had been over for a year now. Perhaps the jurors wanted to put the whole ghastly business behind them.

Jim Lane rode back into the smoking ruins of Lawrence leading a posse of farmers, and about a dozen Lawrence volunteers joined him in pursuit of the raiders. Although Captain Pike at Aubry had not moved against Quantrill, his warning telegrams had sent troops moving out from various posts. They were joined by hastily mustered militia and farmers with muskets, pistols, shotguns and, if nothing else was available, household knives. The word had spread across the prairie like a wildfire on a windy day. Smoke rising from yet more burning farms marked Quantrill's path back towards Missouri. The residents of Brooklyn, a small trading settlement on the Santa Fe Trail fled for their lives shortly before the bushwhackers' arrival. The village went up in flames and disappeared from the map, never to be rebuilt, but the delay allowed the vengeful pursuers to close in. Shots were exchanged with Jim Lane's men as a running fight took place. The bushwhackers could have turned back and wiped Lane's small party out, but Quantrill well knew any further delay could be fatal.[45] Troops under Major Preston Plum converged with Lane and the pursuit continued. The bushwhackers left a trail of dumped plunder, and George Todd came to earth, his horse shot from under him. To avoid being shot by his own men, he threw off Captain Bank's Federal uniform coat, the pockets stuffed with stolen greenbacks. He ran after the retreating command and mounted a fresh horse as the skirmishing continued.

The jaded Yankee horses began to give out and the rebels, mounted on fresh horses stolen in Lawrence, began to move ahead. The Yankees were joined by 150 civilian volunteers with fresh mounts, and Major Plumb ordered them forward under the command of Lieutenant Cyrus Leland. They maintained a close chase as Quantrill retreated southeast towards Paola. A 60-man rearguard commanded by William Gregg kept the pursuers at bay, but both sides took casualties. Any wounded rebels who fell into enemy hands did not live to bushwhack another day. At about 4 p.m. an exhausted Gregg was replaced by George Todd.

At sunset Quantrill arrived at the Paola river crossing to find his advance cut off by troops and civilian volunteers under Lieutenant Colonel Charles Clark. The rebels turned back and counterattacked Leland's pursuing force, driving them back, then escaped by turning north into heavy woods. Major Plumb's exhausted force staggered into Paola, many horses literally dying on their feet, and command was taken by Colonel Clark. Scouts brought word of Quantrill's movements, and at 2 a.m. Clark gave the order to resume the pursuit.

Quantrill gave his fatigued command only one hour's rest during the night, and they resumed their retreat back east, crossing into Missouri a few miles from their entry point 36 hours earlier. At dawn they stopped and dismounted at the Grand River to allow men and horses to drink. They stretched painful, saddle-sore limbs, and men went out to gather food from neighboring farms. But Quantrill soon discerned through his telescope Colonel Clark's force crossing the border. Then a farmer arrived in camp. He claimed 1200 Yankees were mustered in the hills four miles to the east. Quantrill ordered about 100 of his men, their horses spent, to disperse. With the others he rode east to reconnoiter the supposed 1200 Yankees for himself. As suspected, he found a far smaller force, about 150 Missouri militia. An assault by the bushwhackers saw them put to flight. But, now back on home turf, Quantrill knew it was time to scatter. His men would reappear as farmers, laborers, parolees and loyal residents of Missouri towns and hamlets.

Clark arrived at the former rebel campsite and, his command worn out, abandoned any major pursuit. But he did carry out a local search for bushwhackers, "picking up scattered ones that had stopped in the brush at Grand River." Those picked up did not live to stand trial. This included the two wounded men in the ambulance and their driver, Jim Bledsoe. The wounded recruits pled for their lives, but the veteran Bledsoe held no such delusions. "Stop it! We are not entitled to mercy. We spare none and do not expect to be spared." They were shot and White Turkey took both their scalps and ears. Andy Blunt found their bodies some time later. "We had something to learn yet, boys," he said, "and we have learned it. Scalp for scalp, hereafter."[46]

Other bushwhackers were hunted down. "Such inhumane wretches deserve no mercy and should be shot down like dogs where ever found," wrote Colonel Bazel Lazear to his wife. "Quantrell is in here yet with some three hundred men but they are so scattered that it is hard to find them." Over the next week Red Legs, jayhawkers, armed civilians, militia units, and regular troops moved through the scrub and woods, watching fords, searching houses and barns. Captives were hung and others shot. Lieutenant Leland hung three men so high a rider beneath them could not touch their feet. "Don't cut them down" was nailed to the tree trunk. Some men died merely on the possibility that they had been involved. On August 27 General Ewing reported that 80 men had been killed. "I think it will largely exceed 100 before any considerable part of our troops withdraw from the pursuit. No prisoners have been taken, and none will be. All houses in which Lawrence goods have been found have been destroyed, as well as houses of known guerrillas, wherever our troops have gone." But key figures like Quantrill, Holt, Gregg, Todd, Poole and Anderson remained on the run.

Even before Ewing wrote this report, he issued his infamous General Order No. 11. This ordered all residents of Jackson, Cass and Bates Counties and part of Vernon County, to vacate their homes within 15 days. Those living within one mile of major population centers were exempt, and others who could prove their loyalty to the Union could move to military posts or western Kansas. All hay and grain stores were to be turned over to the military by September 9 or destroyed. Very soon 20,000 people were on the move, the prey of Red Legs, jayhawkers and Yankee troops who disobeyed orders that no looting should occur.

Missouri state treasurer George Caleb Bingham was one of many Union men who were aghast at Ewing's order. Also a noted artist, he left a vivid image of what he saw by both paintbrush and words: "Bare-footed and bare-headed women and children, stripped of every article of clothing except a scant covering for their bodies, were exposed to the heat of an August sun and compelled to struggle through the dust on foot. All their means of transportation had been seized by their spoilers, except an occasional dilapidated cart, or an old and superannuated horse, which were necessarily appropriated to the use of the aged and infirm. It is well-known that men were shot down in the very act of obeying the order, and their wagons and effects seized by their murderers.... Dense clouds of smoke arising in every direction marked the conflagration of dwellings."[47]

These measures did seriously damage the guerrilla home base, and many applauded Ewing. But others, like Bingham, saw him as having gone much too far. Many of the displaced had been loyal to the Union, and that loyalty had been lost. Young men from these families now chose to ride with the rebels. Ewing was replaced by General Egbert Brown in January of 1864. He had never been in favor of Order No. 11, and decreed that anyone not "disloyal or unworthy" could swear an oath to the Union and return. Ewing protested that "General Brown will let disloyal refugees return, and following them will be the guerrillas." Many exiled families did not return till the war's end, but others did, and Ewing's prediction proved correct. In May of 1864 Colonel James Ford, Union commander in Jackson County, complained it "is full of bushwhackers, and they have friends all through the country who furnish them with food.... I am satisfied that there are many families that are feeding them that have proved their loyalty."[48]

And Quantrill, meanwhile, had struck again. On September 30, 1863, about five weeks after Lawrence, more than 400 men answered his call. They mustered at Captain Perdee's farm on the Blackwater River in Johnson County where the "First Regiment, First Brigade, Army of the South" was organized. Quantrill was given the title of colonel, most likely by election, as no proof of this rank from a Confederate authority exists.[49] Colonel John Holt and his command were present. Captain Quantrill giving orders to Colonel Holt was dysfunctional with the formal organization of a regiment. A formal chain of command was required, and it seems that Quantrill was determined to be a colonel regardless of what the Richmond brass thought. But if John Mosby could be "Captain" Mosby while still a private, why not "Colonel" Quantrill?

Baxter Springs

Winter was coming on, and the "First Regiment" started riding south towards warmer climes in Texas. The ravaged condition of their usual support grounds provided a further inducement. They set out on October 2 and rode into Kansas, then continued south on the Fort Scott-Fort Gibson Road. On October 6 the advance guard under Dave Poole captured two teamsters and, before killing them, learned that a log and earthwork redoubt called Fort Blair had been constructed at Baxter Springs. He sent word to Quantrill who decided this was a Yankee plum ripe for the picking. Quantrill dispatched Gregg's company to join Poole for an assault from the east while he split off with the rest of the command to attack from the north.

Lieutenant James Pond had arrived at Fort Blair with Yankee reinforcements just two days earlier. He now had under his command 185 men. To accommodate the additional troops, he had one wall removed to enlarge the earth and log fortification, and on the morning of the 6th dispatched eight wagons escorted by 60 cavalrymen on a foraging expedition. This left 45 dismounted whites and 50 black infantrymen to hold the fort. Dave Poole, meanwhile, deployed his detachment to attack, but Quantrill, with no guide, had become disoriented in the woods.

Most of the garrison were eating their midday meal around camp tents outside the breastworks. Pond had no pickets on duty, and the bluecoats looked around in astonishment at the sight and sound of Poole's yowling rebels in a headlong charge. It was a bizarre case of Poole versus Pond. The troops raced for the fort but became intermingled with the charging horsemen as they were overtaken. With rebels wearing Federal uniforms, Poole recalled it was difficult to tell friend from foe. Thirteen black soldiers were wounded in this attack, but "the darkies fought like devils," in Pond's words, and they were able to drive the rebels from the fort.[50] His men lined up behind the four-foot walls and opened fire while Pond single handedly manned his howitzer, just outside the earthworks. He fired three shots, the shells exploded and he guerrillas moved behind cover, rebel yells and revolvers no match for artillery.

The bushed Quantrill, meanwhile, had emerged from the woods. He could see no fort but Yankee troops, in stationary position, organizing themselves on the plain several hundred yards away. They were 100 men from the 3rd Wisconsin and 14th Kansas Cavalry escorting General James Blunt, commander of the District of the Frontier. The general had called a halt to prepare his brass band for an impressive arrival at the nearby Fort Blair. Due to the lie of the land and intervening woods Blunt could hear no firing, and was unaware that Dave Poole's much more impressive arrival was already under way. The general took the blue-clad horsemen approaching from the woods to be cavalry from the fort, but "my first suspicion of their being an enemy was aroused by seeing several men, supposed to be officers, riding hurriedly up and down their line, and apparent confusion among the men." Blunt ordered his troops to form a battle line facing the suspected enemy. The wagons and non-combatants, including one lady, were sent to the rear. A second line of horsemen moved from the woods facing Blunt. At about 200 yards the rebels opened fire. First of a couple of Yankees turned tail, quickly followed by a handful of others.

"Charge!" yelled Quantrill. With hideous rebel yells, the guerrillas dashed forward at the gallop. Blunt, riding in the front of his men, turned to see "the whole line broken, and all of them at full gallop over the prairie, completely panic-stricken." He galloped back and joined Major Henry Curtis in an attempt to rally the men.

"We soon closed on them," reported Quantrill, "making fearful havoc on every side."[51] Any who surrendered were shown no mercy, including civilian employees. "It was simply a butchery," recalled one survivor. Blunt and Curtis attempted to rally the men but the onrush of rebels forced them back. Blunt's horse jumped a ditch and he escaped, but Curtis' mount was shot in the hip and fell. The major landed in the dust, then the wounded animal regained its feet and galloped off. A bushwhacker rode up to Curtis, who offered his revolver in a gesture of surrender. The answer was a bullet in the head. "I've killed Blunt! I've killed the old son of a bitch," crowed his slayer by mistake.

Rebel Frank Bledsoe galloped alongside the 15 Union musicians in a fleeing wagon thumping across the plain. His demand for their surrender was answered with a gunshot and he fell dead from his horse. A few more thumps and a wheel came off as the wagon overturned in a flurry of curses and dust. The bruised musicians staggered to their feet waving white hankies as a band of guerrillas rode up. George Todd demanded to know why they had not waved their hankies at Bledsoe instead of shooting him. The musicians died in a blaze of gunfire along with artist and reporter James O'Neil from *Frank Leslie's Illustrated Newspaper*. The wagon was set on fire and a 12-year-old drummer boy, badly wounded, emerged with his uniform on fire and crawled 30 yards before he died.

Lydia Stevens Thomas was present, en route to visit her ill husband, an officer at Fort Gibson. Her buggy driver, Trooper Davis, whipped her two gray mares, and they clattered across the prairie with rebels in pursuit. Not knowing a woman was on board, their shots hit the enclosed buggy several times, but they were forced to give up the chase when their horses played out. Unhurt, Mrs. Thomas and Davis abandoned the buggy in a grassy hollow when her own horses were exhausted. Luckily, two riderless cavalry mounts came their way. Mrs. Thomas and Davis mounted up and rode about half a mile before a cluster of troops came into view, General Blunt with a handful of survivors.

General Blunt "had many very narrow escapes" while trying to rally the men, reported Major Henning, who had ridden to the fort in attempt to get help. Blunt finally "succeeded in collecting about 10 men, and with these he worried the enemy, attacking them in small parties, and, when pursued by too large a force, falling back until they turned, and then in turn following them, so that at no time was he out of sight of the enemy, and most of the time close enough to worry and harass them."[52]

It was a bad day for the general. He had lost not only his escort but also his baggage wagons. On board were his spare clothing, sword, commission papers, letters, official documents and a fine personal flag prepared for him by the ladies of Fort Leavenworth.

By the time Mrs. Thomas rejoined Blunt, he had already sent a small detachment to Fort Scott to bring reinforcements. With one trooper as escort, he sent her after them. That night they halted in a wooded grove by a stream where a few other survivors found refuge. "The soldiers watched while I slept the sleep of exhaustion with the sod for a pillow," she recalled.[53] They arrived safely at Fort Scott the next day.

"On looking over the ground for the wounded," reported Blunt, "I soon discovered that every man who had fallen, except 3, who escaped by feigning death, had been murdered, all shot through the head."

Todd and Anderson, flush with victory, wanted to renew the attack on Fort Blair, but Quantrill decided against such a rash move. The Yankees would have the upper hand, waiting behind earthworks with rifles ready. Before long Lieutenant Pond saw George Todd ride forward with a flag of truce. He demanded the post's surrender, which Pond promptly refused. Todd then demanded "in the name of Colonel Quantrill of the First Regiment, First Brigade, Army of the South, an exchange of prisoners." He falsely offered to exchange Major Curtis and others lying dead, many mutilated, for any prisoners Pond had taken. But Pond said he had no prisoners to exchange. Todd returned to Quantrill who decided to waste no more time on Fort Blair. The guerrillas mounted up and rode south. General Blunt, who Quantrill assumed to be dead, tailed the guerrillas with his few men to see where they were headed. "Is there a braver man living than the general?" asked Pond.

The army brass thought there was.

It was Pond who, 35 years later, received the Congressional Medal of Honor for his actions that day, not General Blunt. After the war Pond left the army and organized celebrity lecture tours. His clients included Mark Twain, P.T. Barnum, Frederick Douglas, Arthur Conan Doyle, and a young Winston Churchill. The English gent came into conflict with Pond, and described him as "a vulgar Yankee impresario."[54] Perhaps Quantrill and Todd had similar thoughts as they rode away, Fort Blair still intact.

Counts differ, but about 103 Yankee soldiers and ten civilians were killed that day, with 18 wounded.[55] Normal battles produce far more wounded then dead. The disparity indicated that most wounded were executed, as claimed by Blunt. In his report of October 13, Quantrill claimed only three guerrillas killed and three wounded, generally thought to be a considerable underestimate. With the killing and mutilation of surrendered soldiers so soon after Lawrence, Quantrill's Raiders were denounced throughout the North as "demons" and "fiends incarnate."[56]

Lawrence and Baxter Springs had been the zenith of Quantrill's career. With time, everything changes, and the notorious guerrilla chief faced difficult times ahead.

Texas

The First Regiment, First Brigade, Army of the South, arrived in North Texas, and set up camp near Sherman. "During the winter we spent our time hunting and fishing," recalled John McCorkle, "and going to dances and during Christmas Week, quite a few of us attended a big ball in Sherman."[57]

Quantrill may have been wined and dined by locals, but General Henry McCulloch, his immediate superior, was not happy with the notorious guerrilla's arrival:

> He has not reported here, and I do not know what his military status is. I do not know as much about his mode of warfare as others seem to know, but, from all I can learn, it is but little, if at all, removed from that of the wildest savage; so much so, that I do not believe for a moment that our Government can sanction it in one of her officers. Hence, it seems to me if he can be an officer in our army, his acts should be disavowed by our Government, and as far as practicable, he be made to understand that we would greatly prefer his remaining away from our army or its vicinity.
>
> I appreciate his services, and am anxious to have them, but certainly we cannot, as a Christian people, sanction a savage, inhuman warfare, in which men are to be shot down like dogs, after throwing down their arms and throwing up their arms supplicating for mercy.[58]

Department commander General Edmund Kirby Smith, however, felt the guerrillas could be useful. Unlike McCulloch, he wanted them to enter the regular service. But the bushwhackers had other ideas. They felt they would face a rope or firing squad if forced to surrender with regular troops. "I have but little confidence in men who fight for booty," wrote McCulloch, "and whose mode of warfare is but little, if any, above the uncivilized Indian and who says they are afraid to enter our army regularly for fear of being captured."

But Kirby Smith replied: "They have suffered every outrage on their person and families at the hands of the Federals, and, being outlawed and their lives forfeited, have waged a war of no quarter whenever they have come in contact with the enemy." Kirby Smith, accepting Quantrill's desire to remain as an independent command, wanted him to hunt jayhawker bands largely consisting of rebel deserters.

McCulloch let Quantrill off the leash, but gave instructions to kill no deserters or conscripts. They were to be brought back still breathing for military reassignment. Quantrill was not pleased with this, and replied that his men would fire in self defense if required. He soon struck a jayhawker camp on Jernigan's swamp. Some of the jayhawkers were killed and others captured. McCulloch was not happy with the deaths, and the gulf with Quantrill widened. Quantrill decided to refrain from such attacks in future, but was prepared to take the trail when Comanche warriors attacked Gainesville. The wily tribesmen, however, proved they could travel faster over Texan plains than the most agile guerrilla band. Quantrill was forced to abandon the pursuit.

An order from McCulloch to destroy the whiskey stills in the Red River Valley resulted in the destruction of one still and the killing of three brewers, but placing the robber in charge of the bank did not work. The other stills were left intact and the citizens of Sherman got a mild impression of Lawrence when drunken bushwhackers galloped through the streets and shot up the town. Along with similar events, discipline disintegrated and men deserted the "First Regiment" as they went back home to Missouri, or even joined the regular army.

William Gregg informed Quantrill that he was leaving. Unhappy with the Lawrence slaughter, he was also dissatisfied with the division of spoils. Quantrill had promised to help out impoverished citizens of Jackson County, but they had received nothing, while Todd's company had been given the bulk of stolen money. Quantrill did not oppose Gregg leaving. Rifts had developed in the command and it was known Todd would be quite happy to see Gregg in his grave. Gregg joined the regular army under General Jo Shelby and was made captain of Company H in Shank's Brigade. He married and survived the war to return to his farm in Jackson County where he served as deputy sheriff.

Over the winter of 1863–64 General McCulloch received reports of robberies by Quantrill's men on Texan citizens. He wrote to his immediate superior, General John Magruder, on February 3 that "so much mischief" was charged to Quantrill's men that "I have determined to disarm, arrest, and send his entire command to you or General Smith. This is the only chance to get them out of this section of the country, which they have nearly ruined, and I have never yet got them to do any service.... They regard the life of a man less than you would that of a sheep-killing dog."[59]

But McCulloch changed his mind; better to send them 500 miles away to Corpus Christie. No doubt he had wondered how many of his men would die while attempting to disarm and arrest the ferocious bushwhackers. He suggested to the Corpus Christie commander, "if they do not act properly" to disarm them and put them "to work on fortifications." But Quantrill had no intention of going to Corpus Christie. On February 24 he wrote to the supposed Confederate Governor of Missouri, Thomas Reynolds, requesting that his command be sent home for a spring campaign. By now Quantrill was no longer a colonel in his own estimation, as he signed the letter "Cap. Comg Partisans." Reynolds replied diplomatically advising that a man of Quantrill's "ability should look forward to a higher future." Guerrilla warfare was no longer an "honorable pursuit," and he "should acquire the confidence of the regular authorities" and "strive to organize a regular command and enter the regular Confederate service." No doubt Reynolds was influenced by the fact that on February 17, Secretary of War Seddon had banned partisan units. For some time he had been receiving complaints from Southern citizens and army officers regarding the activities of rogue outlaw bands calling themselves partisans. Quantrill's reputation would have added fuel to the fire.

And Reynolds warned Quantrill that, in guerrilla bands, sooner or later, "some officer or some private rises up, disputes his authority, gains the men, and puts him down." Prophetic words for William Clarke Quantrill.

No doubt Seddon's ban had some effect back east, but guerrillas out west took no heed of such directives from distant Richmond. The likes of Quantrill, Todd and Anderson were a law unto themselves.

Along with drinking and carousing, Bill Anderson had been taking time out to do some romancing on the side. The result was his marriage, on March 2, to Miss "Bush Smith," full name Mary Erwin Bush Smith. Despite having been called a prostitute, some claim she was church goer and "one of the finest ladies of Sherman." Or, at only 16 tender years, one of the finest blossoming ladies in Sherman, perhaps. The couple had met at the Christmas ball, and Anderson commissioned the building of a home on Cherry Street.[60] Presumably the guerrillas had avoided shooting up the structure when they rampaged through Sherman on their drunken spree.

In late March the body of one Major Butts was found shot and robbed by the Red River, and Colonel Alexander was shot and robbed at his own home. Quantrill was informed that one his own men, Fletch Taylor, was responsible for the murder of these Confederate officers. He placed Taylor and three accomplices under arrest and sent word to General McCulloch that he wanted Taylor court-martialed. It was a further sign of Quantrill's fading authority when sentries allowed Taylor to ride out during the night. Quantrill called the command together, now about 75 men. One of these, W. L. Potter, wrote a letter in 1896 claiming that Quantrill "told them if there was a Man in his Command that had been guilty of Robbing any Person While in Texas, that if they would come out and acknowledge their guilt & Promise that they Would Never again repeat it & that they were sorry for it, that they would remain in the command the same as ever & He would not permit them to be punished for it." If they did not comply, and he found out they were guilty, he "Would have them punished to the full Extent of the Law & he would also Expel them from his command." No one came forward, and he went on to say if anyone did not like his style of command "they could take their Horses & Weapons and they were welcome to go wherever they pleased."[61]

Considering General McCulloch's complaints against the command, it seems impossible that Quantrill could have been so naive regarding the activities of his men. Perhaps he merely said it was time to turn over a new leaf and act within the law.

But, whatever was said, "I won't belong to any such a damned outfit," replied Bill Anderson. He and 20 others mounted up and rode out.[62] They rode into McCulloch's headquarters in Bonham to find Fletch Taylor had already arrived. Taylor told the general that Quantrill had ordered Major Butts' killing, and Anderson claimed Quantrill was responsible for a whole list of crimes. McCulloch sent word for Quantrill to come with his witnesses, and the guerrilla chief arrived with his command. George Todd had been left in camp behind with a dozen men.

When Quantrill walked into McCulloch's office, he was astonished to be told he was under arrest. McCulloch told him to unbuckle his side arms and place them on the bed.

This done, he offered to dine with Quantrill while they discussed the whole business. "No, sir! I will not go to dinner. By God, I do not care a god damn if I never eat another mouthful in Texas!" McCulloch had no intention of missing dinner, and left Quantrill with two armed guards. Quantrill, pretending to get a cup of water from a cooler, promptly sprang to the bed and the astonished soldiers found themselves staring into his revolver. He made them drop their guns, and in a flash was out the door, locking it behind him. He bolted down the stairs, covering two more soldiers with his revolver, then ran into the street to see his men in a casual chat with Anderson's party. "Boys, the outfit is under arrest," he shouted, "get on your horses, and lets get out of here!"[63] Rebel yells echoed along the street as the fugitives galloped out of town.

Men who had just been trading yarns now traded bullets as Anderson's band joined Texas militia in the pursuit of Quantrill. Bring him back dead or alive, was the order. Quantrill sent a galloper to Todd with orders to rendezvous on the Sherman-Bonham road. Anderson broke off the chase, but soon clashed with Todd's party. Again former comrades exchanged gunfire and two men were wounded. Todd, outnumbered, broke off the fight and rejoined Quantrill. They crossed the Red River into Indian Territory, and formed a line to meet Colonel Martin's pursuing militia. The troops approached the ford, but instead of opening fire, Martin rode to the center of the river with a white flag. Quantrill rode out to meet him. He had no desire to fire on Confederate soldiers, he told Martin, but would do so if followed. Martin had no desire to tangle with the dreaded guerrillas, and said he had no jurisdiction in Indian Territory. He turned and led his command back to Bonham while Quantrill continued north, happy to distance himself from his former, ostensible commander, General McCulloch.

Overall, the Texas stay had not been a happy one. McCulloch wrote to his department commander that he could do nothing about the "Captain Quantrill command" because his own troops lacked the "physical and moral courage to arrest and disarm them."[64]

Anderson had gone his own way, the former comrades now enemies. But, strangely enough, the day would come when Quantrill and Anderson would join forces again.

Missouri Again

More than 400 guerrillas had ridden into Texas under Quantrill, but only about 65 remained as they plodded through April rain and swollen streams on their trek back to the bluffs and plains of Missouri. Anderson led his band back at about the same time. He had promised his bride that he would return to Texas, but the bloody career of Bill Anderson would ensure that the two never met again.

General Egbert Brown, commander of the Central District of Missouri, sent Colonel James Ford's 2nd Colorado Cavalry, 1200 "hardy mountaineer boys," into Jackson County to suppress guerrillas. But most civilians had little faith in their ability catch Quantrill. "Lonely and weary, with continual watching," wrote Julia Lovejoy of Baldwin City, Kansas, on May 10, "we are looking every hour for 'Quantrill,' with his horde of fiends to sweep through this entire region, and murder indiscriminately and burn every house, in his march of death! 'Our nigger' has a 'six shooter,' every barrel loaded to sell his life as dearly as possible, for he well knows no mercy will be shown him. I had him learn me how to fire it and I surely shall if I am not shot before I can seize it, if they begin their murderous work here."[65]

But Mrs. Lovejoy had little to fear from Quantrill. As predicted by Thomas Reynolds, the notorious guerrilla chief would soon be deposed.

11

"An honorable foe"
Mosby, 1863–1864

General Lee was not happy with Major Mosby. "I fear he exercises but little control over his men," he wrote on August 18, 1863, three days before the Lawrence Massacre. "He has latterly carried but too few on his expeditions apparently, and his attention has been more attracted towards the capture of wagons than military damage to the enemy. His attention has been called to this."[1]

This rebuke was the result of malicious tongues falsely accusing Mosby of selling $30,000 worth of booty in an auction at Charlottesville.[2] "I always had a Confederate fire in my rear as well as that of the public enemy in my front," Mosby recalled.[3] But, if Lee was concerned about Mosby not inflicting enough military damage, he had no cause for concern. Only two weeks before, Union Colonel Grimshaw had received the following: "Fairfax Court House has been surrounded all day by Mosby's guerrillas. Every team going down and returning has been captured. They are 200 strong."[4] On this occasion Mosby had only 27 men. Giving the impression of 200 rebels capturing supply trains was certainly damaging the enemy, and they were forced to deploy hundreds of troops in an attempt to hunt him down. Once again Jeb Stuart recommended Mosby for promotion.

Six days after Lee wrote his report, Mosby set out with 30 men to inflict the military damage that the general required. He was going to burn three railway bridges to the east of Bull Run. But the small trestles involved could be quickly repaired by army engineers who could achieve wonders in a short time with post and beam construction.

Mosby left his command concealed in a grove of woods to the east of Fairfax Court House, and scouted ahead with three men. But a more tempting target than railway trestles came in sight. One hundred horses bound for General Meade's cavalry were moving along the pike guarded by 25 men of the 2nd Massachusetts Cavalry, a regiment raised by Amos Lawrence, the abolitionist who had bankrolled Lawrence. The bluecoats stopped to water their throats and horses at Gooding's Tavern. "My men went at them with a yell that terrified the Yankees and scattered them in all directions," reported Mosby.[5] Bullets flew as the rebels came at the gallop from both directions down the pike. Some Yankees returned fire from beneath houses, and nine men of the 13th New York Cavalry arrived to reinforce their comrades. Mosby felt a sharp pain in his side as a bullet hit home, and another bullet passed right through his thigh before killing his horse. But the Yankees, with two dead and five wounded, soon surrendered. Mosby suffered two dead and three wounded, including himself, but captured 12 bluecoats and 85 horses.

Fortunately for Mosby, he had recruited Dr. William Dunn for his command. The bullet in his side had passed around his ribs without breaking bone. Neither thigh nor body wound were mortal. But there were still those trestles to attend to. Mosby dispatched Lieutenant William Turner with several men, and they managed to set one ablaze before disappearing into the hills once more.

First the Gettysburg disaster; now this. Perhaps winds of change were in the air? Mosby must have wondered if his luck was running out. Escaping bluecoats had seen him go down, and rumors of the Gray Ghost's death soon spread. One woman reported seeing him being escorted in a wagon with "the ghastly hue of death" upon his face. It must have been amusing for the "dead" man to read his obituary, *Sketch of Mosby, Guerrilla Chief*, which appeared in the *New York Herald* on August 31. Then rumors of his survival circulated. Was he alive or dead? The Washington correspondent for the *New York Herald* decided it was impossible to tell.[6] An enquiry was held by the Yankee brass into the loss of so many valuable horses. The highly esteemed Colonel Charles Lowell, commander of the 2nd Massachusetts Cavalry, took responsibility, saying he should have detailed a stronger escort, but wrote to his fiancée that a captain "went insane" during the fight, which allowed Mosby's victory. Lowell and Mosby had previously crossed swords, and would do so again. When ordered to burn the homes of guerrilla supporters, Lowell wrote to Mosby stating that he would only burn homes actually used for rebel rendezvous. He had come to respect the Gray Ghost, and wrote home that "Mosby is an honorable foe, and should be treated as such."[7]

Other Yankees, however, frustrated with their inability to outwit Mosby, were not so kind in their assessments. They chose to consider the furtive raider little more than a despicable highwayman.[8] One Union soldier wrote to a newspaper condemning Mosby. "The gallant Chevalier of Southern Maidens, Mosby, continues to dash out on sutlers, where he can find them unguarded or broken down, and he generally takes them without loss of a man. Now and then an ambulance or two, full of sick men, is taken by him without a loss."[9]

As Mosby healed, he paid a visit to Lee at Orange Court House. The general apologized to the wounded hero for the confusion regarding auctioned booty, and suggested that he pay attention to the Orange & Alexandria Railroad. Perhaps he could disrupt supplies, capture prominent Union officials traveling by rail, or snatch them from coaches on public roads? Influential relatives of important men would be anxious to see the war over so the captive could be restored to hearth and home.

Mosby mounted a fresh horse, supplied courtesy of Uncle Sam, and took to the hills and valleys once more, capturing men, arms and stock. On October 26 he bluffed a train of 40 wagons to halt, and made off with 103 horses, 42 mules and

Major Mosby remained very much alive, despite the *New York Herald* having reported his death (Library of Congress).

30 prisoners. The cavalry supposed to be protecting the train galloped to the rescue, and the rebels fled before having a chance to burn the wagons. "The train had an escort," George Meade wrote to General Halleck, "which was in front and rear, but was unable to reach the center of the train before the guerrillas had made off with the animals."

"Hurrah for Mosby!" said Jeb Stuart, "Mules! And fat too!"[10]

West Virginia had stayed with the Union to become a new state in her own right. The governor appointed for all Virginia by the Federals was Francis H. Pierpont, considered by Mosby the "Bogus Governor."[11] His headquarters were in Alexandria, on Virginian soil, about five miles south of Washington. Mosby cased the town, and Pierpont was appalled to receive a note, "I'll get you some night, mighty easy." Taking the well guarded governor would not be mighty easy, in fact, but Mosby hatched another plot that would strike close to home.

Dulaney Taken

Families split in civil wars, as seen with Union General Philip St. George Cooke. Not only did Cooke fight his son-in-law, Jeb Stuart, but he also had a son who became a Confederate general. Riding with Mosby was Private French Dulaney, the son of Governor Pierpont's aid, Colonel Daniel Dulaney. On September 27, under cover of night, French led Mosby and four others to Dulaney's home, Rose Hill, about four miles from Alexandria. Mosby knocked on the door, and a top window swung open. "Is Colonel Dulaney in?" Mosby asked. "Yes," came the reply. Mosby explained that he had dispatches from the governor, and within a few minutes Colonel Dulaney opened the door and invited the new arrivals in. "My name is Mosby," the visitor said as he entered. And then Dulaney's son walked in. "How do, Pa, I'm very glad to see you." Dulaney stared in disbelief. "Well, sir, I'm damned sorry to see you."

Once the shock wore off, the bewildered colonel gave his word not to escape if they allowed him time to prepare for a journey he would rather not make. He told his son he had better take some old shoes from the house. They were scarce in the Confederacy, he'd been told. But French held up one leg displaying a fine pair of cavalry boots recently taken from a Yankee sutler. "What do you think of that?" he asked.[12]

The rebels rode off with their prisoner, but took time out to cause mischief along the way. Yankees in the two forts west of Alexandria saw the night sky light up as the trestle at Cameron's Run burst into flames. Troops rushed out and extinguished the blaze, and searched for the culprits, but by that time Mosby's party was long gone. "Guerrillas seem to be about as plentiful in Fairfax County as our own troops and much more active." reported the *New York Herald*. "Until a regiment is stationed at Fairfax Court House, and another at Vienna, we may anticipate the continued and frequent depredations of these bands."[13]

Following this raid, Jeb Stuart recommended Mosby for promotion yet again. But army red tape was not to be beaten. "I have hoped that he would have been able to raise his command sufficiently for the command of a Lieutenant-Colonel," Lee replied, "and to have it regularly mustered into the service. I am not aware that it numbers over 4 companies."[14]

Mosby continued to hit the Yankees, but valued men were either killed or captured along the way. Some taken prisoner, having violated paroles, were considered outlaws and faced a Yankee rope. And the O & A Railroad was proving a hard nut to crack. "It is very difficult to do any thing on the railroad," Mosby reported on November 22, "as they have sentinels stationed all along in sight of each other, in addition to the guards on each train. Rest assured that if there is any chance of effecting anything there, it will be done."

"Major Mosby is very vigilant and very active," Stuart wrote three days later. "The importance of his operations is shown by the heavy guard the enemy is obliged to keep to guard the railroad from his attacks."[15]

In November of 1863, the *New York Times* received a letter from a reporters who had been captured by Mosby. "The first intimation we received of the presence of his formidable and almost mythical individual, the mysterious and ubiquitous Mosby, was the scream of the ladies which apprized us of the fact. Shortly after we were summonsed to open the door, which we reluctantly obeyed, and found two gentlemen courteously tending us the contents of two revolvers if we did not surrender." The reporter was taken prisoner and spent some time on the road with his captors. He observed that Mosby "is a perfect gentleman," and his men, "such as I have seen, are intelligent beyond the average, and seem to revere their leader, who, to use their own words, can wear out any four of them by his labors."[16] Based on the lengthy letter, an article appeared in the paper on November 27 headed "A modern Rob Roy." "Our correspondent speaks in the highest terms of the treatment which he and his companion received from their captor, who, like his famous Scotch prototype of the Scottish Border, can, it appears, be very much the gentleman when he chooses. He did all he could to make them comfortable, and they seem to have had a capital time with him, all things considered. The only property belonging to them that he has appropriated were the animals that they rode—'those gay *Herald* horses'—as he styled them."[17]

With the capture of Stoughton, and then Dulaney, every Yankee worth kidnapping was on the alert. Fearing the dreaded night visit, they ensconced themselves amidst bluecoats and bayonets. The ultimate would be, of course, to snatch Abraham Lincoln. On one scout along the Potomac during 1864, the flags and buildings of Washington in plain view, Mosby encountered one Mrs. Barlow driving a wagonload of farm produce. From her he borrowed a pair of scissors, removed his hat, and took a snip of hair. "Please take this lock of my hair right into Lincoln," Mosby said, "and say to him that I am coming to see him soon and will expect a lock of his hair in return." Lincoln duly received the gift and was, characteristically, highly amused. But the *Daily National Republican* was not: "It is reported that Moseby, the guerrilla, sent a lock of his hair to the President a few days ago," wrote the indignant correspondent. "It wouldn't be a bad idea to send 'Hole-in-the-Day,' or some other of the Indian chiefs lying around here loose, to bring in the balance of Moseby's hair, scalp and all."[18] The Indian chiefs stayed put, and "Moseby's" scalp remained securely in place. If the Yankees had employed Indian trackers, as when fighting wild tribes out west, perhaps the elusive Mosby would have been easier to scalp.

Loudoun Heights

The cold winds and snows of January 1864 caused the Potomac to freeze over for the first time in several years, ideal conditions for a winter raid. The Yankees would be more interested in keeping warm than fighting—so the rebels thought. This included rebel Captain Frank Stringfellow, an outstanding scout, commended for bravery, who had worked for Jeb Stuart. He had earned Mosby's trust by acting as guide on a raid towards Warrenton the previous November. Despite being on the Yankee "wanted" list, Stringfellow often visited his sweetheart, Emma Green, who resided in Yankee-held Alexandria.

Major Henry Cole's 200-man 1st Potomac Maryland cavalry battalion was stationed on the eastern base of Loudoun Heights, half a mile south of Harpers Ferry. They stood guard over a strategic bridge crossing the Shenandoah River. Cole had authority to act independently against partisans, and clashed with Mosby on various occasions. On January 1, with 32 men, Captain William "Billy" Smith had routed an 80-man detachment of Cole's troops commanded by Captain A. N. Hunter. "Cole's men threw away bags of corn, sabres, carbines, pistols and everything they could well rid themselves of," recalled one rebel, "and some, as though thinking their horses not fleet enough, jumped down, and leaving them in the road, ran through the woods on foot."[19] Fifty-seven Yankees had been killed, wounded or captured. It would be quite a coup if Mosby could now capture Cole's home base. Stringfellow scouted the position and felt that, with a little daring, the whole camp could be taken, lock, stock and barrel, with no casualties.

Major Cole and his staff resided in a two-story house 100 yards away from the main campsite. The men slept on their arms, ready for action should a shot be fired by outlying pickets. But Stringfellow had seen no sentries in the camp itself. On the freezing night of January 9 he led Mosby and about 110 men along a steep cliff path from the Potomac River. The footing was so narrow they had to proceed single file, the men dismounted and leading the horses across slippery snow.[20] Avoiding the Yankee pickets, they emerged on the road near the camp. Mosby was confident of success, and sent Stringfellow with ten men to capture Cole and his staff in the headquarters house. Mosby, meanwhile, made his way towards the camp. It was about 4:30 a.m., and the bluecoats would be in their deepest sleep and least able to resist. Detailed accounts of what happened next, as with most gunfights, are contradictory. One claim is that a sentry on duty outside Cole's quarters fired on Stringfellow's detachment,[21] but Cole's report made no mention of this.

Mosby ordered the charge. But his men mistook Stringfellow's party for enemy cavalry, and fired on them while the real Yankees dashed from their tents. Many were clad only in underwear, but they all had guns in hand. "No one who has not experienced a night attack from an enemy," recalled one soldier, "can form the slightest conception of the feelings of one wakened in the dead of night with the din of shots and yells coming from those thirsting for your blood."[22] Horsemen, pistols blazing, galloped about the camp in wild confusion. Cole reported that 400 (actually 100) rebels "made an impetuous charge, with a loud yell, on the right of the camp. In consequence of the charge, the right Company, B, offered but a feeble resistance, but in the meantime, the second Company in line, Company A, was speedily rallied."[23]

"Shoot every soldier on horseback," the Yankees yelled. All was confusion as Mosby's plan went askew. One of his original 15, Lieutenant William Turner of Company A, was mortally wounded. Ranger Walter Franklin steadied Turner in his saddle, and led him to the rear. Yankee Captain George Vernon was hit in the head, the bullet destroying his left eye, but "rally here men," he yelled, "they're nothing but a set of damn horse thieves." As the mounted rebels dashed about they made good targets at close range for the troopers on foot, and several dropped from their horses into the cold snow. Mosby could see the day was lost. "Retreat, boys, they're too many for us," he yelled.

"Gallant Repulse of Mosby's Guerrillas" proclaimed the Northern press. Cole was wined and dined, and his men were given a 30-day furlough. But Mosby put the blame squarely on Stringfellow's shoulders: "All my plans were on the eve of consummation, when suddenly the party sent with Stringfellow came dashing over the hill towards the camp, yelling and shooting. They had made no attempt to secure Cole. Mistaking them for the enemy, I ordered my men to charge."[24] Mosby retreated with six prisoners and over 50 horses, but had four of his own men killed outright, four mortally wounded, three wounded, and one captured. Cole reported four killed and 16 wounded. Among Mosby's dead were two men he had come to depend on, Captain William Smith and Lieutenant William Turner. They were being trained to lead independent commands, and the Yankees took special delight in bagging Smith, who had routed Captain Hunter on January 1.

But, once again, the Gray Ghost had lived to fight another day. His report concluded, "In numerous other affairs with the enemy, between 75 and 100 horses and mules have been captured, about 40 men killed, wounded and captured. A party of this command also threw one of the enemy's trains off the track causing a great smash up."

Despite Loudoun Heights, Jeb Stuart still had nothing but praise for Mosby. He had been an outstanding leader for one year now, and should have "the evidence of the appreciation of his country," Stuart wrote, and "that evidence is promotion. If Major Mosby has not won it, no more can daring deeds essay to do it." But even before Stuart penned these words on February 9, the cogs of bureaucracy had been turning. Lee had recommended Mosby's promotion to lieutenant colonel, and War Secretary Seddon gave his stamp of approval on January 21. It seems ironic that the Yankee hero of the day, Major Cole, was also promoted to lieutenant colonel for his efforts in punishing Mosby at Loudoun Heights.

Seddon banned partisan units on February 17, 1864. In doing so, he was supported by Lee. "The evils resulting from their organization more than counterbalance the good they accomplish," he wrote. The exceptions from the banning, however, were those two units that had achieved notable legitimate success for the Confederate cause. One was Mosby's Rangers, and the other was McNeill's Rangers. John H. McNeill had moved from West Virginia to Missouri where he mustered a company of the pro-rebel Missouri State Guard. Imprisoned by the Federal authorities, he escaped and made his way back to Virginia where he raised an effective partisan band. He plagued the Baltimore and Ohio Railroad, and amongst other exploits burned the railway machine shops at Piedmont. Later in the year he would lead a raid on the railway bridge at Mt. Jackson, Virginia, and meet the same fate as his hero, Stonewall Jackson, mortally wounded by "friendly fire."[25]

Both Stuart and Lee wanted Mosby's command raised to regimental strength and integrated into the regular cavalry, but the Gray Ghost had other ideas. Mosby had a powerful ally in Seddon, who took great pleasure in reading his reports and admired his exploits. He wanted the guerrilla chief to stay out there in Mosby's Confederacy, bewildering the Yankees with his will-o-the-wisp, hit-and-run tactics. The demoralized Yankees could never feel safe behind their own lines, and were obliged to keep defensive troops in the rear.

"I am making an effort to have Colonel Mosby's battalion mustered into the regular service," Lee wrote on April 1, 1864. "If this cannot be done I recommend that his battalion be retained as partisans for the present. Lt. Colonel Mosby has done excellent service, & from the reports of citizens & others I am inclined to believe that he is strict in discipline & protection in the country in which he operates."

Shortly after Lee wrote these words, the stage play, *The Guerrilla, or, Mosby in Five-Hundred Sutler-Wagons*, opened in Alexandria.[26] Fighting a hit-and-run war was how Mosby had achieved his renown, and others were happy to make money exploiting the guerrilla's name.

At this time Herman Melville, the author of *Moby Dick*, spent three days with Lowell's 2nd Massachusetts Cavalry while out on a Mosby hunt. He later penned *The Scout Towards Aldie*, a 114-verse poem based on the ride, which read in part:

All spake of him, but few had seen
Except the maimed ones or the low:
Yet rumor made him every thing—
A farmer—woodman—refugee—
The man who crossed the field but now;
A spell about his life did cling—
Who to the ground shall Mosby bring?[27]

12

"I will kill you for being fools"
Quantrill and Anderson, 1864

Quantrill returned to Missouri during May of 1864, and riders spread word for his men to muster in Fayette County. Although General Brown had reversed Ewing's Order No. 11, Johnson County still suffered, and scorched chimneys were all that remained of many farms. And the 1200 men of Colonel Ford's 2nd Colorado Cavalry patrolled the area. They were spoiling for a fight with Quantrill or any other bushwhacker band.

But, along with an erosion of the old unity, friction between Todd and Quantrill was on the rise. As is so often the case, the junior officer desired command. And the war would not last forever. The split with Bill Anderson showed that Quantrill had lost his grip. Things came to a head in the Fayette County camp. Some accounts say it was over a card game when Quantrill accused Todd of cheating. Others say Todd pulled a gun on Quantrill, and others combine the two.[1] Whatever precisely happened, Quantrill and a handful of followers mounted up and rode out around the end of May 1864, leaving Todd in command. Kate King later recalled that she and Quantrill went into Howard County where they set up house in a tent with a separate kitchen attached. Here they "whiled away many hours beside the stove, planning the future."[2]

Throughout the summer men died on both sides as various guerrilla bands skirmished with troops, burned bridges, stole horses, plundered homes, and attacked steamboats. Orders were given that all pilot houses and engine rooms must be "ironclad" and pilots were paid $1,000 per safe trip from St. Louis to Leavenworth. But, unable to beat the menace, on July 13 General Brown called a halt to all river traffic "until further notice."

As the guerrillas wore captured blue uniforms, passwords and elaborate signals were devised by Brown to tell friend from foe. "The signal to be given and answered, where the nature of the ground will permit, before the parties have approached nearer than 300 to 350 yards." And on alternating days red or white strips were to be worn on hats and caps.[3]

Within a week of these orders being issued, Captain Seymour Wagner and seven troopers of the 2nd Colorado died when they were ambushed by Todd's men on the Independence-Glasgow Road. Todd placed his one wounded man in a captured stage coach and led his men back to the Sni Hills. Despite the victory, the bushwhackers were impressed with the performance of the Colorado men, hardy miners who had acquired fine mounts.

Bill Anderson was also on the prowl. Lexington newspapers urged civilians to arm themselves to resist guerrillas, and on July 7 Bill had a literate member of his gang write four letters to the editors under the Anderson name. "Listen to me, fellow citizens ... do not take up arms if you value your lives and property. It is not in my power to save your lives if you do. If you proclaim to be in arms against the guerrillas I will kill you. I will hunt you down like wolves and murder you. You cannot escape. It will not be the Federals after you. Your arms will be no protection to you.... I will kill you for being fools. Beware men, before taking this fearful leap." Anderson went on to justify himself, saying, "I lived in Kansas when this war commenced. Because I would not fight the people of Missouri, my native state, the Yankees sought my life, but failed to get me. Revenged themselves by murdering my father, destroying all my property, and have since that time murdered one of my sisters and kept the other two in jail for twelve months. But I have fully glutted my vengeance. I have killed many. I am a guerrilla."[4]

In a letter to Colonel James McFerran, Anderson criticized his lack of accuracy in reports and the marksmanship of his troops. He made an offer: "Send them out and I will train them for you."

Anderson took time out from dire threats for some humor in a brief letter to one adversary, Captain Milton Burris: "Burris, I love you: come and see me. Good-by, boy: don't get discouraged. I glory in your spunk, but damn your judgment."

Miss Anna Fickle of Warrensburg had been given three years behind bars for attempting to aid a bushwhacker's escape, and a soldier had been killed in the process. As before the Kansas City collapse, other women had been jailed for aiding guerrillas. Anderson addressed one letter to General Brown: "I do not like the idea of warring with women and children, but if you do not release all the women you have arrested in La Fayette County, I will hold the Union ladies in the country as hostages for them. I will tie them by the neck in the brush and starve them until they are released, if you do not release them. The ladies of Warrensburg must have Miss Fickle released. I hold them responsible for her speedy and safe return. General, do not think I am jesting with you. I will resort to abusing your ladies if you do not quit imprisoning ours." After demanding the release of a condemned male prisoner named Ervin, Anderson finished, "If he is killed, I will kill twenty times his number in Lexington. I am perfectly able to do so at any time. Yours, respectfully, W. Anderson Commanding Kansas First Guerrillas. (Editors will please publish this and other papers copy)."

Anderson never carried out his threats against women, and the letter to Brown was not published until it appeared in the *Official Records of the Union and Confederate Armies* more than 20 years later.[5] But on July 11 Anderson and Co. crossed into Carroll County where, in a four-hour spree, they murdered nine civilians. One victim made the mistake of cursing Anderson and had his throat cut instead of being mercifully shot.

William T. Anderson did his best to earn the nickname "Bloody Bill" (State Historical Society of Missouri).

Huntsville, Randolph County, had been Anderson's home town till eight years earlier when he moved to Kansas with his family. Just before dawn on July 15 Anderson arrived in town and let his men loose on a pillaging spree while he socialized with a few old friends. A salesman, George Damon, was seen to be wearing a U.S. Army belt. He made a bolt for freedom only to be wounded by gunfire as he ran. Anderson galloped down the street and shot him again he scaled a fence. Damon painfully crawled into a hotel dining room where the sobbing owner's wife pleaded with two bushwhackers not to finish him off. "We would shoot Jesus Christ or God Almighty himself if he ran from us," said one ruffian. But there was no need to waste a bullet, as Damon was already dead.

The rebels rode out with booty and $40,000 in cash from banks and shops. The command split up to baffle pursuit, Bill leading one party and his brother Jim the other. A Yankee patrol caught up with Bill, and a running fight followed for several miles. Plunder was dropped along the road, but Anderson kept a tight grip on the valise holding the money. With superior mounts, the rebels soon made their escape.

Anderson rode into Rocheport, a village beneath bluffs overlooking the Missouri River, where his men enjoyed the carousing hospitality of the pro-rebel locals. Passing steamboats were forced to turn back when used for target practice.

On July 23 Anderson struck Renick, to the north of Rocheport, with 65 men, looting and setting fire to the North Missouri Railroad depot. They then rode to Allan township (present-day Moberly) intent on seizing a train. The plan, however, was derailed when they encountered a 40-man Yankee detachment in town to take delivery of an arms shipment. Although taken by surprise, the bluecoats quickly barricaded the railway station with bales of hay and barrels of salt. The rebels "amused themselves during the 'siege' by shooting the horses [of] the militia ... of which animals they killed nine," reported the *Missouri Statesman*. A woman managed flag down the expected train before it pulled in at the station. The engineer reversed back to Sturgeon to take on guards, and then another train arrived in Allen carrying cargo Anderson had not counted on: Yankee troops. The telegraph operator had sent an urgent message when the rebels arrived. Shots were exchanged and the guerrillas beat a hasty retreat, leaving two dead men in the dust. Thirty-nine soldiers and civilians mounted up and gave chase. They killed another three bushwhackers and wounded several more, but the main body made their escape by dispersing through the scrub.

The telegraph wires sung with the news, and troops closed in to finish Anderson off—they hoped. The following day 55 soldiers and civilians rode along the Fayette Road. With the rebels having been dispersed, there was no real danger—so they thought. Then horsemen were seen ahead. With rebel yells they charged. Lieutenant Knapp ordered his men to dismount and form a line. The guerrillas opened fire and the untrained Yankee horses bucked and bolted amidst curses and confusion. While most Yankees fled into the woods, a few held their ground and delivered a volley. One guerrilla was killed, and another wounded—Anderson himself. The Yankees then fled leaving two dead on the road. Anderson's right-hand man, Archie Clement, dismounted and went to work with his scalping knife. Once finished, Anderson scrawled a note and pinned it to the collar of one victim: "YOU COME TO HUNT BUSH WHACKERS. NOW YOU ARE SKELPT. CLEMYENT SKELPT YOU. WM. ANDERSON."[6] At just over five feet tall and about 130 pounds, the 18-year-old Clement was commonly known as "Little Archie." But what Clement lacked in height, he made up for in ferocity.

Having shot 21 captured horses, the guerrillas rode north into Shelby County where the Hannibal and St. Joseph railway felt their wrath. Water tanks, depots, and the 150-foot Salt River Bridge went up in flames. Three days later Anderson was joined by brother Jim and gang, and they decided to visit the 72-year-old father of Lieutenant Colonel Denny, the Union garrison commander at Huntsville. The old man was strung up and let down from a gateway repeatedly while being whipped. They demanded money, but he refused to talk. A brief respite came when a small girl with tears in her eyes begged them to stop hurting her grandpa. She was bustled back inside the house and the torture resumed. Thinking the victim dead, the rebels rode off but, still breathing, he managed to crawl and stagger the two miles to Huntsville, the rope still about his neck.

Bill and Jim split off into two parties once more, and on July 31 Jim captured 32 young men and boys holding a religious service in a schoolhouse. They were marched to a Macon County church and questioned. Eight failed to declare their allegiance to the Bonny Blue Flag and found themselves stripped and whipped, but were allowed to live. If brother Bill had been around, that may well have not been the case.

The following day Bill's band of 11 men, led by two captives, stopped at the Mitchell farmhouse in southeast Carroll County. Anderson ordered four women present to prepare food for his men. As they relaxed after eating, there was a blast from outside and bullets ripped through the windows. A dozen civilians had followed their trail and opened fire with shotguns and rifles. Pellets slightly wounded two women and an infant, and only one rebel received a scratch. They took cover and blazed back with their revolvers. Amidst the mayhem, Mrs. Mitchell bolted from the house. Anderson brought her to the ground with a bullet to the shoulder when she refused to stop. Both the captive guides made a bid for freedom but one, taken for a rebel, was shot down and killed by his would-be rescuers. Realizing their firepower was no match for the rapidly firing Colts, the civilians turned tail and fled. The guerrilla leapt into their saddles and gave chase. John Kirker, fleeing, was thrown to the ground by a stumbling horse. Rebel John Maupin caught up, shot him, then jumped from his mount. Brandishing a Bowie knife, he ignored Kirker's scalp and hacked off his whole head. Maupin held it aloft as a trophy of a good night's work. All things considered, this would not have raised too many eyebrows within the murderous band. But shooting an unarmed, fleeing woman was another matter. "Well, it has got to come to that before long anyhow," Anderson replied when asked why he had broken the taboo.[7]

Anderson's gang went on, dressed in Federal uniforms, skirmishing, burning and killing. A father and son were shot down in their yard while engaged in conversion with apparently friendly Union troops. After stripping the bodies, the bushwhackers rode off with "the wailings of the murdered men's family in their ears," so the newspaper account read. A few miles down the track they encountered a young man riding a mule. Misled by their uniforms, he declared himself to be all for the Union. He was stripped and whipped before being tied, almost dead, behind his own mule. The animal was whacked in the expectation that it would bolt and drag the owner to his death. But it only took a few paces, then stopped. No amount of cursing and whacking would make the stubborn animal budge. The frustrated bushwhackers mounted up and rode away, no doubt thinking the mule would have to move off sooner or later in any case. But the victim got free and lived to tell the tale of how his stubborn, trusty mule saved his life.

Anderson made a 300-mile ride across Missouri skirmishing, burning buildings and shooting civilians. On August 20 *The Osage Chronicle* wrote, "The most heartless, cold blooded bushwhacking scoundrel that has operated in Missouri since the breaking out of the war is Bill Anderson. His acts are characterized by a fiendishness and diabolism, worthy of a devil incarnate. Quantrill, Todd, Thornton, Thrailkill, and others we might name have written their names high on the pages of infamy, but Bill Anderson overtops them all in crime…. Indiscriminate plunder and murder seem to be his mission, and as we trace his career it is impossible to find where he has exhibited the least trait of humanity. At Huntsville, Randolph County, he robbed friend and foe, and relentlessly shot down unoffending and unarmed citizens.... It is reported that a few days ago he took a Union man prisoner, and after torturing him in various ways, wound up by cutting off the nose and ears of his victim, after which he shot him to death, riddling his body with bullets.... We hope ere long to chronicle Bill Anderson's capture, when a punishment swift and terrible as he deserves should be dealt out to him."[8]

Military minds agreed. "Anderson is the worst of all, and he must be killed, or he will cause the death of every Union man he can find," wired General Clinton Fisk, commander of Missouri's North District. He ordered that a dedicated Anderson extermination party be put in the field.

But Anderson's notoriety had brought him a flood of recruits and he now had more than 100 men. This included seasoned bushwhacker Frank James. Accompanying Frank was his 16-year-old brother Jesse.[9] On August 13 General Fisk's Extermination Party, a mounted militia force of 150 men, followed a string of dead bodies left by Anderson in Carroll County. The following day the militia advance of 50 men paused to water their horses in Wakenda Creek. The rebel yell was heard, and howling guerrillas splashed through the shallows on their charging mounts. Revolvers banged and several Yankees fell from their saddles as the others beat a hasty retreat. The main Federal body, coming up behind, heard the firing and mistook their own retreating men for charging rebels. They opened fire and emptied more saddles. The Extermination Party lost about 15 killed while the guerrillas lost one killed, and Anderson was amongst several wounded once more. The most serious wound was sustained by Jesse James, struck in the chest with a pistol ball. Frank, grazed himself, left Jesse in the care of a rebel family. He made a full recovery, but bore the scar as a badge of honor for the rest of his life.

The skirmishes, burnings, and deaths continued as the Yankee troops failed to catch their pray. Major Matlock at Glasgow pointed out to General Fisk, "With our muskets we can well defend, but pursuit and attack is another thing."[10] The slow loading long-barreled muzzleloaders were a burden to cavalry who required repeating, short-barreled carbines and pistols for effective use in a running fight. The guerrillas finding out the identification signals used by Federals either from informers or prisoners added to the Yankee woes.

On August 28 a large mounted squad of the 4th Missouri State Militia crossed on the ferry from Boonville and set out on a guerrilla hunt. Two horsemen soon appeared on the Fayette Road and the Yankee commander, Captain Joseph Parke, took the bait. He ordered his men to pursue and they were greeted by a blast of lead as the concealed bushwhackers opened fire from the woods. The militiamen fled leaving seven wounded on the road. They were stripped of their uniforms, then the rebels went to work with their Bowie knives. One skinned and bleeding corpse was strung up and left dangling from a tree as an example. This is what happened to those who challenged Bloody Bill.

As more troops closed in, the band scattered through the nearby Perche Hills. Anderson led about 30 men to Rocheport once more where they got drunk and caroused with the locals. "My capitol," Anderson called the town. On August 30 the steamboat *Buffington* docked. The captain resisted a demand for surrender and was killed for his trouble. Anderson used the vessel to ferry his men for a raid across the river into Cooper County. He stayed in Rocheport for two weeks halting river traffic on the Missouri between Boonville and Jefferson City. Federal authorities decreed that the residents of Rocheport must pay $10,000 to the family of the murdered captain,[11] but Anderson devised revenue raising plans of his own. Those on outlying properties would pay a "contributory tax" to support the "king" of Rocheport in a manner befitting his rank. This tax was "altogether voluntary," according to one collector, providing you did not mind being shot or having your home reduced to ashes. On the drizzly morning of September 12, five of Anderson's tax men took refuge in the barn of a widow, Mrs. Turner, without posting a picket. Even Yankees had sense enough to stay under cover in this weather, it was assumed. But a determined Union patrol arrived in the farmyard, and a black servant was asked if he had seen any sign of guerrillas. A silently pointed finger gave the tax gatherers away. Seeing the Yankees closing in, two rebels charged out, Anderson style, pistols in hand. But first one and then the other fell in a blaze of musket fire. The other three fled into woods but were soon overtaken and shown the same mercy guerrillas meted out. Seven rebel horses were captured, some with scalps hanging from the bridles[12]

The news reached Rocheport later the same day. According to guerrilla Hemp Watts, Anderson was "pitiable to behold. Great tears coursed down his cheeks, his breast heaved, and his body shook with vehement agitation." If true, it seems probable Anderson took this as a personal affront—and no time was to be lost in revenge being sought.

The word went out for the band to muster once more. On the evening of September 23 a wagon train of 18 vehicles plodded along the road between Columbia and Fayette escorted by 80 men of the 3rd Missouri Militia. The rebel yell was heard as the guerrillas burst from the woods. Most of the militia fled while a dozen surrendered to the tender mercies of Bloody Bill. After being stripped of their uniforms, they were shot through the head along with three black teamsters. Most wagons were set ablaze, and the band dispersed into smaller groups to baffle pursuit. A squad of the 9th Missouri Cavalry, however, picked up the trail of one party numbering seven bushwhackers. They struck, killing and scalping six, but taking one man, Sergeant Cave Wyatt, prisoner, possibly for interrogation. This was another coup for the 9th Missouri, stationed in Fayette. This regiment had also killed Anderson's tax collectors at Turner's farm.

The Fayette Fiasco

Anderson resolved to teach the 9th Missouri and Fayette a lesson they would not forget. General Sterling Price was invading Missouri from Arkansas and wanted the guerrilla bands to disrupt the Yankee defense.[13] Old grievances were put aside as Anderson, George Todd, Tom Todd (no relation), John Thrailkill and other guerrilla leaders reunited with their bands to fight for the common good. "And to our delight," recalled John McCorkle, "Colonel Quantrell with his friends who had been with him in this country, came to us." With more than 400 gathered, this was the largest muster of guerrillas since Lawrence and Baxter Springs. A conference was held. Convinced of his own invincibility, Anderson wanted an immediate attack on Fayette. Fresh from recent successes, Todd had no qualms, but Quantrill was opposed. He had not forgotten the failed attacks at Fort Blair and Lamar the year before. "Here was a command of Federals under Colonel Reeves Leonard," recalled McCorkle, "who were fortified in the courthouse and the college building and on a hill southwest of the college. They had fortifications built of logs."[14] Even if the assault was successful, said Quantrill, how many men would the guerrillas lose?

"We are going into Fayette no matter what," said George Todd. "If you want to come along, all right. If not then you can go back into the woods with the rest of the cowards."[15]

Quantrill took his leave, but not back into the woods. He would stay close and assess events as they unfolded. Anderson volunteered his band to lead the assault, and at 10:30

the following morning, September 24, the citizens of Fayette took little notice as bluecoats rode up the main street towards the courthouse square. The town was defended by 150 men under Lieutenant S. S. Eaton, most of the garrison out guerrilla hunting. There had been warnings of a coming rebel attack but, as with Lawrence, this was not unusual and had been ignored.

But then a shot rang out. People looked around to see a black man wearing a military jacket fall into the street. Chaos followed as the rebels charged and civilians and soldiers ran for cover. "We dashed into the town up the street leading from the graveyard to the court house square," recalled McCorkle, "and when we reached the corner of the square, we turned west one block, then turned south a block, then back again, all of us riding at the top of our speed and were passing down a side street when the Federals from the court house poured a perfect volley into us."[16] Men dropped from their saddles, and McCorkle led a wounded friend out of harm's way. "I there found Colonel Quantrell with Jim Little, who had received a bad wound in the right arm." McCorkle turned to continue the fight, but Quantrill said, "Come on back. There's no use in trying to shoot through brick walls and logs with pistols."[17]

"We charged up to a blockhouse made of railway ties filled with port holes and then charged back down again," recalled Frank James. "The blockhouse was filled with Federal troops and it was like charging a stone wall only this stone wall belched forth lead."[18] Hemp Watts' faith in Anderson and Todd took a severe blow: "Leading men, armed only with revolvers, charging an invisible enemy in block-house, to simply imbed bullets in logs, with no possible chance to either kill or inflict injury on the foe, was both stupid and reckless."[19] Some rebels did make it to the walls and start fires, but it was futile. They all fell back to a ravine to regroup and lick their wounds. They feigned another charge to draw fire while wounded men were retrieved.

Fayette fell silent as the defeated rebels formed up and moved out leaving a trail of blood from wounded men. They had just learned what happens when bushwhackers give up bushwhacking and try to fight like regular troops without artillery support. Thirteen guerrillas had been killed outright and 30 wounded, some of whom would die later that night. The Yankees had lost only one killed, a man caught in the open, and two wounded. But Anderson was not ready to accept blame. Where was Quantrill? He had taken the wounded Jim Little to Boon's Lick township to seek medical treatment. It must be Quantrill's fault for hanging back, Anderson decided. He demanded that his old chief be brought in and shot. But the men knew he was not at fault and refused. Todd then said he would kill Quantrill, but his men said it may be he who ended up dead, and calmed him down.

That night the bushwhackers camped about ten miles from Fayette and next day continued on past Huntsville. Anderson dispatched a farmer with a demand for the town's surrender. The commander, Lieutenant Colonel Denny, was the son of the 72-year-old man strung up and whipped by Anderson's men. "Tell them to come in and get us if they want us," was Denny's reply. "Captain Anderson wanted to go in and attack them," recalled McCorkle, "but Captain Todd, who was in command, refused, saying he had enough experience in trying to shoot through brick walls with pistols."

As these events unfolded, Union soldiers on furlough from the Atlanta campaign in Georgia were many miles away, traveling north by train. "A feeling of disquietude, of restlessness, a something indescribable yet surely felt and almost seen, harassed my mind," recalled Sergeant Thomas Goodman of the First Missouri Engineers. "I arose, let down the car window, and looked out upon the somber shadows, chasing each other with lightning speed, as onward moved the train."[20]

Centralia

Three days following the Fayette fiasco, September 27, Anderson and his band of 80 men rode into Centralia, a small town on the North Missouri Railroad. George Todd and his men, about 120, remained behind in camp. Apart from supplies, Anderson wanted word of how Old Pap's Missouri invasion was coming along. William Tecumseh Sherman had captured Atlanta on September 2, but if Price could take St. Louis, sagging Confederate spirits may well receive a boost.

The guerrillas dismounted and immediately began looting Centralia's two small stores and the railroad warehouse. Among other spoils they found four crates of very useful boots, and to their delight a large barrel of whiskey. In no time at all the precious liquid was refreshing parched throats.

The Columbia stage rattled into town at 11 o'clock, the passengers horrified to see drunken guerrillas on all sides. The door was pulled open. Were any Union soldiers on board? There were none, but three men were Union delegates to a Democratic Congressional Convention in Mexico township, Missouri. Claiming to be Southern men, they provided false names. They watched in trepidation as their luggage was searched. Documents, if read, would reveal their true identities. But the search was interrupted. "The train! The Train! Yonder comes the train." All looked down the track to see the huffing smoke of an approaching locomotive, small Union flags on either side of the headlamp. It pulled three passenger coaches, a freight car and a baggage car on their scheduled run from St. Louis to St. Joseph.

Engineer James Clark was not concerned with the sight of troops ahead. They were wearing blue uniforms. But then he saw ties being thrown across the tracks. Guerrillas were known to wear Yankee blue. Instead of slowing down, he opened the throttle to crash straight through the barrier. But at the same time, the brakemen set the carriage brakes to stop. Despite the open throttle, the train slowed as it moved into the station, the wheels slipping on the rails, and "we were inside a line of blazing, murderous weapons," recalled Sergeant Goodman, "and volley after volley was poured into the train, until we came to a dead stop." But with the brakes hard on, the screeching wheels of the stationary engine were still turning, slipping on the track. Some rebels kept shooting until, "seeing they had me foul," recalled Engineer Clark, "I raised up and shut off the throttle and dropped on the deck again. In a short while half a dozen men surrounded me and my fireman, demanding our money, watches and valuables. The fireman was shot in the breast but it was a flash wound, though the blood was running freely. He said, 'For God's sake do not kill us.' Some one said, 'We do not want to hurt any of you men, but consider yourselves prisoners under orders.' This relieved us greatly."[21]

Back in a passenger car, "scarcely had the motion of the train ceased, ere with yells and shouts the guerrillas, in a body, rushed towards the cars," recalled Goodman. The door was burst open "and in crowded our grim, fierce captors, shouting 'Surrender! Surrender!' You shall be treated as prisoners of war."

"We can only surrender," replied one man. "We are totally unarmed."

In an instant the "the olive branch of peace" was withdrawn, and the guerrillas "became the lawless free-booters, the inhuman monsters, Rumor had always designated them." Each man was robbed at gunpoint, "not one man escaped, so systematic was their plan, and so eager their greed for plunder," recalled Goodman.[22] All the other passengers, including women and children, received the same treatment.

Twenty-three uniformed Federal soldiers were shoved from the train, along with a

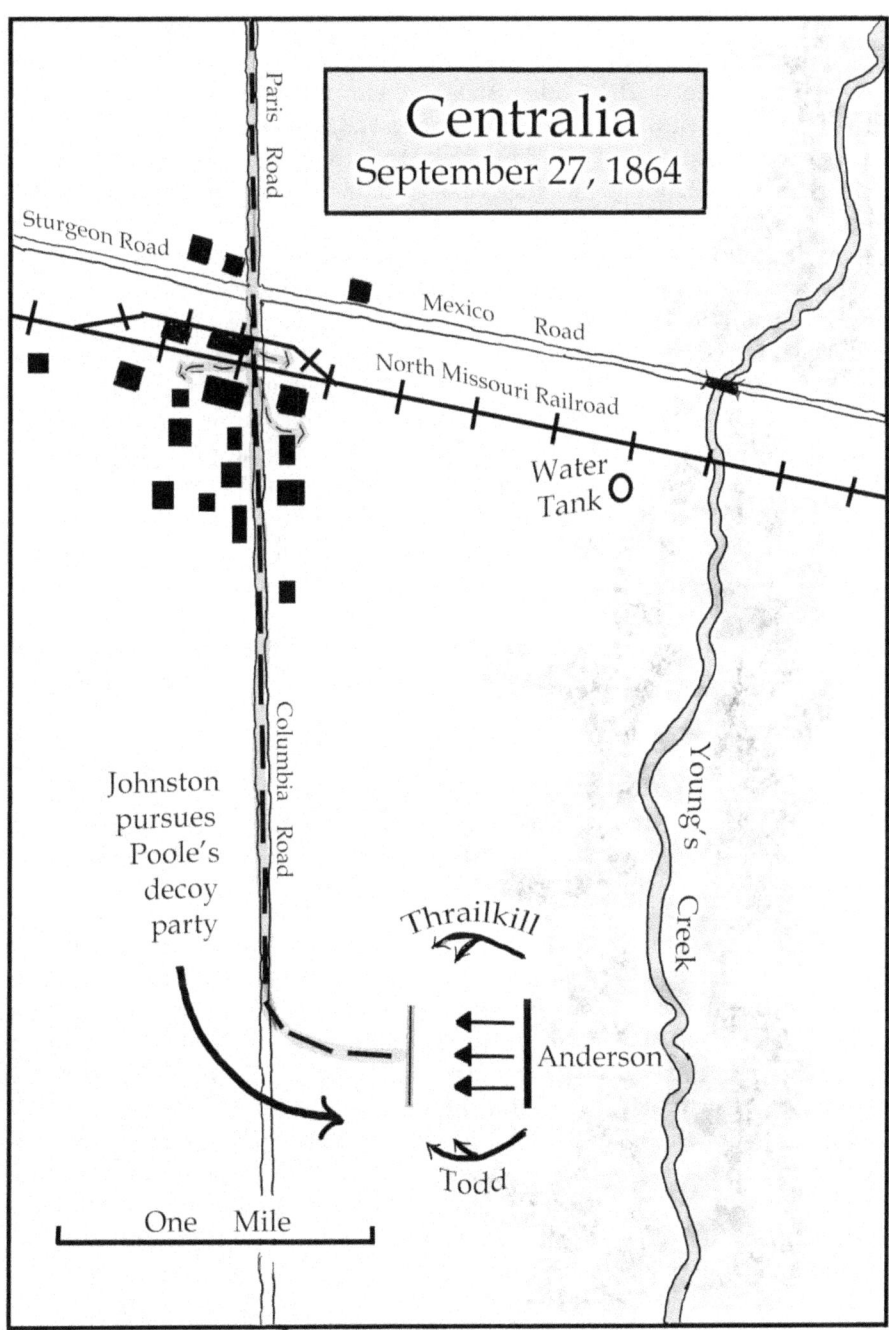

Centralia, September 27, 1864 (author's rendition).

German unfortunate enough to be wearing a blue shirt. Having little command of English, he could not correct the mistake. But guerrillas tended to shoot "Dutch" prisoners, as they called Germans, in any case. The other passengers were also ordered off, and they clustered in small, frightened groups near the tracks. A few civilians stayed behind, hiding beneath the seats. As the robbers took valuables from the passengers, one affluent looking gent handed over only a few dollars. He was warned that he would be searched and, if hiding anything, killed. He pulled off a boot and retrieved $100. But it was too late. Bloody Bill shot him where he stood. His mother, standing with the other passengers, screamed in anguish as other women and children burst into tears. One bushwhacker recognized a man who had once testified against him in a trial. He fired at him and missed, and the man ducked into the crowd. But he was dragged out and the second shot left him crumpled by the tracks.[23]

Bill Anderson and Frank James forced a railway employee to hand over the keys to the safe in the express car. Once opened, the rebels found themselves richer by $3,000. But a bigger haul was discovered when they ransacked the baggage car, one trunk yielding $10,000. The soldiers, meanwhile, had been forced to strip off their uniforms and stood in their underwear. They were ordered to move and line up, but two men refused and called for the others to do the same. Anderson shot them both and they fell between railway cars. He had a quick conference with Archie Clement who suggested keeping some men to exchange for Cave Wyatt, captured before the Fayette fiasco. But Anderson thought one man of equal rank would do. He looked along the line. "Boys," he said, "do you have a sergeant in your ranks?" No one answered. Again he asked. Once more, all remained silent. The question was asked a third time. "If there is one, let him step aside?" Goodman saw the man who had taken his coat, adorned with sergeant's stripes, move towards Anderson. "Almost involuntarily," recalled Goodman, "I moved beyond the rank, still wondering what could be his purpose." Anderson directed two men to take Goodman to one side.

> I had scarcely stopped in the position assigned me, when a volley from the revolvers of the guerrillas in front, a demonic yell from those surrounding, mingled with the cries and moans of pain and distress from my comrades smote upon my ear. I turned, and, God of Heaven, what a sight I beheld!
> The line had disappeared. Many of my late comrades lay dead upon the ground; others were groaning in the agony of their wounds, and yet others, wounded and suffering, were making a last struggle for existence in seeking to avoid further injury.[24]

Sergeant Valentine Peters, a large 24-year-old of great strength, though badly wounded, managed to knock a number of the murderers down. He broke through the line and crawled beneath the station house. But, not to be outdone, the guerrillas immediately set the structure on fire. They would kill Peters, one way or another. The intense heat soon forced him into the open, but he was still not done. Brandishing a piece of firewood, he knocked down two men before being brought down in a shower of bullets.

The first blast of gunfire had not killed all the victims, and wounded men staggered about, bleeding from their wounds. Sergeant Goodson watched in horror. "The yells and horrid curses of the wretches intermingled with the piteous moans of my suffering, wounded comrades and now and then I could hear the dull thud of the carbine stroke that ended forever the suffering of some prostate form." Goodman came close to be shot himself, his guards having to fend off several threats.

The guerrillas set fire to the railway coaches and a local man, Thomas Sneed, dashed on board to warn a woman with three children hiding beneath a seat. But she was so frozen with terror it took repeated urgings to have her move her brood away from the spreading flames.

The railway crew were ordered to pull the ties from across the tracks, and the engineer to start the train. He jumped from the cab as it steamed away, and the metal monster sped down the line with the carriages ablaze and the whistle, set open, screaming. It traveled over three miles before losing steam and coming to a grinding halt in a swirl of fire and smoke.

At the burning station, meanwhile, "the flames roared and flashed about this scene of blood," recalled Goodman, "and the dense, black cloud of smoke hung around the spot, as though to hide it from the light of day. The guerrillas, with horrid oaths and wild, fierce looks, gloated over the bodies of the slain, or spurned them from their path with brutal violence. Civilians stood trembling by, eager perhaps to express their sympathy for the dead in words and tears, but fear of a like fate forbade." Goodman, still clad in underwear, was told to mount a mule. Anderson warned the civilians not to move the bodies or extinguish the flames, and ordered his men to mount up.

"Can we go on with our trip?" a woman asked. Perhaps she was so horror-struck with the bloodbath insanity had set in.

"Go to hell for all I care," was Anderson's response.

Carrying stolen boots filled with whiskey slung over their mounts, the bushwhackers cheered and laughed as they formed up and began to ride out of town. But then more smoke was seen approaching, a railway maintenance train. Anderson and most of his cohorts continued back to camp, but others turned back to form a welcoming committee. The rebels halted the train just short of the burning depot and proceeded to rob the engineer, fireman and crew. Then the protesting engineer was forced at gun point to run his locomotive over a corpse thrown across the tracks. The dead soldier's legs were sliced off at the knees, the impact forcing the front wheels from the tracks.[25] More black smoke billowed skyward as the tender and caboose were set ablaze, then the remaining rebels followed Anderson back to camp. Behind them, bewildered men, women and children looked on in horror at the blood-soaked ground strewn with corpses amidst the smoke from the burning train, station and warehouse.

Anderson arrived back in camp and boasted to Todd of his day's achievements. But, according to John McCorkle, "Captain Todd severely reprimanded Anderson for doing it, telling him he did not endorse such actions." Considering Todd's own track record, boasting of having killed 17 men in Lawrence, this appears hard to believe—unless said as a joke.

In camp, Sergeant Goodman looked closely at his captor and left the following vivid description: "William T. Anderson, the leader of the most blood-thirsty and inhuman gang of wretches that ever infested Missouri, was a man of about five feet, ten inches in height; round and compact in form, slender in person, quick and lithe in action as a tiger—whose nature he at times possessed. His complexion naturally was soft and very fair, but had taken a tinge of brown from his exposed manner of life. His face was in no sense attractive or winning, neither was it repulsive." His eyes were "a strange mixture of blue and gray, the opposing colors sustained by opposing forces, in the war he waged. They were cold, unsympathizing and expressionless, never firing in anger or lighting with enthusiasm in battle.... His hair was his greatest ornament, and hung in thick, clustering masses about his head and neck; in color, a rich dark brown." His clothes "seemed to blend something of taste, something of roughness, and much that was indicative of his inclinations and pursuits, in its ornament and the fabric of which it was composed. To be never called 'unarmed' was his great pride and care, one would suppose; for, see him when and where you might, a brace or so of revolvers were stuck in his belt."[26]

"In the afternoon," John McCorkle recalled, "our pickets came in and reported that there was a command of Federals coming with a black flag hoisted. Captain Todd ordered Dave Poole to go out and see who they were."[27] The new arrivals were a detachment of the 39th Missouri Volunteers. Although infantry, commanding officer Major Andrew Vern Emen "Ave" Johnston had procured a variety of mounts including ageing plough horses and mules. Johnston was a former schoolteacher and "Christian gentleman" of impeccable character who had gained respect for his successful pursuit of guerrillas in the past. Those under his command today, however, were mainly green volunteers armed with muzzle-loading Enfield rifles and bayonets—no revolvers. Attracted by the rising smoke, Johnston rode into Centralia where he surveyed the carnage and dead bodies with disgust. Anderson had about 80 men, he was told, but many more were out there in camp, perhaps as many as 400, twice the real number. But Johnston, appalled by the slaughter, allowed passion to overcome common sense. He insisted that his rifles would have the advantage over pistols at a distance, and he was going to fight the murderers, come what may. He climbed to the hotel attic and saw a small band of guerrillas not far down the Columbia Road. Despite being warned not to attempt battle with the savage bushwhackers, Johnston rode out at the head of 125 men. His wagons, teamsters and Captain Adam Theiss with 33 men were left in town, and a courier rode for Sturgeon to bring reinforcements.

As Johnson approached, Dave Poole and ten men paused to fire a few shots now and then. The major, impassioned by his desire for revenge, took the bait. A rebel scout, meanwhile, galloped back to camp with the news. The guerrillas mounted up and rode out. Johnston pressed ahead, his men having to be ordered not to break formation in their eagerness to catch the decoys. On the other side of a rise the main body of rebels prepared for combat, scouts keeping them informed of Johnston's advance. "Detaching Todd and some hundred and twenty-five men," recalled Goodman, "he divided his force; sending Todd with half their number (62 men) by the left, around the south side of an old field, skirted by brush and scattered timber. The remaining half, led by Thrailkill, marched by the right." Johnston's command edged slowly forward. They topped a rise and saw a broad, gently sloping field lined with woods on the opposite side. From the trees emerged a line of mounted bushwhackers making a slow advance. There appeared to be only about 80, a number the Johnston felt he could handle. The rebels dismounted to check weapons, discard blue coats, and tighten saddle girths. They remounted, obviously preparing to charge.

Johnston's men were mounted infantry, not cavalry, and he correctly ordered them to dismount, fix bayonets, and prepare to fight on foot. Stories are told of the guerrillas being surprised by this—most unlikely. The well-known fact was that an infantryman on horseback with a long Enfield musket was virtually useless. He had to dismount to take steady aim, fire, and reload. Johnston sent 23 men to the rear to hold the horses while the remaining 90 formed the battle line, standard procedure.

The two sides remained motionless for a few minutes, and Johnston rode foreword. "We are ready! Come on!" he yelled.

Anderson rode along his line. "Boys, when we charge, break through their line and keep straight on for their horses. Keep straight on for their horses."[28] He rode to the front and signaled to the flanking commands by waving his hat three times. With a nudge of spurs, the guerrillas made a steady advance, pistols in hand. Johnston watched them, waiting for the right moment. A direct volley once they were in range should reap a substantial harvest of rebels and horses. But the captive Sergeant Goodman saw the full picture: "I knew at a glance the battle was already won by the guerrillas," he recalled.[29] "The cry 'charge!' broke shrill and clear from the lips of their leader, and with one, long, wild shout, the guerrillas dashed forward at the full run upon the little line of dismounted Federals in the field. At the same moment both Todd and Thrailkill, their men yelling like so many fiends, appeared on either flank." Rattled to find themselves under attack from three sides, the Yankees fired an awkward volley. But only a few rebels dropped from their saddles and some bluecoats, terrorized by the sight and sound of 200 screaming bushwhackers, simply froze, unable to pull the trigger. Those soldiers who had fired frantically thrust ramrods down barrels in an attempt to reload, but in the next few seconds the rebels were riding through their ranks, firing left and right, and heading for the Yankee horses as ordered. The horse holders, abandoning their charges, turned and galloped off. Most were overtaken and cut down. Other guerrillas rode amidst the dismounted bluecoats. "Some of the Yankees were at 'fix bayonets,'" recalled Frank James, "some were biting off their cartridges, preparing to reload. Yelling, shooting our pistols upon them we went."[30] Major Johnston, his horse killed, held his ground, firing his pistol, till a lethal enemy bullet brought him down. Frank James later claimed that brother Jesse was responsible, but doubt remains that Jesse was even there.

"Surrender! Surrender!" the Confederates cried amidst a haze of gun smoke. The soldiers dropped their muskets and raised their hands. The rebels stopped shooting and closed in. "No sooner was this accomplished than Hell was suddenly transferred to earth," recalled Goodman, "and all the fiends of darkness summoned to join the carnival of blood. Centralia, with all its horrors, was eclipsed here in the enormity and infamous conduct of the bloody demons!"

The surrendered men were shown no mercy, executed with pistol shots to the head. The bushwhackers dismounted and stripped the bodies before carving them up with Bowie knives.

Lieutenant Thomas Jaynes, having survived the carnage, galloped into Centralia. "Get out of here, get out of here!" he shouted to the remaining troops. "Every one of you will be killed if you don't." Most bolted, but not all. They probably realized their horses and mules would be no match for the fine rebel mounts in a race for life. They sought hiding places in town only to be dragged out and shot once the bushwhackers arrived. Alcohol stores were ransacked again, and a few women were given a rough time, knocked down or pistol whipped, when confronting the drunks. Most bluecoats galloping for Sturgeon were overtaken and killed along the way, but others rode in to tell the horrific tale.

That night the townsfolk of Centralia groaned and women wept again. Another horrific massacre had taken place while the bodies of the murdered soldiers still lay around. The following day Union reinforcements arrived in town. Lieutenant Colonel Daniel Draper telegraphed the battle site as "a scene of murder and outrage at which the heart sickens. Most of them were beaten over the head, seventeen of them were scalped, and one man had his privates cut off and placed in his mouth. Every man was shot in the head. One man had his nose cut off."[31] Goodman's account also stated that men were beheaded but, if so, Draper made no mention of this. Civilians were given the task of burying the dead on Johnston's field. On arrival, they were surprised when one badly wounded man staggered to his feet. Taken back to town, he died later that night. Most bodies were buried in a trench near the railroad track, but four were shipped east for family burial.[32] In 1873 the bodies at Centralia were reinterred in Jefferson City. It was reported that every skull revealed a bullet hole in the forehead between the eyes. The exact number of dead is not known, some soldiers being unaccounted for, but it would appear that 23 had been killed when the train was captured, and 123 had been killed during the following slaughter. With three civilians shot, a total of 149 dead. Only three guerrillas were killed, and some wounded by bayonets who were treated by Dr. Sneed at Anderson's demand following the fight.

"The land will be swarming with blue-coats by tomorrow eve," one guard told Goodman back in camp. As was usual, the guerrillas decided to split up to confuse pursuit. Todd and Anderson camped several miles apart in preparation for marching separately the following day. Anderson's men were allowed three hours sleep before riding out, Goodman still a prisoner. "Their march was conducted in a manner peculiar to their discipline, yet with much more order and *empressement* than I had anticipated," he recalled. Over the next few days the guerrillas carried out night marches to the southwest, Goodman now clad in old coat discarded by Anderson.

But the Yankees were out for blood, and the rebels skirmished with pursuing bluecoats before rejoining Todd's band a few days later. After a night of drunken revelry, "like so many savages," during which Anderson, "rode wildly through the crowd; firing his revolvers indiscriminately, and yelling like one possessed," recalled Goodman.[33] The decision was made to split into smaller squads to avoid further pursuit, and a mustering point was selected near Boonville, on the Missouri River. Anderson, with Goodman still in tow, set out. With a small party, they were able to travel during daylight hours. When near Anderson's "capitol," Rocheport, where, "we could witness the burning of part of the town, which had been fired by a detachment of federal cavalry," recalled Goodman. The troops had just been out on an Anderson hunt.

After 10 days of captivity, October 6, Goodman seized his chance. The guerrillas, preoccupied with getting skittish horses to swim the Missouri, dropped their guard. The captive slipped into a group of waiting men and, clad like a guerrilla himself, "I passed carelessly through the crowd and emerged near a dense mass of bushes and brush-wood on the river side." He entered the brush and kept walking until well clear. "I now paused for a few moments and sought out the North Star as a guide on my course." Next day he sought refuge in a barn, slept soundly, and continued his journey that night. Exhausted and famished, he encountered a man at dawn who delivered joyous news; the Union garrison in Fayette was only one mile down the road. He soon saw pickets "dressed in the 'bonnie blue' of my beloved country's uniform." The sole survivor of the Centralia Massacre soon walked into the hands of the Ninth Missouri Cavalry. "I ever shall remember these boys with the kindliest of feelings and lasting gratitude."[34]

13

"Wipe Blazer out"
Mosby, 1864

February 22, 1864. A battalion of 150 Yankees under Captain James Reed rode up the Alexandria turnpike. In the distance, the rumble of heavy guns could be heard from the forts around Washington. But no battle raged; the salvos were fired in honor of George Washington's birthday. The nation's first president had been a Virginian who owned slaves. But he had willed for his slaves to be freed when he died, a good indication he knew all was not rosy with the South's "peculiar institution." Some firing those guns must have wondered what flag George Washington would have fought under were he alive today.

Three videttes rode in advance of Captain Reed's 25-man advance guard. No doubt Reed realized they were in the vicinity Miskel's Farm, the place where Mosby had scored his victory on April Fool's Day the preceding year. The videttes paused when three men, clad in blue overcoats, appeared to their front. "Who are you? What command do you belong to?" a Yankee asked the strangers.

"Fifth New York Cavalry. What command do you belong to?"

"We are the California Battalion, but believe you are Mosby's Men. If you are not, advance and make yourself known."

"If you are the California Battalion, advance and make yourself known, but we believe you are Mosby's men."

"I'll find out damn quick who you are," replied the Yankee, and raised his carbine.

"There was an unnatural, an unearthly stillness around us at that moment," recalled rebel James Williamson, "a stillness which seemed to creep over our flesh like a chill, and to be seen and felt; when out of this ghostly silence there came that shrill, warning signal, like the fierce, wild shriek of the wind rushing through the trees of the forest, giving warning of the coming storm."[1]

The shrill, wild shriek came from a whistle blown by John Mosby. Why carry a 'horn" when a whistle will do? A blast of carbine fire erupted from the undergrowth, and Yankees in the advance guard dropped from their saddles. Captain Reed halted the main body some distance behind, and rapped out orders. But then the dreaded rebel yell was heard as gray-clad horsemen, led by Mosby, charged from the woods. Then others under Captain William Chapman charged the Yankee right flank. Guns cracked and men cursed as the horsemen clashed in a swirl of gunsmoke. A scarlet lined cape, plumed hat and flashing saber were seen amidst the turmoil. It must be Mosby, the Yankees thought. But it was Baron Robert Von Massow, a Prussian out for adventure with Mosby's Rangers. Captain Reed shot him from his horse, but a moment later fell himself, shot and killed by Chapman.

Mosby, meanwhile, fought on. He was unscathed, but his horse had received two wounds. The rebels, with 160 men, slightly outnumbered the surprised bluecoats who had little chance against the onslaught. A fence alongside the road was smashed down as they fell back and scattered, retreating into the pines and back down the road leaving dead and dying on the ground. Some threw down their arms and surrendered before they met the same fate. Once the smoke cleared, there were ten dead Yankees, seven wounded, and 70 captured, while Mosby had one dead and five badly wounded. This included Von Massow, who survived to return to Europe and fight in the Austro-Prussian War of 1866.[2]

Mosby received praise from Stuart and Lee again, but in Washington, D.C., meanwhile, significant changes were under way. Ulysses S. Grant was promoted to lieutenant general, a supreme rank last held by George Washington. Grant was now general-in-chief. This followed his successes at Fort Donelson, Shiloh, Vicksburg, and Chattanooga. When rumors surfaced of him having been drunk at Shiloh, Old Abe was not deterred. "I can't spare this man, he fights," he said. Grant came east to command the war's direction from his headquarters with of the Army of the Potomac, still nominally commanded by George Meade. Lincoln felt Meade had not pressed the rebels after his victory at Gettysburg, thus losing a prime chance to crush the Confederacy once and for all. William T. Sherman was given Grant's former command of the western armies, and Philip Sheridan came east to take charge of the Union cavalry. It had taken nearly three years, but Lincoln now had his three best generals, Grant, Sherman and Sheridan, in a position where they could do the rebels most harm.[3]

The Confederacy had suffered serious setbacks. Rations had been short through a long, cold winter, and Jefferson Davis was having trouble keeping enough troops in the field. Those men whose three-year enlistments were about to expire were ordered to remain with their units, and the age of those eligible for the draft was increased. The Confederacy had been the first American government to introduce conscription in 1862, originally from 18 to 35 years of age, then 18 to 45, and in February of 1864, 17 to 50. Despite these measures, the Confederacy could only muster half the Yankee numbers. But not all these blueclad troops could be brought to front line battle. As the Yankees advanced, they were obliged to detach troops to police thousands of square miles of conquered territory. And strikes by rebel cavalry leaders, like Mosby, required the deployment of thousands to protect rail and communication lines. Despite Gettysburg and Vicksburg, and the shortage of food and adequate clothing, the morale of Lee's troops remained high. "If victorious," said Lee, "we have everything to hope for in the future. If defeated, nothing will be left for us to live for." Many veterans reenlisted even before the deadline of February 17, 1864, the same day the Partisan Ranger Act was repealed.[4]

The Yankees, on the other hand, did not demand their three-year men stay with the army, seeing the original contract as ironclad. But they wanted these veterans to reenlist, and cajoled them with inducements: a special chevron for their sleeves, a $400 Federal bounty in addition to state bounties, and a 30-day furlough. "If they can't kill you in three years they want you for three more," said one man, "but I will stay." Some 136,000 veterans reenlisted, augmented by fresh recruits. The Union had introduced its own Conscription Act on March 3, 1863, and there was no shortage of black men who wished to fight.

Grant devised his grand strategy for the spring offensive of 1864. This must win the war. His reputation and future depended on it; there was no going back. The plan called for Sherman to advance from Chattanooga towards Atlanta, a vital railroad and communication center in Georgia. In the east, the Army of the Potomac would cross the Rapidan River in a push towards Richmond, while General Ben Butler's Army of the James would moved towards the same goal from the south. General Franz Sigel would march from West Virginia southwards through the fertile Shenandoah Valley and destroy the farms providing the enemy with food.

Confronting this, Lee had to play a guessing game. His future strategy was obscure due to conflicting assessments of the enemy's next move. And even the Gray Ghost was not infallible, some information he provided proving to be off the mark.[5] But on April 30 he sent word to Lee that Yankee troops under General Burnside had passed from Alexandria through Centreville two days earlier. This was correct, and could only mean that they were not sailing south for a seaborne assault on Richmond, as had McClellan in 1862. Burnside would join up with Grant in preparation for a major offensive across the Rapidan into the wild, wooded area known as the Wilderness.

Mosby's command grew to over 200 men, and he formed companies for independent operation. The loss of Turner and Smith had been a blow, but other natural leaders came to the fore, men like William Chapman, Adolphus "Dolly" Richards and Richard Montjoy.

German-born Union General Franz Sigel had a Teutonic desire for rigid discipline and order. But, "The Flying Dutchman," as he was called by the rebels, ultimately failed to fly. The operation of unorthodox guerrilla bands did not fit his view of the military world, and it would appear that he chose to pretend they did not exist. On April 29 he left Martinsburg with 9000 men for the Shenandoah Valley, but he left scant resources behind to defend the vital Baltimore & Ohio Railroad and his horse drawn supply trains. Over the next few weeks about 1000 rebel horsemen struck his flanks and rear. This included not only Mosby's and McNeill's Rangers, but also men under former partisan leaders Gilmore, Imboden and White.[6] Their commands had been absorbed into the regular cavalry, but now harassed Sigel in guerrilla-like mode. Sigel was forced to deploy 1650 of his cavalry to chase guerrillas through woods and ravines. Mosby struck Martinsburg, and 800 cavalry were redeployed to defend the Yankee home base.

"Captain Richards had a skirmish near Winchester in which several of them were killed and wounded," Mosby reported, and "Captain Chapman attacked a wagon train, which was heavily guarded, near Strasburg, capturing about 30 prisoners with an equal number of horses, etc. Near Belle Plain, in King George, I captured an ambulance train and brought off 75 horses and mules, and 40 prisoners, etc. ... about May 10, I attacked a cavalry outpost in the vicinity of Front Royal, capturing 1 captain and 15 men and 75 horses and sustained no loss."[7]

Sigel was perplexed. "My forces are insufficient for offensive operations in this country," he telegraphed from Woodstock on May 13. "The enemy is continually on my flank and rear ... have sent out parties in every direction. Skirmishing is going on every day."[8]

Two days later a disillusioned Sigel met the Confederate army of General John C. Breckinridge at the small village of New Market. Breckinridge had hastily mustered a force of about 5000 troops, including young cadets from the Virginia Military Institute. The following battle saw Sigel beaten back, burning a bridge to prevent pursuit. Grant was most displeased. "There will be no turning back," he had told Lincoln.[9] Sigel was replaced with 61-year-old David Hunter, a hard-fighting West Point man who had been wounded at First Bull Run. Hunter was a no-nonsense man who wore a permanent scowl, and had no time for pomposity or needless show. He wore a faded linen coat, army issue shoes, and an old slouch hat with ventilation holes to vent his steam. The ardent abolitionist had been the first to bring black soldiers into Union ranks. If captured, Hunter was to be executed, Jefferson Davis decreed.

Mosby's friend and mentor Jeb Stuart had a "physical endurance which seemed to defy all natural laws," Mosby recalled.¹⁰ But crushing news arrived that must have pierced Mosby's heart; Stuart had been killed.

Previously, Ulysses S. Grant had crossed the Rapidan and fought Lee in the Wilderness on May 4–7, 1864. And once again 'Bobby" Lee had inflicted massive casualties and blocked the Yankee advance. The new lieutenant general, it would seem, would have to limp back north, no more successful than his predecessors. But to the delight of both officers and men, instead of turning left, Grant gave the order to turn right. There would be no going back. He continued marching south. Lee scrambled to cut Grant off, and the two clashed once more at Spotsylvania Court House on May 8–21. While this battle raged, Grant dispatched Sheridan's cavalry to bypass Lee and strike straight for Richmond. They met Jeb Stuart's outnumbered cavalry at Yellow Tavern on May 11. In the following clash Stuart was mortally wounded by a pistol shot from a dismounted cavalryman of George Armstrong Custer's Wolverines. Sheridan won the day, and could have pressed on to capture Richmond. But such a capture would have been brief. A closing net of rebel forces forced his retreat.¹¹ The flamboyant Jeb Stuart died of his wound the next day, and part of the Old South died with him. Both men and women alike wept for their fallen "beau sabreur."

General David Hunter earned the nickname "Black Dave" for his incendiary activities down South (Library of Congress).

But John Mosby was still very much alive. If anything Stuart's death hardened his resolve to inflict as much damage on the Yankee invader as possible. But David Hunter, called "Black Dave" by his men, still pushed along the Shenandoah Valley leaving smoking ruins in his wake. On May 21 Mosby and 103 Rangers crossed the Shenandoah River in skiffs while their horses swam the swift current. Hunter had stationed 150 men of the 15th New York Cavalry on Guard Hill. But 30 men were posted as pickets in a pine grove half a mile away: a tempting target for the Gray Ghost. Having scouted their position, William Chapman sent 15 dismounted Rangers charging through the trees, shooting and venting wild rebel yells as though the whole Confederate army was following them. Mounted Rangers followed, and they swept into the camp as most of the Yankees fled on foot. Captain Michael Auer, billeted a short distance away, galloped into the chaos. Not realizing the camp was under attack, he demanded to know what the fuss was about. "Mosby has got you," he was told. "Well, this beats hell, don't it?" he said.¹² Three months earlier, he had been wounded in a skirmish with Mosby near Upperville. Now captured, his future looked bleak: an indefinite stint in a prisoner-of-war camp. Mosby captured another 10 men besides Auer, along with 45 horses, arms and equipment.

Hunter was furious. Without a chance to defend himself, the captured Auer was dishonorably discharged as an example of what to expect if you let Hunter Down. Auer did not get to give his side of the story till after the war. A mollified Hunter, the war won, not only changed Auer's discharge to honorable, but also promoted him to major.

Two days following Auer's capture, a shot was fired at a supply train from a homestead yard. Black Dave, in a dark frame of mind, ordered the house and outbuildings burned. Word went out that any repeat would result in every building within five miles of the attack going up in flames. Hunter marched from Cedar Creek on May 26. Three days later rebel Major Harry Gilmore struck. Leading a detachment of Maryland cavalry fighting in guerrilla mode, he captured 16 wagons carrying supplies. The next day Mosby struck an unloaded northbound train. Two Yankees were killed, and two men and eight horses captured.[13] In retribution, Hunter dispatched 200 cavalry under Major Joseph Stearns to set Newtown ablaze. A citizen deputation, however, insisted that Confederate soldiers were to blame; the townspeople were innocent of any wrongdoing. Convinced, Stearns only burned the homes of three prominent citizens, one a known guerrilla haunt.[14] On Stearns' return, Hunter accepted his explanation and continued south.

On June 5 Mosby's old commanding officer, William "Grumble" Jones, now a brigadier general, confronted Hunter with 5000 men to the north of Piedmont. Jones died when shot through the head while leading a futile charge. The Yankees won, taking 1000 rebel prisoners.

With Stuart and Jones both gone, who would be next? Mosby must have wondered if he would ever see old age himself. He already bore both saber and bullet wounds. Who knows what damage the next encounter might bring.

The day following Jones' death, Hunter occupied Staunton on the Virginia Central Railroad, and two days later generals Crook and Averell arrived with reinforcements. This brought the Yankee force to 18,500 men—more mouths to feed. Thanks to the operations of Mosby and other guerrilla bands, only one wagon train had got through since May 20. The Yankees foraged from civilians and burned what they could not carry away. "Many of the women look sad and do so much weeping over the destruction that is going on," one soldier wrote. "We feel the South brought on the war and the State of Virginia is paying dear for her part."[15]

Hunter arrived in Lexington to find a "violent and inflammatory" proclamation by the former governor of Virginia, John Letcher, "inciting the population of the country to rise and wage a guerrilla war on my troops." Letcher was long gone, but his property went up in flames for "abetting such unlawful and uncivilized warfare."[16] On June 12 the Virginia Military Institute was also torched. V. M. I. Cadets had captured a Union artillery position during Sigel's defeat at Newtown. Numerous Confederate officers, including 15 generals, were former graduates, and Stonewall Jackson had taught there before the war. The institute's statue of George Washington was carted away as the conquerors marched towards Lynchburg, a vital transport and supply center. But Robert E. Lee had no intention of losing Lynchburg without a good fight.

General Jubal "Old Jubilee" Early was dispatched by Lee, and by the time the Yankees approached Lynchburg they were confronted by about 10,000 rebels well stocked with ammunition. Black Dave, on the other hand, was running short. Much ammunition had been spent defeating Grumble Jones, and Dave's supply lines were under attack. Phil Sheridan's cavalry was supposed to reinforce Hunter but, as the V.M.I. burned on June 12, they were taking a beating at Trevilian Station from Confederate Cavalry under Wade Hampton and Fitzhugh Lee. Sheridan was forced to turn back, leaving Hunter to tackle Lynchburg alone. Unable to break the Confederate line, his powder and ball running out, Hunter became the hunted as he beat a retreat on the night of June 18. He scurried back into West Virginia leaving the Shenandoah Valley in Confederate hands. Jubal Early could now strike north towards a thinly defended Washington, D.C., most Union troops being with Grant besieging Lee in Petersburg.

John Mosby, meanwhile, had been on the move, striking wherever possible, capturing men, horses and arms. It had been hard work during March and April, potential targets well guarded by bluecoats on the alert.[17] But then the B&O Railroad and several posts were stripped to a skeleton guard, troops being required to escort ammunition wagons bound for Hunter's troops. Instead of splitting his strength as usual, Mosby decided to hit the enemy in strength, and requisitioned a 12-pounder Napoleon cannon. Now with over 200 men, he had a much greater chance of defending his gun from falling into enemy hands. On June 29 he unlimbered the Napoleon in front of the bluecoats at Duffield's Depot, on the B&O Railway near Harper's Ferry. Outgunned and outnumbered, the Yankees wasted no time in raising the white flag. Groceries, drygoods, clothing, and rolls of calico were taken, making this venture "The First Calico Raid." The telegraph line was cut, and what was left went up in flames as the graybacks rode off with prisoners and horses. The engineer of an approaching locomotive saw the rising smoke, and brought his train to a grinding halt. He steamed back to Martinsburg and wasted no time in spreading the alarm. Lieutenant Nelson of Mosby's Company A, meanwhile, had been left at Charles Town to defend Mosby's rear. He routed a Yankee cavalry force sent against him from Harper's Ferry, taking 19 prisoners and 27 horses. The rebels disappeared back into the hills with no casualties of their own.

Point of Rocks

July 4 saw Mosby's appearance with 250 Rangers at Point of Rocks, a hamlet and depot about 12 miles east of Harper's Ferry. Here the Potomac River, the adjacent Chesapeake and Ohio Canal, the B&O Railroad, and the overland telegraph merged as they passed through the Catoctin Mountains. Jubal Early was advancing towards Washington, and Mosby was intent on supporting him by severing Yankee communications between Harper's Ferry and Washington. The town was garrisoned by two infantry companies and two companies of the mounted Loudoun Rangers, totaling 350 men. One infantry company held Patton's Island in the Potomac, and the other a small fort overlooking the canal and river. The cavalry were encamped in the town itself.

Mosby placed his cannon high on the Virginia side of the river. The island was his first target, and a party of sharpshooters under Lieutenant Albert Wren waded into the water. A cloud of gunsmoke shrouded the water as they exchanged rifle fire with the infantry defenders.[18] A few shells burst on the island, and that was enough. The bluecoats fled across a footbridge to the opposite bank, then crossed the canal on a another small

General Jubal Early frustrated Mosby with his lack of contact and written orders, forcing the guerrilla chief to go his own way (Library of Congress).

bridge. The timbers were torn up and flung into the canal, and the Yankees fell back to the fort while Mosby's Rangers crossed the river. Stalled at the canal, they hastily pulled timbers from a nearby building, threw an improvised bridge across, and ran to the opposite bank. The Yankees lost heart and fled from both town and fort, but two were wounded and seven captured. A locomotive steaming down the track came to a halt just short of logs placed over the rails. Bullets flew as Mosby's sharpshooters opened fire, wounding the fireman, and shells exploded around the train as it was thrown into reverse.

Then the steamboat *Flying Cloud* chugged into view. Seventeen clerks from the Washington Treasury Department were enjoying an Independence Day river trip. They were astonished to see fountains of water erupt as shells splashed about. The boat was forced to halt at a canal lock, and they were horrified to see rebel horsemen galloping towards them. Both clerks and crew abandoned ship, and clouds of smoke soon billowed into the sky as the *Flying Cloud* went up in flames. A detachment of 12 rebels rode six miles along the river bank. They sacked the camp of the 8th Illinois Cavalry and torched four canal boats before returning with two prisoners and two horses.[19] The rebels cut the telegraph line, plundered the stores, and draped their horses with colorful bunting. During "The Great Calico Raid" They took more calico, food, confectionary and clothing including women's bonnets and hoop skirts, fine presents for Southern belles back home.

Before abandoning his post at Point of Rocks, the Yankee telegraph operator had wired "rebels in force" to Washington. This, combined with Early's advance towards the capitol, caused panic throughout the north. Mosby's raid across the Potomac was magnified out of all proportion, and Governor Curtin of Pennsylvania heard that 20,000 rebels had crossed. Imaginative boatman came into Washington reporting rebels crossing at every ford. An alarmed General Halleck mustered 2800 dismounted cavalrymen from the Washington fortifications, and they marched towards Harper's Ferry. General Albion Howe had orders "to force his way to Harper's Ferry" through the apparent enemy hordes.[20] But he arrived without a rebel in sight. Mosby's supposed "20,000" had withdrawn. Grant, meanwhile, was obliged to weaken his force outside Petersburg to reinforce the Washington defenses.

Major William H. Forbes of the 2nd Massachusetts Cavalry was known as "Lowell's fighting major."[21] Two days after Mosby's assault on Point of Rocks, Forbes was bivouacked at the Mount Zion Church on the Little River Turnpike to the east of Aldie. Under Forbes' command were 100 men of his own regiment, and 50 of the 13th New York Cavalry. They were armed with the formidable, seven-shot Spencer carbines. Forbes had been scouting through Mosby's Confederacy for any sign of Early's approach. But when news arrived of five wagon loads of Mosby's plunder from Point of Rocks passing through Leesburg, Forbes decided to hunt the guerrillas instead.

As it turned out, he did not have to look far. At 6:30 p.m. there was a rattle of gunfire from the east. Forbes had pickets in that direction. Mosby had found Forbes. The order was given to mount up and form battle lines. The officers rode to the front of their companies and, with a flourish, sabers were drawn. The firing drew closer, louder, and the bluecoat pickets rode from the woods into the open field. Then Mosby's cannon boomed. A shell exploded with a loud crash and smoke overhead, the first seen by Forbes' command. Both man and horses were already rattled when Mosby's Rangers appeared. The grayback skirmishers pulled down two sections of an intervening fence about 220 yards from the bluecoat ranks. Mosby led the men through the gap and, without any formal lines, they slowly advanced. Mosby was playing games, intimidating the enemy, waiting for a Yankee mistake. Forbes fulfilled his wish. A volley erupted from the Spencers but, while doing no harm to the enemy, "It created confusion among the horses," Colonel Lowell reported, "and the squadron in the rear added to it by firing a few pistol shots."[22] Forbes attempted to redeploy his unsettled first rank. Seeing the enemy vulnerable, Mosby ordered the charge. "Mosby and his rangers were upon us," recalled Chaplain Charles Humphreys," swooping down like Indians, yelling like fiends, discharging their pistols with fearful rapidity, and threatening to completely envelop our little band." Pistols banged and sabers flashed as horses and men became intermingled. Ranger John Munson recalled, "One of our boys, Willie Martin, was so closely surrounded by Forbes' men that they were obliged to club him into insensibility because there was no room to fire a carbine with safety to their own men."[23] But Yankees fell, and most in the rear fell back in disorder while some others held their ground. "Form in the woods! Form in the woods," Forbes shouted. "Attempts were made, with some success, to rally parts of the first squadron in the next field, and again near Little River Church, one mile off," Lowell reported. Forbes dashed about waving his saber. "Now rally around your leader," he shouted. "They rallied and attempted to form three times," recalled Ranger James Williamson, "but Mosby pressed on and drove them in disorder each time."

Then Mosby and Forbes came face to face. Forbes swung his blade at Mosby, but Dolly Richard's brother Tom thrust his pistol in the way. The saber deflected into Tom's own shoulder, then sprung from Forbes' hand. Mosby fired, but the bullet hit Forbes' rearing horse in the head. The animal came crashing down with the major pinned underneath. Lieutenant Amory galloped forward to assist his fallen commander, but was shot from his saddle. Men cursed, guns banged, rebels yelled, and the remaining bluecoats turned and fled. Captain Goodwin Stone bravely rallied several men before a bullet smashed into his spine. He managed to remain in the saddle and escape back to base. But his wound was mortal, and he died 12 days later.

"The ground was strewn with guns, pistols, blankets and equipment of all kinds," recalled Williamson, "dead and wounded were lying around; horses wounded and maddened with pain and fright, dashed wildly over the battleground, while others lay trembling, or rearing and falling, unable to stand."[24]

Chaplain Humphreys escaped the carnage. His fleet horse, an unusual shade of roan. stood out. In 1886 Mosby gave a talk about Stuart's ride around McClellan to former foes in Boston. Humphreys was present and reminded Mosby of their encounter. "Do you remember me?" he asked. Mosby looked closely. "No," he replied. "But I remember your horse."[25]

The Yankees lost 14 dead and 37 wounded. Major Forbes was captured along with 54 other men and 100 valuable cavalry mounts. Mosby's loss was eight wounded, one of whom died.[26] After the war in later years, Forbes and Mosby would be reunited and become close friends.

Jubal Early, meanwhile, pushed on towards the apprehensive Yankee capitol. Mosby wished to cooperate with Early, and sent word that he would follow his orders. It would appear, however, that the old West Point man had no more regard for guerrilla warfare than did Fitz Lee. He felt the ordinary soldier did the hard slogging and fighting for little money, while the guerrillas profited from spoils—and reaped glory along the way. He sent Mosby no word of his own movements, or congratulations for successes, and what few instructions arrived, came by word of mouth. Both Stuart and Lee always sent written orders. This was correct procedure to avoid misinterpretation and later disagreement as to what exactly the orders were. It was as though Early did not take Mosby seriously enough to put pen to paper, an apparent rebuff. The guerrilla chief, therefore, simply ignored Early's verbal instruction and went his own way.

On July 9 Early defeated General Lew Wallace, future author of *Ben-Hur*, at the Battle of Monocacy. This news caused panic in Washington, but the delay allowed Union reinforcements to arrive from Grant and man the city fortifications. On July 11 and 12, the two sides skirmished and exchanged artillery fire. Mosby, meanwhile, was destroying a deserted fort of the 18th Illinois Cavalry 15 miles in Early's rear. The garrison had been withdrawn in haste to help fend off Early's threat to Washington. A timber blockhouse and much abandoned equipment went up in flames.

Old Jubilee, feeling that Washington's defenses were too strong, ordered a withdrawal. "We haven't taken Washington," he said, "but we scared Abe Lincoln like hell."[27] But if Lincoln was scared he did not show it. He viewed the action first-hand from the walls of Fort Stevens, and a surgeon standing alongside received a bullet wound. The shot may well have been intended for the tall, lanky figure in the stovepipe hat.

After his withdrawal, Old Jubilee and the Gray Ghost came face to face for the first time. The meeting was cordial—on the surface at least. Early presented Mosby with a small rifled cannon, and commended him for his energy and dash. But, once Mosby went his own way, the lack of contact resumed. Early defeated Crook at Kernstown on July 24, but Mosby had been unable to provide support by attacking the enemy rear. In early August Mosby met Early again at Bunker Hill. He asked why the general had not sent word of his plans, but it would seem the reply, if any, was evasive. Early was not obliged to reveal his reasoning to a subordinate officer, especially as he had won the battle in any case. Jealousy, combined with a dislike of partisan warfare, was probably the reason. Mosby had become a dashing cavalier of the South, while Early was under fire for having failed to take Washington. Following the war, Early wrote that Mosby had not supplied intelligence on enemy strength in the capitol. In reply, he received a letter from Mosby detailing his attempts to cooperate and reconnoiter on his behalf.[28]

On July 30, 1864, a detachment of Early's cavalry entered Chambersburg, Pennsylvania. They wanted $100,000 in gold or 500,000 in greenbacks as compensation for Black Dave's incendiary activities down South. While the town leaders pondered this, the troops looted shops and homes. Such a sum could not be paid, the rebels were told, and hundreds of buildings went up in flames. Half the population of 6000 found themselves with no roof over their head. No person was injured, but the damage was three times the ransom demand, and greater than that inflicted by Quantrill on Lawrence.[29]

Combined with the Washington assault, the Chambersburg affair convinced Lincoln that resources must be found to crush Old Jubilee forthwith. On August 7, 1864, Phil Sheridan took command of the newly created Middle Military Division, headquartered at Harpers Ferry. The Division reached southwards from Southern Pennsylvania through Virginia's Shenandoah Valley and included the area to the east known as Mosby's Confederacy. Jubal Early's army was the main target, but the rich farmlands of the region would also come under Sheridan's heel. He would finish off what Black Dave had failed to complete. While Secretary of War Edwin Stanton had concerns about the 33-year-old Sheridan being given such an important post, William Tecumseh Sherman had no doubts. "He will worry Early to death," he told Grant. "Let us give those Southern fellows all the fighting they want, and when they are tired we can tell them we are just warming to the work."[30]

The fact that "Little Phil" Sheridan was only five feet five inches tall did not count for much once mounted on Rienzi, his fine black charger, 16 hands high. The animal was, in Sheridan's words, "an animal of great intelligence and immense strength and endurance.... I doubt if his superior as a horse for field service was ever ridden by any one."[31] Which was just as well. Sheridan now had had his work cut out for him. The West Point graduate and former cavalry commander of the Army of the Potomac was ordered to destroy Early's army, advance on Staunton, and cause general havoc. Ulysses S. Grant wired General Halleck in

Despite the efforts of these Union generals the Gray Ghost stayed on the loose. Left to right: Wesley Merritt, Phil Sheridan, Thomas Devlin, George Forsyth and George Custer (Library of Congress).

Washington, "I think Sheridan should keep up as advanced a position as possible towards the Virginia Central railroad and be prepared with supplies to advance on that road at Gordonsville and Charlottesville at any time the enemy weakens himself sufficiently to admit of it. The cutting of that road and canal would be of vast importance to us."[32] Lee would be forced to weaken his Petersburg defenses by sending reinforcements to Early in the Shenandoah Valley.

The Berryville Raid

The notorious Mosby was in Sheridan's sights the very day after taking command. The Rangers had been spotted only five miles away foraging for corn. Sheridan ordered the diversion of 600 men to protect his rear against Mosby, then, on March 10, moved south at the head of 30,000 men. He hoped to bring Early to battle within a few days, but the wily old grayback did not cooperate. Looking for a position of strength, he ordered a withdrawal. Sheridan had only three days rations, and sent orders for wagons to move south from Harper's Ferry loaded with provisions. The massive train, 325 wagons, hit the trail, but there were too few escort troops, and became fragmented and strung out over miles.

At Berryville on August 13, wagons at the rear of Sheridan's supply train began to pull out through the dawn mist. "The flush of the morning began to blow over the beautiful valley landscape—there are few lovelier spots than the Valley of Virginia around Berryville," recalled Ranger John Munson. But as Mosby's howitzer was set up, the rebels found themselves under attack. It was the buzz of wasps, however, and not bullets that nearly destroyed Mosby's plans, "the fun of which is more apparent now then it was then," he recalled. "The howitzer was unlimbered over a yellow-jacket's nest."[33] Mosby's Rangers could handle any number of Yankees, but the wasps were too much. The gun was rapidly deployed to a safer spot. Then, "Frank Rahm sent a twelve-pound shell over the train," recalled Munson, "It exploded like a clap of thunder out of a clear sky, and was followed by another which burst in the midst of the enemy." A panic was already under way by the time a third shell hit. Then the dreaded rebel yell was heard. The ominous, dark shapes of 250 horsemen charged from the mist, pistols in hand. Chaos ensued as teamsters cracked whips in a mad dash to escape. Wagons crashed into one another amidst a flurry of curses as guns banged and Yankee officers bellowed orders not heard. Their Infantry dashed about, almost trampled by their own bewildered cavalry. "Colonel Mosby was dashing up and down the line of battle on his horse," recalled Munson, "urging the men by voice and gesture. I never saw him quite so busy or interested in the total demolition of things.... Our men were yelling, galloping, charging, firing, stampeding mules and horses and creating pandemonium everywhere."[34] The Yankee infantry made for the woods towards Berryville township. A stone fence, some houses and a brick church offered protection. Here a few officers managed to organize a rally. The bluecoats fired an ineffectual volley or two, then fled in disorder as the rebels charged. While most escaped, dozens threw up their hands in surrender.

Once the battle smoke cleared, Mosby held the field. The Rangers had killed six, wounded nine, and captured 200, along with 420 mules, 200 cattle, and 36 horses. Mosby had lost two killed and three wounded.[35] About 40 wagons had been captured. After being ransacked, smoke billowed into the summer sky as they went up in flames. By the time Yankee reinforcements arrived, Mosby was gone with his prisoners and booty.

"We lived off the country where we operated" recalled Mosby, "and drew nothing from Richmond except the gray jackets my men wore. We were mounted, armed and equipped entirely off the enemy, but, as we captured a great deal more than we could use, the surplus was sent to supply Lee's army."[36] One thing Mosby could have used, however, was the Union army payroll that had gone up in smoke at Berryville. This valuable trifle had been missed during a wagon search. Mosby learned of the mistake from Northern newspapers. "There's a cool million gone after it was fairly earned," he said, exaggerating the amount involved. "What other man could sustain such losses with so little embarrassment."[37]

But Sheridan was embarrassed—very embarrassed. He was obliged to detach General Currie's 3rd Infantry Brigade, one of his best, to reinforce his rearguard—1800 soldiers Early would not have to fight. Sheridan informed Grant that Mosby had burned a mere six wagons. But Southern newspapers, read in the North, printed a report written by General Lee: "Colonel Mosby reports that he attacked the enemy's supply train near Berryville on the 13th, captured and destroyed 75 loaded wagons and secured over 200 prisoners, including several officers, between 500 and 600 mules...."[38] General Halleck in Washington wired Sheridan if it were true that 70 to 80 wagons had gone up in flames and 500 mules captured? Sheridan then admitted that it was about 40 wagons, but still underestimated the mules, claiming only 200 rather than the actual 450.

"Where any of Mosby's men are caught with nothing to designate what they are, hang them without trial," wired Grant.[39] On August 17 Sheridan replied, claiming that he had hanged one of Mosby's men and shot six. And two days later, "guerrillas give me great annoyance, but I am quietly disposing of numbers of them." On August 22 he wrote that "We have disposed of quite a number of Mosby's men."[40] After the war Mosby read this in the *Official Records*, and accused Sheridan of cold-blooded murder—but at the same time was confused. Who exactly had he disposed of? The men of Mosby's command captured at this time were still living after the war. He concluded that Sheridan either fabricated the reports to keep Grant happy, or the men executed were regular troops, or members of other irregular bands who still operated without official sanction.[41]

Sheridan ordered cavalry commander General Alfred Torbert to burn crops and farm buildings, kill livestock, and set slaves free, but "No houses will be burned, and officers in charge of this delicate but necessary duty must inform the people that the subject is to make the valley untenable for the raiding parties of the rebel army." Most in Sheridan's command had joined up to fight rebels, not make war on civilians. "It was a phase of warfare we had not seen before," wrote a Pennsylvanian trooper, "and though we admitted the necessity, we could not but sympathize with the suffers."[42]

Sheridan still found Jubal Early a dire threat, and pulled back to Charles Town. Five days following Mosby's Berryville raid Sheridan had the redoubtable George Custer's Wolverines protecting his right rear flank. "The rebs say thy dasent shoot a cannon for if they do general Custer is shure to go for it and take it away from them," wrote Private Jessup of the 5th Michigan Cavalry, "they call his men the flying devils of Michigan."[43]

Mosby sent no cannon with William Chapman when he ordered him to take on the flying devils. While Mosby and Richards carried out separate raids near Charles Town, Chapman led 150 men on a scout along the Shenandoah River in close proximity to Custer's command. Night had fallen when Chapman, close to the home of a Mrs. Sower, ordered a lone vidette of the 5th Michigan to surrender, "which he refused," recalled Chapman. "We both fired and the result was the death of the picket."

Next day, August 19, the Wolverines found their comrade's dead body and chose to believe he had been "bushwhacked," shot down in cold blood. Regardless of Sheridan's orders, Custer decided that the homes of five prominent local citizens be put to the torch. Captain George Drake was given the task, and rode out with 50 men. That afternoon Chapman rode to a plume of smoke to find the McCormick house ablaze, the anguished owners standing in the yard. Then more smoke was seen. They rode on to find Mrs. Sower's dwelling going up in flames. Women and children stood outside, and their tears flowed along with the drizzling rain. Mrs. Sower yelled out, "We are rebels still if we are burned out of house and home." She pointed at the home of Ben Morgan, not far away. Drake's troopers were at work, setting fire to house and barn. "We kept on at a brisk pace," reported Chapman, "believing that we could get nearer to them before they discovered who we were than if we traveled more rapidly." But the Yankees were suspicious of the new arrivals. Captain Drake ordered his men to draw up in line of battle. When within 100 yards, Chapman gave the order to charge. The Yankees held their fire until 40 yards, then their carbines opened up. But the ill-aimed volley took no effect. Perhaps the wild rebel yells had done their work, unsettling the Wolverines' nerves and aim. "We struck them in the center and threw them into confusion," recalled Chapman, "and they fled in the direction of their camp. We pursued them almost to their camp. Not a single man of my command was wounded."[44]

Chapman, however, had provided a whitewashed version of events. When the Yankees broke and fled, over a dozen were trapped and surrendered. Destroying crops and barns to deprive rebel troops made military sense, but house burning in this theater of war was another matter. Kansas rules did not apply here. Mosby had given orders to shoot house burners. Chapman gave the order and all but one captive died where they fell. One man, shot in the face, survived to tell the tale by feigning death.

Mosby makes no mention of this event in his published memoirs, but his report to Richmond stated "Such was the indignation of our men at witnessing some of the finest residences in that portion of the State enveloped on flames that no quarter was shown, and about twenty-five of them were shot to death for their villainy." He later admitted issuing such orders, but added that "the order was superfluous."[45]

"Massacre by Mosby—Rebel Treachery—Cowardly Cruelty," screamed the *New York Times*.[46] General Wesley Merritt, Custer's immediate superior, issued orders to "stir up and kill as many of the bushwhackers as possible who are between you and the river," and Merritt's superior, General Torbert, sent the 1st Rhode Island Cavalry out with orders "to bring in no prisoners." Sheridan ordered a roundup of suspected Mosby guerrillas, and 20 wagons crammed with males aged 16 to 60 rattled into Charles Town. Orders were given to be vigilant, and arrest any Union soldier who strayed from camp without arms.

By early September 1864, Mosby's Rangers had grown to six companies, totaling 300 men. He divided this force to hit various targets at the same time. The bewildered Yankees had no idea of where the Gray Ghost would strike next.

On September 13 Union Colonel Henry Gansevoort heard that Mosby and two Rangers had been seen turning off towards Centreville after riding through Fairfax Court House. Little confidence was placed in the report, with the result that only five men of the 13th New York Cavalry were sent to investigate. Gansevoort could not believe that the elusive Gray Ghost could be waylaid in open daylight: too good to be true. But in any case, a large party may well give their approach away.

Mosby and his companions, Guy Broadwater and Tom Love, were riding towards Centreville when they found themselves confronted by the five troopers.[47] Pistols were whipped from holsters and bullets flew. Three of the Yankees turned and galloped off while Mosby and his men rode in the opposite direction. The remaining two Yankees gave chase for about a mile with shots being exchanged. But, with no other pursuers in sight, the rebels reined their horses about and charged back. Mosby blazed away with one revolver in each hand, and both Yankee horses crashed to the ground. But Private Henry Smith, one leg trapped beneath his horse, took careful aim and fired. Mosby was seen to "throw up his hands and give signs of pain," Gansevoort reported.[48] The bullet had glanced off the handle of a pistol in Mosby's belt, then into his left groin.[49] But he remained in the saddle, reined his horse about, and galloped off. He was taken to the home of an elderly woman who helped tend his wound. The rebels probably wondered if Jeb Stuart's death was a portend of Mosby's: mortally wounded with a pistol shot from a dismounted trooper. But, despite the bullet being too near an artery for surgery, the wound was not mortal. Private Smith's good shooting was rewarded with a promotion to sergeant, and Mosby would carry Smith's bullet for the rest of his life.

The wounded rebel recuperated at his mother's home, but during September managed a visit to Lee's headquarters near Petersburg. The general, conversing with General Longstreet, looked up to see his famous guerrilla chief supported by a crutch under each arm. "Colonel, the only fault I have ever had to find with you is that you are always getting wounded."

"Such a speech from General Lee," Mosby recalled, "more than repaid me for my wound."[50]

On September 19, Old Jubilee clashed with Little Phil at Winchester. The badly outnumbered rebels lost the day. Their retreat through Winchester was not halted by townswomen who joined hands in a futile attempt to have them return to the fight. One of those killed during the battle was Confederate Colonel George S. Patton, grandfather of the legendary World War II general. In later years the Mosby and Patton families would become friends, young George inspired by Mosby's stories of his Civil War exploits.

"We have just sent them whirling through Winchester," Sheridan wired, "and we are after them tomorrow." With one-fourth of his army captured, wounded or killed, Early fell back 20 miles and threw up fortifications on Fisher's Hill. But again Sheridan went after him with zest and Early was forced to fall back another 60 miles to a defensible pass in the Blue Ridge Mountains.[51]

Front Royal

At Front Royal, on September 23, two of Mosby's Rangers swung from a stout tree branch. Not far away, four others lay dead with gunshot wounds.

Earlier the same day, Captain Sam Chapman had encountered a Yankee ambulance train escorted by cavalry. He split his 120 man force to hit front and back, but saw too late that hundreds more Union cavalry were moving up the road. The Yankee reinforcements came forward at the gallop. "We pitched into them," recalled Private Corbett," driving them into the mountains killing seventeen and taking four prisoners.... I had the pleasure of capturing one of them myself." Exactly how many guerrillas were killed and captured varies with different reports. Mosby's old antagonist Colonel Charles Lowell, usually accurate, was present and reported 13 rebels killed.[52]

Once the dust settled, a mortally wounded Union Lieutenant Charles McMaster was found on the Chester road. Although hotly denied by the rebels, McMaster claimed he had been robbed and shot after his surrender. This appeared to be a repeat of Morgan's farm. The bluecoats were baying for blood, and four rebel prisoners were led away to be summarily shot. One was a local boy of 17, Henry Rhodes, who had joined Chapman that day on a borrowed horse to ad a bit of excitement to his life. Captured by Custer's men, he was pulled along on foot between two mounted troopers through the center of Front Royal. The boy's mother ran out and cast her arms about him, pleading for his life, but there was to be no mercy this day. She was thrust to one side, and Rhodes was dragged into a field. Custer's band struck up "Love Not, The One You Love May Die" as taunting Yankees marched around Rhodes. A volunteer stepped forward and emptied his revolver into the cowering boy. His body, left in a pool of blood, was picked up by residents and delivered under a sheet to his weeping mother by wheelbarrow.

Two other rebels had already been questioned by General Torbert. They refused to cooperate and he ordered them hanged. The *Richmond Examiner* reported the affair. One of the condemned was William Overby from Georgia: "When the rope was placed around his neck by his inhuman captors, he told them he was one of Mosby's men, and that he was proud to die as a Confederate soldier, and that his death was sweetened with the assurance that Colonel Mosby would swing in the wind ten men for every man they murdered."[53] The two rebels swung from a walnut tree. One body was adorned with a placard, "This will be the fate of Mosby and all his men." Many felt vengeance had been served, but cooler heads were not so sure. "I was sorry enough the other day," wrote Colonel Lowell in a private letter, "that my Brigade should have had a part in the hanging and shooting of some of Mosby's men who were taken,—I believe that some punishment was deserved,—but I hardly think we were within the laws of war, and any violation of them opens the door for all sorts of barbarity.... The war in this part of the country is becoming very unpleasant to an officer's feelings."[54]

If George Custer found the proceedings unpleasant it was not apparent at the time. The flamboyant and colorful "boy general" was present when the Rangers swung, and Mosby laid the blame at his feet. It made sense, after all, Custer had ordered the house burnings, and it was his Wolverines who had been killed at Morgan's farm. Those home burners had deserved what they got, Mosby felt, but his men had been captured in fair combat and deserved to be treated as prisoners of war. Despite Torbert having ordered the hangings, the belief persisted for years afterwards that Custer was to blame. Confederate General Thomas Rosser was an old West Point friend of Custer. They clashed during the war, but resumed their friendship afterwards. Custer told Rosser that he did not order the hangings. "I have no doubt of Custer's innocence," Rosser recalled, "for he was not in command, and his superior officer was present." But Mosby was not impressed. In 1899 He wrote, "a man who would burn houses for revenge over the heads of woman and children as Custer did would commit murder—a murderer generally denies it. So I attach no importance to what Rosser says Custer said."[55]

Perhaps, with hindsight, Mosby felt that the killings at Morgan's farm affair should never have occurred. This unfortunate event had brought on the Yankee retribution, when all said and done, and prisoners taken by Mosby in following raids were treated in a humane manner. Following the war, Mosby said he stood by Morgan's farm, and would do the same thing again. But he was not in a position to say anything else.

The scarcely healed guerrilla chief, still carrying lead from Private Smith's revolver, was helped onto his horse on September 29, 1864. The executions, only six days before, may well have provided his determination to resume command.

Six days later Mosby caused havoc when he struck bluecoats guarding a repair crew at Salam on the Manassas Gap Railroad. The 200 rebels tore up track and, with two cannon, skirmished with Yankee reinforcements over the next few days. One rebel fatality was Lieutenant "Big Yankee" Ames, killed on October 9. Mosby was upset, Ames having become one his most valued men. The following day the railway's military superintendent, M. J. McCrickett, was killed when his train was derailed and crashed down an embankment.[56] An outraged Secretary of War Edwin Stanton ordered that all males suspected of "belonging to, or assisting the robber bands of Mosby" to be sent to the Old Capitol Prison in Washington. Houses within five miles of the track not required by the military, or "occupied by persons known to be friendly" were to be burned, and the livestock confiscated. Anyone found in the exclusion zone to be treated as "robbers and bushwhackers."[57] Union officers ignored this, but Stanton's order that foliage "within musket shot" of the track be burned was obeyed. Trees and undergrowth along a ten mile stretch went up in flames.

The day following Stanton's directive, however, Colonel William Powell, a few miles southeast of Front Royal, received word of the "willful and cold-blooded murder" of a U.S. soldier. Two rebels, Myers and Chancellor, supposedly of "Mosby's gang of cut-throats and robbers" were known to be the guilty parties. Mosby Ranger Albert Willis had been captured the day before, and Powell was in no mood for mercy. The rebel was soon swinging from a tree with a placard attached: "A. C. Willis, member of Company C, Mosby's command, hanged by the neck in retaliation for the murder of a U.S. soldier by Mssrs. Chancellor and Myers."[58] These rebels were not, in fact, attached to Mosby's command. The exact details are obscure, but one story has it that the Yankee had been arrested as a spy. They were riding for the provost marshal's office at Gordonsville when he was shot by Chancellor while "attempting to escape." As well as the hanging, Powell sent a detachment to Chancellor's farm where all structures were put to the torch, and the livestock driven off. The execution of Willis would have tragic consequences for some of Custer's men.

On October 11 Rangers under Dolly Richards mortally wounded Sheridan's medical director, Dr. Emil Ohlenschlager, and his quartermaster general, Colonel Cornelius Tolles. According to the rebels, they had been shot while running instead of answering a call to surrender. Their ambulance, escorted by 25 cavalry, had been ambushed on the road between Winchester and Sheridan's headquarters at Cedar Creek. A newspaper man who witnessed the fight claimed they were shot after surrender.

Sheridan, infuriated, had too few troops for guard details, and this included an eight-mile stretch of the B&H Railroad between Harper's Ferry and Duffield's Station. Rebel scouts found a gap, and Mosby selected a suitable place for derailment. In a cutting, it would prevent the civilian carrying train from crashing too far off the track. A rail was lifted on the clear, frosty night of October 14. Mosby and most of his men, exhausted after a long day's ride, were soon sound asleep near the rails. "I was aroused and astounded by an explosion and a crash. The engine had run off the track, the boiler burst, and the air was filled with red-hot cinders and escaping steam." The hiss and whoosh was intermingled with "the screams of passengers—especially women." But the only person injured was the engineer. Rangers James Wiltshire and Charles Dear boarded two different carriages as Mosby, shouting orders, moved along the bank with the aid of a walking cane. One foot was in a cavalry boot, and the other in a sock—not the heroic image artists like to paint. During a recent skirmish, he had been injured by a charging Yankee horse after his own mount was shot down.[59]

Charles Dear barged into one carriage, Colt in hand. It was filled with frightened passengers and a handful of troops. He called for their surrender, but one soldier drew his pistol as he rose from his seat. Dear fired first and women screamed as the Yankee fell. A group of horrified officers stood around a stove. One, the rebel noticed, was clutching a satchel for dear life. He demanded that it be handed over, but the officer refused. The others, however, fearing for their lives, demanded that he comply.[60] The satchel was soon in Mosby's hands and he found, to his delight, wads of greenbacks inside. A payroll for thousands of Yankee troops became a very lucrative windfall for the 84 rebels taking part, to be known thereafter as "The Greenback Raid."

The passengers were ordered off the carriages, lined up, and relieved of their valuables. But one group of Germans refused to move. Either they did not understand or, "They had through tickets and thought they had a right to keep their seats," recalled Mosby. Newspapers bound for the Yankee troops were liberally spread through the carriages. Matches were struck, the paper ignited, and "The Germans now took in the situation and came tumbling, all in a pile, out of the flames.... They ought not to blame me, but Sheridan: it was his business, not mine, to protect them."[61]

The burning carriages lit up the night sky as the Confederates, with booty and prisoners, rode off. Mosby nudged his mount up alongside a German officer riding among the prisoners. The young gent was superbly dressed in a beavercloth coat, shiny boots and new hat embellished with gilt cord. Mosby asked why he come had come so far from home to fight against the South. "I only come to learn the art of war," he replied. Later the German, now wearing battered rebel garb, rode up alongside Mosby. He complained of having being forced to swap.

"Did you not come to learn the art of war?" asked Mosby.

"Yes," he replied.

"Very well. This is your first lesson."[62]

A horse with those riding in advance fell, and the satchel broke open, the precious greenbacks being spread amongst the grass. "We gathered it up hastily," recalled Lieutenant Grogan. "As to the loss, if any, we knew little and cared less, as a few thousand out of the pile was of small concern to us." Grogan stated that 168,000 was distributed, each of the 84 men receiving $2000. But confusion eventually emerged about how much was taken. The two Union paymasters were accused of colluding with Mosby. Following the war paymaster Major Moore approached Mosby to certify that $173,000 was actually taken, not $168,000 as stated in Mosby's report. The missing $5000 was probably lost in the grass that night, to be pocketed by some farmer who could not believe his luck. Regardless of the amount, Federal money was preferred over the failing Confederate currency thus, the greenbacks, "were circulated so freely in Loudoun that never afterwards was there a pie or blooded horse sold in that section for Confederate money," recalled Grogan.[63]

As the carriages burned, Captain William Chapman was carrying out a separate raid with 80 Rangers. They torched canal boats near White's Ford, cut the telegraph line and plundered two stores in Adamstown, Maryland. They skirmished with the Loudon Rangers, taking seven captives, then exchanged shots with infantry tearing up a canal bridge. The rebels relayed the planks, and crossed safely back into Virginia without losing a man.

These two raids received big coverage in the Northern papers—Sheridan humiliated by the Gray Ghost, yet again. But there had been a price to pay. The Yankees took comfort in the capture of four cannon under Mosby's command. A deserter, John Lunceford, informed Colonel Gansevoort that the guns were parked on Little Cobbler Mountain, just one mile from his Piedmont headquarters. As the guerrillas burned the derailed train, New York troopers climbed the slopes and seized both the guns and a small detail under Sergeant Babcock. These captives soon found themselves in Yankee boxcars traveling the rails to deter Mosby from derailing trains and injuring his own men.

Lee congratulated Mosby on yet another success, but warned that "owing to recent heavy losses of artillery in the Valley," it would take some time to replace the guns. Things had not been going well for Old Jubilee in the Shenandoah Valley. His army had taken a final, decisive hit at Cedar Creek on October 19, just five days after the Greenback Raid. Lee felt the best way for Mosby to replace the lost guns was to "capture some from the enemy." And an informer was responsible, so, "as your command increases it will be necessary to be extremely watchful as to the character of the men you enlist."[64]

Colonel Charles Lowell, the man who considered Mosby "an honorable foe" was mortally wounded at Cedar Creek. He died, aged 29, and had the rare distinction of being promoted to brigadier general after death. "He was the perfection of a man and a soldier," said Sheridan."

No doubt Edwin Stoughton was delighted to hear that he would not go down in history as the only Union general captured by John Mosby. A problem shared is a problem halved, when all said and done. On October 25 Mosby mustered his largest force yet, 375 men. Various companies were divided and dispatched in different directions to disrupt Sheridan's supply lines and communications. Mosby's own detachment encountered a Union wagon rattling along the pike north of Winchester guarded by only 10 cavalrymen. A larger escort of 50 troopers had foolishly been left behind. The rebels swooped, and four men were captured. This included General Alfred Napoleon Alexander Duffie, on his way to take charge of a remount depot. Sheridan was not overly upset when he received the news, having recently removed the dapper Frenchman from command of a cavalry division. Earlier successes for Duffie had been replaced with failed ventures as the war went on. Sheridan wrote to Halleck that Duffie was "a trifling man and a poor soldier. He was captured by his own stupidity."[65] Rumors spread that Duffie had been shot down in cold blood. The *Richmond Examiner* stated that if Duffie was still living, Mosby should place him in front of his next cavalry charge in retaliation for hostages being placed in trains. But Duffie, very much alive, was safely imprisoned until paroled in February of 1865.

Just six days after Duffie's capture, Mosby penned a letter to Lee. The execution of Ranger Albert Willis by the Yankee Colonel Powell, along with the Front Royal executions, had been playing on his mind, and he requested permission to strike back. In response, Lee gave Mosby permission to hang seven of Custer's men. A few days later 14 woebegone Wolverines were brought in by Dolly Richards, giving Mosby 27 prisoners in hand. Others, like Duffie, had been sent back behind the Confederate lines.

On November 6, in Rectortown, the 27 prisoners were lined up. Mosby was in town, but not present, when the Yankees were given the bad news. Perhaps he wished to distance himself from the unpleasant retribution. Some Yankees prayed and some wept as a man walked along the line, hat in hand. Each prisoner took a piece of paper. If marked, that man was to pay the price. "Tell my mother I died like a man," said one. Drummer boy James Daley fainted when he saw the fatal mark. But two marked papers were still in the hat at the deadly raffle's conclusion. Someone in Mosby's command could not count, apparently. A second draw was required. The drummer boy was spared because of his age, so three papers were still to be drawn. Three men who thought they had been spared now found themselves condemned. The seven victims were tied up and taken away on horseback under the charge of Lieutenant Ed Thompson. At Ashby's Gap, however, they encountered Captain Richard Montjoy with yet more prisoners in hand. Montjoy, a Mason, "ascertained in the usual way that two of the condemned men were brother Masons," recalled John Munson, "and that they would be glad to enjoy any fraternal assistance that might be available at the moment; so Montjoy took them from Thompson in exchange for two of his own prisoners and passed on."

When Mosby heard of these proceedings he took Montjoy to task. "I want you to understand my command is not a Masonic lodge," he said.[66]

The prisoners were taken on horseback by eight rebel guards to Beemer's woods near Berryville. Darkness fell and a light rain added to the bleak mood of the somber procession. They arrived and "The first man was gotten up," recalled Acting Union Sergeant Charles Marvin, "his hands tied behind him, a bed-cord doubled and tied around his neck; he was marched to a large tree beside the road, from which a limb projected. He was lifted in the air, the rope taken by one of the men on horseback and tied to the limb, and there was left dangling. Two more were treated in the same manner." A sign was placed on one body: "These men have been hung in retaliation for an equal number of Colonel Mosby's men hung by order of General Custer at Front Royal, measure for measure." But the rebels felt uneasy. "This hanging is too damned slow work," one said. The remaining Yankees were lined up to be shot. But to the rebels' surprise they now had only three prisoners left, not 4. In the darkness, Private George Sowle had dropped from his mount while crossing a ditch and made his escape.

Pistols were pointed at the remaining three captives, Charles Marvin in the center. But

Marvin had managed to loosen his bonds. "The revolver on my right went off," he recalled, "the revolver on my left went off, and the revolver in my face failed to explode. The click of the hammer on the tube went through me like an electric shock. I caught my breath, raised onto the balls of my feet, knocked the revolver to one side, hit him in the head, jumped over as he fell into the road, and as they sang out, 'There goes the big Yankee ——,' I seemed to find new life, and went at the speed of a streak of lightning down the road about 100 yards, where I entered the same woods as they were in and climbed a shellbark hickory tree.... I don't think I ever saw a squirrel go up a tree faster than I went up that one."[67] Marvin remained hidden amidst the dark, damp leaves till the rebels rode off. He climbed down and searched in the gloom for the other two men, shot and left for dead. But Private Hoffnagle had only been hit in the elbow, and rolled down as though killed. Corporal Bennett had been hit in the shoulder with the first bullet. "For God's sake kill me if you are going to!" he had wailed, "Don't torture me to death." The rebel obliged with a second shot from his Navy Colt. The bullet entered his cheek bone near his left eye and destroyed his right eye as it passed right through his head. He fell down, but still breathing.

Marvin searched about, found Hoffnagle, and took him to a civilian home. From there they made it to the army hospital at Winchester. The following morning, a passing civilian and his daughter found Bennett perched against a tree. He was taken to a doctor, and then reunited with Hoffnagle at the same hospital. Both survived to tell their stories, but with damaged lives. Hoffnagle had his right arm amputated, and Bennett was left with a paralyzed left arm, blind in the right eye, and damaged vision in his left.[68] As good as Mosby's men may have been in the saddle, some left much to be desired when it came to be executioners, it would appear.

Mosby was forced to defend himself when this event was brought up in the press many years later. Aged 78, he claimed he was pleased with the escape of some prisoners, "as they carried the story to Sheridan's army which was the best way to stop the business." It was a "disagreeable duty," he wrote, and "If my motive had been revenge I would have ordered others to be executed in their place."[69]

It would appear however, that those who bundled the executions did not admit to it at the time, as disclosed in a letter written by Mosby to Sheridan on November 24, 1864

> GENERAL: Some time in the month of September, during my absence from my command, six of my men, who had been captured by your forces, were hung and shot in the streets of Front Royal, by the order and in the immediate presence of Brig.-Gen.-CUSTER. Since then, another (captured by Col. POWELL, on a plundering expedition into Rappahannock) shared a similar fate. A label, affixed to the coat of one of the murdered men, declared "that this would be the fate of MOSBY and all his men. Since the murder of my men not less than seven hundred prisoners, including many officers of high rank captured from your army by this command, have been forwarded to Richmond, but the execution of my purpose of retaliation was deferred in order, as far as possible, to confine its operation to the men of CUSTER and POWELL. Accordingly, on the 6th inst., seven of your men were, by my order, executed on the Valley pike—your highway of travel. Hereafter any prisoners falling into my hands will be treated with the kindness due to their condition, unless some new act of barbarity shall compel me, reluctantly, to adopt a line of policy repugnant to humanity.
>
> Very respectfully, your obedient servant,
> JOHN S. MOSBY, Lieutenant-Colonel."[70]

The acts "of barbarity," ceased—as far as hanging prisoners went. But by now Yankee domination of the Shenandoah Valley was complete, and there were still plenty of farms east of the Blue Ridge awaiting Sheridan's attention. The Gray Ghost had given Little Phil a bad time, and Mosby's Confederacy would feel his wrath.

And, to make matters worse, William Tecumseh Sherman had captured Atlanta on September 2. This victory along, with Sheridan's success, virtually ensured the re-election of Abraham Lincoln. Unlike his peace-seeking political opponents, the wily Kentuckian had vowed to keep fighting until the rebellion was crushed.

Blazer

On September 4, 1864, the 75 men of Mosby's Company A, under Lieutenant Joseph Nelson, took a break. They were on the east bank of the Shenandoah River at Myers's Ford, about six miles from Charles Town. A few watered their horses, and others stood about chatting while they smoked a pipe. Some took time off to catch a few winks while there was a chance.

A sudden blast of fire and smoke erupted from nearby woods. Some cried out as Spencer bullets hit home, There was a mad dash for horses while others fled on foot. The Yankees burst from the woods and pursued the rebels for three miles, but some "fought with a will," reported Captain William Blazer, "but the seven-shooters proved too much for them."[71] Blazer killed 13 men, wounded six, and captured five along with 17 horses. The disproportionate number of dead to wounded would indicate executions having taken place. Nelson, who had failed to place videttes to his rear, was wounded and captured. Mosby was off scouting to the north with 15 men at the time, and was appalled to hear of the rout. "You let the Yankees whip you," he said. "I'll get hoop-skirts for you!"[72]

Thirty-five-year-old Captain William Blazer had been given a special task. "I have 100 men who will take the contract to clean out Mosby's gang," Sheridan wrote to General Augur on August 20, "I want 100 Spencer rifles for them."[73]

From Gallipolis, Ohio, Blazer had a well-earned reputation as a guerrilla fighter from exploits in West Virginia while serving under General Crook. Like Mosby, he dispensed with the saber and employed irregular tactics to achieve his goals. He relied on Union sympathizers amidst the Virginian population for information, and sent out "Jesse Scouts,"—spies in Confederate uniforms. "Capt. Blazer was not only a brave man and hard fighter," recalled Ranger Williamson, "but by his humane and kindly treatment, in striking contrast with the usual conduct of our enemies, he had so disarmed our citizens that instead of fleeing on his approach and notifying all soldiers, thus giving them a chance to escape, but little notice was taken of him."[74] And Mosby was impressed. He described "Old Blaze" as "a bold but cautious commander," all of which helped his successes against rebel guerrillas.[75]

The affair at Myers's Ford was Blazer's greatest triumph against Mosby's Rangers, but not the last. Two months later Captain Richard Montjoy was leading 30 men and 17 prisoners back home from a successful raid. When nearing Ashby's Gap, the undergrowth suddenly erupted in gunfire. Informed of their movements, Blazer had laid an ambush. About half a dozen rebels were wounded, one mortally, and they fled into the woods. It was another victory for Blazer, and the Yankee prisoners fell back into friendly hands.

"Wipe Blazer out!" Mosby ordered, "Go through him!"[76] On November 17 he sent Dolly Richards with about 100 men through Snicker's Gap, and William Chapman with an equal number through Ashby's Gap. Disabled by illness, Mosby stayed behind.

The following morning Richards closed in on the telltale sign of camp smoke wisping above the trees. Blazer was camped with 75 men near Meyerstown, to the south of Charles Town. "When the woods were reached," recalled Williamson, "the command moved on at a gallop and dashed into the camp, but found it deserted. The fires, still burning, a huge pile of corn in the center of the camp, and a bundle of newspapers lying unopened near by, showed the enemy had left but a short time before."

Blazer had got wind of Richards' arrival in the area and, like a cat chasing its own tail, had set out from the camp to track him down—all while Richards came after him from behind. The rebels left the deserted campsite, and scouts soon located Blazer's command. "As we moved along the road," recalled Williamson, "a couple of Federal cavalrymen were observed dashing across a field from one piece of woods to another, and the whole column soon came in sight, moving slowly along." The Yankees had some prisoners, including Ranger John Puryear of Richard's command, captured while scouting that morning. Blazer's second, Lieutenant Cole, had strung Puryear up by the neck a number of times in a vain attempt to make him talk. Gasping for air, he was only allowed down each time when about to black out.

The Yankees were armed with 7-shot Spencers that could easily outrange the rebels' pistols, but Richards had no intention of allowing a long distance duel. The rebels fell back towards Meyerstown to make Old Blaze think they were moving back through Snicker's Gap, thus avoiding a fight. Once in Meyerstown, Richards led his men down the road to the left, then veered right through a stand of woods before riding into an open field. This descended into a hollow from where the ground rose again forming a hill crested by a timber fence. Richards scanned this terrain, and deployed his men.

Rebel decoys opened fire to lure the Yankees on. Blazer took the bait and followed. He dismounted his men in the woods at the edge of the field, hoping to open fire at long range, but then saw the rebels beating a hasty retreat through a gap in the distant fence. They were not going to give battle; they may well escape—or so it appeared. Blazer ordered his men to remount and charge. The bluecoats bolted across the field but, to their astonishment, a grayclad line rose from the hollow to their front like demons charging from hell. They hit with "the fury of a tornado" and those feigning retreat on the hill swung about and charged back to join the fight. "Blazer's men used their carbines at first," recalled Williamson, "until we got fairly among them, when they drew their revolvers. They fought desperately, but our men pressed on, broke them and finally drove them from the field."[77] Ranger Charles McDonough was wounded by a man he recognized, Trooper Harrell. He had deserted from the Confederate regulars and now fought with the Yanks. "Harrell, you——, I am going to kill you," yelled McDonough. He fired his last bullet and Harrell's horse came down with a crash. Harrell lay with one leg pinned underneath, and McDonough rode up with a second, borrowed pistol. He aimed. *Snap! Snap!* The gun misfired. But, "At the third trial the weapon exploded," recalled Williamson, "and the ball struck him in the top of the head, the blood spurting up like a fountain."

The shocked Yankees fell back in a mad scramble towards Meyerstown. Blazer attempted to rally his men and take cover behind buildings, but they were having nothing of that. They rode off at the gallop. Seeing the day lost, Blazer joined them, the rebels in close pursuit. Ranger Sydnor Ferguson, only 18, had no idea who his target was as he closed in. Blazer had a good horse, but Ferguson's mount "Fashion," had the speed. Ferguson rode alongside Blazer and hit him in the head with his empty revolver. The captain dropped from his saddle and rolled into a fence corner.

Ranger John Alexander, meanwhile, caught up with the fleeing Lieutenant Cole. Riding alongside, he demanded Cole's surrender. Already wounded, Cole reined in his mount, and raised his hands. But then another man galloped onto the scene. Puryear, the man he had strung up earlier in the day, had escaped during the fight. His "face was distorted with anger or excitement," recalled Alexander, "and he was pointing a cocked pistol at the officer's head."

"Don't shoot this man," yelled Alexander, "he has surrendered."

"The rascal tried to hang me this morning," said Puryear. Alexander turned to Cole and asked if this was true. "There was a moment's hesitation and no response; then the crack of a pistol, and Lieutenant Cole fell against my side and rolled to the ground between his horse and mine." Alexander dismounted and unbuckled Cole's empty pistols and belt. "As I moved away he rolled his dying eyes towards me with a look I shall never forget and I would gladly have tarried to give him such comfort as I could. But this was no time for sympathy, and I hurried back to the road."[78]

The Federals lost 21 dead, 12 wounded, 22 captured, and 50 Union horses joined the rebel stock. Dolly Richards had eight wounded, including one mortally. Blazer was found bruised but alive on the roadside. "Boys," he said, "you have whipped us fairly. All that I ask is that you treat us well." He was sent off to a Richmond prison, and from there to Danville, Virginia. He was partially disabled by kidney disease and, following the war, returned home to Gallipolis. In 1878 he and others died after the infected steam tug *John Porter* spread Yellow Fever from New Orleans.

Since the Cedar Creek defeat, the remains of Old Jubilee's force had been moved east to support Lee at Petersburg. But Mosby's Rangers and other rebel bands kept up the fight in the west of the state. They captured couriers, bushwhacked Yankee detachments and torched supply trains.[79] From November 20 to 27 Mosby struck various targets in the Shenandoah Valley and Loudoun County. His detachments took about 100 prisoners and 250 horses and mules. Seven of Mosby's men were captured, but in one case it was not for long. Frank Angelo, nicknamed the "Mocking-bird" was cast into the Martinsburg jail, but by morning had broken out and made his escape. But tragedy struck on November 27. Captain Richard Montjoy and Company D were in pursuit of fleeing Yankees when one fired a chance shot over his shoulder. Montjoy dropped from his mount, the bullet in his head. "Every man in the company who witnessed the tragedy," recalled one man, "reined in his horse voluntarily and groaned."

Montjoy, still alive, was taken to Leesburg, but soon died. His body was moved to Warrenton where the bad news was broken to his fiancée, Annie Lucas. He was buried in the local cemetery where a headstone was later erected with this inscription: "His death was a costly sacrifice to victory. He died too early for liberty and his country's cause, but not too early for his own fame."[80]

"There is no doubt about the necessity of clearing out that country so that it will not support Mosby's gang," Grant wrote to Sheridan on November 9.[81] Grant, no doubt, would have choked on his cigar if he had gazed into a crystal ball. He and Mosby were destined to become good friends. On November 28, one day after Montjoy's death, and 11 days after Blazer's rout, General Merritt's Cavalry Divisions rode east through Ashby's and Snicker's Gaps. Behind them, the Shenandoah Valley had been crushed under the Yankee heel, and now it was Loudoun County's turn. The people there had supplied Mosby with men, food and shelter. The time had come to pay the price. There was to be no "personal violence," Sheridan ordered, but he was intent on burning the county out.

On the very first day of the Yankee arrival, Amanda "Tee" Edmonds saw blueclad horsemen ride through her gate. Her brothers were known to ride with Mosby and the rebel cavalry. "The Yankees burned our barn," was that day's single diary entry. Next day, Catherine Broun near Middleburg wrote, "The farms all around us are on fire burning all the hay, corn, and wheat, driving off all the cattle, sheep, hogs, etc." That night she observed, "The whole heavens are illuminated by the fires." Her brothers rode with Mosby, but the Yankees miraculously missed her farm. The purge went on, however, and thousands of farm animals were driven off, and barns, crops, mills and outbuildings put to the torch. "We thought we had fathomed the depths of Yankee malice and rapacity," recalled Catherine Cochran, "but we had only skimmed the surface. From every quarter come tales of brutal insolence." Some Yankees relished this work: "We burned out the hornets," wrote one Rhode Island cavalryman. Army Chaplain Humphreys had barely escaped Mosby at Mount Zion Church, but he was one of many who took a different view: "This was the most unpleasant task we were ever compelled to undertake." Families cried and begged to have their life's work spared. "It was a terrible retribution on the country," he wrote. One Yankee captain recalled, "The task was not a pleasant one, for many innocents were made to suffer with the guilty, but something was necessary to clear the country of those bands of Guerrillas that were becoming so formidable."[82]

Even Sheridan was not made of stone. On Christmas Day he wired General Henry Halleck for permission to distribute military rations to hungry families. But Halleck refused: "While the men of Virginia are either serving in the rebel ranks, or as bushwhackers are waylaying or murdering our soldiers, our Government must decline to support their wives and children."

By the time the cold winds of January swept the scorched Loudoun countryside, the people around Middleburg were living in a "pitiable condition," and people went hungry. "Our children, indeed all of us, nearly live on milk and butter," recalled Catherine Broun.[83] General Merritt informed General Stephenson at Harper's Ferry, "Should complaints come in from the citizens of Loudoun County tell them they have furnished too many meals to guerrillas to expect much sympathy."[84] As the bleak winter wore on, however, humanity prevailed and emergency rations were dispatched to Winchester by rail for distribution amongst the starving populace.[85]

By December 1864, Mosby's command had swelled to nearly 400 men. But the lack of food and forage, and the thousands of Yankee troops in Loudoun county, meant a change of tack was required. Mosby shared his 31st birthday, December 6, with General Lee over a meal in Petersburg. The dire situation was discussed, and Lee agreed with Mosby's suggestion that he divide his command. Half would be sent to the "Northern Neck," an area on Chesapeake Bay between the Potomac and Rappahannock Rivers.[86] Here food and forage would be available for men and horses. Mosby wished to appoint Chapman and Richards as majors, each commanding separate battalions, and Lee advised him to approach War Secretary Seddon with the idea.[87] Seddon not only agreed, but had further good news for Mosby. He was promoted to Colonel, while Lieutenant Colonel Chapman would command one battalion, and Major Richards the other. This became official on January 9, 1865, with Mosby's colonelcy backdated to December 7, and the 43rd Battalion became the 43rd Regiment of Virginia Cavalry. The departure of Chapman's battalion for the Northern Neck on January 3, however, meant that the regiment would never campaign as a single unit. Chapman's battalion would operate independently until war's end, now only a matter of months away.[88]

Despite fire and destruction, and the looming collapse of the Confederacy, some happy events still came to pass. A few weeks before the reorganization, and Mosby's promotion, he attended the marriage of Sergeant Jake Lavinder to Judith Edmonds on December 21, 1864. Word was received that 600 cavalry under Major Douglas Frazar were on the road to Salem, just a few miles away. Mosby and Ranger Thomas Love left the festivities to reconnoiter the icy terrain. Before leaving, Mosby threw his black beaver overcoat and a scarlet-lined cape over a fine new uniform trimmed with gold. His hat was adorned with an ostrich plume, gold cord and star. They rode cross country to avoid the troops on the road, but soon encountered Yankee flankers. Bullets cut the cold air as the enemy opened fire, "So Love and I galloped away a few yards and then halted on an eminence," recalled Mosby. "They did not pursue, and we soon saw the whole column in blue moving on the road to Rectortown."[89] Mosby cut a fine, mounted figure overlooking the bluecoats as a brisk wind swirled around. "Scarlet Cloak" they called him, a lasting, chivalric image of the Old South. Many young soldiers, including Mosby, would live to see mounted warriors replaced with wartanks and airplanes as the 20th century saw romantic delusions regarding warfare swept away.

As dusk approached, the Yankees stopped in Rectortown. From a distance, Mosby saw fires kindled and assumed they would bivouac there for the night. He sent word to Chapman and Richards to prepare the men for an attack on the northern-most Union campsite at dawn. Mosby and Love set off to spread the word to other officers, but the welcoming lights of Ludwell Lake's home proved too much of a temptation. A cold drizzling rain was falling and icicles hung in clusters from the trees. Love offered to stand guard, but Mosby insisted that he too come in from the cold. Mr. Lake was famous for setting a good table, when all said and done. Their horses were left tethered, their pistols in saddle holsters. Mosby felt there was no danger; the Yankees were all huddled around campfires in Rectortown.

Mosby and Love were enjoying coffee, hot rolls and spareribs when the alarming tramp of horses' hooves was heard around the house. Mosby's usual sharp instincts had let him down. The Yankees had only stayed in Rectortown for a break, then moved out. Mosby flew to the back door to see cavalrymen in the yard. He turned back to the front door to be confronted by blueclad officers entering the room. He quickly covered the twin stars of rank on his collar by raising his hands in a gesture of surrender. A few words passed between them, then a soldier outside saw the rebel uniform through a window. Glass shattered as he fired. Mosby winced. "I am shot," he cried. In the next few moments pandemonium broke out as more bullets flew and both officers and the Lake family ducked for cover. The table was knocked over and the candle lights went out. Lake's daughter screamed as people thrashed about in the dark. Bleeding profusely, Mosby staggered into an adjoining bedroom and pulled off his uniform coat. He thrust it under a bureau so the enemy could not see his rank. Thinking fast, he lay on the floor and smeared blood around his mouth. Perhaps the Yankees would not take him prisoner if they thought the wound was mortal.

The firing ceased, people shuffled about in the darkness, then someone struck a match. Soon the rooms were bathed in candlelight once more. Mosby lay there groaning, as though about to take his last breath. When questioned by the officers, the "dying" man muttered that he was Lieutenant Johnson of the 16th Virginia Cavalry. "I was sure they would drag me away as a trophy if they knew who their prisoner was."[90] His bleeding abdomen was examined. A mortal wound was the consensus; there was no point in taking him away. The ruse had worked. But his trousers and fine cavalry boots were another matter. They were stripped off. As the Yankees walked out, Major Frazar said, "He will die in 24 hours."[91] Another officer, an Irishman, looked back with suspicion. "He is worth several dead men yet," he said.

Mosby heard the Yankees ride off. They took Tom Love as a prisoner, along with Mosby's ostrich plumed hat, overcoat and scarlet-lined cloak. One would think these items would have raised an alarm, but, "There was good deal of whiskey in the crowd." Mosby recalled. "My own belief is that I was indebted to whiskey for my escape."

The Lakes, meanwhile, were calming their rattled nerves around the log fire, happy to be alive. The bullet that downed Mosby had also taken Ludwell's waistcoat button away. Then there was a movement at the bedroom door. The family looked around to see the Gray Ghost, resplendent in socks, flannel shirt and blood-soaked underclothes, enter the room. Quite a change from his flamboyant arrival. "They were as much astonished to see me as if I had arisen from the tomb; they had thought me dead and were now sure the general resurrection had come."

Mosby was taken by ox-cart through a howling snow storm, and arrived at a safe house two miles away. Despite being wrapped in a quilt and blankets, his body was rigid with cold, and his hair stiff with ice. But, before dawn, help arrived, including two surgeons. They examined the wound and saw that the ball had not gone deep, but traveled around just under the surface to the victim's right side. Mosby was fortunate that they had chloroform, a luxury not always on hand, and the ball was extracted in the early hours of the morning.

The Yankees, meanwhile, were finally sobering up. Frazar looked at the plumed hat and scarlet-lined cloak. Who exactly had been shot? Prisoners denied they belonged to Mosby, but the word soon spread that the elusive Gray Ghost had escaped yet again. Frazar's superior, Colonel William Gamble, was not pleased. "I exceedingly regret that such a blunder was made," he wrote to General Augur. Gamble ordered that all wounded enemy, "be hereafter bought in, although any officer ought to have brains and common sense enough to do so without an order." He was, furthermore, "informed that Major Frazar was too much under the influence of liquor to perform his duty at the time."[92] Gamble ordered Frazar back into the area with 300 men. They searched every stable, barn and attic, but without success, Mosby being moved from house to house and kept out of reach.

As Chapman's battalion departed for the Northern Neck on January 3, 1865, Mosby arrived at his parents' home near Lynchburg. The Richmond press, however, had announced his death at Charlottesville on December 27, 1864. And the Northern press agreed. On December 30 the *New York Herald* carried: "The Fate of Mosby, Death of the Notorious Pirate of the Valley." The writer had no time for Mosby's heroics, even comparing him with Bloody Bill Anderson and others of "like character." Mosby's career, said the paper, "has been short and inglorious. He added nothing to the cause of the rebellion by his conquests. He has only served to disgrace the country and degrade the profession of arms."[93] The following day the same paper published an article which falsely claimed that Mosby opened fire from the doorway, slammed it shut, and was shot through a window by Corporal Kane in reply. The officers then entered and found him mortally wounded. Subsequent enquiries revealed the shot man to have been the notorious guerrilla chief, John Mosby.

But, by then, other rumors were doing the rounds. "If we believe the rebel stories, Mosby is not yet dead," said the paper. "He may possibly recover: 'The devil takes care of his own.'"[94]

14

"The optics of the dead"
Anderson, 1864

On October 11, 1864, two weeks after the Centralia Massacre, a group of horsemen rode into Boonville, Missouri. They were "well clad," recalled one observer, "in black or dark suits, and had their hats fantastically decorated with ribbons." They carried "at least four revolvers in their belts," and scalps were seen dangling from the bridles of their mounts.[1] Anderson had arrived in town to meet with General Price, who had arrived the day before. Yankee prisoners were being paroled. "Shoot the sons of bitches," the guerrillas shouted as they reached for revolvers. But Old Pap had a different set of rules. He promptly ordered his "allies" to desist.

Anderson rode forward on a fine black mount and started talking to Price, but the would-be Confederate governor of Missouri, Thomas Reynolds, was standing alongside. Appalled by the sight of the scalps, he angrily cut in, upbraiding Anderson and his men for dishonoring the Confederate Cause. Price agreed, and said he would have nothing to do with the guerrillas till the scalps were gone.

With the offending trophies removed, Anderson presented Price with a fine wooden box containing a pair of silver-mounted pistols. Regardless of what Price thought of Anderson, they were both fighting on the same side, and he was obliged to accept the gift. And Price needed all the help he could get. His campaign to take Missouri had not been going well. On the very same day Anderson had inflicted carnage at Centralia, 7,000 of Old Pap's troops had been repulsed with heavy losses at Fort Davidson by 1,500 bluecoats under General Ewing, author of the infamous Order No. 11. To make matters worse, the Yankees had managed to slip away during the night and blow up the fort. Price's loss of men and munitions during the assault had ended any hope of planting rebel colors over St. Louis. He took Fort Davidson, but the dubious victory had cost him the campaign.

Governor Reynolds later damned the handling of the expedition, and the conduct of Price's troops. It would appear they were no better than the guerrillas. "It would take a volume to describe the acts of outrage; neither station, age, nor sex was any protection," he wrote. "Southern men and women were as little spared as Unionists; the elegant mansion of General Robert E. Lee's accomplished niece and cabin of the negro were alike ransacked ... the clothes of a poor man's infant were as attractive spoil as the merchant's silk and calico or curtain taken from the rich man's parlor; ribbons and trumpery gee-gaws were stolen from milliners, and jewelled rings forced from the fingers of delicate maidens whose brothers were fighting in Georgia in Cockrell's Missouri brigade."[2] Price, of course, did not condone such conduct, but the officers under his command had either little control or profited them-

Here rebel guerrillas lynch Yankee sympathizers. But the Yankees did some lynching of their own (*Thrilling Adventures of Daniel Ellis*, 1867).

selves. And murders occurred, black and white bodies being left by the roadside. On October 13 the St. Louis *Missouri Democrat* reported attacks on women including Mrs. Charles Schmidt who "was ravished and her person violated by a number of the fiendish ghouls." Another woman was saved from the same fate by "some rebel soldiers less brutal than their fellows, who rescued the poor woman from their clutches."[3]

Shortly after his arrival in Boonville, Bloody Bill received the following orders from

Price: "Captain Anderson and his command will at once proceed to the north side of the Missouri River and permanently destroy the North Missouri Railroad, going as far east as practicable. He will report his operations at least every two days." This order gave Anderson official status and recognized him, at least in Old Pap's eyes, as holding a captain's rank. No doubt there would be many in Richmond who would not agree, but Richmond was a long way off. Price also dispatched orders to "Colonel" Quantrill to strike the Hannibal & St. Joseph Railroad. This was another convenient recognition that belied the truth. Quantrill was now commanding only a small band, but many on both sides still believed him to be the supreme chieftain of the Missouri guerrillas. In any case, the order never reached Quantrill.

Anderson's command crossed the Missouri from Price's camp on the Boonville ferry. On October 14 some of his men burned railroad depots at Florence and High Hill while Anderson himself led the looting of Danville, which had no connection with the railroad he had been ordered to destroy. They shot five former Union shoulders and burned several buildings. Ignoring Price's verbal order to burn the important railroad bridge in St. Charles County, he turned back west and followed Price's army. Joined By George Todd and his band in Lafayette County, the guerrillas murdered dozens of "Dutch" farmers and plundered homes along the way. There was no profit in burning railway bridges and, regardless of Southern sentiments, that's what these gentlemen were primarily about.

And Quantrill was out to do a bit more profiteering of his own. On the evening of October 17 he arrived in Glasgow township and had two men abduct bank manager W. E. Dunnica from his home. Once at the bank, Quantrill emptied the safe of its contents, $21,000, and led his robbers back to their lair in the Perche Hills. No doubt he was well pleased with the night's work, but would have been infuriated to know the wily banker, fearing such a robbery, had buried $32,000 in his back yard just the day before.[4]

Bloody Bill was the next guerrilla to arrive in Glasgow. Perhaps he had heard of Quantrill's good fortune and decided to try his own luck. He and his orderly, Ike "Weasel" Berry, invaded Glen Eden, the opulent home of wealthy Union supporter Benjamin Lewis. Despite Old Pap's brother-in-law being a house guest, Anderson told Lewis he would die if he did not hand over the substantial cash said to be on hand. The $1000 in notes and silver gathered by Lewis did not satisfy Anderson. Women screamed as Lewis was knocked to the floor, beaten, trampled and kicked, all the time protesting there was no more money in the house. The barrel of a revolver was thrust up and down in his mouth, lacerating his throat. Then, according to the St. Louis *Missouri Democrat* Anderson and Weasel "took a negro girl of 12 or 13 years old into another room and both of them ravished her by turns." The battered and bleeding Lewis still insisted there was no more money at hand, and he was subjected to more torments such as knife pricks, having his clothes slashed, and a revolver fired through his pants and alongside his face causing powder burns. He was then dragged out into the street where Anderson's horse trampled him underfoot.

Two previously hidden women appeared and pleaded with Anderson to desist. Lewis had previously proposed $5000 be levied on the town's rebel sympathizers, and Anderson informed the women that $5000 was the victim's fine. He would die if the sum was not paid out. The women set out to raise the money while Lewis was taken into the nearby township and laid out on a liquor store counter. Battered, burnt and bruised, he went into convulsions while the rebels drank whiskey. Eventually one of the women, a cousin of Lewis, returned with the required $5000 in paper and silver, provided by Mr. Dunnica. No doubt the banker was thankful he had not received the same treatment from Quantrill. Anderson told the cousin that he would rather kill Lewis than have the money but, being a man of his word, would stick to the deal. He took the money, gathered his band, and they rode out of town.[5]

Next morning Lewis, racked with pain, fled Glasgow with his wife and two children, a wise move as it turned out. Apparently Anderson's account of the night's activities inspired a return visit by some of his men. They turned up next morning and raped two black girls after having them provide breakfast. Lewis never recovered from the attack, and died of his injuries on February 2, 1866.

"Are the diabolical murders, robberies, and other outrages of the demon, Bill Anderson, never to cease in Northern Missouri?" clamored the St. Louis *Tri-Star Missouri Republican*, on October 19. "Is there no power in our troops or people to drive him and his gang of cutthroats from the State, or to exterminate them? Can there not be raised a volunteer force especially for this purpose?"[6]

George Todd and his band, meanwhile, were doing a bit of bushwhacking of their own. According to John McCorkle, George Todd said, "Boys, when Price gets here, I will join him and, in the first battle I am in with him I shall be killed."[7] Todd joined Price on October 18. Accounts vary as to how exactly he died, but it was during the Second Battle of Independence on October 21. Apparently he was shot from his horse on a scouting mission. Some sources credit the marksman as being Lieutenant Colonel George Hoyt, who had been a defense lawyer for John Brown at his trial in 1859. Todd was buried in the Westlawn Cemetery in Independence, and Dave Poole merged his band with Todd's to take over as leader. But the day following Todd's death, Price ordered the guerrillas from his army for having executed prisoners.

The Yankees may not have been able to drive Bloody Bill from the state, but they were having more success with Old Pap. After a series of battles to the east of Kansas City, Price was routed by Union forces at the Battle of Westport on October 23, called by some the "Gettysburg of the West."

Anderson, meanwhile, free ranged through Carroll County and murdered six more Union supporters. One had acted as their guide before being "paroled," as Anderson put it. Little Archie Clement took the old "Dutchman" into the brush where he was killed. His body was found with his hands appearing to hold his decapitated head on his chest.

On October 26 Anderson rode up to a farmhouse near Albany in Ray County where he ordered the woman living there to prepare breakfast. He took time out to wash his face and comb his hair, then grinned into a mirror. "Good morning, Captain Anderson, how are you this morning?" Then, "Damn well, thank you," he answered himself.[8]

That same morning a woman arrived in the Yankee quarters of Sam "Cob" Cox. She divulged news of Anderson's camp near Albany. Cox was now serving as a volunteer militia commander without formal rank. He had routed 200 guerrillas at Cameron on July 24, and had been brought in for one purpose: "I believed he would find and whip Anderson," reported General James Craig.[9]

Bugles blew, and soon 300 men of the 33rd and 51st Missouri Militia rode out. About one mile from Albany Anderson's pickets were seen by the Yankee advance troop. They mounted up and retreated back through the town. Cox arrived in Albany with the main force at about midday, and scouts brought word of the enemy camp some way ahead. Like Johnston's men at Centralia, Cox's troops were mostly armed with muzzle-loading rifles, but a few companies carried the guerrillas' favorite weapon, the revolver. Cox had his infantry dismount, every fourth man holding the horses. Using guerrilla tactics himself, he ordered a cavalry squad forward to lure Bloody Bill out rather than launch an all out assault. His remaining men were then deployed across a laneway and in the woods along either side. Then Cox waited. "Everything seemed to stand still," recalled Lieutenant Hankins, "not even a horse appeared to move." But things soon happened down the lane. "'Bang,' a single shot, then a sharp volley, followed by the 'rebel yell'—once heard, never to be forgotten."[10] The Yankee bait came galloping back down the lane with the guerrillas in hot pursuit. Cox allowed his own men to pass, then gave the order to open fire. A few guerrillas dropped from their saddles, but the rest continued on, revolvers blazing. Cox had his men fire in stages, and at about 40 yards the rebel charge wavered, the horsemen milling about in some confusion, neither retreating nor continuing on—except two men. Seemingly impervious to the hail of lead, they passed right through the blueclad lines, reigns between their teeth and a Colt in each hand. Bluecoats turned and fired after them. At about 50 yards, one reeled in his saddle and fell to the ground, to be quickly followed by the other. The latter, mortally wounded, regained his feet and staggered into the woods. The main party of bushwhackers turned and retreated in confusion as the Yankee cavalry countercharged.

The dead man was found to have two balls in his head. A wide-brimmed white hat with a long black plume lay nearby. He wore a dun-colored frock coat, a blue vest, and an embroidered black shirt. He held a revolver in each hand. Two more were found in hip holsters, and yet another two in saddle holsters. Scalps dangled from the bridle. A pocket search revealed two watches, gold and silver, $600 in paper and gold coins, a lock of woman's hair, a photograph of himself with a woman, and a letter, signed "Bush Anderson." The discovery of Price's orders of October 11 and a small Confederate flag inscribed, "PRESENTED TO W. T. ANDERSON BY HIS FRIEND, F. M. R. LET IT NOT BE CONTAMINATED BY FEDERAL HANDS," confirmed that Cox had bagged Bloody Bill himself.[11] Gazing at the dead guerrilla, no doubt some felt cheated that Anderson had died so quickly rather than "dancing a hornpipe," at a rope's end. Legend has it that a buckskin pouch was also found containing a silken cord adorned with 53 knots—one for each of Bloody Bill's victims.

News of Anderson's demise caused rejoicing in every Union camp, but a quick death seemed inappropriate for Bloody Bill (State Historical Society of Missouri).

Anderson's body was hauled by cart to Richmond, Missouri, where it was put on display and photographed, revolver in hand. The staff of the St. Louis *Missouri Republican* viewed pictures "of the celebrated murderer and robber, Bill Anderson, taken while he lay, cold and stark, in the arms of his only master, Death. His mouth is partially open, disclosing his front teeth and imparting to the expression a half-sardonic, hideous grin; while the eyes—whose scorching orbs, which have often sent terror to innocent hearts—are partially open, with that woeful and expressionless appearance belonging to the optics of the dead, induce a peculiar and contradictory estimate of the general contour. Thinking of his demonic life, and looking upon him helpless and forever powerless to murder and pillage, a strange feeling is excited—a contention between a desire to spurn the hideous body of a serpent, dead, and that natural emotion of pity which ever arises on view of the remains of a human being. But the memory of his crimes soon drives away the last vestige of the latter feeling, if any should arise. It is gratifying in looking upon the picture, to know that there is one devil less in the world."[12]

An Anderson family tradition has it that the body was mutilated, dragged through the streets and beheaded in an attempt to show Bill's slayers were as barbarous as himself. But a witness stated his body was placed in a "decent coffin," for burial, "a respect due not to him but to ourselves and to humanity."[13]

Two days following Anderson's death, Price fought an engagement with General Blunt's cavalry near Newtonia in southwestern Missouri. Shelby's troops, including his Iron Brigade, drove the Yankees back for the moment, but Old Pap was now in full retreat, his ideas of conquering Missouri a shattered dream. This was the last engagement of the campaign, and after retreating through Indian Territory and Texas, Price arrive back in Arkansas on December 2, 1864, with 6,000 men—half the number he marched with, the others having been killed, badly wounded, captured or deserted.[14]

Price was gone, and Bill Anderson lay dead. But the guerrilla curse did not die—yet. Archie Clement took command of Anderson's band and continued on. And Bill's brother Jim led another lot calling themselves "Anderson Avengers." Apart from gaining further plunder, however, their activities were a waste of time, and both would be killed after continuing as outlaws following the war's conclusion.

Meanwhile they rode through Howard and Boon Counties, burning and killing as though nothing had changed. A little over two weeks after Bloody Bill's demise, The *St. Louis Democrat* complained that "This whole region is sprinkled with the blood of Union men, and dotted with fresh-made graves, in which they lie, and in many cases their unburied corpses furnish food for the swine of the woods. Yes, the spirit of Bill Anderson yet lives."[15]

And so did William Clarke Quantrill. But it was now apparent that the Confederacy had no future; Missouri was a lost cause. Quantrill decided to head east.

15

"Unconquered"
Mosby, 1865

John Mosby was out of action after being shot at Lakers's farm, but his Partisan Rangers kept up pressure on Sheridan's supply lines. Union infantry companies protecting the W&P and B&O tracks were backed up by the 12th Pennsylvania Cavalry commanded by Colonel Marcus A. Reno. But a gap was created when Sheridan received orders to dispatch the 2nd Eastern Shore Infantry Regiment from Duffield's Depot to Baltimore.[1] Informed of the opportunity, Dolly Richards mustered a combined force of rangers and regular cavalry, and set out on January 18, 1865. Colonel Preston Chew of the Horse Artillery came along for the ride. That night a rail was removed and the arrival of a locomotive saw it clatter off the tracks leaving 15 cars stranded on the rails. The horsemen swooped with rebel yells. Their plunder included sugar, ale, canned oysters, raisins, wines, and an immense consignment of coffee beans, all intended for a big Yankee do in Martinsburg. As the cars were ransacked a sentry saw a light approaching through the woods, the regular Yankee night patrol, unaware of the raid. The bluecoats were surprised to find themselves surrounded, and gave up without a fight. Then the cars went up in flames as each man took away all he could carry. This included numerous bags of coffee beans, the exploit becoming known as the "Coffee Raid."[2]

Colonel Mosby, while stating he had little "spirit of knight-errantry in him," was not shy when it came to a photo shoot (Library of Congress).

On February 3, the rebels struck again one mile to the east.

A detachment of the 12th Virginia Cavalry under Lieutenant George Baylor, learning guerrilla tactics, was operating with Mosby's Rangers. A train carrying a Union payroll was expected. "Our waiting was not long," recalled Baylor, "the rumble was heard in the distance: nearer and nearer it came, until the iron horse with its fiery head appeared in full view. All were eager and excited. The prize seemed in our grasp. The engine struck the obstruction; a great crash followed, and the train stopped. But, alas! it was only a special freight, running on express time. Our financial hopes were again blasted."[3] Ironically, in later life George Baylor would serve as chief legal officer for the B&O.

The rebels plundered the cars and escaped. But Colonel Reno was on the alert, having received warning of the rebels crossing the Shenandoah River the day before. He dispatched two parties of 50 cavalry under lieutenants Harland Guild and Deloss Chase to hunt them down. But, according to Reno, Guild disobeyed his orders and moved in the wrong direction. The two Yankee columns came in contact and Guild opened fire. One man was wounded before the mistake was realized.

Secretary of War Stanton was not happy. "Another train was thrown off the track and robbed last night within three and a half miles of Harper's Ferry, in the immediate vicinity of a recent occurrence of this kind," he wired Sheridan. "Will you please give this matter attention? The interruption of trains there seems to be chronic, and may spread if not checked."

Sheridan promptly fired off a telegram to Reno: "The country in your vicinity and out for a distance of ten miles is full of Confederate soldiers. With a regiment as strong as yours you should be able to capture many of them, and I will look to you to do so. At every house where you make a capture drive off all stock except one milch-cow, and notify the people that I will put them out of my lines and let their rebel friends take care of them."

Reno wired back his side of the story. "I have placed Lieutenant Guild in arrest, and now report him for immediate dismissal…. He is always full, and when not stupefied with whiskey, he is with opium. His performance last night is sufficient to hang him." Reno wanted Guild dismissed immediately. A court martial would be a waste of time, he claimed, and Guild was discharged on February 14. "Poor Guild was the scapegoat," recalled Lieutenant Baylor. "After the capture we passed back within a half-mile of Reno's camp, and in a quarter mile of Lieutenant Chase's company, and they must have been stupefied also."[4] Ironically, Reno would be accused of being "full" at the Battle of the Little Bighorn 11 years later.[5]

But while these vexing telegrams changed hands, the Yankees could take

Union secretary of war Edwin Stanton had no time for Mosby and wanted him excluded from surrender terms offered to other rebel officers (Library of Congress).

heart from one success against rebel rangers. Union Major Henry Young led a band of 60 scouts who, often dressed as Confederates, gathered intelligence about enemy movements. Posing as rebel recruits from Maryland, Young surprised the camp of Colonel Harry Gilmore on February 4. Gilmore, asleep, found himself under Young's pistol before he could reach his own revolvers, kept under his pillow.[6]

But then, on February 21, McNeill's Rangers more than evened the score. Emulating Mosby's capture of Stoughton, they took Union Generals George Crook and Benjamin Kelly in their beds at their headquarters hotel in Cumberland, Maryland. Taken under guard to Richmond, the embarrassed generals were exchanged the following month. Kelly resigned in June while Crook went on to become a famed frontier Indian fighter.

Mount Carmel Church

On February 18, two deserters From Richards' battalion offered to act as guides to General Merritt. Major Thomas Gibson was dispatched with 237 men to search homes where the deserters said guerrillas slept during the night. Gibson divided his force, and 100 men under Captain Henry Snow searched houses in Upperville. Dolly Richards and two others were rumored to be at his parents' home on a farm a few miles out of town. But, when a search was made, Richards' new Confederate uniform was the only thing found. As the Yankees rode off, uniform in hand, the rebels emerged from behind a hidden trapdoor. Captain Snow was even more disappointed when back in town he found about one-third of his men drunk. Two barrels of apple-jack had been captured along with three disgruntled rebels.

Gibson, meanwhile, had more luck. Despite 11 of his men getting lost in the dark, he managed to bag 18 rebels and 50 horses in and around Markham. While on the job, his troops pillaged homes and farmyards. Due to a confusion of orders, the two Federal columns missed reuniting at Piedmont, and Gibson rode to Upperville to learn that Snow had already departed. Meanwhile, word of their arrival spread. "I was roused from my sleep early in the morning by one of the little black boys clattering up the stairs—his feet being encased in a pair of old shoes many sizes too large for him," recalled James Williamson. "At every step he called out 'Yankees! Yankees!'"[7]

Gibson's plan had been to leave Mosby's Confederacy before daybreak, but the division of his force caused confusion and delays. In mid-morning his column was passing through Paris, at the entrance to Ashby's Gap. Here a handful of rebels opened fire from behind a stone wall on an overlooking hill. Unable to return any effective fire, the bluecoats dashed on. Then Dolly Richards, dressed in clothes borrowed from his father, arrived with reinforcements. He was welcomed with three huzzahs, but the rebels still had only 43 men against Gibson's 125. The Yankees passed through Ashby's Gap and, heading for the Shenandoah River, turned right at Mount Carmel Church into Shepherd's Ford Road. The narrow path meandered between rocks and undergrowth in mountainous terrain. Despite being outnumbered, the rebels caught up with their rear and "charged them on sight," recalled Williamson. "They attempted to form and delivered a volley with their carbines; but the carbine was no match for the revolver at close range and our men broke and routed them completely." The Yankees fled, the road "strewn with hats, belts, carbines, turkeys and chickens—both living and dead—clothing and plunder of all kinds, which the pillagers in their flight had thrown away. The blood from the wounded men and horses crimsoned the snow along the road."

I was "unable to engage in a melee successfully with an enemy armed with at least two revolvers per man," Gibson reported. By the time the smoke cleared, Richards had killed or wounded 25 bluecoats, and captured another 64 along with 90 horses. The rebel prisoners were all freed, but the deserter guide, Spotts, made good his escape. One rebel had been killed by "friendly" fire, and another wounded. "I have always said it was the most brilliant thing our men ever did," Mosby later wrote.[8]

The guerrilla chief himself, meanwhile, was on the mend. Just one week following the Mount Carmel Church fight, Mosby's mother wrote in her diary: "The day has come and the hour has passed that we saw our dearest one leave once more the household group to go back to battle for his country and all that is dear to man and woman. It is one of the saddest events of my life, when I have to part from my dear boys, to go the Army, yet I know God is there as well as around the peaceful and secure fireside.... A crisis is upon us. We are beset on all sides by a powerful enemy."[9]

And the powerful enemy was closing in fast. The day Mosby had been shot, December 21, William Sherman had completed his famous, or infamous, March from Atlanta to the Sea. He wired Abe Lincoln offering Savannah, just captured, as a Christmas present. Sherman then marched north through the Carolinas destroying anything of military value.[10] He continued through North Carolina with the intention of joining Grant's host outside Petersburg. His army of 60,000 met and defeated General Joe Johnston's 21,000 at Bentonville on March 19–21.[11]

Despite these victories, the Confederacy doomed, the Union cavalry on the early-warning screen protecting Washington remained under threat. The dreaded Mosby was still on the loose. Over a 13-mile stretch the Yankees built defensive, frontier-style blockhouses two or three miles apart, and only ventured into Mosby's Confederacy with forces of at least 600 men.[12] On February 27 Sheridan moved with the bulk of his troops east to join Grant at Petersburg. Winfield Scott Hancock took command of his former post. The handsome and popular Hancock was considered the prime hero of Gettysburg, having been wounded while holding Cemetery Ridge against Pickett's Charge.

Hancock deployed the 1st Veteran Infantry Regiment of 800 men, under Lieutenant Colonel Charles Bird, to Keyes's Ford, a few miles south of Harper's Ferry. He was to support Colonel Marcus Reno's cavalry stationed at Charles Town. This provided strong defense for the Baltimore and Ohio Railway, much to the satisfaction of his friend, Secretary of War Stanton.

But the Gray Ghost was still at large. Hancock dispatched a clumsy column of 1800 infantry, cavalry and artillery to bring the vexing rebel to bay. Sheridan, however, had learned that small, night-time sorties were virtually the only path to success when it came to rooting out partisan rangers.

Reno was placed in charge of Hancock's primary strike force, 300 cavalry and 700 infantry with two cannon in tow. On March 20 they crossed the Shenandoah River at Harper's Ferry, and marched south. A Confederate supply base said to be at Upperville was to go up in flames, and troops were deployed to catch fleeing rebels at strategic points like Ashby's and Snicker's Gaps to the west, and the Little River Turnpike to the east. The first night Reno camped near Hillsboro, and next morning his cavalry did a sweep through Leesburg, then swung back to rejoin the infantry at Purcellville. Mosby's scouts watched their movements from the hilltops, and reported back.

Near the Quaker settlement of Hamilton, six rebels fired on the Yankee cavalry and, taking the bait, a large detachment under Lieutenant John Black galloped off in pursuit. Mosby was waiting with 128 rebels spoiling for a fight. Lieutenant Channing Smith of the

Confederate regulars was serving with Mosby, and observed the action. As the Yankees approached, rebel Captain Alfred Glascock led his guerrillas from woods at the trot, "and as he struck the open, gave the command to charge and the whole band broke into a gallop and hurled themselves upon the flank and front of the astonished foe," recalled Smith. "They stood for a short while, but only for a few minutes, but then gave way and fled back towards Hamilton pursued by Glascock and his men, who rained bullets among them.... The colonel sat upon his horse in the field on top of the bank, his eyes flashing, his long black plume tossing in the wind, waving on his men, who with loud cheers followed up the chase."[13]

The Yankees took refuge in the township, but the rebels charged on, only to be met with a surprise volley from infantry lined up behind a hedge. "The fire of the infantry then became so hot that Colonel Mosby ordered the men to fall back," recalled James Williamson. "Some, not hearing or heeding the order went through both cavalry and infantry and back again safely to the command.... The men cheered, waved their hats, and used every means to draw the cavalry away from the infantry. Some of our men, venturing too close to the enemy's lines, were fired on, and one, Joseph Griffin was wounded and his horse was killed. He attempted to gain the shelter of the woods, but was pursued and captured."[14] The rebels pulled back with two men killed, six wounded, and six taken prisoner. The Yankees lost nine killed, 12 wounded, and 13 taken prisoner along with 15 horses.

Over the next three days Reno marched his command to Snickersville, Bloomfield, Upperville, and Middleburg in a quest to destroy rebel supplies. Along the way Mosby harassed his flanks, trying to draw the cavalry out. But, having no wish to tangle with the Gray Ghost, they stayed safely within infantry lines. The Yankees found and destroyed some rebel supplies but, overall, the expedition was a failure. Reno claimed that he had to contend with Mosby leading about 500 men.[15] The weary troops trudged back into Harper's Ferry, "having accomplished much less than I expected it to do," admitted Hancock.[16] The same could be said for an Indian hunting expedition Hancock led the following year. His burning of a deserted Indian village would serve only to inflame the Southern Cheyenne.[17]

On April 3 Hancock received word that his Union headquarters at Harpers Ferry was under threat; General Pickett's Division was marching his way. Bluecoats marched out to counter the menace, leaving only 500 troops to guard the B&O Railway. Pickett was, in fact, retreating towards Appomattox Court House with Lee and the battered remains of The Army of Northern Virginia. The Confederate trenches at Petersburg had been overrun while Pickett was enjoying a shad bake with fellow officers a few miles in the rear.

On April 5 Mosby organized the 8th company of the 43rd Partisan Rangers under the command of Captain George Baylor. Despite many of Mosby's men having been killed or captured during the previous two years, there had been no shortage of fresh volunteers. But time was running out for the Confederacy, and Baylor's company was the last to be organized for the 43rd.

Mosby dispatched Baylor to breach the weakness caused by Hancock's redeployment, and do what damage he could. The Loudoun Rangers, having heard of Richmond's fall, felt the war as good as won, and they relaxed about the river bank enjoying a yarn, a smoke— and possibly a shad bake of their own. The dreaded rebel yell was heard as Baylor charged from the woods with 50 men. They rode amongst the astonished Yankees, most quickly surrendering while others ran for their lives. The rebels killed two men and wounded four while capturing 65 men and 81 horses.

On April 8, 215 rangers mustered in Upperville. Divided into two squadrons, Mosby dispatched them on separate missions. The following day, however, Lee lowered his colors at Appomattox Court House. Grant had won, the war virtually over. But other Confederate troops were still in the field, and President Jefferson Davis, having fled Richmond, had set up government in Danville, Virginia. He was in no mood to surrender, and urged other rebels to fight on.

On April 10, George Baylor's detachment took a break at Arundel's Tavern, only 2.5 miles from the Union fort at Fairfax Station. The tables were turned when the rebels were attacked by 250 men of the 8th Illinois Cavalry. The rebels were outnumbered 2 to 1, and perhaps news of Richmond's fall had an effect. "I endeavored to urge our men to charge," recalled Baylor, "but they had now become somewhat dispirited and disorganized, and all attempts in that direction were futile ... our line began to waver and break, and retreat was inevitable ... my horse was shot in the nostrils and foreleg and nearly succeeded in unhorsing me." Baylor fled along with his men, and Colonel Charles Albright reported that he had "whipped him like thunder."[18]

William Chapman returned with his battalion from the Northern Neck to a dispiriting scene. But, with the regiment reunited, the 43rd Virginia Cavalry still had a fighting force of eight companies of about 400 men. A copy of the *Baltimore American*, however, fell into Mosby's hands. This carried news of Lee's surrender. "I thought I had sounded the profoundest depth of human feeling," he recalled, "but this is the bitterest hour of my life."[19] On April 10, on instructions from Secretary of War Stanton, Hancock put out a circular offering other Confederates the same generous conditions as those afforded Lee. But— "The guerrilla Chief Mosby is not included."

Grant, however, disagreed, and on April 11 Hancock's chief of staff wrote to Mosby offering to receive the surrender of his command under the same conditions. Hancock received no immediate reply and commenced preparations to hunt Mosby down, promising more fire and destruction on the civilian population. But, shortly before the troops marched on April 15, Hancock received the news of Lincoln's assassination. The campaign was postponed, and that same day William Chapman and three other officers arrived under a flag of truce carrying a letter from Mosby. He had received no official word of Lee's surrender, Mosby stated, and asked for "a suspension of hostilities for a short time, in order to enable me to communicate with my own authorities or until I can obtain sufficient intelligence to determine my future actions. Should you accede to this proposition, I am ready to meet any person you may designate to arrange the terms of the armistice."[20] The following day Hancock wrote back giving Mosby 48 hours to communicate with the Confederate government. An officer of equal rank would meet with him at the Millwood Hotel on April 18 to receive his surrender, should that be his decision.

Hancock honored Mosby by sending not an officer of equal rank, but Brigadier General George Chapman. Mosby and several officers faced the Yankee delegation on opposite sides of a long table, and an amicable exchange followed. The Confederates officers expressed their regret regarding Lincoln's assassination. Mosby said his men had his permission to take paroles, but he personally was not convinced that the Confederacy was finished. He wanted more time to ascertain if Johnston's army was still in the field. If Johnston surrendered, he would disband the regiment, but he himself would leave the country and go into exile rather than surrender.

Hancock wired a favorable report of Chapman's meeting with Mosby. Grant, however, felt the rebel had outstretched his luck. "If Mosby does not avail himself of the present truce, end it and hunt him and his men down," he ordered.[21] A second meeting with Mosby took place on April 20, where he was informed that Hancock would devastate Loudoun and Fauquier Counties if he did not capitulate. "Tell General Hancock it is in his power to do it," Mosby hotly replied, "and it is not in my power to resist it; but I will not accept a parole before Joe Johnston has surrendered." During this exchange one of Mosby's Rangers, John Hearn, burst in. "Colonel, the damned Yankees have got you in a trap: there is a thousand of them hid in the woods right here. Let's fight 'em, Colonel. We can whip 'em." Mosby stood up, one hand on his holstered revolver. "If the truce no longer protects us we are at your mercy, but we shall protect ourselves."[22] He gave his silent hand signal to attack, then led his officers from the room. "Mount and follow me," he said. "We galloped rapidly from Millwood to the Shenandoah River," recalled James Williamson, "closely followed by a cloud of Yankee cavalry." The Yankee delegation rode back to headquarters, and gave Hancock the bad news. "If Mosby is in Loudoun County," he said, "I will Hunt him out."[23]

Mosby's refusal to surrender gave Southerners heart. "God bless his *noble, brave, unyielding Southern heart*," one lady exclaimed. "Oh Mosby, must we give up thee?" On the other hand, Federals rejoiced when a false rumor of his wounding and capture swept their ranks.[24]

On April 21, in Salem, Mosby sat astride his horse in front of the 43rd Partisan Rangers. This was his command's final muster; he was not a happy man. John Munson was present, and later recalled, "Failure of the cause for which we had fought made the chilly winds of early spring seem colder and the drizzle from the trees all the drearier."

The despondent colonel rode along the line of grayclad riders he had led through many a skirmish and raid. Mosby had written an address, and this was read to each battalion by Richards and Chapman: "Soldiers: I have summonsed you together for the last time. The visions we have cherished of a free and independent country have vanished, and that country is now the spoil of the conqueror. I disband your organization in preference to surrendering it to our enemies. I am no longer your Commander. After an association of more than two eventful years, I part from you with just pride in the fame of your achievements and a grateful recollection of your generous kindness to myself. And at this moment of bidding you a final adieu, accept the assurance of my unchallenging confidence and regard—Farewell."[25]

The men clustered about Mosby, shaking hands, some weeping. They could do whatever they chose, he told them. A parole from Hancock would provide protection for their homes and families, but he did not intend surrendering. He was riding South, possibly to connect with Johnston's army. Bidding comrades goodbye, Mosby rode towards Richmond with half a dozen men. They paused outside the city, and two men rode forward to get the latest news. It was a very different and desolate city now, many fine buildings burned out shells, the result of fires breaking out when the rebels blew up discarded ammunition as they departed.

While waiting, Mosby saw a canal boat moving from the city, and sent Ben Palmer to get an update. He hailed the craft and came back with a Richmond paper which carried more bad news. Joe Johnston, the South's last hope, had also surrendered.

But John Munson felt the war was still on. He returned from Richmond with a scheme. He suggested capturing the Yankee commanders now residing in Jeff Davis' former home, the Confederate White House, and steal their horses from the stables. It would have been "the most audacious and sensational and destructive forays of our career," he felt. But, "Too late," said Mosby. "It would be murder and highway robbery now. We are soldiers, not highwaymen."

With all hope gone, the remnant of Mosby's Rangers dispersed for a final time.

16

"Dark clouds are above me"
Quantrill, 1864–1865

There could be no honorable surrender and parole in Missouri for the man who had led the Lawrence Massacre. According to those who rode east with Quantrill in December of 1864, Virginia was their destination. If Robert E. Lee should surrender, and they did likewise as part of his army, they may well get the same terms. Or perhaps Quantrill even thought of joining up with the Gray Ghost—if he would have him.

Quantrill sent Kate King to the safety of St. Louis, and put out a call for men to muster at the Dupee farm in Lafayette County. Times had changed since Lawrence days and only 33 men arrived, including Frank and Jesse James. Clad in Yankee uniforms, the remnants of Quantrill's Raiders rode into Saline County and headed southwest through chilly December winds and across frozen streams. They arrived in Tuscumbia where Quantrill presented a commission taken from a Union officer, Captain Clarke.[1] After gleaning all available intelligence regarding Yankee dispositions, Quantrill produced a pistol and forced the commanding officer to order his troops, ensconced in the local hotel, to surrender. "They all promptly obeyed," recalled John McCorkle, "except one man who attempted to get out of a window, when Frank James gently tapped him on the head with his pistol and told him to get back in line or he might be seriously hurt." The rebels then selected the best blankets and clothing from the Yankee supplies. Having paroled the prisoners, Quantrill ended his last Missouri raid by escaping across the Osage River by ferry. The craft was sent to the bottom to prevent pursuit. A few men were taken along as guides, and they too were paroled when of no further use. They faired much better than guides earlier in the war who had been executed. "We never fired a shot or hurt a man," recalled McCorkle.[2] Perhaps Quantrill now wished to present a more merciful image to help get a parole at war's end rather than a rope.

They rode into Arkansas where, near Pocahontas, Joe Hall became ill. It appeared smallpox was the culprit, and he dropped out along with his brother Ike. It was not long before six other men decided to head south and join the regular Confederate army in Texas. This included young Jesse James, but brother Frank decided to stay with Quantrill.

Late December saw Quantrill on the banks of the Mississippi. How best to cross to Tennessee? The rebels encountered an old Missouri man, Murray Boswell, who had "an old yawl hid in the swamps," recalled McCorkle. But it was in no condition to cross the broad waters of the Mississippi. Using material pilfered from houses and fences, repairs were carried out, and at dusk on January 1, 1865, the bushwhackers took to the water, their horses swimming behind on leads. It took more than one trip, and there were anxious moments when a Federal transport came in sight. The rebels maneuvered the yawl into the bank and sheltered beneath weeping willows as the oblivious Yankees steamed by.[3]

Once all had crossed, the bushwhackers continued east. A congenial plantation owner provided food, and allowed what appeared to be blueclad Federal boys to camp in front of his home. But next morning an armed stranger arrived in camp. The plantation owner was an "outrageous rebel," he said, who did all he could to help the South. Kill him, was his advice. Leaving the visitor in camp, Quantrill went to the owner where "after being seated," recalled McCorkle, "told him that he was Colonel Quantrell and was taking his command through to Virginia and also told him what our visitor had said about him." The man was a known Union spy, the owner replied, who informed the Yankee invaders in Memphis when men returned after fighting for the South. They would be placed under arrest or even killed, the owner claimed. Quantrill returned to camp and the guerrillas moved out, taking the informer along for the ride. "The next report that this traitor made was to Him who receives final reports from us all," recalled McCorkle.

Kentucky

The rebels continued through Tennessee in a north easterly direction, avoiding towns. Best not to reveal that the notorious Quantrill was on the prowl. Unsuspecting commanders of small Yankee posts provided food and forage for the supposed 4th Missouri troopers, who crossed the border into Kentucky, a slave state which, like Missouri, had not formally left the Union. Many there supported the Confederacy, and Kentucky provided an entry point for Confederate horses, mules, food, leather, and military supplies.[4]

The guerrillas rode through Canton township, and picked up a trail of several horsemen. At sunset they arrived in a farmyard where several horses were seen tethered. Six Yankees were inside the house. To them, the new arrivals looked like comrades, but best to make sure. One bluecoat yelled out demanding the current countersign. There was an awkward pause as no response came. A blaze of gunfire erupted from the windows.

"John, I am shot, my leg is shattered," cried out Jim Little. "Four of us boys placed him in a blanket and carried him across the hill," recalled John McCorkle, "the Federals shooting at us all the time, and one of the bullets tore the heel off my boot," Frank James and Peyton Long crept forward, covered by fire from behind. They were intending to set fire to the house and drive the Yankees out. The outnumbered besieged did not like their chances. "We will surrender if you treat us as prisoners," one called out. Quantrill agreed to the terms, and the Yankees surrendered. Quantrill kept his word, paroling the prisoners, but Jim Little was too badly wounded to continue on. The Yankees promised to care for him, which may well have been the case, but he died of his wound a few days later.[5] Jim Little had been a close friend and comrade to Quantrill from early days. These were somber times for the guerrilla chief, but he was not through yet.

On January 22 Colonel Q.C. Shanks at Hartford greeted the supposed Missouri soldiers and provided them with supplies: "Their uniform[s] and good behavior whilst in this place and the conservation we had with said Clarke sufficiently satisfied us that he and his company were Federal." Quantrill's command rode out with a Yankee guide, Lieutenant Barnett, and two others, an enlisted man named C. J. Lawton and a discharged cavalry trooper called Lownsley. But any new leaf Quantrill may have previously intended to turn was now forgotten. Perhaps the loss of Jim Little had changed his mind. A week later Lownsley's body was found swinging from a tree three miles down the road, Lawton's body, shot, was found nine miles beyond that, and Lieutenant Barnett was found with a bullet hole in the forehead seven miles further on.[6]

The bushwhackers wound their way through the Kentucky countryside arriving in Hustonville at dawn on January 29. Fresh mounts were required, and not much notice was taken when the blueclad riders went from stable to stable in search of suitable mounts. But Lieutenant G. F. Cunningham was far from pleased to see 16-year-old Allen Parmer astride his fine horse. "If this horse leaves this stable, it will be over my dead body," he said.

"That's a damned easy job," Parmer replied. Cunningham fell, shot through the face. Two of the victim's relatives fled from the stable as bullets ripped through their clothes. With their cover blown, the rebels galloped from town, and the alert quickly spread that "the desperate outlaw and blood-thirsty scoundrel Quantrell, of Kansas notoriety," had invaded Kentucky. But this did not prevent Danville from feeling the rebels' wrath. Still posing as Federals, they entered the town and "Quantrell drew up in line and gave the order to dismount," recalled McCorkle, "which we understood to mean to dash forward and compel every soldier and man in the town to fall in line."[7] The telegraph office was wrecked, more horses stolen, citizens robbed, and a boot store looted. Then the raiders galloped off down the Perryville pike.[8]

Three hours later Union Captain James Bridgewater rode into Danville leading 45 men. He heard accounts of Cunningham's murder, and set out to track the culprits down. The guerrillas, meanwhile, split into three different groups near Harrodsburg to obtain food from different farmhouses. John Barker and 11 others were eating at one place when they realized they were not alone. Bridgwater had followed their trail and his troopers were surrounding the house. Guerrillas preferred attack rather than defense, and they burst from the house, pistols blazing. But the Yankees were ready and the brush erupted in a blaze of musket fire. Three rebels died where they fell and the others, including three wounded, quickly surrendered. John McCorkle was with seven other guerrillas at a nearby house. Chad Renick rushed out, mounted his horse, and rode towards the sound of the guns. "I followed him," recounted McCorkle, "Just as he reached the top of the hill, I heard Chad exclaim 'Quit firing down there,' and then I met his horse coming back without a rider."

Bridgwater took eight prisoners to Lexington from where seven were removed to Louisville prison. On suspicion of having killed Cunningham, Tom Evans was kept in Lexington, but was released after the war when John McCorkle identified Allen Parmer as the culprit. Parmer would be amongst the last guerrillas to surrender on July 26, 1865. With others, he was paroled and allowed to go home. He would marry Susan James, sister of Jesse and Frank, in 1870, and live to 1927.[9]

On January 31 George D. Prentice of the influential Louisville *Daily Journal* urged discharged veterans to join the militia and "swear not to cease chasing the guerrillas until the last one of them is driven from or *into* the soil of Kentucky." Prentice was pleased to note that "Captain Terrell of the Independent Scouts is after them with untiring energy." Being only 20 years old, Captain Edwin Terrell could well have untiring energy. But his reputation for loyalty to the Union was dubious, being known to fraternize with rebel guerrillas and rob civilians from either side. Nevertheless, he had been employed by Colonel Fairleigh of the Louisville garrison to hunt rebel guerrillas down. But "Terrell was a bad man," said John Langford, one of Terrell's own band, "perhaps as bad as the man he was hunting down."[10]

Quantrill had lost about one third of his men in Bridgwater's attack, but only a few days later struck Midway in company with another notorious guerrilla chief, Jerome Clark. Because of his youth and appearance, many thought Clark was a woman by the name of

Sue Mundy, a mistake he did nothing to dissuade.

About 30 raiders took possession of the Midway railway depot which also housed the telegraph office. They relieved the safe of its contents, and set the brick building on fire. They then robbed the town's inhabitants of "pocket books, watches, and other articles of value; stole such horses as answered their purposes," reported the Lexington *Observer & Reporter*. Having cut down telegraph poles, they set out for the farm of R. A. Alexander, known for his fine stock. Seventeen prime horses were stolen despite Alexander supposedly being prepared for such a raid. A neighbor, Frank Kinkead, was taken from his home and used as a guide to the Kentucky River before being set free.

On February 4 Quantrill's gang, now operating independently, captured a Yankee wagon train, killing three soldiers and capturing another four. They set off leaving seven wagons ablaze, but a running fight ensued when a force of partially disabled volunteers from the "Invalid Corps" caught up. The volunteers dismounted to fight as infantry when the guerrillas counterattacked, but the invalids, "could not master

It takes a thief to catch a thief. Captain Edwin Terrell, considered no better than Quantrill himself, was dispatched to bring the notorious guerrilla down (author's collection).

their horses and load their long guns," reported Major Thomas Mahoney. They retreated in confusion while the rebels escaped once again. Quantrill's four prisoners from the wagon train paid the price, being shot and killed as the band rode towards Hustonville.

They camped for the night on the Little South Fork, but the determined Captain Bridgewater was on their trail again. He struck the camp at 2 a.m., killing four, while seven made their escape on horseback. Another 35 fled on foot to be tracked through the snow, and the careers of another four bushwhackers ended under the stars that chilly night.

Jim Dawson, residing near Taylorsville, Kentucky, was one of those who provided comfort and lodgings for Quantrill when required. In late February Dawson's daughter Nannie asked their noted guest to write a few lines in her autograph album. Mixing a few of his own words with those of Lord Byron, he happily obliged:

> My horse is at the door,
> And the enemy I soon may see,
> But before I go Miss Nannie
> Here's a double health to thee.
>
> Here's a sigh to those who love me
> And a smile to those who hate.
> And whatever sky's above me,
> Here's a heart for every fate.

> Though the cannons roar around me,
> Yet it still shall bear me on.
> Though dark clouds are above me
> It hath springs which may be won.
>
> In this verse as with the wine
> The liberation I would pour
> Should be peace with thine and mine
> And a health to thee and all in door.
>
> Feb. 26, 1865 Very respectfully
> your friend
> W. C. Q.[11]

How incongruous that the last known written words by the architect of the infamous Lawrence Massacre should be so poetic. Bloody Bill Anderson's seem more appropriate for a Missouri guerrilla, something about being "skelpt."

In March General John Palmer in Louisville learned that Jerome "Sue Mundy" Clark and two others were sheltering in a barn on a tobacco plantation about 40 miles to the southwest. They were licking their wounds after being ambushed by home guards armed with repeaters rather than the usual muzzle-loaders. One guerrilla had been killed and another badly wounded. Palmer dispatched 50 Wisconsin Infantry under Major Cyrus Wilson, who surrounded the barn at dawn on March 12. After an exchange of gunfire in which four Yankees were wounded, Wilson advanced under a flag of truce and parleyed with Clark. Convinced to surrender, the prisoners arrived in Louisville the following day by river steamer. Clark and Henry Metcalf were placed behind bars while the badly wounded Henry Magruder was placed in the prison infirmary. "It is thought he will yield up the ghost before morning dawn," wrote the Lexington *Observer and Reporter*.[12] But Magruder lived on to be hanged on October 19. Metcalf escaped the gallows when Palmer commuted his death sentence to five years behind bars due to "mitigating circumstances."

But their leader received no mercy. "Jerome Clark, 'alias Sue Mundy' will be hanged by the neck until he is dead on Wednesday the 15th day of March 1865, at 4 o'clock p.m., at Louisville, Ky." As Palmer wrote this *before* the trial, one could get the impression that the court, despite the official facade, was of the kangaroo variety. "The fall was not more than three feet, and did not break his neck; he choked to death," wrote George Prentice of the Louisville *Journal*. "We have seen a great many persons hung, but never before did we witness such hard struggles and convulsions. It was feared for a time that he would break the lashings."[13]

William Clarke Quantrill, a keen newspaper reader, must have felt a choking sensation when he read these words. Anderson, Todd, Jim Little and now Sue Mundy were gone. Would he too soon be convulsing at the end of a rope? Then another ill omen arrived. Guerrilla Jack Graham was attempting to reshoe Old Charley when a sudden reflex jerk caused a leg tendon to snap. The horse was crippled, perhaps the ultimate result of many grueling charges and chases over the previous few years. "This means my work is done," said a distraught Quantrill. "My career is run. Death is coming, and my end is near."[14] But not just yet. Miss Betty Russell was happy to lend a fine mount to the guerrilla chief. The animal, however, had no experience with the rigors and clamor of battle.

On April 1 General Palmer employed the dubious Captain Edwin Terrell and his 30-man squad as unofficial "scouts." Their specific job was to rid Kentucky of Quantrill. If the guerrilla still had any thoughts of going to Virginia for an honorable capitulation, they came to an abrupt halt with news of Lee's surrender to General Grant on April 9. On April

13, in company with local bushwhacker Billy Marion, Quantrill skirmished with Federal troops near Bloomfield. Two men were killed on each side, then the guerrillas split up. Two days later Marion was shot from his horse after Captain G. W. Penn's company of state guards attacked his band in a "still house" at Manton. Penn's troops went off in pursuit of others, then Terrell and company arrived on the scene. Marion's body was loaded onto a railway car and taken to Louisville where Terrell claimed to have killed "one of the most bloodthirsty and desperate outlaw leaders operating in the state." He also claimed to have rescued a hostage who had, in fact, escaped under his own steam. General Palmer acknowledged Terrell's claims, possibly to preserve his own health. "Terrell was an exceedingly dangerous man," he recalled, "I never let him enter my quarters without keeping a revolver at hand."[15] Terrell was considered a necessary evil by the Union authorities; "it takes a thief to catch a thief" seems to have been their thinking.

Following the jubilation of Lee's surrender and the satisfaction of Marion's death, shocking news arrived for the Yankees. President Lincoln had been shot by an assassin at Ford's Theater in Washington. He died the following day, April 15.

"The purest man of the age has fallen," wrote Palmer in General Order No. 23, "and the whole nation which was rejoicing over the prospects of a speedy peace is mourning." But not all felt that way. Quantrill read of Lincoln's death to his men. "Before the colonel had finished reading it," recalled McCorkle, "we all began to cheer and, breaking ranks, we all started at a gallop and never stopped until we had reached Jim Dawns' still house, where we stayed for a day or two."[16] While the drunken bushwhackers reveled in the news, wiser Confederate heads back east, like Mosby, knew Lincoln's death was, in fact, another blow. He had wanted reconciliation with the defeated South, not, like many others, retribution.

The Wakefield Farm

"In the spring of 1865, in March, I think, a man who went by the name of Captain Clarke, came to my place with a squad of men," recalled farmer James Wakefield. "I had not been in the army on either side, but had been buying stock and forage for the Union troops in Louisville." Captain Clarke "treated us very well" and, with his men, "came often to my place, but never stayed long at a time. After we got pretty well acquainted, Captain Clarke told me his real name was Quantrill, but he did not want it known."

Before noon on May 10 Quantrill and his band arrived at the Wakefield farm once more. At a 1909 reunion of Quantrill's Raiders, researcher William E. Connelley was told "that Quantrill had started for Louisville that morning to surrender himself and his men."[17] If so, James Wakefield seems to have been unaware of the fact. It received no mention in his account, and may well have been a fabrication by old rebels. It seems unlikely Quantrill would have ever considering surrendering once the war was over. The gallows would have been his only reward.

The clouds opened up, and the guerrillas took refuge in Wakefield's barn. Quantrill and some others fell asleep in the hayloft while others stood about sheltering and chatting outside under 15 foot eaves.

"Here they come," yelled Clark Hockensmith. Shots rang out as Terrell's band of 30 men galloped down the lane, carbines in hand. An African blacksmith on the Taylorsville Road had seen 21 men ride into the farm and informed the Yankee Rangers. From his shop, the barn roof could just been seen above a rise, and Terrell ordered his men forward at the gallop. As bullets flew the guerrillas scrambled for horses, but some bolted and their owners fled into the woods on foot. Quantrill's untrained horse reared amidst the gunshots and confusion, and he was unable to mount while others rode down a bridle path to the south. Quantrill followed them on foot calling for help. Dick Glasscock and Clark Hockensmith reined about and gave covering fire while Quantrill attempted to mount behind Glasscock, but the horse, shot in the hip, bucked and reared. Still on foot, Quantrill turned and got off a few shots before running alongside Hockensmith in an attempt to mount behind him, but suddenly pitched forward into the mud with blood streaming from his back left shoulder blade. The Yankee bullet had deflected against Quantrill's spine, and the once elusive guerrilla chief lay paralyzed from the lower chest down. Hockensmith and Glasscock paid for their loyalty with their lives, shot and killed a little further down the path. Fate decreed that the trigger finger of Quantrill, the man responsible for the Lawrence Massacre, should be shot off by a Yankee as he galloped past.

"I went along down," recalled Wakefield, "and found Quantrill so badly wounded that he could neither sit nor stand. They had taken his pistols and stripped off his boots. He was conscious and they rolled him over on a blanket and carried him up to my house and laid him on the lounge." The victors started ransacking the house, but stopped when Wakefield gave Terrell $20 and Lieutenant John Thompson $10, along with a jug of whiskey.[18]

Wakefield remained tight lipped while the ailing prisoner told Terrell that he was not Quantrill, but Captain Clarke of the 4th Missouri Cavalry. He asked to be allowed to stay in the house to die. Initially Terrell refused, but then relented, saying he would hold Wakefield responsible if the prisoner went missing. Terrell departed to continue his guerrilla hunt, and Wakefield sent for medical help. Dr. Isaac McClasky arrived, and upon examination, declared the wound to be fatal.

Frank James had been out scouting when Terrell attacked, but he and some others arrived that night. "Frank," said Quantrill, "I have run a long time, but they have got me at last." James offered to have Quantrill removed to safety, but he had given his word to remain. "I will die," he said. "It's no use." The following night more of his men turned up. Again he was urged to be taken beyond Yankee reach. But, only able to move arms and head, Quantrill realized the game was up. To move would only prolong the inevitable, and he did not want to see Wakefield burned out in reprisal. The guerrillas left in despair. Lee had surrendered and now Quantrill was down. The bleak future had arrived.

Next morning Terrell returned. By now he knew that Clarke and Quantrill were one and the same. The prisoner was placed on straw and pillows in a mule-drawn wagon, and Terrell set out for Louisville with his prize catch, a mounted guard riding along each flank. They moved slowly to preserve the prisoner's life, much better to see him hang than expire en route. That night, in Jeffersonville, two doctors were summonsed to Quantrill's side. Their examination confirmed his paralysis, due to a broken back.

Word of Quantrill's capture spread and a story appeared in the Louisville *Daily Union Press* under the heading "DANGEROUS SYMPTOMS." Two Southern belles had presented Quantrill with a bouquet of flowers, and the card read, "'Compliments of Miss Maggie Frederick and Sallie Lovell to Mr. Quantrell.' This was presented to the distinguished bandit, we suppose, as a testimonial of his valor, A strange way some people have of showing their loyalty."

By a quirk of fate, the same day Quantrill was shot, May 10, President Jefferson Davis was captured in Georgia, the official end of the American Civil War. The false story spread that "Jeff Davis is caught disguised in petticoats. The god of the rebellion in crinoline!" reported the *Daily Union Press*. "Can't one of our mantus-makers send a messenger to procure the identical *female* dress which Jeff Davis wore at the time of his capture? If she is so

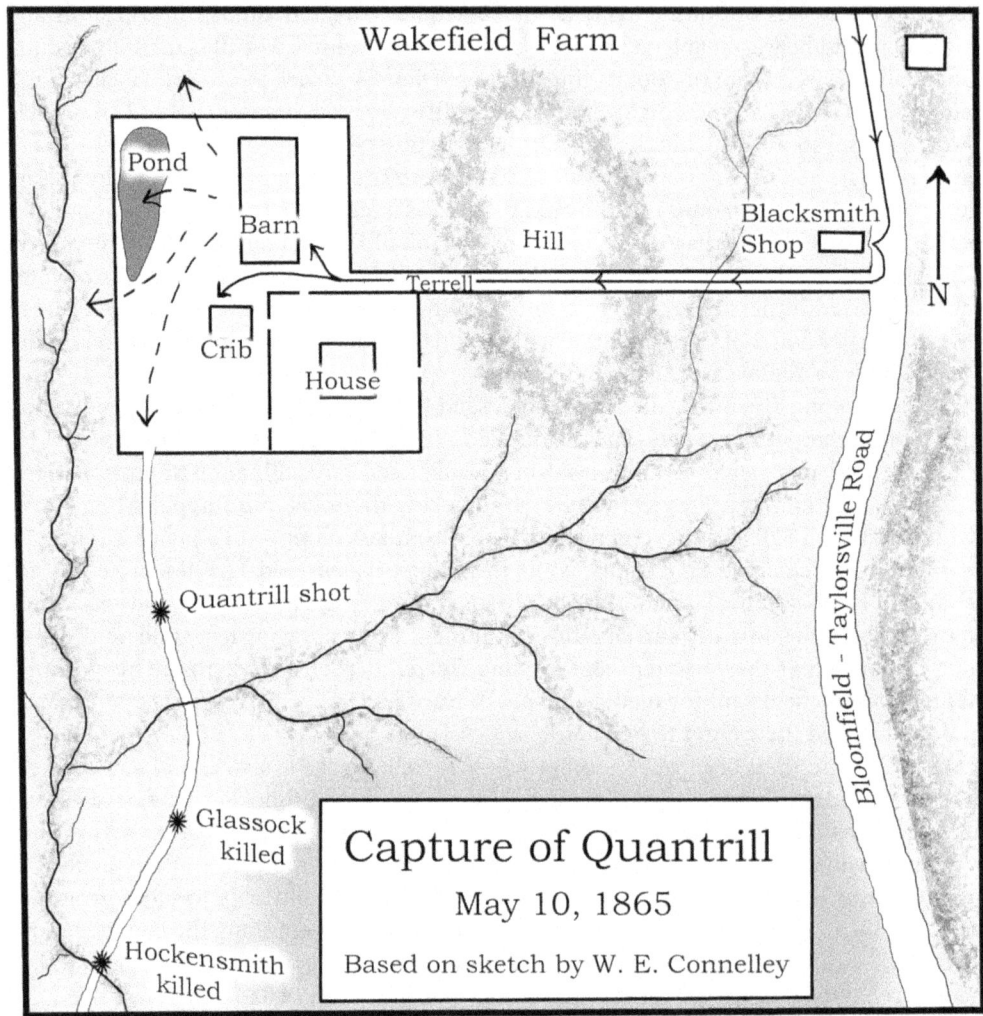

Capture of Quantrill, May 10, 1865 (author's rendition, based on a sketch by W.E. Connelly).

lucky as to obtain it, she will doubtless make her fortune, as it is expected to become the fashionable style of dress for all she-rebels in out city. Orders for the above my be left at our office. So hurry up, ladies."

Yet another article complained of "rebel officers and soldiers dressed in the uniform of the quondam confederacy swaggering about in the same insolent, overbearing style that ever characterized the 'chivalry.' How long is this to be permitted? How long are our brave soldiers, many of them mutilated and crippled for life, to be insulted by this public parade of the insignia of falsehood, barbarity and treason?"[19]

There were quite a few rebels crippled for life too, including William Clarke Quantrill. But his crippled life was destined to be short. On May 13 he was confined to the Louisville military prison's infirmary. "All the honor for his capture is due to Captain Terrill and his company of 'decoy guerrillas,'" wrote the *Louisville Daily Journal*. "The news of his capture will cause great joy throughout the Union." But false stories immediately emerged of Terrell having bagged the wrong man, the real Quantrill still serving as a colonel with General

Sterling Price. In his 1914 memoir, John McCorkle recalled, "There has been in late years a number of sensational articles appearing in the public press, claiming that Quantrell was not dead and at various times some one, to gain notoriety, has published a statement that Quantrell was still alive, but I know he died at Louisville. Kentucky."[20] One claimant told such a convincing, well publicized yarn that he was beaten to death by persons unknown at Coal Harbor, Vancouver, in 1907.[21]

Like the James and Younger brothers, a life of peace was not for Edwin Terrell. Following the war, he became an outlaw wanted for robbery and murder. On May 26, 1866, apparently convinced of his own invincibility, Terrell rode into Shelbyville with his uncle, John Baker, and John Wethers, "all armed to the teeth," according to the *Louisville Daily Journal*. "This blood-seeking party dashed into town and began to abuse and threaten the citizens, drinking and carousing and disputing the power of any man or set of men to arrest them." The town marshal, under judicial orders, formed a posse of 35 men. In the ensuing gunfight and chase Wethers escaped but both Terrell and Baker were brought down. Terrell must have realized how Quantrill felt when "one shot entered his back, near the spinal column inflicting it is believed, a mortal wound." Shotgun pellets also hit home, and Terrell was put behind bars in Louisville. Balls were extracted, but one leg remained paralyzed. In chronic pain and failing health, he was eventually released and died of his wounds on December 13, 1868, aged 23.

By that time another of Quantrill's enemies, Senator Jim Lane, was also dead. Apparently deranged and accused of fraud, the Grim Chieftain shot himself and died ten days later, June 11, 1866, near Leavenworth, Kansas.

Quantrill did not live to hear of either demise. Father Michael Power tended the dying 27-year-old, converted him to Catholicism, and administered the last rites. According to those who saw him, Quantrill maintained a cheerful disposition to the last, but made no attempt to contact his mother or other family back east. He died in the Louisville military prison hospital at 4 p.m. on June 6, 1865, to be buried in an obscure grave in Louisville's St. Mary's Catholic Cemetery.[22] In 1887 William W. Scott, a boyhood friend and Quantrill researcher, exhumed his remains. During the following decades his skull and various bones were bartered, used in fraternity rituals, and displayed in museums before being laid to rest. Today there are Quantrill grave markers in Kentucky, Missouri and Ohio.

Many saw Quantrill's lingering death as a just ending for a callous murderer who fought to divide the United States and prolong slavery. There is just evidence for this. Others, however, saw him as a brave cavalry commander who fought in retaliation for the actions of men like Jim Lane and Charles Jennison. According to John McCorkle, "the spirit of one of the truest, bravest men that ever lived passed from earth to appear before his maker and render an account of the deeds done here."[23]

17

"The South was my country"
Mosby, 1865–1916

Jefferson Davis was behind bars, but the Gray Ghost was still on the run with a $5,000 price on his head. Although Mosby's original thought was to go into exile, he finally rejected the idea. "To have run away would have at least have looked like a confession of guilt," he recalled. "So I took my chances and remained in Virginia."[1] He lay low with various relatives, and wrote to Robert E. Lee with a request that he intercede with Grant to allow his parole. Lee did so, saying he held Mosby in the highest regard, but on June 6 Grant's chief of staff issued an edict precluding Mosby from an amnesty announced by President Johnson on May 29.

Lee, however, wished to set an example for reconciliation, and on June 13 applied for his own pardon on condition that Grant not prosecute former Confederate soldiers. Lee's capitulation angered diehards who felt that the South would rise again, but the Federal government appreciated his example, and "Grant had the outlawry withdrawn," Mosby recalled. On June 13 Mosby, in full uniform, and his brother Willie went into Lynchburg for a meeting with Union officers. Not trusting his former foes, he had two pistols loaded in a holster lying at his feet—with good reason. The Yankee spokesman said that Mosby's parole offer had been revoked by General Halleck, now commanding in Richmond. He was to be placed under arrest. Mosby placed the still holstered revolvers on the desk. "I will not submit to arrest," he said. "I will kill the first man who attempts it." The Yankees made no attempt to intervene as he left and stood to leave. "I threw my holsters with my pistols across my shoulder and with my brother walked down the street," he recalled. "A great crowd of citizens and soldiers had collected but there was no hostile demonstration."[2] Captain Charles Blackford stepped forward with an offer from supporters to finance Mosby's departure from the country, but the offer was declined. Mosby felt he should receive the same treatment as any other Confederate officer. The brothers climbed into their borrowed buggy, and left town in some haste.

The following day, bluecoats searched various homes, including that of Mosby's parents, without result. But Halleck, it would appear, was quickly overruled by Grant. Three days after Mosby's hasty departure word went out that the original parole offer was, in fact, valid. Mosby and Willie returned to Lynchburg on June 17, and the famous guerrilla chief finally signed the terms of parole.

But Mosby was soon under arrest. Having resumed his law practice in Warrenton, he arrived in Alexandria on August 10, and a virtual riot hit the streets when Mosby supporters and detractors clashed. He was arrested by soldiers with orders to escort him out of town,

Colonel Mosby (center, with a plume in his hat) with a group of his most trusted compatriots, men who spread fear and carnage behind Union lines (*The Photographic History of the Civil War*, 1911).

but he demanded to see district commander, General Henry Wells. Mosby arrived in Wells' office to be told the arrest was for his own protection. He left town in safety, but was deemed by some officials to be violating his parole conditions by traveling to neighboring counties to attend court sessions. On August 27 he wrote Pauline: "the infernal Yankees were in Lynchburg which made it dangerous to remain there longer. Uncle John made John Hipkins go to Richmond, as we were anxious to learn the designs of the Yankees towards me."[3] On January 8 he wrote Pauline from Leesburg: "I was just in the act of starting home this morning when an order came for my arrest. I am now under arrest here, awaiting orders from General Ayers. Don't be uneasy."[4]

Grant issued orders for Mosby's release, but the threat of arrest remained a constant, dark shadow he could not lose. In January of 1866 Pauline told Mosby she was going on a shopping trip to Philadelphia, but arrived at the White House with their five-year-old son Beverly instead. President Andrew Johnson had been a family friend before the war, and she asked him for help. But Johnson had no time whatever for rebel guerrillas, former or otherwise. Having been the notorious Mosby's wedding guest was something the president of the United States would sooner forget.

Next stop was Grant's office. The all-conquering general heard Pauline out, and promptly wrote an order granting Mosby freedom of travel and exemption from arrest. The general-in-chief who defeated Robert E. Lee had the clout to overrule the president, and Grant was destined for the White House himself.

Mosby never forgot Grant's support. He treasured the handwritten note, and eventually gave it to his daughter, May, who had it framed and displayed with pride on her parlor wall.[5] Mosby would repay Grant for his support with interest a little further down the track—to his own detriment.

During a trip to New York in 1867, Mosby visited the gold market where he caused a minor sensation. One group of members hurled abuse while the other cheered. "My friends said that my breaking up the Gold Board is my greatest exploit," he wrote Pauline.

On March 8, 1870, Mosby visited General Lee in Richmond. He was "pale and haggard, and did not look like the Apollo I had known in the army," recalled Mosby. They discussed current topics and avoided rehashing the doomed Confederate cause. What was left to be said? As Mosby left the hotel room, he encountered George Pickett, of failed Gettysburg charge and shad bake fame. Pickett said he too would visit Lee if Mosby would accompany him. Mosby agreed, and recalled that the meeting was frosty, formal and embarrassing. Afterwards, Pickett referred to Lee as "that old man" and said, "He had my division massacred at Gettysburg."

"Well, it made you immortal," Mosby replied.[6]

The immortal Robert E. Lee died later the same year following a stroke and a bout of pneumonia.

Mosby's law practice, in the meantime, flourished. There was no shortage of clients for the famous partisan chief. In 1871 his annual income was $6000 compared to a laborer's of about $600.[7] He purchased a fine home, lavishly decorated by Pauline with fine furnishings and works of art. Some may have settled back and enjoyed the fame and success, but not Mosby. Material objects meant little to him. He needed conflict and a good cause to fight. Rampant corruption in the corridors of power provided a worthwhile target. "The whole administration of affairs in Virginia is in the hands of a lot of bounty jumpers and jailbirds," he said, "and their only qualification is that they can take the iron clad oath! But they generally take anything else they can lay their hands on."[8] Following an exchange of insults, Mosby challenged one corrupt sheriff to a duel. The offender promptly packed his carpetbag and left town.

The presidential election of 1872 saw a choice between Ulysses S. Grant and Horace "On to Richmond" Greeley, editor of the *New York Times*. Both Yankees were hated in the South. But Mosby did the unthinkable and threw in his hand with the Republican Party, becoming Grant's advocate in Virginia. It was time to forget the past and reunite, Mosby said, and Grant had supporters who would give Dixieland better treatment than the Greeley camp. He arrived at the White House with Beverly and met Grant for the first time on May 8, 1872. "When I walked in with my son into the room where Grant was sitting his presence inspired something of the awe that a Roman provincial must have felt when first entering the palace of the Caesars. His manner soon relieved me of embarrassment and restored my self confidence."[9] Years later, Mosby recalled, "He immediately began telling me how near I came to capturing the train on which he went to take command of the Army of the Potomac in 1864. I remarked, 'If I had done it, things might have been changed—I might have been in the White House and you might be calling on me.'"

"'Yes,' he said."[10]

Mosby felt he could carry Virginia for Grant in the forthcoming election if Congress enacted a proposed Amnesty Bill which would finalize pardons for former rebels. With Grant's support, the bill passed, and a fine friendship was born. "Since the close of the war I have come to know Colonel Mosby personally, and somewhat intimately," Grant recalled. "He is a different man entirely of what I had supposed. He is slender, not tall, wiry, and looks as if he could endure any amount of physical exercise. He is able, and thoroughly honest and truthful. There were probably but few men in the South who could have commanded successfully a separate detachment in the rear of an opposing army, and so near the border of hostilities, as long as he did without losing his entire command."[11]

But the memories of those scorched farms and the thousands killed while fighting for the Lost Cause were seared into many Southerners minds. And the slaves they once owned were now free. Perhaps some remembered, as Mosby no doubt did, that he had opposed secession in the first place. The former hero received death threats, his boyhood home was burned down, and his once thriving law practice went into decline. But, thriving on conflict with a cause at stake, Mosby went on, giving speeches supporting Grant and debating the opposition. He "speaks as fiercely as he fights," wrote the *Washington Evening Star*. "Take him all in all, he is an ugly customer to tackle, either in the field or on the rostrum."[12]

With many old rebels refusing to vote for either Yankee candidate, "Virginia casts her vote for Grant, peace and reconciliation," Mosby wired the White House on November 7. "Col. Mosby, the notorious guerrilla chief of the war, is to be rewarded, it is said, with a fat government office for his services in behalf of General Grant and the Republicans in Virginia," reported the *Home Journal* on November 28.[13] But Mosby declined a job offer from Grant. He had no intention of validating claims that he had a vested interest in supporting his election as president.

On May 2, 1875, however, he wrote Grant saying he had become loathsome in the Virginian public eye, his legal practice was in trouble, and he was having to borrow money to survive. He could not visit Grant in the White House as it would damage them both. "There was more vindictiveness shown to me by the Virginia people for my voting for Grant than the North showed to me for fighting for four years against him," Mosby recalled.[14]

And tragedy struck in 1876. Pauline, aged 39, died on May 10 after giving birth to a young son, Alfred, who also passed on the following month. Mosby and his five surviving children packed their bags and moved from Warrenton to Washington, D.C., where his legal practice continued to suffer hard times. Mosby campaigned for Republican Rutherford B. Hayes who succeeded Grant as president in 1877. Although Hayes too had been a Yankee general, the war had been over for 12 years, and Mosby's financial situation required a pragmatic approach. He requested a position in the Justice Department, but was instead offered the position of United States consul to Canton, which he respectfully declined. A more auspicious post, Hong Kong, was put on offer, and Mosby, not noted for diplomacy, arranged for relatives to care for his brood as he prepared to embark on his new diplomatic career.[15]

On February 2, 1879, Mosby arrived in Hong Kong. The consular service was known for corruption, and the new man's first act was to peruse the books. On the second day Vice-Consul H. Seldon Loring got the sack. During the war Union generals had considered bribing Mosby to desert and fight for the North. "Do not hesitate as to the matter of money," General Ingalls wrote on June 12, 1863.[16] This revealed a complete ignorance of Mosby's incorruptible character. The new consul's scrutiny revealed that Loring and the previous incumbent, David H. Bailey, had been involved in various fraudulent schemes. Charging $10,000 per annum for licensing the legal shipment of opium into the United States from Macao was one. Mosby charged the correct fee of $2.50.[17] The honest consul wrote to his superior, Frederick W. Seward, regarding Bailey's schemes, but the letter was shelved. An investigation would reveal that Frederick's cousin, George F. Seward, the Minister to China, was also involved.

Ulysses S. Grant, now retired, arrived in Hong Kong, and the two friends were reunited during May of 1879. With his wife and son, Grant was on a two-year tour of the world. It was his first overseas excursion, and enthusiastic crowds waited at every port.[18] Mosby was aware of the corrupt practices of David B. Sickles, the American consul in Bangkok. Grant, also aware, advised Mosby to approach President Hayes directly with his allegations against Bailey and Sickles, rather than go through channels. And he would take it up with Hayes personally once back in the United States. Bailey, however, had powerful connections, and was appointed consul in Shanghai before Grant's return. And newspaper stories began appearing that portrayed Mosby as an unbalanced eccentric causing carnage within diplomatic circles, a repetition of his performance with supply trains during the war. Other papers backed him, however, publishing his suppressed letter, and Hong Kong Governor John Hennessy certified that Mosby's conduct was without reproach.[19]

Mosby's old foe, ex-general Julius Stahel, was now a State Department investigator. Despite being a friend of the accused, he was obliged to verify Mosby's fraud allegations. As a result, Frederick Seward, George Seward, David Bailey and David Sickels were forced to resign their posts. In Mosby's words, President Hayes had "at last swept the China Coast."[20] And to help keep the coast clean, Beverly Mosby, now 24, arrived to serve as vice-consul for the last two and a half years of Mosby's time in Hong Kong.

Mosby, scrupulous with financial affairs, insisted that all incoming funds go through government coffers for correct accounting. This included money ultimately owed to himself. These funds, he expected, would then be reimbursed. But treasury officials claimed all such deposits became U.S. property, not to be reimbursed. Over time, Mosby was forced to take legal action, and the court found in his favor. "Mosby Victorious" said one paper. An appeal launched by treasury lawyers was overturned. The judge commended Mosby for his honesty, and he was finally paid $11,783.50—but not until 1890.[21]

In 1885 Grover Cleveland became president, and Mosby was recalled by the new administration. With Grant's help, he secured a position as a lawyer with the Southern Pacific Railroad. At the same time, he wrote newspaper articles about his Civil War exploits, and traveled on a speaking tour through the New England states. In 1887 he published *Mosby's War Reminiscences and Stuart's Cavalry Campaigns* which contained a passionate defense of Jeb Stuart's actions at Gettysburg. Many, like General Longstreet, claimed Stuart had been responsible for the defeat.

When the Spanish-American War broke out in 1898, the 64-year-old Mosby offered his services to the American Army. He received a rebuff, however, and was probably irked that four old Confederate generals, including Fitz Lee, went to war under the Stars and Stripes with the rank of major general. Mosby prepared for action regardless, and commenced training a cavalry company called Mosby's Hussars. The *San Francisco Call* wrote that he was drilling them in Oakland, "instilling the same vim that he showed when at the head of his raiders."[22] But the war lasted less than four months, and Mosby's Hussars returned to peaceful pursuits.

Upon the assassination of William McKinley in 1901, Theodore Roosevelt became the 26th president of the United States. Mosby's tenure with the railroad ended, and he sought a position in the Justice Department once more. Roosevelt had led his Rough Riders to victory at San Juan Hill, and no doubt felt an affinity with Mosby. Not only were they both cavalry leaders, but both fought corruption, and had no time for cartels. But rather than the Justice Department, Roosevelt felt Mosby was just the man for a job out West. Dispatched as a special agent for the Department of the Interior, he was to deal with illegal fencing of open range land by cattle barons in Nebraska and Colorado. He had success in Colorado, but struck trouble in Nebraska. Powerful men with an axe to grind wanted Mosby gone, and he refused requests from implicated senators to cease his activities. Mosby sealed his own fate with characteristic honesty that lacked the diplomatic touch: "Every effort has been made to protect the cattle barons in their occupancy of the lands. Senators Millard and Dietrich are interested in aiding the barons because both are at the head of national banks which hold heavy mortgages on the stock of the ranges."[23] Pressure was brought to bare, and Mosby was recalled, "probably to keep him from being eaten, blood, boots, nippers and all, by the ferocious tribesmen who inhabit the sandhill regions in western Nebraska," said the *Lincoln Daily Star*.

Mosby was reassigned to handle illegal settlement in Alabama forest lands. In a letter to friend and newspaper publisher, Joe Bryan, he described the position as "very distasteful to me.... I am really in exile now."[24] Roosevelt, however, based on Mosby's revelations, sent attorneys to Nebraska who secured fines and jail terms for Bartlett Richards and William Comstock, two prominent cattle barons involved in fraudulent land claims.

Mosby finally gained employment with the Department of Justice. He worked for his brother-in-law, Charles Russell, who headed up the Bureau of Insular and Territorial Affairs. His daughter Stuart and her family lived within easy walking distance of his Washington office, and he took up lodgings with them. In 1905 Mosby was sent to Alabama once more to investigate alleged fraud in the Port of Mobile. Then it was out west again to the broad plains of Oklahoma to investigate corruption against the Chickasaw tribe. Within two weeks Mosby secured indictments against seven men. Charles Russell wired Mosby with a request to give a "square deal" to three lawyers involved, as they had been helpful in the past. "I feel very sure that if there is a square deal they will land in the penitentiary," Mosby replied.[25]

This was the death knell for Mosby's career in the Justice Department. They "kept the lid on me," he recalled. But he was not shown the door. Far easier to keep the old troublemaker on the books—but give him no work. This, however, gave Mosby time to write articles, and ward off those who would dispute his defense of Jeb Stuart.

In June of 1907 he wrote to Sam Chapman, "Now, while I think as bad of slavery as Horace Greeley did, I am not ashamed that my family were slave holders. It was our inheritance." Mosby was annoyed with those who claimed slavery was not the cause of the Civil War. "South Carolina went to war—as she said in her Secession Proclamation—because slavery wd. not be secure under Lincoln. South Carolina ought to know what was the cause of her seceding." But "I am not ashamed of having fought on the side of slavery—a soldier fights for his country—right or wrong—he is not responsible for the political merits of the cause he fights in. The South was my country."[26]

In 1909, he and others took the University of Virginia to task for allowing violent rules in football games which saw students killed. "I had no taste for athletics

John Mosby, aged 73, in 1907. The old rebel's fight against corruption ensured continued conflict throughout his life (author's collection).

and have never seen a ball game," he wrote. "My idea of manhood is a sense of honor and courage; such qualities may exist in a weak body." The following year, changes were made to the football rules.

Finally, in 1910, at the age of 76, the old rebel was tapped on the shoulder. Time to retire from public service and enjoy his remaining days in the sunshine of old memories, and the admiration of fellow Virginians. By now Mosby had been forgiven for supporting Grant, and his name was high in the pantheon of Confederate heroes; only a handful like Lee, Jackson and Stuart were as well known. (And perhaps, for dubious reasons, Quantrill.) Mosby had never surrendered his command, and had lived on to old age, writing and giving talks to enraptured audiences about those critical, war-torn years that had so divided the nation.

In January of 1915, the University of Virginia invited Mosby to a ceremony to honor himself and President Taft, under whom he had served. Initially he accepted, but then heard that he was to be awarded a special bronze medal and written tribute. He withdrew the acceptance. "The reason I didn't go was that…. They intended to give me a testimonial that would be an atonement for their having expelled me from the University for shooting a bully. That determined me not to go. It is crucifixion to me to undergo any kind of a ceremonial." The awards were sent to him after the event and, despite his previous refusal, he received an invitation from the University Colonnade Club to give a talk about his wartime experiences. This was a different matter, and he gave the talk on May 1, 1915. The packed audience included old comrades like Dolly Richards and William Chapman. "For the first time in my life I felt like a rich man," he recalled, "that the kindness and consideration shown me where I was raised and educated convinced me that I possessed something that gold could not buy and that I have not lived in vain."[27]

By the end of 1915 Mosby's health was in serious decline. On Memorial Day, May 30, 1916, he passed away, aged 82, during surgery at the Garfield Hospital in Washington, D.C. No fewer than 3000 people gathered for his funeral at Warrenton on June 1. This included Sam Chapman, Fount Beattie, and 25 other surviving Rangers. A special funeral train arrived from Washington, and three companies of the National Guard, along with the Warrenton Rifles, formed the honor guard as Mosby's casket was carried by friends and family to a large, black hearse. The solemn procession moved to the Town Hall where the hero lay in state for four hours before being moved to the cemetery. He was laid to rest between wife Pauline, and his daughter May, who had died in 1904.

Newspapers across the country published eulogies praising Mosby's honest character and dash under fire. The *Richmond Virginian* concluded with "With the bitterness of war all gone, there remains to Americans, North and South, a precious heritage of valor, of self sacrifice, of sturdy never-give-up spirit, a heritage which, in future days of possible stress, will prove inspiration to us. Mosby is dead—peace to his ashes."[28]

Chapter Notes

Chapter 1

1. George R. Turpin, Students of University of Virginia, 1825–1874 (online).
2. Siepel, *Rebel: The Life and Times of Mosby*, 21.
3. Connery, *Mosby's Raids*, 15.
4. Williams, *Jackson, Crockett and Houston on the American Frontier*, 140.
5. Mosby, *Mosby's Memoirs*, 5.
6. Ibid., 3.
7. Peter Parley biography, Peter Parley Schoolhouse (online).
8. Mosby, *Mosby's Memoirs*, 4.
9. Ramage, *Gray Ghost*, 17.
10. Mosby, *Mosby's Memoirs*, 2.
11. Connery, *Mosby's Raids*, 17.
12. Monteiro, *War Reminiscences*, 11, 12.
13. Ramage, *Gray Ghost*, 20.
14. *Baltimore Sun*, Jan. 15, 1911.
15. Leake, Shelton Farrar, Biographical Directory of U.S. Congress (online).
16. How Arlington National Cemetery Came to Be, Smithsonian.com (online).
17. Ramage, *Gray Ghost*, 23.
18. Richard Henry Field, Dictionary of Virginia Biography (online).
19. John A. G. Davis, Encyclopedia Virginia (online).
20. Citizens Petition from Leake to Johnson, June 21, 1853.
21. Maupin letter to Johnson, June 10, 1853.
22. Ramage, *Gray Ghost*, 26.

Chapter 2

1. Border Ruffians, Dictionary.com (online).
2. David Rice Atchison: The Chief Border Ruffian, Random Thoughts on History (online).
3. Phillips, *The Conquest of Kansas*, 29.
4. Cordly, *A History of Lawrence, Kansas*, 82.
5. Leslie, *The Devil Knows How to Ride*, 15.
6. Gladstone, *The Englishman in Kansas*, 35, 36.
7. Cordly, *A History of Lawrence, Kansas*, 91.
8. Gladstone, *The Englishman in Kansas*, 40, 41.
9. Kansas-Nebraska Act, Primary Sources of American History (online).
10. Ibid.
11. Bleeding Kansas, New World Encyclopedia (online).
12. Leslie, *The Devil Knows How to Ride*, 6, 7.
13. Spurgeon, *A Kansas Soldier at War*, 21.
14. Thayer, *A History of the Kansas Crusade*, 31.
15. Monaghan, *Civil War on the Western Border, 1854–1865*, 20.
16. Bogus Legislature, Kansas Historical Society (online).
17. Leslie, *The Devil Knows How to Ride*, 10.
18. Andrew Horatio Reeder. Kansas Historical Society (online).
19. Goodrich, *Bloody Dawn: The Story of the Lawrence Massacre*, 58, 59.
20. Tim Rues, "Samuel J. Jones," Lecompton, Kansas (online).
21. Wakarusa War, Civil War on the Western Border (online).

Chapter 3

1. Clarke, Beverly L., Biographical Directory of the U.S. Congress (online).
2. Siepel, *Rebel*, 6.
3. Ashdown and Caudill, *The Mosby Myth*, 18.
4. Mosby, *Memoirs*, 17.
5. Lincoln, *Speeches and Letters of Abraham Lincoln*, 85.
6. Mosby, *Memoirs*, 17, 18.
7. Williams, *The Last Confederate Ship at Sea*, 21.
8. Mosby, *Memoirs*, 11.
9. Gen. William E. "Grumble" Jones, Shenandoah 1864 (online).
10. Mosby, *Memoirs*, 23.
11. Ramage, *Gray Ghost*, 34.
12. Mosby, *Reminiscences*, 206.
13. Mosby, *Memoirs*, 18.
14. Ibid., 28, 29.
15. Mosby Writes Home to His Mother, Heritage Auctions (online).
16. Letcher, John, Encyclopedia Virginia (online).
17. Siepel, *Rebel: Life and Times of Mosby*, 18.
18. J.E.B. Stuart, Civil War Trust (online).
19. Mosby, *Reminiscences* 12.
20. Mosby, *Memoirs*, 32.

Chapter 4

1. Battle of Black Jack, Kansas Public Library (online).
2. Battle of Osawatomie, Kansas Historical Society (online).
3. Connelley, *Quantrill and the Border Wars*, 110.
4. Leslie, *The Devil Knows How to Ride*, 37.
5. Connelley, *Quantrill and the Border Wars*, 43, 44.
6. Ibid., 28.
7. Ibid., 33, 34.
8. Letter from Quantrill to his mother, Aug. 8, 1855.
9. Letter from Quantrill to Edward T. Kellem, Oct. 2, 1855.
10. Leslie, *The Devil Knows How to Ride*, 46.
11. Letter from Quantrill to his mother, Feb. 21, 1856.
12. Castel, *William Clarke Quantrill*, 26.
13. Letter from Quantrill to his mother, May 16, 1857.
14. Leslie, *The Devil Knows How to Ride*, 52.
15. Connelley, *Quantrill and the Border Wars*, 80.
16. Letter from Quantrill to his sister, Mar. 23, 1860.
17. McPherson, *Battle Cry of Freedom*, 206.
18. Letter from Quantrill to his mother, Jan. 26, 1859.
19. Connelley, *Quantrill and the Border Wars*, 95.
20. Petersen, *Quantrill at Lawrence*, 143.
21. Connelley, *Quantrill and the Border Wars*, 129.
22. Leslie, *The Devil Knows How to Ride*, 74.
23. Connelley, *Quantrill and the Border Wars*, 176.
24. Letter of Andrew J, Walker, Feb. 22, 1883.
25. Leslie, *The Devil Knows How to Ride*, 78, 79.
26. Marshall, *Army Life: From a Soldier's Journal*, xiii.
27. Castel, *William Clarke Quantrill*, 44, 45.
28. Chesnut, *Mary Chesnut's Diary*, 34.

Chapter 5

1. McPherson, *Battle Cry of Freedom*, 342.
2. Letter from Mosby to his wife, July 24, 1861.
3. Mosby, *Memoirs*, 53, 54.
4. "On to Richmond! Or Not," *The New York Times* (online).
5. Mosby, *Memoirs*, 49.
6. Letter from Mosby to his wife, July 24, 1861.
7. Ibid.
8. McPherson, *Battle Cry of Freedom*, 342.
9. Letter from Mosby to his wife, July 29, 1861.
10. Ramage, *Gray Ghost*, 40.
11. Letter from Mosby to his sister, Sept. 17, 1861.
12. Mosby, *Memoirs*, 91.
13. Letter from Mosby to his wife, Sept. 14, 1861.
14. 14th Infantry Regiment, DMNA (online).
15. McPherson, *Battle Cry of Freedom*, 367.
16. Mosby, *Memoirs*, 94.
17. Mosby, *Reminiscences*, 20.
18. Mosby, *Memoirs*, 101.
19. Perret, *Ulysses S. Grant*, 174.
20. Letter from Mosby to his wife, Apr. 1, 1862.
21. Ramage, *Gray Ghost*, 45.
22. Mosby, *Reminiscences*, 22.
23. Mosby, *Memoirs*, 109.
24. Gen. William E. "Grumble" Jones, Shenandoah 1864 (online).
25. Partisan Ranger Act, Apr. 22, 1862 (online).
26. Ramage, *Gray Ghost*, 132.
27. Ibid, 46.
28. *Southern Historical Society Papers* XXVI, 247.
29. Lee's orders to Stuart, June 11, 1862.
30. Black, *Cavalry Raids of the Civil War*, 17.
31. Mosby, *Reminiscences*, 224.
32. *Blackwood's Edinburgh Magazine*, July 1865, 284.
33. Mosby, *Memoirs*, 116.
34. Stuart's Report to Lee, June 17, 1862.
35. Mosby, *Memoirs*, 114, 115.

Chapter 6

1. McPherson, *Battle Cry of Freedom*, 290–291.
2. Leslie, *The Devil Knows How to Ride*, 85.
3. Castel, *General Sterling Price*, 45.
4. Stewart, *Custer's Luck*, 162.
5. Edwards, *Noted Guerrillas*, 51.
6. Leslie, *The Devil Knows How to Ride*, 91.
7. *Harper's Weekly*, Oct. 19, 1861, 658.
8. Palmer, *Civil War Sketches and Incidents*, 177.
9. Monaghan, *Civil War on the Western Border*, 197.
10. Connelly, *Quantrill and the Border Wars*, 202.
11. Castel, *William Clarke Quantrill*, 67.
12. Connelly, *Quantrill and the Border Wars*, 204–205.
13. Gilmore, *Civil War on the Kansas-Missouri Border*, 181.
14. Leslie, *The Devil Knows How to Ride*, 98.
15. Bronaugh, *The Youngers' Fight for Freedom*, 33, 34.
16. Younger, *The Story of Cole Younger, by Himself*, 3, 4.
17. Report of Capt. W. S. Oliver, Seventh Missouri Infantry (online).
18. Leslie, *The Devil Knows How to Ride*, 106.
19. Younger, *The Story of Cole Younger, by Himself*, 17.
20. Letter from A. Ellis to W. W. Scott, Jan. 5, 1879.
21. Ibid.
22. Leslie, *The Devil Knows How to Ride*, 109.
23. Indian Expedition, Oklahoma Historical Society (online).
24. Nester, *The Age of Lincoln*, 297.
25. Mudd, *With Porter in Northern Missouri*, 385, 386.
26. Barton, *Three Years with Quantrill*, 119.
27. Castel, *William Clarke Quantrill*, 73.
28. Connelly, *Quantrill and the Border Wars*, 237.
29. Leslie, *The Devil Knows How to Ride*, 115.
30. Castel, *William Clarke Quantrill*, 76.
31. Report by Col. R. Mitchell, Mar. 22, 1862.
32. Castel, *William Clarke Quantrill*, 77.
33. Leslie, *The Devil Knows How to Ride*, 117.

34. Gilmore, *Civil War on the Missouri-Kansas Border*, 190.
35. Lt. G. W. Nash (1834–1897), Find a Grave (online).
36. Erwin, *Guerrilla Hunters in Civil War Missouri*, 175.
37. Leslie, *The Devil Knows How to Ride*, 119.
38. Banasik, *Cavaliers of the Brush*, 202.

Chapter 7

1. Mosby, *Memoirs*, 121.
2. McPherson, *Battle Cry of Freedom*, 525.
3. Rafuse, *McClellan's War*, 237.
4. Mosby, *Memoirs*, 126.
5. Ramage, *Gray Ghost*, 51.
6. Akers, *Years of Glory*, 46.
7. Glazier, *Three Years in the Federal Cavalry*, 52.
8. Letter from Mosby to his wife, July 23, 1862.
9. Mosby, *Memoirs*, 129, 130.
10. McPherson, *Battle Cry of Freedom*, 526.
11. Mosby, *Memoirs*, 135.
12. Williamson, *Life of J,E.B. Stuart*, 39.
13. Grummond, *Jeb Stuart*, 75.
14. Mosby, *Memoirs*, 142.
15. Letter from Mosby to his wife, Sept. 5, 1862.
16. McPherson, *Battle Cry of Freedom*, 555, 556.
17. Mosby, *Memoirs*, 144.
18. Ramage, *Gray Ghost*, 55.
19. Brewster, *Lincoln's Gamble*, 181.
20. Leidner, *Lincoln's Gift*, 166.
21. Letters from Mosby to his wife, Nov. 24, Dec. 2 and 9, 1862.
22. Mosby, *Memoirs*, 149.
23. McPherson, *Battle Cry of Freedom*, 574.
24. O'Neill, *Chasing Jeb Stuart and John Mosby*, 59.
25. Mosby, *Memoirs*, 148.

Chapter 8

1. Brownlee, *Gray Ghosts of the Confederacy*, 70.
2. Leslie, *The Devil Knows How to Ride*, 123.
3. *War of the Rebellion*, Serial 019, Chapter XXV, 131.
4. Official Records, Series 1, Vol. XIII, 157.
5. Capt. W. A. Martin's report, July 12, 1862.
6. Ibid.
7. Leslie, *The Devil Knows How to Ride*, 127.
8. Castel, *William Clarke Quantrill*, 86.
9. Gilmore, *Civil War on the Missouri-Kansas Border*, 198.
10. Leslie, *The Devil Knows How to Ride*, 136.
11. Official Records, Series 1, Vol. XIII, 227.
12. Banasik, *Cavaliers of the Brush*, 143.
13. Britton, *The Civil War on the Border*, 325.
14. Nichols, *Guerrilla Warfare in Civil War Missouri*, Vol. 3, 283.
15. Bronaugh, *The Youngers' Fight for Freedom*, 35.
16. Dedmondt, *The Flags of Civil War Missouri*, 117.
17. Leslie, *The Devil Knows How to Ride*, 145.
18. 1918, KS & Kansans, John T. Burris (online).
19. Official Records, Series 1, Vol. XIII, 267, 268.
20. Ibid., 312, 314.
21. Leslie, *The Devil Knows How to Ride*, 149, 150.
22. Ibid., 153.
23. Warner Lewis, Civil War Survivor Story (online).
24. Edwards, *Noted Guerrillas*, 157.
25. Leslie, *The Devil Knows How to Ride*, 159.
26. Barton, *Three Years with Quantrill* (throughout book).
27. Ibid., 48.

Chapter 9

1. Mosby, *Reminiscences*, 43, 44.
2. Ramage, *Gray Ghost*, 59.
3. Sir Percy Wyndham, HistoryNet (online).
4. Mosby, *Memoirs*, 284, 285.
5. Ramage, *Gray Ghost*, 61.
6. Wert, *Mosby's Rangers*, 42.
7. Ibid., 45.
8. Mosby, *Memoirs*, 170.
9. Ramage, *Gray Ghost*, 62.
10. Collea, *The First Vermont Cavalry in the Civil War*, 121.
11. Mosby, *Memoirs*, 157.
12. O'Neill, *Chasing Jeb Stuart and John Mosby*, 102.
13. Mosby's report to Stuart, Mar. 11, 1863.
14. Ramage, *Gray Ghost*, 62.
15. O'Neill, *Chasing Jeb Stuart and John Mosby*, 63.
16. *New York Times*, Mar. 10, 1863.
17. Antonia Ford, Encyclopedia Virginia (online).
18. Mosby, *Memoirs*, 172.
19. Ibid., 173.
20. Mosby report to Stuart, Mar. 11, 1863.
21. Sardanapalus, Encyclopedia Britannica (online).
22. Mosby, *Reminiscences*, 80.
23. Ramage, *Gray Ghost*, 69.
24. Ibid.
25. Mosby, *Memoirs*, 177.
26. Ibid., 181.
27. Mosby, *Memoirs*, 182, 183.
28. Ramage, *Gray Ghost*, 71.
29. Wert, *Mosby's Rangers*, 48.
30. Antonia Ford, Civil War Women (online).
31. Ramage, *Gray Ghost*, 73.
32. Mosby, *Memoirs*, 187.
33. Sir Percy Wyndham, HistoryNet (online).
34. Ramage, *Gray Ghost*, 72.
35. Mosby, *Memoirs*, 163.
36. Letter from Lt. P.C.J. Cheney to Mosby, Dec. 19, 1910.
37. Mosby's report to Stuart, Mar. 18, 1863.
38. William Wells (General), Civil War Wiki (online).
39. Mosby, *Memoirs*, 192.
40. Mosby, *Reminiscences*, 89.
41. Mosby's report to Stuart, Apr. 7, 1863.

42. Mosby, *Reminiscences*, 87.
43. Scott, *Partisan Life with Mosby*, 62.
44. Pavlovsky, *In Pursuit of a Phantom*, 105.
45. Sutherland, *A Savage Conflict*, 166.
46. Mosby, *Memoirs*, 285.
47. Mosby, *Reminiscences*, 98.
48. Ramage, *Gray Ghost*, 78.
49. Mosby, *Reminiscences*, 105.
50. Bonan, *The Edge of Mosby's Sword*, 70, 72.
51. Ibid., 71.
52. General Stahel's report of Apr. 2, 1863.
53. O'Neill, *Chasing Jeb Stuart and John Mosby*, 145.
54. Pavlovsky, *In Pursuit of a Phantom*, 105, 106.
55. Mosby, *Reminiscences*, 131.
56. General Stahel's report of May 5, 1863.
57. Mosby, *Reminiscences*, 135.
58. Ramage, *Gray Ghost*, 217–218.
59. Williams, *The Last Confederate Ship at Sea*, 185.
60. Ramage, *Gray Ghost*, 85.
61. Mosby, *Reminiscences*, 142, 143.
62. O'Neill, *Chasing Jeb Stuart and John Mosby*, 198.
63. Mosby, *Reminiscences*, 145, 146.
64. Wert, *Mosby's Rangers*, 66.
65. Bonan, *The Edge of Mosby's Sword*, 76.
66. General Stahel to General Heintzelman, May 30, 1863.
67. Mosby, *Reminiscences*, 151.
68. O'Neill, *Chasing Jeb Stuart and John Mosby*, 201.
69. Ramage, *Gray Ghost*, 89.
70. Mosby, *Reminiscences*, 213.
71. Ibid., 157.
72. Ibid., 160.
73. Mosby's report to Stuart, June 10, 1863.
74. Williamson, *Mosby's Rangers*, 71.
75. Stuart's endorsement, June 16, 1863.
76. O'Neill, *Chasing Jeb Stuart and John Mosby*, 225.
77. Mosby, *Reminiscences*, 166, 167.
78. Williamson, *Mosby's Rangers*, 72.
79. Ramage, *Gray Ghost*, 92.
80. Ryan, *Spies, Scouts and Secrets in the Gettysburg Campaign*, 220.
81. Report of Captain Harvey Brown, 14th Infantry, June 22, 1863.
82. General G. Meade to General O.O. Howard, June 22, 1863.
83. Williamson, *Mosby's Rangers*, 79.
84. Mosby, *Reminiscences*, 176, 177.
85. Mauro, *A Southern Spy in Northern Virginia*, 73.
86. McPherson, *Battle Cry of Freedom*, 653.
87. Williamson, *Mosby's Rangers*, 80.
88. Lee's endorsement from Culpeper, July 31, 1863.

Chapter 10

1. Castel, *William Clarke Quantrill*, 104.
2. Connelly, *Quantrill and the Border Wars*, 281.
3. Castel, *William Clarke Quantrill*, 109.
4. Leslie, *The Devil Knows How to Ride*, 169.
5. *Confederate Veteran Magazine*, Jan. 1903, 158.
6. Leslie, *The Devil Knows How to Ride*, 187.
7. Ibid., 181.
8. E. D. Ladd's letter, Kansas Historical Society (online).
9. Gilmore, *Civil War on the Missouri-Kansas Border*, 233.
10. Barton, *Three Years with Quantrill*, 76.
11. Castel and Goodrich, *Bloody Bill Anderson*, 27.
12. Peterson, *Quantrill at Lawrence*, 185.
13. Barton, *Three Years with Quantrill*, 78.
14. Leslie, *The Devil Knows How to Ride*, 198.
15. Schimeal, Judge Barker and the Vengeance of "Bloody Bill," New Prairie Press (online).
16. Castel and Goodrich, *Bloody Bill Anderson*, 19.
17. Who Was William T. Anderson's Friend, FMR? (online).
18. Gilmore, *Civil War on the Missouri-Kansas Border*, 232.
19. Petersen, *Quantrill at Lawrence*, 231.
20. Gilmore, *Civil War on the Missouri-Kansas Border*, 346.
21. Leslie, *The Devil Knows How to Ride*, 246.
22. Castel, *William Clarke Quantrill*, 126, says beaten to death while Quantrill apologist, Petersen, *Quantrill at Lawrence*, 236, says struck, then shot.
23. Connelly, *Quantrill and the Border Wars*, 328.
24. Cordley, *A History of Lawrence, Kansas*, 202.
25. Leslie, *The Devil Knows How to Ride*, 201.
26. Petersen, *Quantrill at Lawrence*, 238.
27. Castel and Goodrich, *Bloody Bill Anderson*, 28.
28. E. D. Ladd's letter, Kansas Historical Society (online).
29. Cordley, *A History of Lawrence, Kansas*, 203.
30. *The Kearney County Advocate*, Aug. 27, 1887.
31. Connelly, *Quantrill and the Border Wars*, 343.
32. *The Kearney County Advocate*, Aug. 27, 1887.
33. Ibid.
34. Leslie, *The Devil Knows How to Ride*, 207.
35. E. D. Ladd's letter, Kansas Historical Society (online).
36. Sarah Finch letter to her parents, Sept. 2 1863.
37. Castel and Goodrich, *Bloody Bill Anderson*, 29.
38. Petersen, *Quantrill at Lawrence*, 269.
39. Leslie, *The Devil Knows How to Ride*, 207.
40. Castel, *William Clarke Quantrill*, 135.
41. Barton, *Three Years with Quantrill*, 81, 82.
42. Cordley, *A History of Lawrence, Kansas*, 224.
43. Leslie, *The Devil Knows How to Ride*, 237.
44. Bayens, *Frontier Kansas Jails*, 76.
45. Gilmore, *Civil War on the Kansas-Missouri Border*, 247.
46. Bayens, *Frontier Kansas Jails*, 253.
47. Bingham letter to the *St. Louis Republican*, Feb. 26, 1877.
48. Castel, *Winning and Losing in the Civil War*, 59.
49. Leslie, *The Devil Knows How to Ride*, 270.

50. Pond Report to Col. Blair, Oct. 7, 1863.
51. Quantrill Report to Gen. Price, Oct. 13, 1863.
52. Henning Report to Col. Blair, Oct. 7, 1863.
53. Holmes, *A Genealogy of John Steevens*, 130.
54. Gilbert, *Churchill and America*, 42.
55. Nichols, *Guerrilla Warfare in Civil War Missouri*, Vol. 11, 286.
56. Sutherland, *A Savage Conflict*, 199.
57. Barton, *Three Years with Quantrill*, 97.
58. Castel, *William Clarke Quantrill*, 156.
59. Leslie, *The Devil Knows How to Ride*, 292.
60. The True Story of Bush Smith (online).
61. Connelly, *Quantrill and the Border Wars*, 442, 443.
62. Leslie, *The Devil Knows How to Ride*, 296.
63. Castel and Goodrich, *Bloody Bill Anderson*, 36.
64. Ibid.
65. Letters of Julia Louisa Lovejoy, The Kansas Collection (online).

Chapter 11

1. Lee to War Department, Aug. 18, 1863.
2. Ramage, *Gray Ghost*, 111.
3. Mosby, *Reminiscences*, 100.
4. Williamson, *Mosby's Rangers*, 88.
5. Mosby's report to Stuart, Sept. 30, 1863.
6. Ramage, *Gray Ghost*, 114.
7. Wert, *Mosby's Rangers*, 104.
8. Wheelan, *Terrible Swift Sword*, 122.
9. McPherson, *Battle Cry of Freedom*, 738.
10. Ramage, *Gray Ghost*, 124.
11. Mosby's report to Stuart, Sept. 30, 1863.
12. Letter from Mosby to his wife, Oct. 1, 1863.
13. Ramage, *Gray Ghost*, 114.
14. Lee to War Department, Nov. 17, 1863.
15. Stuart to War Department, Nov. 22, 1863.
16. Williamson, *Mosby's Rangers*, 445.
17. *New York Herald*, Nov. 27, 1863.
18. Hughes, *A Thousand Points of Truth*, 25.
19. Williamson, *Mosby's Rangers*, 119.
20. Scott, *Partisan Life with Mosby*, 180.
21. Ramage, *Gray Ghost*, 127.
22. Wert, *Mosby's Rangers*, 134.
23. Cole's report to Gen. Sullivan, Jan. 11, 1864.
24. Mosby's report to Stuart, Feb. 1, 1864.
25. The McNeill Rangers, West Virginia History (online).
26. Wert, *Mosby's Rangers*, 157.
27. Bonan, *The Edge of Mosby's Sword*, 86.

Chapter 12

1. Nichols, *Guerrilla Warfare in Civil War Missouri*, Vol. 111, 140.
2. Leslie, *The Devil Knows How to Ride*, 302.
3. Brownlee, *Gray Ghosts of the Confederacy*, 195.
4. Castel and Goodrich, *Bloody Bill Anderson*, 16, 17.
5. Ibid., 42–44.
6. Castel, *William Clarke Quantrill*, 181.
7. Nichols, *Guerrilla Warfare in Civil War Missouri*, Vol. 111, 335.
8. *The Osage County Chronicle*, Aug. 20, 1864, 2.
9. Dyer, *Jesse James and the Civil War in Missouri*, 40.
10. Castel and Goodrich, *Bloody Bill Anderson*, 57.
11. Nichols, *Guerrilla Warfare in Civil War Missouri*, Vol. 111, 256.
12. Castel and Goodrich, *Bloody Bill Anderson*, 58, 59.
13. McPherson, *Battle Cry of Freedom*, 787.
14. Barton, *Three Years with Quantrill*, 110, 111.
15. Castel and Goodrich, *Bloody Bill Anderson*, 61.
16. Barton, *Three Years with Quantrill*, 111.
17. Ibid., 112.
18. Banasik, *Cavaliers of the Brush*, 115.
19. Leslie, *The Devil Knows How to Ride*, 318.
20. Goodman, *A Thrilling Record*, 14.
21. *Moberly Weekly Monitor*, Sept. 28, 1908, 2.
22. Goodman, *A Thrilling Record*, 22.
23. Castel and Goodrich, *Bloody Bill Anderson*, 82.
24. Goodman, *A Thrilling Record*, 24.
25. Castel and Goodrich, *Bloody Bill Anderson*, 85.
26. Goodman, *A Thrilling Record*, 30, 31.
27. Barton, *Three Years with Quantrill*, 113, 114.
28. Castel and Goodrich, *Bloody Bill Anderson*, 91.
29. Goodman, *A Thrilling Record*, 34.
30. Banasik, *Cavaliers of the Brush*, Vol. 5, 105.
31. Report of Lt. Col. D. N. Draper, Sept. 29, 1864.
32. Leslie, *The Devil Knows How to Ride*, 328.
33. Goodman, *A Thrilling Record*, 48.
34. Ibid., 63.

Chapter 13

1. Williamson, *Mosby's Rangers*, 144.
2. Lonn, *Foreigners in the Confederacy*, 194.
3. McPherson, *Battle Cry of Freedom*, 718.
4. Ibid., 719.
5. Ramage, *Gray Ghost*, 144, 145.
6. Sutherland, *The Savage Conflict*, 240.
7. Mosby, *Memoirs*, 273.
8. Lepa, *The Shenandoah Valley Campaign*, 30.
9. Smith, *Grant*, 334.
10. Mosby, *Reminiscences*, 206.
11. Wheelan, *Terrible Swift Sword*, 79.
12. Pavlovsky, *In Pursuit of a Phantom*, 157.
13. Ramage, *Gray Ghost*, 152.
14. Sutherland, *The Savage Conflict*, 240.
15. McPherson, *Battle Cry of Freedom*, 738, 739.
16. Carnahan, *Lincoln on Trial*, 126.
17. Mosby, *Memoirs*, 272.
18. Connery, *Mosby's Raids*, 85.
19. Ramage, *Gray Ghost*, 156.
20. Schairer, *Lee's Bold Plan for Point Lookout*, 123.
21. Parson, *Bear Flag and Bay State in the Civil War*, 45.
22. Lowell's report of July 8, 1864.

23. Munson, *Reminiscences of a Mosby Guerrilla*, 96.
24. Williamson, *Mosby's Rangers*, 188.
25. Humphreys, *Camp, Field, Hospital and Prison in the Civil War*, 104.
26. Ramage, *Gray Ghost*, 160.
27. Gordon, *The Last Confederate General*, 114.
28. Ramage, *Gray Ghost*, 163.
29. Sutherland, *The Savage Conflict*, 242.
30. Wheelan, *Terrible Swift Sword*, 98.
31. Rienzi or Winchester, *CivilWar@Smithsonian* (online).
32. Catton, *U.S. Grant*, 272.
33. Mosby, *Memoirs*, 291.
34. Munson, *Reminiscences of a Mosby Guerrilla*, 105, 106.
35. Ramage, *Gray Ghost*, 191.
36. Mosby, *Memoirs*, 190.
37. Ramage, *Gray Ghost*, 191.
38. Simpson, *Custer and the Front Royal Executions*, 139.
39. Wheelan, *Terrible Swift Sword*, 122.
40. Alexander, *Mosby's Men*, 140.
41. Ramage, *Gray Ghost*, 194.
42. Wheelan, *Terrible Swift Sword*, 122.
43. Urwin, *Custer Victorious*, 274.
44. Williamson, *Mosby's Rangers*, 451.
45. Wert, *Mosby's Rangers*, 196.
46. Ramage, *Gray Ghost*, 197.
47. Pavlovsky, *In Pursuit of a Phantom*, 201.
48. Gansevoort Report to Lansing, Sept. 15, 1864.
49. Mosby, *Memoirs*, 296.
50. Ibid., 375.
51. McPherson, *Battle Cry of Freedom*, 777.
52. Parson, *Bear Flag and Bay State in the Civil War*, 155.
53. Mosby, *Memoirs*, 302.
54. Emerson, *Life and Letters of Charles Russell Lowell*, 353.
55. Caudill and Ashdown, *Inventing Custer*, 125.
56. Ramage, *Gray Ghost*, 204.
57. *Official Records*, Series 1, Volume XLIII, 348.
58. Neely, *The Civil War and the Limits of Destruction*, 132.
59. Mosby, *Memoirs*, 322.
60. Williamson, *Mosby's Rangers*, 456.
61. Mosby, *Memoirs*, 316.
62. Ibid., 318.
63. Williamson, *Mosby's Rangers*, 263.
64. Ibid., 266, 267.
65. Sheridan to Halleck, Oct. 29, 1864.
66. Munson, *Reminiscences of a Mosby Guerrilla*, 150.
67. Williamson, *Mosby's Rangers*, 456.
68. Ramage, *Gray Ghost*, 214.
69. Ashdown and Caudill, *The Mosby Myth*, 88.
70. *Richmond Examiner*, Nov. 24, 1864.
71. Sizer, *The Glory Guys*, 135.
72. Ramage, *Gray Ghost*, 225.
73. Mosby, *Memoirs*, 316.
74. Williamson, *Mosby's Rangers*, 301.
75. Mosby, *Memoirs*, 320.
76. Ramage, *Gray Ghost*, 225.
77. Williamson, *Mosby's Rangers*, 305.
78. Ibid., 308, 309.
79. Wheelan, *Terrible Swift Sword*, 162.
80. Wert, *Mosby's Rangers*, 257.
81. Sheridan, *Memoirs*, 367.
82. Sutherland, *A Savage Conflict*, 244.
83. Bonan, *The Edge of Mosby's Sword*, 141.
84. Wheelan, *Terrible Swift Sword*, 162.
85. Ibid., 165.
86. Ramage, *Gray Ghost*, 232.
87. Mosby, *Memoirs*, 355, 356.
88. Ramage, *Gray Ghost*, 232.
89. Mosby, *Memoirs*, 335.
90. Ibid., 341.
91. Frazar's report to Col. Gamble, Dec. 31, 1864.
92. Gamble's report to Gen. Augur, Jan. 1, 1865.
93. Ashdown and Caudill, *The Mosby Myth*, 137.
94. *New York Herald*, Dec. 31, 1864.

Chapter 14

1. Castel and Goodrich, *Bloody Bill Anderson*, 113, 114.
2. Neely, *The Civil War and the Limits of Destruction*, 52.
3. Leslie, *The Devil Knows How to Ride*, 330.
4. *St. Louis Daily Missouri Democrat*, Nov. 12, 1864.
5. Castel and Goodrich, *Bloody Bill Anderson*, 120–122.
6. *St. Louis Tri-Weekly Republican*, Oct. 13, 1864.
7. Barton, *Three Years with Quantrill*, 122.
8. Castel, *William Clarke Quantrill*, 198.
9. Gilmore, *Civil War on the Kansas-Missouri Border*, 354.
10. Stiles, *Jesse James*, 137.
11. Leslie, *The Devil Knows How to Ride*, 338.
12. *St. Louis Missouri Republican*, Nov. 6, 1864.
13. Leslie, *The Devil Knows How to Ride*, 338, 339.
14. McPherson, *Battle Cry of Freedom*, 788.
15. *St. Louis Daily Democrat*, Nov. 16, 1864.

Chapter 15

1. Ramage, *Gray Ghost*, 238.
2. Scott, *Partisan Life with Mosby*, 444.
3. Baylor, *Bull Run to Bull Run*, 297.
4. Ibid., 300.
5. Williams, *Custer and the Sioux; Durnford and the Zulus*, 100.
6. Wheelan, *Terrible Swift Sword*, 162, 163.
7. Williamson, *Mosby's Rangers*, 342.
8. Ramage, *Gray Ghost*, 240.
9. Mosby, *Memoirs*, 354.
10. McPherson, *Battle Cry of Freedom*, 829.
11. Ibid., 830.
12. Ramage, *Gray Ghost*, 242, 243.
13. Williamson, *Mosby's Rangers*, 356.
14. Ibid., 357, 358.
15. Gen. Thompson to Gen. Augur, Mar. 22, 1865.
16. Williamson, *Mosby's Rangers*, 359.
17. Wellman, *Death on the Prairie*, 79.
18. Baylor, *Bull Run to Bull Run*, 324.

19. Ramage, *Gray Ghost*, 262.
20. Mosby, *Memoirs*, 360.
21. Simon, *The Papers of Ulysses S. Grant*, 410.
22. Munson, *Reminiscences of a Mosby Guerrilla*, 268.
23. Bonan, *The Edge of Mosby's Sword*, 154.
24. Sutherland, *A Savage Conflict*, 269.
25. Munson, *Reminiscences of a Mosby Guerrilla*, 270.

Chapter 16

1. Leslie, *The Devil Knows How to Ride*, 343.
2. Barton, *Three Years with Quantrill*, 130.
3. Ibid., 133.
4. McPherson, *Battle Cry of Freedom*, 294.
5. Leslie, *The Devil Knows How to Ride*, 346.
6. Gilmore, *Civil War on the Kansas-Missouri Border*, 291.
7. Barton, *Three Years with Quantrill*, 140.
8. Leslie, *The Devil Knows How to Ride*, 352.
9. Parmer, Allen, Handbook of Texas (online).
10. Leslie, *The Devil Knows How to Ride*, 345.
11. Castel, *William Clarke Quantrill*, 206.
12. *Lexington Observer & Reporter*, Mar. 13, 1865.
13. *Louisville Journal*, Mar. 16, 1865.
14. Connelley, *Quantrill and the Border Wars*, 467.
15. Leslie, *The Devil Knows How to Ride*, 362.
16. Barton, *Three Years with Quantrill*, 149–150.
17. Connelley, *Quantrill and the Border Wars*, 473.
18. Letter of James H. Wakefield to W. W. Scott, June 13, 1888.
19. *Louisville Daily Union Press*, May 16, 1865.
20. Barton, *Three Years with Quantrill*, 152.
21. Leslie, *The Devil Knows How to Ride*, 404, 405.
22. Ibid., 369.
23. Barton, *Three Years with Quantrill*, 152.

Chapter 17

1. Ramage, *Gray Ghost*, 267.
2. Siepel, *Rebel*, 155.
3. Mosby, *Memoirs*, 361.
4. Ibid,. 364.
5. Ramage, *Gray Ghost*, 270.
6. Mosby, *Memoirs*, 381.
7. Ramage, *Gray Ghost*, 272.
8. Russell, ed., Mosby, *Memoirs*, xvi, xvii.
9. Ramage, *Gray Ghost*, 274.
10. Mosby, *Memoirs*, 392.
11. Grant, *Personal Memoirs*, 282.
12. *The Evening Star*, Aug. 9, 1872.
13. Hughes, *A Thousand Points of Truth*, 155.
14. Mosby letter to Sam Chapman, May 9, 1907.
15. Siepel, *Rebel*, 190.
16. Mosby, *Reminiscences*, 158.
17. Siepel, *Rebel*, 190.
18. Perret, *Ulysses S. Grant*, 449–456.
19. Ramage, *Gray Ghost*, 294.
20. Siepel, *Rebel*, 227.
21. Ramage, *Gray Ghost*, 303.
22. *The San Francisco Call*, June 24, 1898.
23. Ramage, *Gray Ghost*, 326.
24. Goetz, *Hell Is Being a Republican in Virginia*, 394.
25. Ramage, *Gray Ghost*, 329.
26. Brown, ed., *Take Sides with the Truth* (Mosby letters), 74.
27. Ramage, *Gray Ghost*, 332.
28. Ibid., 341.

Bibliography

Online Sources

Bogus Legislature—Kansapedia—Kansas Historical Society, https://www.kshs.org, *Research, Kansapedia, Theme.*
Border Ruffians—dictionary definition of Border Ruffians, www.encyclopedia.com, *History.*
Centralia Battlefield—full report, www.centraliabattlefield.com/uploads/4/8/4/7/48471379/doug_scott_report.pdf.
Civil War Smithsonian: Reinzi or Winchester, http://www.civilwar.si.edu/cavalry_winchester.html.
Colonel William Jones House—Wikipedia, https://en.wikipedia.org/wiki/Colonel_William_Jones_House.
Cornel University Library: The War of the Rebellion: A Compilation of Official Records of the Union and Confederate Armies, http://ebooks.library.cornell.edu/m/moawar/waro.html.
David Rice Atkinson: The Chief Border Ruffian, randomthoughtsonhistory.blogspot.com/.../david-rice-atchison-chief-border-ruffian.html.
Dictionary of Virginia Biography—Richard Henry Field, www.lva.virginia.gov, *Dictionary of Virginia Biography.*
How Arlington National Cemetery Came to Be | History | Smithsonian, www.smithsonianmag.com/.../how-arlington-national-cemetery-came-to-be-1451470...
Kansas Bogus Legislature—John Stringfellow, kansasboguslegislature.org/members/stringfellow_john.html
Library of Congress: Kansas-Nebraska Act: Primary Documents of American History, https://www.loc.gov/rr/program/bib/ourdocs/kansas.html.
The McNeill Rangers: A Study in Confederate Guerrilla Warfare, www.wvculture.org/history/journal_wvh/wvh12-1.html.
Missouri Museum of History, http://collections.mohistory.org/search/.
Peter Parley Schoolhouse: Historic Ridgefield, Connecticut, www.peterparleyschoolhouse.com/Pages/PeterParleyBio.aspx.
The Sack of Lawrence, Kansas, 1856—EyeWitness to History, www.eyewitnesstohistory.com/lawrencesack.htm.
"Samuel J. Jones" by Tim Rues | Lecompton Kansas, www.lecomptonkansas.com/samuel-j-jones-by-tim-rues/.
Students of the University of Virginia 1825–1874, https://uvastudents.wordpress.com/2014/.../george-r-turpin-13-aug-1832-6-aug-1858/.
Territorial Kansas Online—Biographical Sketch—William A. Phillips, www.territorialkansasonline.org/~imlskto/cgi-bin/index.php?.../phillips_william_a.
Wakarusa War | Civil War on the Western Border: The Missouri..., www.civilwaronthe600westernborder.org/encyclopedia/wakarusa-war.
Who Was William T. Anderson's Friend, FMR?—Outlaw Jesse James, https://jessewjames.files.wordpress.com/2014/07/william-t-andersons-friend-f-m-r.pdf.

Newspapers and Periodicals

Baltimore Sun
Blackwood's Edinburgh Magazine
Chicago Tribune
Confederate Veteran Magazine
Daily Lawrence Republican

Daily Missouri Democrat
Harper's Weekly
Kansas City Star
Kansas Historical Quarterly
Kearney County Advocate

Lexington Observer and Reporter
Lexington Weekly Union
Lincoln Daily Star
London Times
Louisville Daily Journal
Louisville Daily Union Express
New York Herald
New York Times
Osage County Chronicle
Richmond Enquirer
Richmond Examiner
St. Louis Daily Missouri Republican
St. Louis Tri-Weekly Republican
San Francisco Call
Southern Historical Society Papers
Washington Evening Star

Books

Akers, Monty. *Year of Glory: The Life and Battles of Jeb Stuart and His Cavalry.* Philadelphia: Casemate, 2012.
Alexander, John H. *Mosby's Men.* Boston: Olde English Books, 1987.
Ashdown, Paul, and Edward Caudill. *The Mosby Myth: A Confederate Hero in Life and Legend.* Lanham: Rowman & Littlefield, 2002.
Banasik, Michael. *Cavaliers of the Brush: Quantrill and His Men.* Iowa City: Camp Pope Bookshop Press, 2003.
Barton, O. S. *Three Years with Quantrell: A True Story Told by His Scout John McCorkle.* Armstrong Herald Print, 1914.
Bayens, Gerald J. *Frontier Kansas Jails.* Charleston: The History Press, 2017.
Baylor, George. *Bull Run to Bull Run or Four Years in the Army of Northern Virginia: Containing a Detailed Account of the Baylor Lighthorse, Company B, Twelfth Virginia Cavalry, C.S.A.* Charleston: CreateSpace, 2012.
Black, Robert W. *Cavalry Raids of the Civil War.* Mechanicsburg: Stackpole Books, 2004.
Bonan, Gordon B. *The Edge of Mosby's Sword: The Life of Confederate Colonel William Henry Chapman.* Carbondale: Southern Illinois University Press, 2009.
Boughton, J. S. *The Lawrence Massacre.* Lawrence: J. S. Boughton, 1884.
Brewerton, G. Douglas. *The War in Kansas (1856).* Freeport: Books for Libraries Press, 1971.
Brewster, Todd. *Lincoln's Gamble: The Tumultuous Six Months That Gave America the Emancipation Proclamation and Changed the Course of the Civil War.* Grand Haven: Brilliance Audio, 2014.
Britton, Wiley. *The Civil War on the Border.* Charleston: Nabu Press, 2010.
Bronaugh, W. C. *The Youngers' Fight for Freedom.* Charleston: Bibliolife, 2009.
Brown, Peter A. *Mosby's Fighting Parson: The Life and Times of Sam Chapman.* Westminster: Willow Bend Books, 2001.
Brown, Peter A., ed. *Take Sides with the Truth: The Postwar Letters of John Singleton Mosby to Samuel F. Chapman.* Lexington: University Press of Kentucky, 2007.
Brownlee, Richard S. *Gray Ghosts of the Confederacy: Guerrilla Warfare in the West 1861–1865.* Baton Rouge: Louisiana State University Press, 1983.
Carnahan, Burrus M. *Lincoln on Trial: Southern Civilians and the Law of War.* Lexington: University Press of Kentucky, 2011.
Castel, Albert E. *General Sterling Price and The Civil War in the West.* Baton Rouge: Louisiana State University Press, 1993.
Castel, Albert E. *William Clarke Quantrill: His Life and Times.* Norman: University of Oklahoma Press, 1999.
Castel, Edward E. *Winning and Losing in the Civil War: Essays and Stories.* Columbia: University of South Carolina Press, 2010.
Castel, Edward E./Tom Goodrich, *Bloody Bill Anderson: The Short, Savage Life of a Civil War Guerrilla.* Lawrence: University Press of Kansas, 1998.
Catton, Bruce. *U.S. Grant and the American Military Tradition.* Boston: Little, Brown, 1954.
Caudill, Edward, and Paul Ashdown. *Inventing Custer: The Making of an American legend.* Lanham: Rowman & Littlefield, 2015.
Chesnut, Mary B. *Mary Chesnut's Diary.* London: Penguin Classics, 2011.
Clark, Thomas D. *A History of Kentucky.* Lexington: The John Bradford Press, 1954.
Collea, Joseph D. *The First Vermont Cavalry in the Civil War.* Jefferson: McFarland, 2009.
Connelley, William E. *Quantrill and the Border Wars.* Cedar Rapids: The Torch Press, 1910.
Connery, William S. *Mosby's Raids in Civil War Northern Virginia.* Charleston: The History Press, 2013.
Cordly, Richard. *A History of Lawrence, Kansas, from the First Settlement to the Close of the Rebellion.* Lawrence: Lawrence Journal Press, 1895.
De Grummond, Lena, and Lyn Delaune. *Jeb Stuart.* Gretna: Pelican, 1979.
Dedmondt, Glenn. *The Flags of Civil War Missouri (The Flags of the Civil War).* Gretna: Pelican, 2009.
Dyer, Robert L. *Jesse James and the Civil War in Missouri.* Columbia: University of Missouri, 1994.

Edwards, John N. *Noted Guerrillas, or, the Warfare of the Border*. Charleston: Nabu Press, 2010.
Eldridge, Shalor W. *Recollections of Early Days in Kansas*. Topeka: Kansas State Historical Society, 1920
Emerson, Edward W. *Life and Letters of Charles Russell Lowell*. Columbia: University of South Carolina, 2005.
Erwin, James A. *Guerrilla Hunters in Civil War Missouri*. Charleston: The History Press, 2013.
Fellman, Michael. *Inside War: The Guerrilla Conflict in Missouri During the American Civil War*. New York: Oxford University Press.
Flood, Charles Bracelen. *Lee: The Final Hours*. Boston: Houghton Mifflin, 1981.
Gilbert, Martin. *Churchill and America*. New York: Free Press, 2005.
Gilmore, Donald. *Civil War on the Kansas-Missouri Border*. Gretna: Pelican, 2005.
Gladstone, Thomas H. *The Englishman in Kansas: Or Squatter Life and Border Warfare*. New York: Miller & Co., 1857.
Glazier, Williard W. *Three Years in the Federal Cavalry*. F Q Books, 2010.
Goetz, David. *Hell Is Being a Republican in Virginia: The Post-War relationship between John Singleton Mosby and Ulysses S. Grant*. Bloomington: Xlibris, 2012.
Goodman, Thomas M. *A Thrilling Record Founded on Facts and Observations Obtained During Ten Days' Experience with Colonel William T. Anderson (the Notorious Guerrilla Chieftain)*. Des Moines: Mills & Co., 1868.
Goodrich, Thomas. *Bloody Dawn: The Story of the Lawrence Massacre*. Kent: Kent State University Press, 1991
Gordon, Larry. *The Last Confederate General: John C. Vaughn and His East Tennessee Cavalry*. Minneapolis: Zenith Press, 2009.
Grant, Ulysses S. *The Complete Personal Memoirs of Ulysses S. Grant*. Charleston: CreateSpace, 2000.
Guy, Anne Welsh. *John Mosby: Rebel Raider of the Civil War*. New York: Abelard-Schuman, 1865
Hale, Donald R. *They Called Him Bloody Bill*. Clinton: The Printery, 1975
Hickman, W. Z. *History of Jackson County, Missouri*. Cape Girardeau: Ramfire Press, 1966.
Hughes, V.P. *A Thousand Points of Truth: The History and Humanity of Col. John Singleton Mosby in Newsprint*. Bloomington: Xlibris, 2016.
Humphreys, Charles A. *Camp, Field, Hospital and Prison in the Civil War, 1863–1865*. Charleston: BiblioBazaar, 2009.
Johnson, Allen, ed. *Dictionary of American Biography*. New York: Charles Scribner's Sons, 1929.
Johnson, L. F. *Famous Kentucky Tragedies and Trials*. Lexington: Henry Clay Press, 1972.
Jones, Virgil Carrington. *Ranger Mosby*. Chapel Hill: University of North Carolina Press, 1944.
Larkin, Lew. *Bingham, Fighting Artist*. St. Lewis: State Publishing Co., 1955.
Leidner, Gordon. *Lincoln's Gift: How Humor Shaped Lincoln's Life and Legacy*. Nashville: Cumberland House, 2015.
Lepa, Jack H. *The Shenandoah Valley Campaign of 1864*. Jefferson: McFarland, 2010.
Leslie, Edward E. *The Devil Knows How to Ride: The True Story of William Clarke Quantrill and His Confederate Raiders*. Boston: Da Capo Press, 1998.
Lonn, Ella. *Foreigners in the Confederacy*. Chapel Hill: University of North Carolina Press, 2002.
Lowman, H. E. *Narrative of the Lawrence Massacre*. Lawrence: Journal Press, 1955.
Malin, James C. *John Brown and the Legend of Fifty-six*. Philadelphia: The American Philosophical Society, 1942.
Marshall, Albert O. *Army Life: From a Soldier's Journal*. Washington, D.C.: Library of Congress, 1886.
Mauro, Charles V. *A Southern Spy in Northern Virginia: The Civil War Album of Sara Ratcliffe*. Charleston: The History Press, 2009.
McPherson, James M. *Battle Cry of Freedom: The American Civil War*. London: Penguin, 1990.
Melville, Herman. *Battle Pieces and Aspects of the War*. New York: Harper and Brothers, 1866.
Mitchell, Adele H. *The Letters of John S. Mosby*. Richmond: The Stuart-Mosby Historical Society, 1986.
Monaghan, Jay. *Civil War on the Western Border, 1854–1865*, Lincoln: Bison Books, 1984.
Monteiro, Aristides. *War Reminiscences by the Surgeon of Mosby's Command*. Charleston: Nabu Press, 2010.
Mosby, John S. *Mosby's Memoirs*. Nashville: J. S. Sanders & Co., 1995
Mosby, John S. *Mosby's War Reminiscences*. New York: Dodd, Mead, 1898.
Mudd, Joseph A. *With Porter in Northern Missouri: A Chapter in the History of the United States*. Iowa City: Pope Camp Bookshop Press, 1999
Munson, John W. *Reminiscences of a Mosby Guerrilla*. Whitefish: Kessinger, 2006.
Neely, Mark E. *The Civil War and the Limits of Destruction*. Cambridge: Harvard University Press, 2010.
Nester, William. *The Age of Lincoln and the Art of American Power, 1848–1876*. Lincoln: Potomac Books, 2014.
Nichols, Bruce. *Guerrilla Warfare in Civil War Missouri*. Jefferson: McFarland, 2014.
O'Neill, Robert F. *Chasing Jeb Stuart and John Mosby: The Union Cavalry in Northern Virginia from Second Manassas to Gettysburg*. Jefferson: McFarland, 2012.
Parish, William E. *Turbulent Partnership: Missouri and the Union*. Columbia: University of Missouri Press, 1963.

Parson, Thomas E. *Bear Flag and Bay State in the Civil War, the Californians of the Second Massachusetts Cavalry*. Jefferson: McFarland, 2007.
Perret, Geoffrey. *Ulysses S. Grant: Soldier & President*. New York: Random House, 1997.
Petersen, Paul R. *Quantrill at Lawrence: The Untold Story*. Gretna: Pelican, 2011.
Phillips, William Addison. *The Conquest of Kansas by Missouri and Her Allies*. Charleston: Nabu Press, 2010.
Rafuse, Ethan S. *McClellan's War: The Failure of Moderation in the Struggle for the Union*. Bloomington: Indiana University Press, 2011.
Ramage, James A. *Gray Ghost: The Life and Times of John Singleton Mosby*. Lexington: University Press of Kentucky, 1999.
Robertson, James I., Jr. *Civil War Virginia*. Charlottesville: University Press of Virginia, 1991
Robinson, Charles. *The Kansas Conflict*. Lawrence. Journal Publishing Co., 1898.
Rodemyre, Edgar T. *History of Centralia, Missouri*. Centralia: Press of the Fireside Guard, 1936.
Rodenbough, Theo. F., ed. *The Photographic History of the Civil War*. Secaucus: The Blue & Gray Press, 1987
Ryan, Thomas J. *Spies, Scouts and Secrets in the Gettysburg Campaign*. El Dorado Hills: Savas Beattie, 2015
Schairer, Jack E. *Lee's Bold Plan for Point Lookout: The Rescue of Confederate Prisoners That Never Happened*. Jefferson: McFarland, 2008.
Scott, John. *Partisan Life with Colonel John S. Mosby*. Gaithersburg: Old Soldiers Books, 1989.
Sheridan, P. H. *Personal Memoirs of P. H. Sheridan*. New York: Charles L. Webster and Company, 1888.
Siepel, Kevin H. *Rebel: The Life and Times of John Singleton Mosby*. Lincoln: Bison Books, 2008.
Simon, John Y. *The Papers of Ulysses S. Grant*. Carbondale: Southern Illinois University Press, 2000.
Sizer, Mona D. *The Glory Guys, The Story of the U.S. Army Rangers*. Lanham: Taylor Trade, 2010.
Smith, Jean H. *Grant*. New York: Simon & Schuster, 2002.
Speer, William. *My Story of the Quantrill Massacre*. Topeka, Manuscript Dept., Kansas State Historical Society.
Spring, Leverett W. *Kansas: The Prelude to the War for the Union*. Boston: Houghton Mifflin, 1896
Spurgeon, Ken. *A Kansas Soldier at War: The Civil War Letters of Christian and Elise Dubach Isely*. Charleston: The History Press, 2013.
Stewart, Edgar I. *Custer's Luck*. Norman: University of Oklahoma Press, 1980.
Stiles, T. J. *Jesse James: Last Rebel of the Civil War*. New York: Vintage, 2003.
Sutherland, Daniel E. *A Savage Conflict: The Decisive Role of Guerrillas in the American Civil War*. Chapel Hill: The University of North Carolina Press, 2009.
Thayer, Eli. *A History of the Kansas Crusade: Its Friends and Foes*. North Stratford: Ayer Co., 1989.
Thomas, Emory M. *Robert E. Lee*. New York: W. W. Norton, 1995.
Urwin, Gregory J. W. *Custer Victorious: The Civil War Battles of General George Armstrong Custer*. Lincoln: University of Nebraska Press, 1990.
Violette, Eugen M. *History of Missouri*. Boston: D.C. Heath, 1918.
The War of the Rebellion: A Compilation of the Official Records of the Union and Confederate Armies. Washington, D.C: Government Printing Office, 1880–1897.
Wellman, Paul I. *Death on the Prairie*. London: W. Foulsham, 1962.
Wert, Jeffrey D. *Mosby's Rangers*. New York: Simon & Schuster, 1991.
Wheelan, Joseph. *Terrible Swift Sword: The Life of Phillip H. Sheridan*. Boston: Da Capo Press, 2012.
Wilder, Daniel W. *The Annals of Kansas*. Topeka: George W. Martin, 1975.
Williams, Paul. *Custer and the Sioux; Durnford and the Zulus: Parallels in the American and British Defeats at the Little Bighorn (1876) and Isandlwana (1879)*. Jefferson: McFarland, 2015
Williamson, James J. *Mosby's Rangers: A Record of the Operations of the Forty-Third Battalion of Virginia Cavalry from Its Organization to the Surrender*. New York: Ralph B. Kenyon, 1982
Williamson, Mary L. S. *Life of J.E.B. Stuart*. Richmond: B. F. Johnson Publishing Co., 1914.
Younger, Cole. *The Story of Cole Younger, by Himself*. St. Paul: Minnesota Historical Society Press, 2000.

Index

Numbers in **_bold italics_** indicate pages with illustrations

Albert, Sylvester 3
Albright, Charles 179
Alexander, John 163, 164
Alexander, R.A. 184
Allan (township) 131
Alley, Riley 49, 50
Ames, James 80–83, 85, 99, 157
Amory, Lieutenant 150
Anderson, Charles 105
Anderson, Ellis 104
Anderson, Jim 105
Anderson, Josephine 104
Anderson, Julia 104
Anderson, Martha 104, 105
Anderson, Mary 104, 105
Anderson, William, Sr. 104, 105
Anderson, William T. 2, 104–106, 111, 115, 118, 120, 121, 129, **_130_**, 131–142, 167–168, 170, 171, **_172_**, 173, 185; background 104, 105; Centralia 136–142; death 172; Fayette fiasco 134–135; splits with Quantrill 120
Angelo, Frank 164
Antietam, Battle of 63–65
Atchison, David R. 9, 10, 13, 15, 16
Atlanta 100, 126, 136, 144, 162, 177
Aubry, Kansas 51, 52, 106, 113
Auer, Michael 146, 147
Augur, Christopher 162, 167
Averell, William 147
Axline, Jacob 70

Babcock, Alexander 159
Bailey, David H. 193, 194
Bailey, Ezra 96
Bailey, Lawrence 108–110
Baker, Arthur I. 05
Baker, John 189
Ball, Charles 32
Ballard, John 98
Banks, Alexander 109, 114
Banks, Nathanial 62

Barber, Thomas 16
Barker, Augustus 83, 84
Barker, Elmer 95
Barker, John 183
Barlow, Mrs. 125
Barnett, Lieutenant 182, 183
Basham, Sol 49
Bates, Edward 54
Baxter Springs 34, 116, 118, 134
Baylor, George 175, 178, 179
Bean, George 91
Beattie, Font 22, 38, 39, 78, 87, 95, 96, 100, 196
Beauregard, Pierre G.T. 34, 37, 81
Beaver Dam Station 60–62
Bee, Bernard 36
Beeson, Harmon M. 25, 27–29
Beeson, Richard 27
Bennett, James 161
Bennings, John 28, 29, 34
Benton, Z.E. 101
Berry, Ike 170
Berryville 86, 152–154, 159
Bingham, George C. 113, 115
Birch, Almond 97
Bird, Charles 177
Black, John 177
Black Bess (horse) 33, 34, 51
Black Jack, Battle of 24
Blackford, Charles 190
Blackford, William 20
Blazer, William 143, 162–164
Bledsoe, Frank 117
Bledsoe, Jim 114
Blunt, Andrew 57, 73, 102, 106, 108, 114
Blunt, James 74, 116–118, 173
Boswell, Murray 81
Bowers, Samuel 108
Bowers, Solomon 108
Bowie, James 3
Boyd, William 96
Brandy Station, Battle of 86, 96
Branson, Jacob 15

Brawner, William 96, 97
Breckinridge, James 70
Breckinridge, John C. 19, 145
Breitenbaugh, Sam 105
Bridgewater, James 183, 184
Broadwater, Guy 155
Bronaugh, Warren 50
Brooklyn (hamlet) 114
Brooklyn Chasseurs 38
Broun, Catherine 164, 165
Brown, Egbert 57, 115, 121, 129, 130
Brown, Frederick 24
Brown, G.W. 11
Brown, Harvey 98
Brown, John 17, 22, 24, 25, 30, 171
Brown, Molly 58
Bryan, Joe 195
Buel, James 66, 68–70
Buffington (steamboat) 135
Buford, John 99
Buhoe, Billy 69
Bull Run, First Battle of 36–38, 41, 46, 145
Bull Run, Second Battle of 62, 63
Burnside, Ambrose 64
Burris, John 71
Burris, Milton 130
Burton, Aaron 18, 38
Byron, Lord 184

Catherwood, Edwin 72
Catlett's Station 62, 94
Cedar Creek, Battle of 159, 164
Centralia 136–142, 168, 169
Chambersburg 151
Chancellor (CSA soldier) 157, 158
Chancellorsville, Battle of 93, 96, 99
Chantilly 75, 80, 86, 88
Chapman, George 91
Chapman, Samuel 91, 92, 94, 95, 156

209

Index

Chapman, William 143, 145, 146, 154, 155, 159, 162, 165, 166
Charles Town 148, 154, 155, 162, 177
Chase, C.M. 111
Chase, Deloss 175
Cheney, P. 87
Chesnut, Mary 34
Chew, Preston 174
Chiles, Dick 72
Churchill, Winston 118
Clapp, Mary 26
Clark, Charles 114
Clark, James 136
Clark, Jerome 183, 185
Clark, Samuel 56
Clement, Archie 131, 133, 138, 171
Cleveland, Grover 194
Cochran, Catherine 165
Cochran, J.F. 66
Cole, Henry 126, 127
Coleman, Franklin 15
Collamore, Hoffman 107
Comstock, William 195
Connelley, William E. 55, 186
Conscription 41, 144
Cooke, Phillip St. George 44, 124
Copeland, Levi 70
Corbett, Private 156
Cordley, Richard 109, 111, 112
Corlew, Tom 112, 113
Cox, Samuel 171, 172
Crook, George 1 47, 151, 162, 176
Cunningham, G.F. 183
Curtin, Andrew 149
Curtis, Henry 117, 118
Custer, George A. 146, *152*, 154, 155-158, 160, 161

Daly, James 160
Damon, George 131
David, Daniel 71
Davis, Jefferson 41, 58, 93, 144, 179, 187, 190
Davis, John A.G. 6
Dawson, Jim 184
Dawson, Nannie 184
Dean, John 31, 32, 33
Dear, Charles 158
Denny, A.F. 132, 135
Dietrich, Senator 194
Donnelly, John 107
Douglas, Stephen 11, 19
Dow, Charles 15
Drake, George 154
Draper, Daniel 141
Duffle, Napoleon A. 160
Dulaney, Daniel 124, 125
Dulaney, French 124
Dunn, William 122
Dunnica, W.E. 170

Early, Jubal 147, **148**, 150, 151-154, 156, 159, 164
Eaton, S.S. 135
Edmunds, Amanda 164
Edmunds, Judith 165
Edwards, John N. 47
Eldridge, Shalor 10, 11
Ellis, Abraham 51-53
Ewell, Richard 40
Ewing, Thomas 104-106, 113, 115, 129, 168

Fairfax Court House 37, 64, 80-86, **87**, 92, 122, 124, 155
Fairleigh, L.B. 183
Farley, Captain 44
Ferguson, Sydnor 165
Fickle, Anna 130
Field, Richard H. 6
Field, William 57
Fisher, Ben 97
Fisk, Clinton 133
Fitch, Edward 110
Fitch, Sarah 110, 111
Flint, Henry 90
Flying Cloud (steamboat) 149
Forbes, William 149, 150
Ford, Antonia 81, 85
Ford, James 115, 121
Fort Blair 16-118, 134
Fort Bridger 29
Fort Davidson 168
Fort Donelson 40
Fort Henry 40
Fort Leavenworth 16, 29, 53, 70, 71, 117
Fort Scott 28, 116, 117
Foster, Emory 70
Foster, James 96, 97
Franklin, Walter 80
Frazar, Douglas 165-167
Fredericksburg, Battle of 64, 65
Frémont, John C. 48
Front Royal 145, 156, 157, 160, 161

Gamble, Hamilton 47
Gamble, William 167
Gansevoort, Henry 155, 159
Gettysburg, Battle of 87, 94, 99-102, 123, 144, 171, 177, 192, 194
Gibson, Thomas 176, 177
Gilchrist, Joe 49, 57
Gill, Mark 33, 34
Gilmer, Joseph 79, 80
Gilmore, Harry 145, 147, 176
Gladstone, Thomas H. 11
Glascock, Alfred 178
Glasgow 129, 133, 170, 171
Glasscock, Dick 187
Glazier, Willard 60
Glen Eden 170
Goodman, Thomas 135, 136, 138-142

Gordon, George 62
Gower, James 67, 68
Grant, Ulysses S. **40**, 99, 144-146, 148, 149, 151, 153, 154, 164, 177, 179, 185, 190-194
Greeley, Horace 9, 12, 36, 37, 192, 195
Green, Emma 125
Greenback Raid 158
Gregg, William 49, 51, 53, 57, 68, 70-72, 74, 102, 108, 114-116, 119
Griffin, Joseph 178
Griffin, Lee 105
Grogan, Lieutenant 159
Grout, Josiah 90, 91
Guild, Harland 175

Halleck, Henry 54, 55, 64, 124, 149, 151, 154, 160, 165, 190
Haller, William 49, 70
Hamilton, Charles 28
Hamner, John 7
Hampton, Wade 61, 147
Hancock, Winfield S. 177-180
Harrell, Trooper 163
Hatch, Ozias 164
Hatcher, Harry 91
Hathaway, James 87, 96
Hayes, Rutherford B. 193
Hays, Upton 66, 70
Hearn, John 180
Heintzelman, Samuel 80
Hendricks, James 49
Hennessy, John P. 94
Hill, A.P. 62
Hindman, Thomas 74
Hockensmith, Clark 186, 187
Hoffnagle, Melchior 161
Holt, John D. 106, 113, 115, 116
Hong Kong 193, 194
Hooker, Joseph 64, 92, 96-99
Horton, James 113
Hoskins, Bradford S. 88, 95
Houser, Samuel 34
Howe, Albion 149
Hoy, Perry 49, 70
Hoyt, George 171
Hughes, John 68, 69
Humphreys, Charles 150, 165
Hunter, A.N. 126, 127
Hunter, David 50, 145, **146**, 147
Hunter, William 84, 91, 96, 151
Huntoon, Franklin 79, 80
Huntsville 131-133, 135

Ide, Sergeant 91
Independence, Missouri, 33, 48, 51, 53, 54, 68-71, 74, 101, 171
Ingalls, Rufus 193
Invalid Corps 184

Index

Jackson, Claiborne F. 33, 46
Jackson, Thomas J. 36, 38, 41, 42, 59, 61–63, 93, 127, 147
James, Frank 107, 133, 135, 138, 141, 181, 182, 187
James, Jesse 25, 133, 141, 181
James, Susan 183
Jarrett, John 50
Jaynes, Thomas 141
Jefferson, Thomas 4
Jennison, Charles 54, 189
John Porter (steam tug) 164
Johnson, Andrew 18, 191
Johnson, Governor 7
Johnson, Lt. Col. 83
Johnston, Andrew V.E. (Ave) 139–141
Johnston, Joseph E. 37, 39, 41, 42
Jones, Samuel 10, 11, 15, 16
Jones, William E. 20, 21, 36, 39, 41, 147
Jurd, E.B. 34

Kane, Corporal 167
Kansas City jail collapse 104
Kansas-Nebraska Act 8, 9, 11–14
Kehoe, Martin 67
Kellam, Edward 26
Kelly, Benjamin 176
Kilpatrick, Hugh 97
King, Rufus 60
King, Sarah (Kate) 102, 129, 181
King, Walter 101
Kinkead, Frank 184
Kirby Smith, Edmund 118, 119
Kirker, John 132
Knowles. James 69
Koger, Edward 49, 50, 68
Koger, John 49

Ladd, Erastus 102, 108, 110, 111
Lake, Ludwell 166, 167
Lamar, Attack on 73, 134
Lane, James H. 14, *15*, 16, 28, 33, 47, 48, 54, 103, 108, 109, 111, 113, 114, 189
Langford, John 184
Latané, William 43–45
Lavinder, Jake 165
Law and Order Party 9, 15
Lawrence, Amos A. 13, 122
Lawrence, Kansas 1, 9–*12*, 13–17, 18, 27, 29–34, 48, 49, 102–104, 106, *107*–115, 118, 119 122 135, 139, 181, 187
Lawton, C.J. 182
Lazear, Bazel 115
Leake, Shelton L. 6–8
Lecompton Constitution 28
Lee, Custis 6
Lee, Fitzhugh 38, 39, 41, 44, 59, 83, 84, 150, 194
Lee, Robert E. 22, 30, 42, 44, 45, **60**, 61–65, 88, 89, 92–94, 96–100, 122–124, 127, 144–148, 150 152, 153, 155, 156, 159, 160, 164, 165, 168, 178, 179, 181, 185, 186, 187, 190–192, 196
Lee, William 44
Leland, Cyrus 114, 115
Leonard, Reeves 134
Letcher, John 21, 84, 147
Lewis, Benjamin 170, 171
Lewis, Warner 73
Lexington, Siege of 47, 48
Liberty (township) 15, 54, 56
Lincoln, Abraham 18–20, 31, 34, 37, 47, 63–65, 80, 85, 92, 96, 99, 125, 144, 145, 151, 162, 177, 179, 186, 195
Lipsey, Chalkley 32, 33
Little, James 49, 135, 182, 185
Little, John 68
Little Blue (steamer) 66
Lone Jack, Battle of 70
Long, Peyton 182
Longstreet, James 155, 194
Loring, H. Seldon 193
Loudon Heights, Battle of 125–127
Love, Tom 155, 166
Lovejoy, Julia 121
Lowe, Jordan 57
Lowell, Charles 123, 127, 149, 150, 156, 157, 158
Lownsley, Trooper 182
Lucas, Annie 164
Lunceford, John 159
Lyon, Nathaniel 46, 47

MacGregor, Rob Roy 3, 125
Maddox, George 49, 67, 113
Magruder, Henry 185
Magruder, John 119
Mahoney, Thomas 184
Marais des Cygnes Massacre 28
Marion, Billy 186
Marion, Francis 1, 4
Marmaduke, John 74
Marr, John Q. 21, 37
Martin, William 67, 68
Maupin, D.W. 7
Maupin, John 132
Mayes, Joel 34
McClasky, Isaac 187
McClellan, George B. 37, 40, 42, 44, 45, 59, 61–64, 75, 81, 98, 145, 150
McCorkle, Christie 104
McCorkle, Jabez 70
McCorkle, John 54, 74, 104, 112, 118, 134, 135, 139, 171, 181–183, 186, 189
McCorkle, Nannie 104
McCrickett, M.J. 157
McCulloch, Ben 47
McCulloch, Henry 118–121
McDonough, Charles 95, 163
McFerran, James 130
McKinley, William 194
McMaster, Charles 156
McNeil, John 53, 54
McNeill, John H. 127, 145, 176
Meade, George 64, 98, 99, 122, 124, 144
Melville, Herman 127
Merritt, Wesley *152*, 155, 164, 165, 176
Meryhew, Charles 69
Metcalf, Henry 185
Millard, Senator 194
Miller, Josiah 108
Miller, Margaret 108
Miller, Robert 108
Miller, William 108
Milroy, Robert 93
Miskel's Farm 86, 89–91, 143
Mitchell, Mrs. 132
Mitchell, Robert 55, 56
Monteiro, Aristides 5
Montgomery, James 28
Montjoy, Richard 95, 145, 160, 162, 164
Moore, Amaziah 55
Moore, Major 159
Moran, Dick 90
Morgan's Farm 156, 157
Morrison, Edwin 32
Mosby, Alfred D. 3, 4, *7*
Mosby, Beverly C. 18, 191, 192, 194
Mosby, Edward 3
Mosby, John S. 2, 3–*5*, 6–8, 18–23, 26, 36–45, 59–65, 75–*82*, 83–100, 116, 121–*123*, 124 -128, 143–167, *174*–180, 190–*195*, 196; captures Stoughton 82; childhood 3, 4; death 196; Hong Kong Consul 193, 194; marriage 18; meets Grant 192; meets R.E. Lee 61; meets Stuart 39; shoots Turpin 3, 5, 6; Stuart raid 42–45
Mosby, Pauline L. 18, *19*, 21, 36, 38, 40, 41, 60, 63, 64, 75, 87, 93, 96, 191–193, 196
Mosby, Stuart 195
Mosby, Virginia C. 3, 7, 8
Mosby, Willie *7*, 190
Mount Carmel Church fight 176, 177
Mount Oread 13, 108, 111, 112
Mount Zion Church 75, 149, 150, 165
Mulligan, James 47
Mundy, Sue *see* Clark, Jerome
Munford, George 7, 8
Munford, Thomas 97
Munson, John 150, 153, 160, 180
Murphy, Captain 56
Myers (CSA soldier) 157, 158

Index

Nash, George 57
Nelson, Joseph 148, 162
New Market, Battle of 145
Newbury, N.M. 72
Newtown 147
Northern Neck 165, 167, 179

Ogden (steamer) 105
Ohlenschlager, Emil 158
Oliver, W.S. 50, 51
Order No. 11 **113**, 115, 129, 168
Osawatomie, Battle of 24, 25, 30

Palmer, Ben 180
Palmer, Henry 48
Palmer, John 185, 186
Palmerston, Lord 63
Pamunkey River 42, 44
Paola 34, 114
Pardee, Captain 106
Parke, Joseph 113
Parley, Peter 4
Parmer, Allen 183
Partisan Ranger Act 1, 58, 59, 73, 144
Pate, Henry 24
Patterson, Robert 22
Patton, George S. 156
Peabody, Albert 56
Pearl Harbor 111
Peck, R.M. 29
Penick, William 101, 102
Penn, G.W. 186
Peters, Valentine 138
Phillips, William 10, 13
Pickett, George 99, 177, 178, 192
Pierce, Franklin 8, 12, 14, 16
Pierpont, Francis 124
Pleasanton, Alfred 96, 97
Plum, Preston 114
Point of Rocks 148, 149
Pomeroy, James 55
Pond, James 116, 118
Poole, Dave 102, 115, 116, 139, 140, 171
Pope, John 50, 54, 59, 60–63
Pottawatomi Massacre 17, 24
Potter, W.L. 120
Powell, William 157, 158, 160, 161
Power, Michael 189
Prairie Cove, Battle of 74
Prentice, George D. 183, 185
Prentiss, Samuel 82, 84
Price, Sterling 46–49, 101, 134, 136, 168, 170–173, 188
Puryear, John 163, 164
Putnam, Israel 4

Quantrill, Caroline C. 25, 26, 31
Quantrill, Jesse 25
Quantrill, Thomas 25
Quantrill, Thomas Henry 25

Quantrill, William C. 2, 17, 25–**27**, 26–35, 46–58, 66–74, 101–121, 129–142, 170, 173, 181–189, 196; ambush at Walker home 32; assumes leadership of gang 49; arrives in Kansas 25; arrives in Kentucky 182; background 25, 26; Baxter Springs 116–118; captured 187; death 189; deposed 129; Lawrence Massacre 106–112

Rahm, Frank 153
Randlett, Reuben 53, 54
Randolph, George W. 59
Ratcliffe, Laura 99
Read, Fred 112
Read, Mrs. 112
Reed, James 143
Reeder, Andrew H. 14
Reid, John 24, 25, 30
Renick (township) 131
Renick, Chad 183
Reno, Marcus A. 174, 175, 177, 178
Reynolds, R.M. 67
Reynolds, Thomas 119–121
Rhodes, Henry 156
Richards, Adolphus (Dolly) 145, 154, 158, 160, 162–164, 165, 166, 174, 176, 177, 180
Richards, Bartlett 195, 196
Rider, George 32
Rienzi (horse) 151
Riggs, Samuel 31
Robertson, William J. 6, 7
Robinson, Charles 11, 14, 16, 33
Robinson, Judge 71
Rocheport 131, 133, 134, 142
Rodewald, William 69, 70
Roosevelt, Theodore 194, 195
Roscoe, Mrs. 25
Rosser, Thomas 157
Rote, Jacob 107
Royall, William 43, 44
Russell, Betty 185
Russell, Charles 195
Russell, Earl 63

St. Louis Massacre 46
Salem 87
U.S.S. *San Jacinto* 38
Sarcoxie, John 31
Schmidt, Mrs. Charles 169
Schofield, John 68
Scott, William W. 189
Searcy, George 49
Seddon, James **73**, 120, 127, 165
Segur, Annis 105
Segur, George 105
Segur, Ira 105
Semmes, Joseph 6
Seven Pines, Battle of 42
Seward, Frederick 193, 194

Seward, George F. 193, 194
Shacklett, Kitty 97
Shanks, Q.C. 182
Shannon, Wilson 16
Sharps rifles 14, 16, 21, 37, 47
Shawneetown 72, 111
Shelby, Joseph 73, 74, 119, 131, 173
Shepherd, Olive 49
Sheridan, Philip H. 144, 146, 147, 151, **152**, 153–156, 158–162, 164, 165, 174, 175, 177
Sherman, William T. 136, 144, 151, 162, 177
Sickles, David, B. 193
Sigel, Franz 47, 64, 145, 147
Skaggs, Larkin 110, 112
Slaughter, George 4, 5
Smith, "Bush" 120
Smith, Channing 177, 178
Smith, Henry 155, 157
Smith, William "Billy" 50, 126, 127, 145
Sneed, Thomas 138, 141
Snow, Henry 176
Snyder, Eli 34
Snyder, S.S. 108
Southwick, Albert 32, 33
Sower, Mrs. 154
Sowle, George 161
Spanish American War 194
Speer, Billy 112
Spencer rifles 78, 149, 162, 163
Sperry, J. Austin 19–21
Spicer, Arthur 109
Spooner, John 5
Stahel, Julius 86, 91–93, 95, 96, 194
Stanton, Edwin 151, 157, **175**, 177, 179
Stearns, Joseph 147
Sterling, William 97
Stone, Goodwin 150
Stone, Joseph 106
Stone, Lydia 112
Stone, Nathan 110, 112
Stoneman, George 92
Stoughton, Edwin 80–82, **83**–86, 88, 93, 96, 98, 125, 159, 176
Stowe, Harriet B. 12
Stringfellow, Frank 125, 126
Stringfellow, John 10
Stuart, James E.B. **22**, 23, 36, 37, 39–45, 59–65, 75, 81–84, 87–89, 92, 93, 96–100, 122, 124, 125, 127, 144–147, 150, 194–196
Sturgis, Samuel D. 47, 54
Sumner, Edwin V. 16, 24
Swan, Robert 36

Taft, William 196
Tate, David 55
Tatum, John 32

Taylor, Fletch 49, 103, 120
Taylor, Walter 87
Terrell, Edwin 183, *184*-189
Thayer, Eli 13, 14
Theiss, Adam 140
Thomas, Aaron 68
Thomas, Lydia S. 117
Thompson, Edward 160
Thompson, Francis 25
Thompson, Gideon 69, 70
Thompson, John 187
Thorne, Joshua 104
Thrailkill, John 132, 134, 140
Todd, George 49, 56, 57, 58, 66, 68–70, 72–74, 101, 102, 106, 109, 113–115, 117–121, 129, 130, 134–136, 139–142, 170, 171, 185
Todd, Tom 134
Tolles, Cornelius 158
Topeka Constitution 16, 24
Torbert, Alfred 154–157
Torrey, Henry 27–29, 33
Totopotomoy Creek 42
Totten, James 57
Trace, Harrison 49
Travis, William B. 55
Tredegar Iron Works 20
R.M.S. *Trent* 38
Trevilian Station, Battle of 147
Tucker, William 67
Tudor Grove 4–6
Tunstall's Station 44
Turner, Edward C. 92
Turner, Mrs. 134
Turner, Thomas 96
Turner, William 123, 126, 127, 145
Turpin, George 3, 5, 6
Twain, Mark 58

Uncle Tom's Cabin 12
Underwood, John 65, 78
University of Virginia 3–5, 196

Vernon, George 126
Vicksburg 99, 101, 102, 144
Virginia Military Institute 145, 147
Von Massow, Robert, 143, 144

Wagner, Seymour 129
Wakarusa War 16
Wakefield, James 186, 187
Wakefield Farm fight 186, 187
Walker, Andrew 32, 33, 48
Walker, Anna 33, 34
Walker, James M. 31–33
Walker, Sheriff 31
Wallace, Lewis 150
Watts, Hemp 134, 135
Weaver, Mortimer 60
Weems, Mason L. 4
Weer, William 54
Wells, Henry 191
Wells, Major William 86, 87
Wells, Private William 55
Wertenbaker, Charles 5
Westport, Battle of 171
Whitacre, Robert 98
White, Martin 25
White Turkey 112, 114
Whitescarver, George 96, 97
Whitfield, John W. 13
Willard, Joseph 85
Williams, R.L. 106
Williamson, James 143, 150, 162, 163, 176, 178, 180
Willis, Albert 157, 158, 160
Wilson, Cyrus 185
Wilson, David 56
Wilson, Mrs. 69
Wilson's Creek, Battle of 47
Wiltshire, James 158
Winchester, Battle of 156
Wistar, Isaac J. 63
Wolfe, James 4
Woodson, Daniel 15
Woodward, John 79, 80
Wren, Albert 148
Wyatt, Cave 134, 138
Wyndham, Percy 75, 76, 78–81, 83, *85*, 86

Yamamoto, Admiral 111
Yeager, Dick 105, 112
Yellow Tavern, Battle of 146
Young, Henry 176
Young, Sallie 107, 108
Younger, Thomas Coleman 50, 51, 57, 69, 70, 104, 189

www.ingramcontent.com/pod-product-compliance
Lightning Source LLC
Chambersburg PA
CBHW081555300426
44116CB00015B/2891